FROM CAMPBELL TO KENDALL
A HISTORY OF THE NFU

GUY SMITH

HALSGROVE

First published in Great Britain in 2008

British Library Cataloguing-in-Publication Data
A CIP record for this title is available from the British Library

ISBN 978 1 84114 696 6

HASGROVE
Halsgrove House
Ryelands Industrial Estate, Bagley Road,
Wellington, Somerset TA21 9PZ
Tel: 01823 653777
Fax: 01823 216796
email: sales@halsgrove.com
website: www.halsgrove.com

Printed and bound by CPI Antony Rowe, Wiltshire

Preface

My intention with this book was to write a history of the NFU built around the 33 men who have been its Presidents since its foundation one hundred years ago. As they were all farmers and countrymen this also provided an opportunity to comment on some of the changes in agriculture and the countryside over the same period. However, the book clearly has limitations that the reader should be aware of. Firstly it cannot possibly cover the story of 20th century British agriculture in its entirety and inevitably leaves a lot out. Nor can it comprehensively tell the story of the NFU. The NFU is a vast organisation with a long detailed history spread out over a wide geographical area. By concentrating on just one man, the President, hundreds of other key individuals in the history of the NFU are overlooked. From Branch Secretaries to County Chairmen, from field officers to Parish Representatives, from members of the legal team to Committee Chairmen, the list of those who merit a mention in any history is endless. A point made repeatedly in the narrative is that to understand the role of the President it is important to remember he stood at the top of an organisation that involved thousands of farmers and hundreds of staff across the length and breadth of England and Wales. Without that mass of people supporting his role, the President would not have had the pre-eminence he did. In particular it should be remembered that alongside the President at the top of the NFU tree stood a General Secretary or, latterly, a Director General. These men must have mention. The list is as follows

Harry Palmer 1909-1917
T.Apps 1917-1920
D.Allen 1920-1924
Sir Cleveland Fyfe and John Guild 1924-1932
Sir Cleveland Fyfe 1933-1945
J.Kenneth Knowles 1945-1970
George Cattell 1970-1978
Professor Asher Winegarten 1978
Roy Watson 1979-1985
David Evans 1986-1996
Richard Macdonald 1996 onwards

What also should be remembered is that although the NFU represented English and Welsh farmers it did not cross the border into Scotland nor the Irish sea into Ulster. Here the NFUS and the UFU were the representative bodies. This book rather ignores these organisations especially in light of the fact that, before devolution, UK agriculture was often dealt with as a single entity in Whitehall and in Brussels. The NFU frequently worked alongside the NFUS and the UFU. Similarly it is difficult to isolate just England and Wales in terms of statistics and national trends. Consequently UK figures are used when technically the ambit of this book is England and Wales.

Guy Smith
2008

Acknowledgements and Dedication

This book is not a full academic history of the NFU. One day soon someone should spend the five years needed to research and write it. It should run to several volumes. Most of the information in this book has been drawn from the NFU Year Books which are a considerable source of information, especially in the first sixty years when they were several hundred pages long. This has been backed up by delving into various farming journals such as the Mark Lane Express, The British Farmer and Stockbreeder and the various NFU Journals. For general histories of British agriculture in the 20th century I recommend 'The History of the Second World War (Agriculture)' by K.A.H Murray and 'British Agriculture since 1945' by B.A. Holderness. Generally there has been very little published specifically about the history of the NFU. Olive Hallam's "Somerset NFU" is one exception. Also there is K.A. Pepperall's biography of Tom Baxter and Lord Plumb's autobiography "The Plumb line". There are two unpublished works about the early days of the NFU. One is a Ph D paper by Tom Brooking "Agrarian Business men Combine" that looks at the origins of the NFU in the UK and the NZFU in New Zealand. The other is "Full Harvest" by L.B.Powell written, but never published, in 1960. I also interviewed many people in the course of the research who are too numerous to mention but I am very grateful for their time and their good company. I am also very grateful to six present members of the NFU staff for their comments and advice, namely: Anthony Gibson, Martin Haworth, Barney Holbeche, Richard Macdonald, Julie Robinson and Carmen Suarez. Finally I would like to thank the staff of that most magnificent of places, the Museum of Rural Life in Reading, who keep an excellent library and are friendly and helpful to visiting researchers. The building which houses the archives also has a fascinating museum that is well worth a visit. The only thing the place lacks is a café, but there is the Esso garage at the bottom of Redlands road if you are really desperate for a coffee, as indeed I frequently was.

DEDICATION

This book is dedicated to the memory of my father Andrew Roger Smith who died in September 2007 while I was writing and researching this book. He was a farmer and an NFU member all his working life, as was his father. He was born in 1926 on a 700 acre Essex farm that was worked with 50 men and 45 horses. When he died the farm was covering twice the acres with three men and three tractors – and some consultants say we are over-staffed! It is appropriate to dedicate the book to him and to the generation of farmers he was typical of. This generation, who are now in their seventies, eighties and nineties, witnessed immense change during their farming careers. They lived through the challenges of war-time and they oversaw the technical and production revolution of the post war era. The great majority of this generation were loyal supporters of the NFU and they were the men on whom the NFU was built. These foundations are still very much in place today and the leave a nourishing legacy. As the NFU reaches its centenary and as this formidable generation of farmers starts to die out, it is appropriate that we should remember them.

CONTENTS

❖ CHAPTER 1 ❖

A Brief 7,000 Years of History

Our story starts on 10 December 1908 in a back-room of the Smithfield Show in North London, where the representatives of various regional farmers' unions came together to discuss the formation of a national union. While some felt the timing was a little premature, there were others who displayed an infectious determination to seize the moment. Action prevailed over caution and the foundation stone of the National Farmers' Union was laid. In due course a mighty organisation would be built to become the unrivalled voice of more than 200,000 English and Welsh farmers.

But first we should bear in mind that our story doesn't really start here at all. We need briefly to discuss how we got to this point in history, and to do so we must consider a potted version of a much longer story... that of farming in Britain. That story goes back into the mists of time when, some 7,000 years ago, prehistoric man arrived on Britain's shores and decided that this green and pleasant land was a very sensible place to practise the civilised art of farming. With its flattish topography and maritime climate that displayed none of the seasonal extremes of the continent, Britain offered a good opportunity to secure that most basic necessity of man... food.

Over the next few thousand years these early farmers cleared Britain of much of its natural deciduous forest and introduced from the Middle East such plant species as wheat, oats, barley and rye into the forest clearings. Early domesticated animals such as cows, pigs and sheep, whose origins also lay in faraway lands, were introduced to graze and grow fat on Britain's abundant pasture. Through a patchwork of fields, ditches, fences, walls, tracks and settlements these early farmers started to lay down some of the core features of what we recognise today as the British countryside. It was, and is, a landscape shaped by those who farmed it rather than as nature intended it.

We then roll forward a few thousand years in this whistle-stop tour to find the Romans improving Britain's capacity to grow food by introducing new farming techniques. They brought with them improved ploughs and scythes, as well cabbages, carrots, parsnips and walnut trees. The countryside was also given new inhabitants through the introduction of species such as rabbits, snails and nettles.

Julius Caeser himself, in 55BC, remarked upon the fertility of British farmland and the abundance of the corn it grew. He also noted that while the south and east of the country supported good crops, the midland plain was largely pastoral and the natives lived off milk and meat. Others recorded how British wheat was exported to Gaul. This is a fact that makes for a cheery thought today amidst the recent tensions over British farm exports to that bastion of agricultural protectionism – France.

During their 400-year occupation the Romans also imported their own social structures based around the 'villa'. Possibly, we can still see a trace of that in today's landed estates. In Roman times the population was approaching four million and urban centres such as Colchester, London, York and Chester were established. For the first time there was a notion of town and country. It was probably very different from the town and country dichotomy we know today, but it is nice to think there were Britons 2,000 years ago sitting around in their respective taverns debating which was preferable: town life or country life. It was a conversation that echoed on through the centuries.

After the Romans retreated from Britain, the Dark Ages and the medieval period did not stand out as ages of agricultural prosperity or improvement. The land was owned, in the main, by the crown, the aristocracy and the church. In turn, these feudal institutions controlled those who worked the land; a motley collection of villeins and free-men. It is an age that we associate with the word 'peasant', with all its uneducated, subjugated and backward connotations. Famine and malnutrition were accepted as a part of life in a society that struggled to feed itself. The population had fallen to three million from its Roman heyday. Open field systems divided into six-metre strips were the basis of land tenure. This system, along with the commons where stock grazed, did not lend itself to agricultural improvement. The intermingling of stock or crops brought everyone down to the lowest common denominator – the worst farmer. The better farmer could do little to isolate himself from the weed seeds and diseases that blew in from those he was obliged to work alongside, cheek by jowl. There was little room for improving stock breeds through selection or improving crop yields through one individual's good husbandry. Cereal yields averaged around less than a half tonne to the acre.

Through this thousand-year Dark Age there is little evidence of any movement amongst those who worked the land to attempt to organise or try to improve their lot through collective representation. In contrast we see the emergence in the towns of the guilds, whereby men of a certain trade came together and sought collectively to promote their trade's interests. There was no such initiative to be found among the food producers out in the countryside. Instead, we witness the Peasants' Revolt in 1381, when a disorganised rabble of thousands of land workers, dissatisfied with their lot, were defeated by a handful of well-organised, properly led king's men.

It is worth noting that while the trades which bought, processed and sold the goods that farmers produced can trace their associations back hundreds of years, farmers cannot. Amongst the Worshipful Companies of Liverymen we can find, for instance, the Butchers (traced to 975 and incorporated 1605), Woolmen (traced to 1180, incorporated 1522), Fruiterers (founded 1463, incorporated 1605) and Leathermen (established 1444).

In the fifteenth century we see the emergence of the terms 'farm' and, indeed, 'farmer' in their modern-day sense. For the first time comprehensive blocks of ring-fenced land were farmed by one man or one family. Farmhouses, as we know them today, began to appear on these consolidated holdings instead of being grouped together in villages. A writer in 1604 notes: 'We may see many of their houses built alone like ravens' nests.' This new farming class stood between the land-owning class and the labourer. Land became not so much an expression of power exercised by a lord of the manor but more of a commercial proposition in which the occupier undertook the business of using cash to buy land or pay rent and wages for the purposes of producing goods which he then sold off the farm, thus achieving profit. It was at this time that, emerging from the commonality of the peasant mass, came a more distinct individual – the yeoman farmer – a man of independent means and independent attitude.

Gregory King, the seventeenth-century commentator, noted of England's farmers that they were a sturdy and independent class, and 'took a jolly pride in voting, as in fighting, on the opposite side of the neighbouring squire'. The yeomanry, wrote Fuller at a similar time:

... is an estate of people almost peculiar to England; he wears russet clothes but makes golden payment, having tin in his buttons and silver in his pocket. He seldom goes abroad, and his credit stretches farther than his travel.

These writers estimated there were 300,000 yeoman and tenant farming families in the English countryside 400 years ago in a population of around five million.

As we shall witness throughout this story, this spirit of individualism is the British farmer's defining characteristic and distinguishes him from his smaller continental peasant cousins. In one analysis, this rugged individualism is his greatest asset, but in another it can be his undoing. Time spent alone within a ring fence makes a man resourceful, hard-working and entrepreneurial, but at the same time it can make him unduly disconnected from non-farmers and obstinate when it comes to co-operating with his fellow farmers for mutual advantage.

This process of land consolidation under one individual's control was at first driven by demand for that most attractive of Tudor farm produce – wool. Towards the end of the medieval period wool from Britain became a prized commodity amongst weavers and fullers, both at home and further abroad in places such as the Low Countries. Consequently, the medieval landscape, dominated by open strip farmed arable land, started to change into one characterised by blocks of pasture where long-wool sheep could be grazed.

This movement from arable land to pasture caused consternation with some, as it increased the risk of famine. In terms of producing calories of food, arable farming easily outperformed its pastoral counterpart. The problem was that arable cropping was expensive and did not always pay as well as stock farming. There was a delicate balance to be found between the financial welfare of the farmer and the needs of the population. As we shall see later in this story, this question as to which should have greater emphasis, arable or pasture, is revisited again and again. Even today it excites debate, and no doubt in the future the question of how many of Britain's acres should be ploughed then cropped and how many should be grazed will continue to be discussed.

Before we move this history on to the eighteenth century and the Agricultural Revolution, we should note that attempts by the state to control or influence agriculture is neither new nor modern. Call it national strategic planning or call it meddling by non-farmers into issues they know little about, either way it seems that the desire of government to intervene in farming is as old as the farmed hills themselves. As we know, the Romans ran Britain as part of a larger empire. Food production and distribution were part of the imperial strategy. The medieval kings seemed equally as interventionist as their Roman emperor forebears. For instance, in AD965 we find King Edgar fixing the price of wool at 120d. per wey so that it did not cheaply get into the hands of the foreigner.

It is a good example of Dark-Age export control and price fixing. In 1351 a statute passed by Edward III fixed the wage paid to agricultural labourers and fixed the price of wheat. Edward's policy was designed to prevent the export of wheat to foreigners. His successor, Richard II, then reversed this policy over concerns that it would encourage livestock farming at the expense of arable production, thus risking famine. Accordingly, it was enacted that wheat could be exported without a licence when it was under 6s.8d. a quarter unless, of course, it was being exported to the king's enemies. A century later we still find the monarch, this time Edward IV, worried that too much land was going out of cropping and so he forbade the import of corn when the price was under 6s.8d. Henry VIII continued this tradition of fixing the price of food by ordaining in 1532 that beef and mutton should be ½d a pound and mutton 5s.8d. a pound.

This control of agriculture by government went to bizarre lengths by today's standards. In Tudor times the desire of the king that every man should be in his estate led him to regulate what farmers and farmer workers could wear. For instance, farm labourers were forbidden to spend more than 14d. on their hosen or wear 'close hosen' (hosen is an old term for clothes and 'close hosen' would now be described as 'figure-hugging'). Some might like to compare this with today's Health & Safety legislation that demands that farm workers, on occasion, wear baggy protective suits and gloves. But it should be remembered that in Tudor times this was about social control and nothing to do with health and safety

Throughout the turmoil of the seventeenth century, with its civil wars, and well into the eighteenth century, we still find British governments prepared to protect the nation's agriculture to ensure supplies of food through price control and export or import licences. In 1665 and 1680 we have laws passed to prohibit the imports of Irish cattle, beef, butter and cheese and to levy duty on Irish wool.

There is still little or no nexus in any of this between government and any collective representation of the farming community, as the latter did not exist. It is true that, through parliament, the landed class were establishing their influence over government, and this clearly gave agriculture some sort of political voice. We should not forget that the hero of parliament and the hammer of King Charles I was a farmer from Huntingdon called Oliver Cromwell. But, even so, it was land ownership rather than farming that was being represented in these embryonic Houses of Parliament.

As we move our story on through to the eighteenth and nineteenth centuries, we find it to be a story of considerable improvement and change. The process of enclosure was made complete and the medieval landscape of commons and open fields farmed by groups of peasants was finally lost to one of hedged enclosures controlled by single farmers. As many as six million acres of English fields were enclosed between 1700 and 1845. The eighteenth century is also a time when we find British farmers becoming world leaders in the development of new techniques and new understandings. One suspects that the two developments, enclosure and progress, are not unconnected. Writing in 1768 in his *Tour of France*, the great eighteenth-century agriculturalist

Arthur Young spoke disdainfully of the inferior and smaller French farms, adding:

The history of enclosure is part of the history of the great revolution in agriculture by which the manorial system was converted into the triumvirate of landlord, tenant farmer and labourer. These enclosures began to change the England of open fields into the country we know, of hedgerows and winding roads.

The 'improvements' of the Agricultural Revolution took many forms. In terms of crop husbandry, the Norfolk four-course system of wheat, turnips and two years' clover and rye was developed by Coke of Holkham. Horse-drawn machinery was improved. We all remember Jethro Tull for inventing the seed drill, but sometimes forget he also devised weed harrows and other cultivators. Iron ploughs became much improved, with the world's first plough factory opened in 1783. Potatoes, introduced from the Americas two centuries before, became a common farm crop, chiefly in Lancashire and Cheshire, where they helped feed the booming population in the industrial towns of the North West. Livestock improvers, of whom Bakewell and the Colling brothers were the most renowned, bred superior lines of cattle and sheep. The pig was transformed in the eighteenth century from something that resembled a ginger wild boar into the fleshy farmyard animal we know today, partly by the introduction of breeds from China. The Longhorn dairy cow became productive enough to supply the British population with fresh milk for the first time. Before that, milk was usually turned into cheese. Fruit and vegetable gardening, which was initially an indulgence made fashionable in the Elizabethan country house, started to cover more acres on a commercial basis and thus became the start of our horticultural industry.

These are just brief highlights in a general agricultural renaissance led by British farmers. It was an age when, everywhere, science and experiment started to take over from tradition and superstition. All areas of farming sought improvement, and the result was increased food production in most sectors. This was important for the British economy at the time, as it allowed the Industrial Revolution, which was also pioneered in our islands.

This spirit of improvement even infected government. In 1793 Sir John Sinclair moved in the House of Commons that:

His majesty would take into his consideration the advantages which might be derived from the establishment of a board of agriculture, for though in some particular districts improved methods of cultivating the soil were practised, yet in the greatest part of these kingdoms the principles of agriculture are not sufficiently understood, nor are the implements of husbandry or the stock of the farmer brought to that perfection of which they are capable.

This resulted in the formation of British agriculture's first quango – the Board of Agriculture – which received £3,000 yearly in government grants. It contained MPs, landed lords and, oddly by today's standards, the Archbishops of Canterbury and York. Part ministry, part advisory service and part research body, the board can be seen as a precursor of many modern-day bodies that concern themselves with British farming.

At a local level, the end of the eighteenth and beginning of the nineteenth centuries saw the establishment all over England and Wales of farmers' clubs, cattle shows, mangel competitions and ploughing matches. These are important in our story as they mark a time when farmers brought themselves together for mutual advantage. But it was not political representation but rather the sharing and development of knowledge. It was technology transfer at the grass-roots level.

So we reach the beginning of the nineteenth century with a dynamic agriculture that has embraced change and improvement. It was in this century that the Industrial Revolution reached full steam. This not only changed the economy of Britain but also its society. Britain was the first nation in the world to move from a rural agrarian society to an urban industrialised one. In 1750 75 per cent of the population lived in rural areas and were employed by the agrarian economy. By 1850 this figure had fallen to 25 per cent. Since the people in the burgeoning cities had to be fed, there existed a strong incentive towards increased farm productivity. But this also stimulated imports, especially of grain. There were significant increases in imports from northern Europe and Russia to help feed Britain's growing, hungry cities.

In the first half of the nineteenth century British farmers still benefited from protection from imports. As we have seen, protectionism for British agriculture was nothing new, but of all the protectionist measures, the Corn Laws of 1815 are the most notorious. They were designed to limit the import of corn when prices fell below the price of 80s. a quarter. Thomas Malthus, a leading political economist of the time, believed that this was a fair price for farmers to receive and that it would be dangerous to rely on imported corn. In contrast, his contemporary, David Ricardo, argued that the Britain thrived most as a manufacturing and trading economy run on the principles of free trade. Protectionism for farmers, argued Ricardo, kept the price of food unjustly high for the working man and falsely raised the costs of the entrepreneurial industrialist.

This debate rumbled on until 1846, when the Corn Laws were repealed and British farmers became exposed to free market forces and unfettered trade from abroad. At first there was little effect on the prospects for farmers. Fired by the Industrial Revolution the British economy was growing rapidly, and so was its population, which increased from 10 million in 1800, to 19 million in 1850, to 34 million in 1900. This increase in mouths to feed gave British farmers healthy expanding home markets. As we have seen, imports were rising but political unrest or war in mainland Europe limited farm output. As yet, the great plains of the American heartland were largely uncultivated.

The middle of the nineteenth century was a 'golden age' for British farmers. In 1950 the great historian, C.S. Orwin, wrote of this period in his *History of Agriculture;*

Never at any other time in its history has the land been better equipped by the landowner, better cultivated by the farmer, nor has food production from it been more intensive. Landlords and farmers collaborated in the means to good farming, secure from effective competition from overseas and thus assured good prices for everything which the land could produce.

In 1875 there were 31 million acres of agricultural land in Britain, 14 million acres of which were under the plough.

Of course, despite this golden age of British food production, there were some who could pick fault with what was happening in the countryside. Writing in 1865, Anthony Trollope observed:

The truth is that if you farm well you must farm ugly. The picturesque nooks and corners have all been turned inside out and the hedgerows abolished because the farmer wants sunshine.

As we shall see later in this story, such criticisms of the impact of farming on the landscape by the chattering classes are not confined to the mid-nineteenth century.

In the 1870s things took a sudden and decided turn for the worse. It was the start of a depression that was to last, more or less, for over 70 years, until 1940. It could be said that for the first time in 500 years British agriculture went into reverse. It was the weather that led the way. Three years of bad harvests

The proposal to repeal the Corn Laws sparked mass protectionist meetings among the farming community.

FUN.——July 2, 1879.

THE BRITISH FARMER

OLD BREED | NEW BREED

STARVATION
BANKRUPTCY
EMIGRATION

FOREIGN COMPETITION

THE ROYAL AGRICULTURAL EXHIBITION.

Specimens which ought to be included in the Show.

"Prosperity," by Management, out of Better Times. | "Adversity," by Foreign Competition, out of Hard Times.

A cartoon depicting the contrasting fortunes of farming before and after the 1870s.

culminated in 1879 with a sunless summer and abnormally high rainfall. This halved the yield of corn on many farms, while over the country generally pneumonia, foot and mouth disease and liver-rot wrought havoc amongst herds and flocks. No doubt today such apocalyptic weather would be blamed on climate change and such levels of disease would be attributed to intensive farming. In those days farmers did not have 'climate change' but rather 'unseasonable weather'. Furthermore, intensive farming was generally considered good for animal welfare, not injurious to it.

To add insult to injury, this run of unseasonable weather coincided with the start of a flood of wheat and meat from the New World. After the disruption of the bloody and bitter American Civil War of 1861–65, which killed a significant proportion of its young men, the young American nation had resumed its relentless move west into the great plains, which it converted into seemingly endless farmland. Ironically, it was often British farming emigrants who led the charge. By the 1870s much of the prairies had been settled and farmed. The growth of the railways in the same period allowed grain to be carried easily to ports. Through the second half of the nineteenth century the US and Canada increased their exports of wheat, from 1.5 million tonnes in 1850 to 60 million in 1900.

In contrast to the situation on British farms, the North American prairie harvests of the late 1870s were good ones. In 1879 Britain imported £40 million worth of wheat and flour – 30 per cent more than in 1875. Soon other countries were farming to supply the British industrial areas. The newly developing technique of refrigeration was turning a small trade in canned meats into a great export of frozen carcases. New Zealand, Australia and Argentina joined the United States and Canada in a great flood into the British markets of grain and animal products. In countries where land was cheap (if not free) it was easy to out-compete farmers in a small, crowded island such as Britain, where high rents had to be found. For those in the industrial centres, whether employer or employee, this cheap imported food was very welcome. In the political sphere, manufacturing and mercantile interests had gained the upper hand over the traditional landed lobby.

In the last quarter of the nineteenth century free trade was the order of the day for British governments. Agricultural protectionism had been consigned to history. Britain had become a global power and, while its Royal Navy ruled the waves, its expanding mercantile fleet chugged out of foreign ports laden with farm produce. This was in contrast to Britain's neighbours and rivals, France and Germany, who protected their agriculture by imposing duties on both cereals and livestock products to the order of one-third of their value. Where Britain chose to follow the free trade teaching of Adam Smith and his disciple Ricardo, the Germans drew inspiration from Friedrich List's school of nationalist economics, with its stress on economic development through protectionism.

By 1900 in Britain there was increasing debate about the wisdom of the free trade policy. Joseph Chamberlain led the proponents of Tariff Reform, but it was debate only and did little to help the prospects of British farmers.

Between 1880 and 1900 the return to the British farmer for beef fell by between 24 and 40 per cent, wool fell by 50 per cent, dairy produce by 30 per cent, potatoes by 30 per cent and cereals by 40 per cent. By the end of the century four million acres of arable land had been converted to grass or abandoned to bramble and gorse. The depression hit the arable farmer hardest, as he suffered the greatest fall in prices and, unlike the livestock man, did not take any

benefit from the decrease in feed prices. By the 1890s the number of farm bankruptcies was escalating: 523 in 1893, 564 in 1895. In 1893 the then Home Secretary, H.H. Asquith, told parliament that between 1875 and 1894 the capital value of agricultural land had declined by £834 million – roughly 50 per cent.

On New Year's day, 1901, a Lincolnshire farmer, Ted Howard, who tenanted a 400-acre mixed farm at Coleby, near Lincoln, wrote in his diary:

The past year 1900, will long remain in the minds of British farmers as the most deplorable of the many bad ones we have been drifting into during the last quarter of the century. I am speaking more particularly of those farming arable land. Never have our acres produced so small a revenue and what is to prevent a repetition (even much worse than a wet harvest?). Many say we hope for a better year. But is it fair to ourselves and those following us to let hoping do? Year after year we see so many good men and true fall to the competitive bullet of our foreign enemy (and who counts the wounded?); they fall singly, or line up. How is our position to be improved? We have a perfect right to demand with the rest of the nation's subjects a living wage. We must co-operate into a united body called, say, the British Farmers' Union.

As you might guess, we are to meet up with Ted Howard again very shortly, but meanwhile, as this story reaches the twentieth century, we complete this whistle-stop prelude. In telling 7,000 years of farming history in such haste, no doubt we have committed the sins of generalisation and lacked attention to necessary detail. But this book is primarily about twentieth-century British agriculture and has not the time or space for a deeper analysis of what went on before. At this point in time there are a number of key developments to bear in mind: British farmers are characterised by their rugged individualism due to consolidation of the way land was comprehensively occupied in large, ring-fenced blocks; this is in contrast to farming on the continent, where farms were smaller and more numerous; unlike other trades and workforces, there is little attempt by working farmers to combine amongst themselves for collective advancement; Britain is the first nation in the world to undergo industrialisation and urbanisation; the British government is the first in Europe to embrace the principles of free trade and to abandon agricultural protectionism.

Now the style and pace of this book change. We have more time to ponder the men who led the NFU through its hundred year history and how they reflected the agriculture of their day.

Colin Campbell

Chairman of Lincolnshire Farmers' Union 1904–08 and first President
of the National Farmers' Union, 1909–17

Throughout the union's history the county of Lincolnshire has claimed Colin Campbell as one of its own, along with the fact that their county was the cradle of the union. It is a fair claim, as they were indeed that cradle and, for most of his adult life, Campbell farmed in the county. The bad news for the proud farmers of Lincolnshire (and many more besides) is that he was actually a Yorkshireman!

Campbell was born in Bransby, North Yorkshire, in 1863, the son of a country parson. As the name would suggest, the family were of Scottish extraction, having moved south to Lancashire after the Jacobite Rising of 1745. As those who have read their Scottish history will know, the Campbells sided with the government troops, invoking bitter hatred from the rebel clans. It is not surprising that some Campbells decided to emigrate. To this day you can find MacDonalds who won't, out of principle, have tins of Campbell's soup in the house.

We know the young Colin was educated at Westminster School in London and rowed at the Leander Club on the Thames. What this suggests is that Campbell was no 'hick from the sticks'. His family must have been reasonably well off and, much later, when the union's work took him to London, he would have had a working knowledge of the Westminster area.

At some time in his youth, we also know, Campbell was a 'farm pupil' at a farm near Norwich. Farm pupilage was a common means of educating would-be farmers on the farms of their elders and betters. We do not know what inspired a country parson's London-educated son to want to become a farmer.

We have brief details of how, as a young man, Campbell went abroad and for some of that time managed a plantation in Mexico. His family also have photos of him further north in the US or Canada. For a young farmer born in Victorian Britain it was nothing out of the ordinary to seek a farming fortune in the New World. It is estimated that between 1830 and 1920 3.5 million Britons emigrated to the US. A census in 1890 revealed that 90,000 farmers and well over 100,000 farm labourers in the United States had been born in England. Many returned, as did Campbell. As we have noted, the creation of productive farmland out of the vast virgin acres of the American prairies was one the main drivers of the British farming recession after the 1870s. It is a considerable irony that much of this breaking of new ground was led by British farming

emigrants who were armed with the considerable knowledge British farming had gained during the agricultural improvements of the eighteenth and nineteenth centuries. The children spawned by British farming skill and ingenuity went abroad to bite the hand that had fed them.

On his return to England Campbell first took a rented farm near Scarborough and then, in 1900, a 640-acre farm called Stapleford Hall in south-west Lincolnshire. Stapleford Hall was owned by Willoughby Estate under the charge of the ninth Lord Middleton. The Middletons were an old-established landed family who owned 100,000 acres across the East Midlands and in Yorkshire, as well as quarries and mines. This was a time when the great landed estates of the aristocracy were at their zenith. It has been estimated that at the turn of the century 18.5 million acres were owned by a little more than 4,000

Colin Campbell, founder of the National Farmers' Union in 1908.

individuals, and 400 ennobled families owned a third of that, 40 of them owning in excess of 100,000 acres (Bateman, *The Great landowners of Great Britain*). The large country house, with its neatly mown lawns and tea parties, is an icon of the Edwardian age. The irony was that it was in this era that the tax legislation that caused its demise was put in place. The Finance Act of 1894 was the first of a number of pieces of legislation that sought to tax land on the death of the owner. By 1945 the 100,000-acre empire of the Middleton family had dwindled to just 10,000. As a generation of mighty landowners died in the first quarter of the twentieth century, the nature of land ownership in Britain was to change fundamentally.

But this was still to come and, as a tenant, Campbell represented the norm in Edwardian agriculture. In 1909 only 13 per cent of land was owner-occupied, the rest being tenanted. A 640-acre farm was not unusual, especially in Lincolnshire at that time, but it was well above the national average of 70 acres. This in turn was much larger than the average size of farm found on the continent. In France, for example, two-fifths of all holding were under 2.5 acres.

Stapleford Hall in the 1900s was a typical arable and livestock farm of south-east Lincolnshire, with wheat, barley and roots in rotation, along with 600 pedigree Lincoln longwool sheep and 150 cattle. Although the soils were mixed, it was described as 'two-horse' land, suggesting it was reasonably easy working. The farm was roughly divided into 350 acres arable and 250 acres pasture. Campbell was reported as being progressive in his enthusiasm to use new labour-saving devices. He had wind-powered water pumps connected to taps to fill drinking troughs and mills, chaff cutters and threshing machines powered by traction engines. In an age before the tractor, Campbell used steam cultivators as well as the traditional horse. Steam cultivators worked by dragging ploughs up to eight furrows

in size back and forth across fields on wire ropes wound on a drum on the engine. The power was provided by steam engines that stood on either side of the field. By modern standards it seems slow and ponderous, far removed from today's hi-tech tractors. Farmers today, however, still subconsciously remember the technique when they talk of taking 'drags' up and down the field with machinery. This use of steam engines for ploughing was the first step towards 'power farming' in the field. Within 50 years this movement towards engines had made the draught horse redundant, but at the turn of the century the horse was still very much the power-house on British farms. Stapleford Hall had 13 draught horses, which suggests Campbell was more mechanised than most. In the early years of the century it was estimated there were a little over a million horses working on British farms, providing 707,000 units of horsepower (for some strange reason, on average, one horse produced a unit of horsepower of 0.7). New ideas such as horse-drawn self-binding reapers were starting to replace man-power on farms at this period, but scythes and sickles were still commonplace. The use of steam engines and motor tractors was still in its infancy. By the 1900s the mechanisation revolution that was to transform farms in the twentieth century had begun, but it was a slow, piecemeal start. Britain was well in advance of the continent when it came to mechanisation, but, even so, human and equine muscles still provided most of the power on farms. Although we don't know the exact figure, we can guess Campbell would have employed around 25 men to run a 640-acre farm. It is a sobering thought that today, thanks to mechanisation, such a farm would probably have a workforce of one or two.

As a man Campbell was known for his straight-talking but was 'well met'. A journalist who interviewed him in 1908 described him as an 'honest John Bull'. Dinner guests were sometimes taken aback by Campbell's habit of shouting from the head of the

Steam ploughing at Campbell's Stapleford Farm. Ploughs were dragged back and forth by cables.

Campbell (centre) in his farmyard at Stapleford Hall.

MORE RURAL DECONTROL.

Chanticleer. "THIS IS THE LIMIT!"
The Pup. "IS IT? YOU WAIT TILL THE LIMIT'S REMOVED."

["Next year in all probability the speed limit, as far as private motor-cars are concerned, will be abolished."—*The Times.*]

A new menace, the motor car and cycle, intrudes on the tranquillity of the countryside. Such inventions suddenly brought town and country closer together.

table when wanting service rather than following the etiquette of the day and pulling the bell-rope to summon the staff.

Campbell had a rather ribald sense of humour. Christopher Nevile, who was NFU president in 1943, recounted to his son that he once attended a tea party where Campbell and some polite young ladies were present. One pretty, innocent young lady asked the assembled company why sheep developed such colourful marks on their backs in November. This being Edwardian England, most of the company were stunned into embarrassed silence, but Campbell relieved the situation by smiling at the young lady and replying: 'They are but autumn tints, my dear, not unlike the pretty marks on your dress.' One can imagine the snorting into teacups and repressed sniggering of the young men present! Elsewhere we note from newspaper reports and union journals that in his speeches Campbell always had a wry remark or two to amuse his audience.

Although Campbell was keen to introduce technology onto his farm, his attitude to motor cars was less than progressive. The 1900s were the first decade when cars appeared on Britain's roads. In 1903 Campbell was to be found on Claypole Parish Council moving a resolution that motor cars be prohibited from driving at more than 10mph on parish roads. The resolution was carried. He later quipped with Ted Howard: 'What is the difference between Dick Turpin and the motor car?' The answer was: 'Dick Turpin took your money or your life. The motor car takes both.' Again, in 1906, Campbell lobbied the government to gaol rather than fine motorists who committed road-traffic offences.

What we must remember here is the huge culture-shock that the introduction of the motor car represented in rural areas. Previously, the countryside had had its tranquillity secured through geographical isolation from the urban hordes. In the first decade of the 1900s the number of motor cars on Britain's roads rose from 10,000 to over 170,000. As we remember from the tales of Mr Toad in *The Wind in the Willows*, the sudden advent of motorised transport meant the teeming hordes from the towns had the means of invading the countryside. The increasing impact and intrusion of the motor car on the lives of farms and farmers is another story that intertwines itself with the history of agriculture in the twentieth century. By 1926 the number of cars on Britain's roads had risen to 1.7 million and today stands at over 27 million.

In his community, Campbell was also typical of his class. Lincolnshire was a rich farming county and, although it suffered recession in the late 1890s, it did not witness the collapse seen elsewhere. Lincolnshire farmers had prospered in the golden age of Victorian farming and retained some of that prosperity. Campbell enjoyed the trappings of the squirearchy. He employed two gardeners and was a keen sportsman. No doubt his time rowing on the Thames as an adolescent had given him an athletic build. His frame was large; in middle age he weighed in at 16–17 stone and, at 5ft 9ins, was tall for his day. We should remember that today we are, on average, six inches taller than our Edwardian counterparts, partly due to better nutrition. Campbell enjoyed the game of cricket and established the first cricket field in Stapleford. Although village cricket traces its roots back to the eighteenth century, it is not until the late-Victorian era that cricket fields became regular features in English villages. There are reminiscences that Campbell went out of his way to employ good cricketers on his farm so that Stapleford might field a worthy team. There are also anecdotes that at one point he fell out with the village team and promptly took back the bats he had provided them with and sawed off all the handles. This was not the only time when it is noted that Colin Campbell's temper got the better of his judgement.

Campbell also enjoyed the hunt and regularly exercised the hounds for Major Cockburn (who really ought to have an associate called Major Eyeswater, but didn't), the master of the local Blankney Hunt. It is this exercising of hounds that led to the very beginnings of the National Farmers' Union, and it is no small irony that, as the NFU reaches its centenary, the government has recently banned the sport that provided the stage for the very spark that ignited the union.

It was the custom with Major Cockburn, once a year, to entertain those who helped with the hunt. This included local farmers such as Campbell, who helped exercise the hounds. And so it was, on the last day of August 1904, that a group of farmers came together to shelter from the rain in a tent at Harmston Park, five miles south of Lincoln. They were farmers similar to Campbell, from the area around Lincoln, and included men such as Ted Howard, the diarist mentioned at the end of the previous chapter.

No doubt their mood was made gloomy by the wet weather that would have been hindering harvest progress and spoiling crops in the field. As ever, the weather proves key in all matters agricultural, even in the history of the NFU. This gloomy mood provoked talk of the difficult times that farmers of their generation had endured. This was probably made all the more pronounced in that, for the older ones amongst them, there would also have been clear memories of a much better time, the 'golden age' for farmers, just 30 years previously.

Mercifully, this gloominess didn't induce a sense of despair and inaction. Unusually for farmers, they decided to not just moan about their problems but to try actually to do something about them. The consensus was that the wrongs and difficulties suffered by farmers were to some extent their own fault because they never combined to take concerted action to find solutions. They all agreed, there and then, to meet again the following Friday in Lincoln. At that meeting they formally agreed to form a farmers' union. To prove they were prepared to put their money where their mouths were, they chipped in £1 each to start a kitty of funds (we are told there was one exception to this, but no one is named and shamed). It was Ted Howard who went to the office of the local newspaper the following day and used some of the kitty to place an advert announcing a public meeting of farmers at the Albion Hotel in Lincoln.

The Albion Hotel was a very sensible place to call farmers together, as it was the traditional haunt for them on market day. Despite the best endeavours of the Lincoln police to stop it, the windowsills of the Albion were used for writing cheques between farmers and related trades. We have no detailed records of the meeting but we do know it was packed to capacity. On the proposal of Campbell the formation of a county union was agreed and Howard was voted first chairman. At the end of the meeting, as a group of farmers, including Howard and Campbell, left the hotel, they bumped into an old friend, Pat Hamilton, the Vicar of Skellingthorpe. Hamilton, a larger-than-life character of Irish extraction, was known to enjoy the company of farmers and a drink or two. The curate and the farmers promptly agreed

to retire to the Saracen's Head to celebrate the formation of the Lincoln Farmers' Union. Over a few pints it was agreed that Hamilton should become the union's honorary chaplain. In hindsight, it is nice to record that in the most earnest moments of NFU history there is still time for pub banter and good humour.

And so the seed was sown. In February 1905 it was reported in the *Lincolnshire Chronicle*:

There is every prospect of the formation of a strong union of Lincolnshire farmers. The advertisement which for some time has been appearing in our columns inviting all farmers who desire not only to see some improvement in the conditions under which they labour, but who are willing to assist in ameliorating them, to communicate with the honorary secretary pro tem, Mr E.W. Howard, of Coleby Lodge, Nocton, has borne fruit. Many applications have been received from farmers all over the county.

A few days later, when the first annual meeting was held, a membership of 91 was reported.

Although this chapter is dedicated to Colin Campbell, a proper history of the NFU must pay tribute to Ted Howard. We should remember from his diary entry at the end of Chapter 1 that in 1901 he had envisaged a national union to be called the

The Lincolnshire pioneers in 1906, including Harry Palmer, the first NFU secretary (fifth from the right at the back).

British Farming Union. Howard was as instrumental as Campbell in these initial days in providing the necessary vision and leadership, but in mid-1905 he decided he had not the time nor the energy necessary to nurture the infant union properly. Howard had no sons, which made leaving the farm difficult for him. He would not be the last good man the NFU lost due to commitments back home on the farm. With Howard taking a back seat, Campbell fully took the reins.

The defining feature of the LFU was that it was to be a farmers' union for farmers alone. The early founding members were adamant on this point. There were already in existence bodies such as the Central Chamber of Agriculture, formed in 1865. In 1892 the Chamber had spawned the National Agricultural Union (Campbell himself was a member of the NAU when farming near Scarborough). The latter was the brainchild of Lord Winchelsea and largely died with him in 1898. These organisations claimed to represent the whole industry – landowners, farmers and farm workers. The Chamber had little democratic structure at grass-roots level and was formed through appointments rather than elections. Many farmers felt the Chamber represented the interests of landlords or was dominated by farm workers to the detriment of the position of the tenant farmer. There were also in existence organisations such as the Yorkshire Farmers' Union, which pre-dated the LFU by four years but, again, which included non-farmers. This is one of the key reasons why we trace the NFU back to the LFU rather than to anything else. But it would be wrong to suggest that, in spreading the farmers' union concept out beyond Lincolnshire, Campbell was working from scratch. He clearly took advantage of existing platforms and existing farmer organisations. As we have already noted, farmers' clubs and organisations had existed in England and Wales since the late-eighteenth century. The key point is that, until Campbell and the LFU arrived, there were no farmer groups dedicated to political representation exclusively for farmers.

One of Campbell's first acts was to appoint H.W. Palmer as the LFU's first secretary. Union offices were also bought in the form of a grimy, derelict pub in Lincoln's waterside area. Campbell knew Palmer personally and appointing him was a shrewd move. Palmer was a university-educated man with an MA from Cambridge. The job of union secretary was poorly paid and expenses were limited. Palmer recollected later that in these early days he happened to bump into a farmer on a train out of Lincoln. Having explained to the farmer he was on union business, the farmer asked him why he was travelling third class. 'Because there isn't a fourth,' was Palmer's droll reply. But Palmer had the good sense to make it clear from the moment he took the job on that he did not consider the position of secretary as a full-time job, and his main source of remuneration remained acting as an insurance agent for the Mutual Insurance Company of New York. No doubt Palmer realised union work might be a good way of getting to meet farmers who might buy insurance. The parallels with this and the later structuring of NFU branch secretaries are striking, but it should be remembered that we are still several years away from the formation of the NFU Mutual.

Although it had been relatively easy to secure an initial membership for the LFU, the job of expanding the union throughout Lincolnshire and beyond was far from straightforward. Later, Campbell recorded, in an NFU *Journal*, the climate of hostility he and Palmer often encountered in the early days:

After being jeered at a good deal and suffering much ridicule because we were cranks in trying to organise the one class of men who would never combine, we began to make headway among a few farmers and it looked as if the movement would go; but it was uphill work in those days.

Another complication was the fact that, for many farmers, a 'union' smacked of radical politics and left-wing agitation. Campbell, on more than one occasion, was greeted with a pitchfork when approaching potential new members.

A key supporter of the LFU at this time was W.A. May, a London publisher based in the Strand. May was the editor of the *Mark Lane Express*, a weekly farming journal. With its national coverage and wide readership, the *Mark Lane Express* was the *Farmers' Guardian* or *Farmers' Weekly* of its day. May took a shine to this new farmers' union in Lincolnshire and gave it crucial profile to the point where the *Express* became, de facto, the union's official journal. This gave the young LFU publicity it could not have afforded out of its own meagre coffers. May was skilled at growing a readership and this skill overlapped into growing a union membership. Discounted advertising rates were offered to union members, which gave farmers another incentive to join up, which in turn increased May's readership. May was also made union treasurer, a position he held for 13 years.

With staff, offices and journal now in place, Campbell used them as a platform to spread the union gospel with missionary zeal. His goal was a national union. One early event smarted with Campbell: he took a delegation of LFU farmers to London to speak to the Board of Trade and was treated dismissively as an irrelevance who represented no great number. It was this sort of setback that brought out the fighter in Campbell and made him more determined to achieve strength in numbers. In the four years between 1904 and 1908 he and Palmer travelled extensively, seeking out opportunities to address gatherings of farmers in towns as far afield as Truro, Berwick, Lampeter and Colchester. When you consider this was in an age when accessing country districts was dependent on steam trains and pony traps, then the extent of Campbell's travel is all the more remarkable. In May 1908 Campbell had a great victory in Devon. He had been invited to Exeter to address some Devon farmers who had decided on the need for some sort of collaboration but couldn't decide whether to join the Chamber of Agriculture or to found a Devon Farmers' Union along the lines of the LFU. Campbell was given a stage alongside a Major Dent from the

Shrewsbury Corn Exchange, a piece of magnificence built in an age of agricultural prosperity in early-Victorian times and now lost to make way for some twentieth-century urban acne in the form of a shopping precinct.

19

Chamber. Campbell won the day and the DFU was duly formed and, by January 1909, had 1,347 members under the chairmanship of the redoubtable John Tremlett.

In 1908 county and branch unions were set up in Nottinghamshire, Cornwall, Yorkshire, Devon, Kent, Leicestershire and Derbyshire.

Campbell's dedication and sheer grit inspired a contemporary to write later:

It was only his courage, enthusiasm and personality that kept the fight going, with little encouragement, with no funds except what he provided himself. But he was a determined man, convinced of the value of his efforts he was making, and refused to be discouraged by slow progress at first.

To help promote the farmers' union movement Campbell, working with his LFU executive, had drawn up the following programme of demands

1. The Agricultural Rating Act to be continued until the whole system of agriculture was dealt with as a raw material.
2. The cost of education to be borne by the Imperial Exchequer.
3. The maintenance of public roads also to be a charge upon the Imperial Exchequer.
4. Preferential railway rates for foreign produce to be abolished.
5. Vendors of foreign meat to be registered and foreign meat branded as such.
6. The beverage called beer to be made solely from barley malt, hops and sugar.
7. Strict adherence to be ensured to regulations respecting the slaughter of all foreign and colonial sheep and swine at ports of entry to avoid disease.
8. The enactment of a Pure Butter Bill.
9. The production of spirit from potatoes for motive power free from excise duty.
10. The provision of legal aid for members.

It is intriguing how many of these 100-year-old demands are still relevant today. Point nine merits particular attention, as it seems to promote bio-fuel for motor vehicles, which is something we assume to be a very modern issue. It is only the fact that potatoes are to be used as the source that dates it. Number six, concerning pure beer, might seem an odd thing for farmers to ask for, but it should be remembered that on the Continent such beer purity laws did and still do exist. It was also calculated that the practice by British brewers of using substitutes rather than proper malt cost British barley growers millions of pounds every year. British consumers never did get the pure beer the NFU wanted them to have and British brewers continued to make beer out of whatever was cheap at the time. Some 50 years later the organisation CAMRA (the Campaign for

Real Ale) was formed and campaigned yet again for pure beer made from proper, traditional ingredients.

Frank Hand, the LFU's self-styled poet and county secretary, summed some of this up in a song he penned, the chorus of which went:

So, come and join the Union
It's bound to do some good,
For we want pure Beer my boys,
As well as pure food.
We want not – anti-foodstuffs
We want the pure thing
So knock your heads together, my boys
And join the Farmers' Union.

Mercifully, in light of this dreadfulness, we have no record of the NFU and the world of poetry colliding again.

In mid-1908 a row brewed between the butchers and the farmers. This was a key moment in the NFU's history and it seems very apt that the debating point was the control of a disease in cattle, namely, tuberculosis. In the years running up to 1908 good progress had been made in eradicating bovine tuberculosis as a human health hazard and establishing higher standards of hygiene in the fresh meat trade. To progress this the government now wanted more stringent measures applied in meat inspection, leading to the condemnation of carcases held to be unfit for human consumption. In order to minimise the butchers' risk, the National Federation of Meat Traders' Associations (NFMTA) proposed that a warranty of health be given with all cattle sold. This placed the risk back with the farmer. If an apparently healthy cow was sold and, on inspection after slaughter, proved diseased, then the farmer would foot the bill. Not surprisingly, cattle farmers were less than enthusiastic about this proposed system, but the NFMTA was well organised and could easily divide and rule those farmers who acted as individual sellers.

Things came to a head on a morning in August 1908 at the cattle market in Wellington, Shropshire. The auctioneers sided with the farmers and called a meeting at which the butchers' demands were to be resisted with the cry of 'No Warranty!'. At a bigger meeting called at Shrewsbury Corn Exchange the following month a new association of Shrewsbury and District Farmers was formed. Some of the local Shropshire men were familiar with Campbell's crusade to form a national union and invited him to speak to a further assembly on 3 November. Campbell accepted the offer and used the occasion to demonstrate how only though united action could farmers hope to take on the likes of the NFMTA and resist their demands. By great good fortune, not long after Campbell had sat down, a telegram arrived from London to announce that the butchers had capitulated. This was in no way the work of

An NFU county dinner in Hereford in 1912. Slowly, the NFU pyramid structure of parish – branch – county – national was establishing itself.

Campbell or in any way due to his vision of a national union, but the effect was to convince farmers that it was indeed united action that had won the day. It was widely reported thus in the press. The Shrewsbury Association promptly became a Shropshire Farmers' Union and sought to work with the Lincolnshire men. There was now an impetus amongst the fragmented farmers' unions across the country to seek a national entity.

From Lincolnshire and Shropshire the focus of our narrative moves to London, where, on 10 December, in an anteroom of the Smithfield Show called the Prince's Chamber, representatives of 20 county or branch farming unions came together to discuss the prospects of forming a national union. Surprisingly, Campbell, who had worked so hard to achieve this end, felt the time was a little premature, but other delegates were keen to seize the moment. Their infectious enthusiasm won the day and the resolution 'that this meeting of delegates from various farmers' unions thinks it desirable that a National Union of Farmers should be formed' was carried. A provisional committee under Campbell's chairmanship was put

together to further explore how a national union would operate; it included men from Lincolnshire, Cornwall, Devon, Kent, Nottinghamshire, Yorkshire and Shropshire.

After two or three exploratory meetings, the first general meeting of the NFU was held on 23 June 1909 in a marquee at the Royal Show in Gloucester. (In those days the Royal Show changed location on a yearly basis.) Here the forerunner of the union's Council was formed – a national executive committee of 15 members from different counties. Campbell was affirmed as the first president, along with three vice-presidents – Richards, Bryan and Turner.

A constitution and rules were approved. At the meeting the first ever resolution of the NFU was passed. It read: 'That in the interests of agriculture, as well as the community at large, the time has come when the Government should make an attempt to stamp out TB.' It is intriguing that 100 years later the NFU is still making this demand, though in 1909 there was no mention of badgers. There was, however, much mention of human TB, which

Left: *The first NFU logo.*

was killing thousands of Britons every year.

On the conclusion of the first annual meeting at the Royal Show Campbell's vision had become the reality. The determined Lincolnshire farmer must have taken great heart in the fact that 500 farmers joined during the show. Somewhat less inspiring was the observation of one delegate who, at the conclusion of the meeting, proudly announced: 'Hitherto farmers have been individual grumblers – now they are going to grumble collectively.' One likes to think that others had more edifying visions of what the newly born NFU was going to achieve for British agriculture.

In 12 months membership had climbed to a respectable 15,000 as county branches duly affiliated. Capitation fees, at 1s. per member, gave HQ an income of £543. Interestingly, only Cornwall, of the existing county unions, refused to affiliate because it felt the capitation fee was too high. One can only sympathise with the embarrassment of the Cornish member of the founding National Executive Committee, who must have returned home across the Tamar full of the exciting news of developments towards national unity only to have it thrown back in his face by the county membership because it was too expensive. Cornwall did not actually affiliate until

BOY: "What does it mean, Father, the Little Loaf and the Big Loaf?"

FATHER: "When I was a boy, PROTECTION gave us the Little Loaf, but, thanks to *FREE TRADE*, sonnie, we now have the *BIG LOAF*, and I mean to

VOTE FOR BETHELL

for he is an out-and-out FREE TRADER, and is against the Conservative-Protectionist Government which has *raised the price* of our SUGAR, TEA AND TOBACCO."

In the 1906 election the Liberals campaigned on the issue of food prices, arguing that Tory plans to protect agriculture would push them up.

1918 and was one of the last English counties to do so, along with Cumberland and Durham. It does seem strange that Cornwall should be there at the very inception of the NFU but be one of the last counties officially to come on board. Some might say this was quite in keeping with the Cornish character, with its combination of a fighting spirit and an inbred suspicion of anything that existed the other side of the Tamar.

A brief mention should be made about the word 'National' in the National Farmers' Union because, to be pedantic about it, it doesn't quite fit the union's ambit. From 1908 it was clear there was to be Welsh as well as English involvement in the NFU – there were Welshmen involved in the Shrewsbury 'No Warranty' protests. The first Welsh branch was Brecon and Radnor, founded at the Lamb Inn, Glasbury-on-Wye, on 20 May 1909. From there on the NFU has always represented both English and Welsh farmers. With the accession of Caernarvonshire and Merioneth in 1918 all Welsh counties had affiliated. The Scots, however, slipped the net. Campbell journeyed north of the border on more than one occasion in the years between 1906 and 1910 to try to convince the Scots of a need for a national union, and it must have been part of the early pioneers' game plan that the NFU would encompass all of Britain. A Scottish Farming Union was formed in 1913, seemingly taking a lead from what was happening in England and Wales. In 1915 there was communication from Scotland of a desire to affiliate with the NFU, but it was felt that the 1s. capitation fee was much too high. The reply from south of the border was that such a fee was low in any analysis. The SNFU never did affiliate and instead steered its own course.

Any flippant suggestion that Scottish miserliness might be the root cause of the NFU's failure to become a truly national organisation would not be appropriate, as it would just play on a tired national stereotype. As might be expected, the SNFU has at times insisted on erroneously calling the NFU the ENFU (the English National Farmers' Union).

If we were able to show by coloured lights on a map the multiplication of branches in the first year or two we would see a cluster of lights in Lincolnshire, which spread north into Yorkshire and then through the counties of the East Midlands as far as Warwickshire and Oxfordshire. Other lights would appear around Shrewsbury and Oswestry, from where the linking of lights would penetrate into mid-Wales. There would be early gleams from Kent and Devon in the south. From Gloucestershire the lights would spread along the Wye Valley through Worcestershire and Hereford into Breconshire and Radnorshire.

Often the creation of local branches preceded that of county branches, with a market town acting as focal point. In its early days the union had a robust cell-like structure that gave it cohesive strength from grass-roots to HQ. Within two years membership increased to 11,065, representing two million acres in 26 counties, with members paying a halfpenny per acre farmed to a maximum of £3.

Sometimes local issues would nudge farmers into seeing the need for combined strength and organisation. For instance, in early March 1909 Oxfordshire farmers were invited to County Hall, Oxford, to discuss the formation of a branch of the NFU. Local farmer Mr John Bryan was in the chair and in his address listed a number of threats to the local agricultural industry.

One such was a plan to ban the spreading of manure on fields that abutted the River Thames for fear it might pollute London's water-supply. (One wonders if Oxfordshire NFU members who meet today to discuss the Water Framework Directive or Nitrate Vulnerable Zones (NVZs) realise such discussions go back 100 years.) After Mr Bryan, Colin Campbell addressed the meeting and explained the need for farmers to combine into one powerful national union. Those gathered were persuaded by Campbell's sales pitch. Another branch was formed and by mid-1909 Oxfordshire as a county was in the NFU fold.

Similarly, in February 1912, a meeting of West Essex farmers was called. This being Essex as opposed to Oxford, the meeting was held not in the town hall amidst the dreaming spires of a university city, but rather at the White Hart pub in Romford. This time it was the recent court case of Ellis v. Banyard that had caused concern in the local farming community. Mrs Ellis, a cyclist, had been "thrown from her bike" by a gang of escapee cows belonging to Farmer Banyard. Although it was agreed that someone other than Farmer Banyard had left his gate open, the county court judge had ruled that the farmer was responsible for his cattle straying onto the highway and the consequent damage.

But all was not lost. The NFU had stepped in with legal aid and appealed the case. The iniquitous decision against Farmer Banyard was duly reversed. At the meeting, Campbell, for once, was not present but had sent a letter, which was read out. W.A. May was there and personally reiterated Campbell's call for unity. The importance of the NFU was duly demonstrated and another branch was duly formed.

Essex as a county affiliated in 1914. Like most of the other eastern counties, it was something of a laggard in joining the NFU. Cambridgeshire came into the fold the same year, with Suffolk joining in 1916 and Norfolk bringing up the rear in 1919.

Another union occasion, this time in 1912, merits a brief mention, as a reminder of the nature of Edwardian society. The LFU annual dinner was held at the Society Assembly Rooms in Woodhall Spa, where 250 guests gathered to hear witty and inspirational speeches from such as the irrepressible Revd Pat Hamilton, Colin Campbell, their president, and their guest speaker, Mr Walter Runciman, who, as President of the Board of Trade, was the Edwardian equivalent of the Minister of Agriculture. Runciman was thus a member of government. During the speeches three young ladies, Miss Crocker, Miss Roberts and Miss Brown, burst in, creating a disturbance and shouting: 'Mr Runciman, when are you going to give us what we want?' They were Suffragettes. After much hilarity and laughter from the farmers, the three women were ushered towards the door by union secretary Palmer. Five minutes later they disturbed proceedings again, bursting through another door and addressing the gathering from the orchestra platform. This time Secretary Palmer was less decorous and, according to press reports, much to the amusement of everyone, 'rushed', Miss Crocker, seized her in a 'double armful' and ejected her from the meeting. Witty and spontaneous as ever, the Revd Hamilton rose to his feet and pointed out that these women were an example to all farmers, in that 'these females could make more trouble in this gathering than all the Lincolnshire farmers combined'.

We have already mentioned that one of the NFU's founding principles was that it should be an organisation for farmers and farmers only. While it was happy to co-operate with landowners and farm workers when making representations to government, it remained staunch in the exclusivity of membership. This, its defining characteristic, differentiated it from other agricultural organisations. The other key founding principle was that it should be apolitical and not form alliances with political parties. It should be remembered that in those days most farmers were tenants and did not necessarily have a natural affinity with either political party of the day – Conservative or Liberal. It was always Campbell's desire to lift agriculture out of 'the mire of party politics'.

This party political impartiality was well tested early on in 1910, when a January election was called which resulted in a hung parliament, each of the main parties picking up around 40 per cent of the vote. The Conservatives had a more nationalistic, protectionist tendency than the Liberals, who were very much in favour of free trade. In their election advertising the Liberals put different-sized loaves of bread on posters and suggested a Tory Government would make tariff reforms seeking to protect UK agriculture, which in turn would lead to more expensive food for the working man. Logically, one might have thought the NFU would lean toward the Tory position that would protect home agriculture, but the union did no such thing. Campbell and his executive refused to have a view on tariff reform other than, if there was such reform, then 'agriculture in all its branches shall receive equal share of any benefits that

Exercising the hounds outside Campbell's farmhouse, an activity that proved the very spark of the NFU.

may accrue to other industries'. What is also interesting is that in its early days the NFU contained both Conservative and Liberal Party activists but managed to maintain its strict neutral stance. In the main, this policy has stayed with the NFU to this day. As we shall see, at times this neutrality has been tested, but the NFU has always remained apolitical and sought to negotiate constructively with the government of the day, no matter what its colour.

From its inception, though, the NFU realised that it must be proactive in lobbying parliament, and a political fund was set up for this purpose in 1910. In terms of policy, the union stuck to a similar list of demands as in the programme previously outlined. There were some extra demands relating to compensation for disturbance of tenanted land and for a uniform system of weights and measures. MPs were then asked to sign up to express their support for the programme. In the second 1910 elections, held on 3–19 December (it was the last of the drawn-out elections that lasted several days), 68 MPs from both parties duly signed.

The Asquith-led Liberal Government began to take the NFU seriously as representing the farming industry after 1912. In 1913 and 1914 regular NFU deputations were made to the Board of Trade and the Board of Agriculture. In 1913 Campbell led a group to Downing Street to speak with Chancellor Lloyd George. It was the opening of a dialogue between the NFU and the government which continues to this day. When present NFU members make delegations to various offices around Whitehall and Westminster they are treading in the well-worn steps of their predecessors.

Campbell's reluctance at this time not to take too many hard-and-fast positions on policy might well have been due to concerns as to the fragility of the NFU in its early days. As we have seen, he knew that forming a union of rugged individualists from a disparity of farming sectors and differing geographical regions would be a challenge. It was like building a house of cards on an unstable table. The trick was to keep a steady hand and to avoid any shocks or jolts. On the other hand, leadership on the issues of the day had to be provided to give the union purpose. A steady course had to be steered between rabble rousing and faintheartedness. It is a challenge that confronted every union president thereafter.

There were times when Campbell's prejudices did get the better of him. From the word go he seldom had time for the smallholder. The LFU had been set up with a membership fee of ¹/₂d. an acre, with a minimum sub of 1s. (12d.), the latter being imposed to deter the small men. The union opposed the action of county councils, who were acquiring some excellent farm land under the provisions of the Small Holdings Act 1892 and 1908 (the latter led to 30,000 families being resettled on the land) Later in 1912 Campbell wrote to the Board of Agriculture:

I am against small men being singled out for help, there is too much spoon feeding already. Land has been taken compulsorily for smallholders whose success under normal conditions was open to grave doubt... I doubt the wisdom of bolstering up insolvent farmers, whether large or small and merely postponing the evil day.

Another issue that caught Campbell's attention was the attack on 'landlordism' in the radical Lloyd George budgets following the Liberal landslide of 1906. Campbell, who was himself a tenant of the large Middleton Estate, felt uneasy about the breakdown of the traditional relationship between tenant and landlord. The Liberal Government's policy of financing the embryonic Welfare State by taxing the rich through increased death duties was causing many large estates to be broken up. While some farmers clearly saw this as an opportunity to buy land and free themselves of a system that bordered on the feudal, Campbell favoured securing the position of trusted tenant and trusted landlord. This sometimes led to tension between the president and the membership.

While this book places much emphasis on the man at the very top of the union, it should not be forgotten that the union's strength largely came from its activity at county and branch level. While at national level the NFU struggled to influence parliament, in the regions NFU candidates were elected onto county councils, especially in Lincolnshire, Kent and Devon, where rating reform and rural education were areas of interest to farmers. The legal services offered by the county branches helped many members win disputes with landlords and secure concessions from railway companies. Some effort was made at local level to improve livestock standards by seeking grants from the Liberal development fund to secure the appointment of specialist livestock instructors. County branches also helped to establish other institutions associated with progressive farming, particularly Milk Record societies.

As the union grew in numbers at local level, with its cell-like structure of parish organisers reporting to branch, who in turn reported to county, HQ struggled to keep up, and dissatisfaction was soon expressed at county level. In 1913 the demand was made that the NFU should establish its own permanent headquarters in London instead of wandering between the *Mark Lane Express* offices, the Holborn restaurant and rooms at the Royal Agricultural Society of England (RASE). There was also a growing need to appoint more full-time staff. Rooms in Wellington Street next to the *MLE* offices were

duly acquired and extra staff were taken on, including a full-time parliamentary lobbyist, Mr C. Weller from Kent.

With the outbreak of war in 1914 Campbell realised the NFU would have to change its approach at this time of national crisis. Times of war are usually profitable ones for farmers, as food supplies get interrupted, creating a seller's market. In his address to the 1915 AGM, and writing in the 1915 Year Book, Campbell was adamant that the NFU must put its patriotic duties first. He also stressed the need to institute a public relations campaign to counter accusations that farmers were profiteering.

The fortunes of agriculture and the NFU during the First World War will be told in the following chapter, but first we should draw a line under Colin Campbell. In its early days the union did not seem to have any clear rules as to how long a president should serve. This excited little controversy in the early years, as Campbell was the obvious choice. By 1913 there were voices suggesting he should give way to another man, but Campbell insisted on putting himself forward each year and each year he was duly re-elected unopposed.

In later years he explained his reasons for this persistence. Until 1918 he felt the NFU was not secure and could still fail, and he did not want anyone else to have to go through the misery of having the fledgling union die under their presidency. He was determined that if the movement failed then he should take responsibility. In early 1918, confident in the NFU's future, Campbell duly stood down after 14 years of leading the LFU and the NFU. By this time union membership had hit the 50,000 mark and was growing rapidly, having doubled in the previous two years. It now represented over 25 per cent of the estimated 200,000 commercial farms in England and Wales. Fittingly, at the 1918 AGM, Campbell was presented with a silver salver and a cheque by Lord Selbourne in recognition of his services. Lord Selborne had known Campbell personally for several years and paid homage to his character and his achievement. Campbell was made an honorary life member of the union.

Despite retirement, Campbell continued to work for the union and sat on a number of HQ committees until his death in 1933. He carried on farming Stapleford Hall until 1925. The 9th Lord Middleton died in 1922 and some of the estate, including Stapleford Hall, was sold to pay death duties. This was undoubtedly one reason why Campbell decided to pack up, the other being that his two sons, George and Colin, had chosen careers in engineering and the military. Campbell retired from farming and lived his days out at the rectory in nearby Thurlby.

Today Stapleford Hall and the village of Stapleford remain much the same as Campbell would have known them. It is a peaceful, unspoilt patch of South Lincolnshire not far from the roar of the A1. The farm is still farmed as a 600-acre unit. The stock has gone and now the typical Lincolnshire arable rotation of sugar beet, wheat, barley and rape is the order of the day. Part of the farm at its northern edge has been excavated for gravel.

Although Colin Campbell's sons chose not to go into farming, the good news is that one of his great-grandsons returned to the fold of his great-grandfather's calling and today farms sheep in Devon. His name is, of course, Colin Campbell, but everyone knows him by his middle name, James.

So, how do we evaluate the position of Colin Campbell in the history of agriculture and the NFU? It must be said that, in its first decade, the NFU did little to transform the prospects for farmers. Its 13-point programme remained largely ignored and, although some MPs signed up to it, theirs remained token support rather than anything more substantial.

Even so, the contribution of Colin Campbell to the history of the NFU cannot be over-estimated. 'What if?' scenarios are seldom worth pursuing, but it is fair to posit that without him there would be no NFU. In his obituary in the 1933 NFU Year Book he is described as 'of Scottish extraction and having the dogged pertinacity of that race'. Although he was several generations removed from his Scots ancestry, the description seems very apt. Without that 'dogged pertinacity' a lesser man would not have had what was needed to found an organisation such as the NFU. Trying to organise farmers has been described as 'trying to herd cats'.

As we shall see, many men have managed to unite and lead the farmers of England and Wales through the presidency of the NFU, but they have all had the benefit of what had been done before. The man who first set out to start the process of corralling farmers was probably the greatest leader of all.

CHAPTER 3

Edward Mials Nunneley, 1918

President Nunneley, looking rather Dickensian in 1917.

The outbreak of war in 1914 brought the emaciated state of British agriculture into sharp focus. Since 1870 the area of ploughed land in Britain had fallen by around three to four million acres, much of which had reverted to grass or scrub. Over the previous 40 years there had been a huge surge of imports. As a result Britain, alone of the major European nations, was dependent on imports for the greater part of its food supply. Overall, about 60 per cent (in calories) of the UK food supply was derived directly from imports.

In the period leading up to the war this dependency caused little concern in political circles. The idea that Britain might be blockaded and its food supplies strangled was seldom considered. Some are of the view that when Germany decided to build up a submarine fleet after 1910 they had this British reliance on food imports at the back of their minds.

The supremacy of free trade as a political philosophy remained unquestioned in the Liberal governments that ruled Britain from 1906 to 1916. Even the Conservative opposition had softened its view on tariff reform. It would seem the British public were happy with cheap imported food and saw no reason why home farmers should receive any favours if they couldn't compete on price. As we have noted, the situation in France and Germany was different, with tariffs of up to a third of the commodity price protecting their home agriculture from foreign competition. In Germany home agriculture contributed 90 per cent of the country's energy supply, and Germany had a much higher proportion of land down to the plough

In 1913, consumers in the UK had spent £669 million on food, at least £216 million of which had been imported. The reliance on imports was most striking in the case of wheat and wheat flour. Four-fifths of the wheat and wheat flour consumed by humans came from overseas, and flour contributed almost a third of the entire energy supply of the nation. In terms of meat, the dependence on imports was less pronounced. A third of beef and lamb and three-quarters of bacon were imported. Butter and cheese were dominated by production in Denmark and Holland. Sugar was entirely imported, as there was little sugar beet grown in the UK until after the war. One-third of the nation's sugar requirement came from cane production in the Americas and the rest came from the sugar beet grown in central and eastern Europe. The latter, after 1914, was enemy territory. Half of the eggs consumed were imported. Only milk and potatoes seemed immune from foreign competition, presumably due to the cost of transport.

At first this potential strategic weakness remained largely ignored. Most thought the war would be over in months and the German U-boats were considered an irrelevance by naval strategists. The Kaiser's Navy remained bottled up in the Baltic, and that is where His Majesty's Royal Navy intended to keep it.

When the war began the president of the NFU offered the government the assistance of its 40 county and local branches in the war effort. The offer was politely acknowledged but that was all. The first thing government wanted from farmers in 1914 was not food security but the conscription of their horses and their labour; even if the 1914 harvest was in full progress. Horses were commandeered by the thousand and many a market town echoed day and night to the clatter of hooves as drafts passed through on their way to Army training centres or the ports. In terms of supplying servicemen, agriculture, with its 200,000 farmers and 800,000 farm workers was one of the first ports of call. There was no attempt to make those involved in food production a reserved occupation, and by the end of 1916 between a quarter and

In the First World War and, to a lesser extent, the Second, one of the first demands on agriculture was the conscription of horses.

a third of agriculture's labour force had been lost to the Services. While the men who worked the mines and the shipyards were kept in place on account of their strategic importance, the men who worked the farms were not. In the first two years of the war the NFU was a lone voice warning of the dangers of depleting the countryside of its workforce.

As the opposing forces on the Western Front dug in, the NFU stood by ready to help with encouraging an increase in the home production of food, but nothing was forthcoming from government in the form of directives or production targets. The 1914 harvest had proven a good one, with cereals averaging 17 cwt an acre and potatoes 6.6 tons/acre. The hay harvest was also good. In 1915 the UK dairy herd of 2.2 million cows was actually two per cent bigger than it had been in 1913. The harvests in America had also been favourable and, in terms of food supply in general, it seemed to be business as usual.

A limited degree of partnership between government and the farming community was introduced in 1915 with the establishment of county war agricultural committees to provide some degree of co-ordination in giving farmers advice on increasing production. While NFU members played an active part in the running of these committees, farmers struggled to take much heed of the committees in the face of the loss of labour to the front line. The fact that crop production required more labour than grazed livestock made farmers very reluctant to plough up grass when faced with declining farm labour. The NFU proposed a lowering of the school-leaving age in rural districts, but this was rejected when vigorously opposed by the teaching and farm workers' unions.

Another piece of government action that rankled with farmers was the introduction of British Summer Time in 1916. The NFU stifled its criticism in case it appeared self-serving and against the national

interest. Even so, it remained unpopular with many in the industry as, indeed, it still does, 90 years later.

As 1916 approached it became clear that the war was going to drag on and that Britain's mercantile fleet – and thus her food supply - was vulnerable to U-boat attack. The Milner Committee, reporting in mid-1915, concluded:

The only method of effecting a substantial increase in the gross production of food in England and Wales for the harvest of 1916 and later consists of restoring to arable cultivation some of the poorer grass land that has been laid down since the 1870s .

The committee calculated that land growing crops would produce five times as much food as pasture supporting livestock. Intriguingly, these were much the same concerns as had exercised the minds of medieval kings 500 years before, when high wool prices encouraged the spread of pastoral farming at the expense of arable crops, thus risking famine.

A system of guaranteeing the wheat price at 45s. a quarter was suggested by the committee, but the government refused to take up the proposal. Arthur Balfour, Admiralty Minister, suggested it was: '... the wildest thing ever proposed. It would be better to take over the land and run it on socialistic principles.' McKenna, the Chancellor, and Runciman, at the Board of Trade, simply rejected the proposal because of the cost. With 60 years of free trade and laissez-faire having left such an indelible mark on the government's attitude to agriculture, it was not going to be easy to shake off these principles.

Things changed radically in mid-1916. The American harvest of 1916 was a poor one in contrast to those of 1914 and 1915. Furthermore, as Caribbean sugar struggled to replace the supply from central Europe, sugar imports were running at 15 per cent less than their pre-war levels. To add to the problem, the U-boat campaign was gaining momentum. In 1915 the tonnage of British shipping lost at sea to enemy action reached 885,471, climbing to 1,231,867 in 1916 and then 3,660,054 in 1917. As Germany unleashed her policy of unrestricted submarine warfare the decision by politicians to allow the country to become dependent on imports for its food suddenly took on a whole new perspective. It was not until after the war that the full extent of the peril to which Britain had been exposed was made known. Lloyd George revealed later that he had been advised in late 1917, at the height of the submarine campaign, that Britain had but two or three weeks' reserves of food. Similar testimony to the mood in 1917 came from the Chairman of the Allied Maritime Commission, who recollected: 'The spectre of famine was more frightening than at any other time.'

In 1916 parliament lost confidence in the way Asquith was running the war, and Lloyd George became Prime Minister in charge of a coalition government. Lloyd George was always going to be more interventionist than his predecessor, Asquith, who, over the previous ten years, had proven unmoved by the plight of agriculture and had always refused any suggestion of intervention or protectionism. Lloyd George backed 'the plough policy', which was to be based on three principles: extension of the arable acreage, compulsory powers and decentralisation. A 'food controller' was appointed and given drastic powers, including that of being able to fix the price of milk and meat. The powers of the food controller often irked farmers, who felt prices were too low, especially of meat and milk, and that the powers were too draconian. In a famous legal battle known as 'the Ivory case', which did not actually find resolution until 1927, William Ivory, a Hertfordshire member, was prosecuted by the Crown for profiteering when selling his milk. As the farmer kept no accounts, whether he had or hadn't profiteered was open to argument. The initial successful prosecution was brought in front of the complaints tribunal of the central profiteering committee of the Board of Trade and the farmer was ordered to pay £147. The NFU then stepped in and assisted the farmer in bringing an appeal to the divisional court, where Mr Justice Darling dismissed the case against the farmer and criticised the court, saying their proceedings reminded him of justice administered 'under a palm tree'.

At county level the County War Agricultural Committees became County Agricultural Executive Committees and were given powers to inspect land, enforce cultivation orders and take over the running of farms if it was felt the occupier was unable or unlikely to comply.

In August 1917 the Corn Production Act was passed. Wheat was guaranteed at 60s. a quarter and oats at 38s. Strangely, barley prices, in deference to the anti-drink lobby, were not guaranteed. The mechanism of support took the form of compensation should the average market price fall below the minimum price. The compensation paid would be equivalent to the difference between the two prices on the assumption that the average yield per acre was four quarters for wheat and five for barley. The farmers simply registered the acreage grown and did not have to prove production or sales.

The Act proved controversial in parliament. Liberal and Labour MPs felt it was enriching farmers to the exclusion of the rest of society. In terms of legislation, this Act was the first significant attempt to protect farmers from low market prices since the Corn Laws of 1816, 100 years before. The irony was it did not actually come into operation. The wheat price remained at around 75s. for the rest of the war. Despite this, it is wrong to think of the legislation as an irrelevance; it gave farmers confidence to plough and sow in the knowledge that prices would not

Five hard-working Land Army women in 1918 with one male supervisor.

collapse in the future. The Act went further than guaranteeing prices. It also guaranteed farm workers' wages by setting up the Agricultural Wages Board, which fixed minimum rates of pay. It was a revolutionary development for agriculture and is the precursor to the AWB we have 90 years later. The first order of the AWB was a standard minimum wage of 25s. Workers' unions complained that this was too low. As the wage for ordinary workers in 1914 had been 17s. and as inflation had run away at 80 per cent subsequently, the minimum should now logically be 30s.

The Act also sought to control rent increases so that landlords could not cash in on the new guaranteed prices. It also allowed tenants to ignore lease covenants that prevented the ploughing of pasture.

The War Cabinet realised that none of these measures would amount to anything unless farmers were also guaranteed the necessary labour, machinery and fertilisers needed to increase production. Accordingly, agriculture was given greater priority in reserving occupations from conscription and in the provision of machinery such as tractors. The German spring offensive in 1918, beginning with the attack on the Somme on 21 March (during which the British incurred losses in excess of 177,000), put pressure on the agreement that farm workers would not be called to the front. In April the War Cabinet waived the exemptions agreed and an additional 30,000 18–23-year-olds were recruited from the agricultural workforce. This caused plans to increase production under the plough policy to be put back. The gap caused by the loss of labour was to some extent filled by prisoners of war and the Women's Land Army.

Meanwhile, the NFU had undergone a change in presidency. At the AGM in February 1918 Campbell handed the presidency on to Edward Mials Nunneley. It was also agreed that it be made clear in the constitution that the president should serve one year and one year only.

At the age of nearly 70, Nunneley was Campbell's senior. Where Campbell displayed the vigour and vitality needed to lead the organisation in its infancy, Nunneley gave the union the wise guidance it needed to take it into adolescence. As photos of him show, Nunneley had a most striking countenance. With a great flowing white beard he looked like a combination of a Dickensian villain and an Old Testament prophet. Our knowledge of him as a farmer is somewhat scant and drawn from the pages of the *Mark Lane Express*. We know he first took a tenancy of a 280-acre farm near the small Northamptonshire village of Ashby St Legers at the age of 20 in 1868. Ashby St Legers has a place in British history in that it was the scene of the hatching of the Gunpowder Plot. From here Guy Fawkes was sent forth to attempt to blow up King James I. Somewhat less romantically, it is now the site of the Watford Gap service station. As you thunder north

on the M1 you may well be speeding across the dirt that Nunneley farmed. In 1878 he took on the lease of his uncle's farm at Orlingbury, where he expanded his farming operation to an impressive 800 acres. It was a typical heavy clay arable farm. Before 1878, when wheat was at over 30s. a quarter, wheat farming was profitable enough, but when the wheat price crashed in the 1880s Nunneley adopted a rotation of four years fallow and four years grass, when he fattened cows and sheep. This was a good example of a farm that reverted from crops to grass and fallow in the recession years. In the 1900s Nunneley left the Orlingbury farm in the charge of his son and bought a 320-acre farm on the Harrowden Road on the northern outskirts of Wellingborough, where he farmed arable, stock and poultry. It was here that he stood as the Liberal candidate for North Northamptonshire, but failed to get elected.

He had been involved in the NFU from the start and was trusted to put the interests of agriculture before any wider political ambition. He was an acknowledged expert on taxation and rating. It should be remembered that in those days farmland was rated. In 1912 Nunneley had given evidence to the Treasury on behalf of Northamptonshire NFU in which he made much of the iniquity of farmers having to pay a large share of local taxation through rates while they got few of the benefits. He made the point that tradesmen in towns paid less in rates and yet made better profits than farmers and got the benefit of good roads with pavements, electricity and sewers, none of which were to be found in the countryside. Nunneley was also a champion of tenants' rights. We should remember that in those days the vast majority of NFU members were tenant farmers.

In his social life, he was a keen member of the Pytchley Hunt and, just as with Campbell, exercised the young hounds. NFU minutes in 1918 report Nunneley's absence due to the fact that he had broken his arm after falling off his horse. One suspects he was not the first or last septegenerian farmer to have learned the frailty of age in this way. We do not know how Nunneley and ground met, but we do know from writings that he was irked by the tarmacking of country lanes, which made rural roads safer for the townman's infernal car but more dangerous for the countryman's horse. We also know that the NFU made strong representations about this issue at the Ministry of Transport to the relevant body, which was called, rather predictably, the Slippery Road Surfaces Committee. In 1919 experiments were carried out jointly between the NFU and the MOT on horseshoe design. This issue rumbled on for several years, and in 1929 the Somerset branch was still lobbying its county council to put sand down onto tarred roads.

As NFU leaders, both Campbell and Nunneley were both clear that efforts to grow the union should be put to one side in favour of concentrating on the war effort. Little was done by way of systematic recruitment. Despite this, between 1916 and 1918 union membership grew at the fastest rate in its history and, by the time the armistice was signed in November 1918, stood at 60,000. This momentum of the war years was maintained through to 1920, when membership hit the 100,000 mark.

One of the ironies of the national crisis brought on by the First World War was that for both agriculture and the NFU it provided a great opportunity. With Britain cut off from her considerable external food supplies, home farmers were in a strong position and markets turned in their favour. Furthermore, with government forced to intervene in farming affairs, those who represented the farming community were well placed to put themselves forward as the official representatives.

In many ways the First World War was the making of the NFU. For an organisation that had freshly established itself in the farming community, the timing of the war was most opportune for a number of reasons. Firstly, farmers were better off, with most commodity prices rising significantly after 1915. The payment of union subs became less of a burden. Secondly, just as a war unites a nation and concentrates its mind, farmers too recognised that the crisis was a time for united action and not a time to indulge individualism. Finally, the increasing role of government in agriculture after 1916 gave the NFU a chance to prove itself as the voice of the farmer and become a reliable partner for government. As the food production campaign gathered momentum and the challenge of managing farms through directives became more complex, liaison between Whitehall and the NFU leadership became more frequent. When the government formed the NAC in 1917 to oversee agricultural strategy the NFU, initially, had no places. The union made a loud protest and was duly given five seats. At county level the fact that the NFU county structure overlapped the county war executives and the agricultural wages boards also helped the NFU achieve permanent places in the committee rooms of local government. This, in turn, encouraged more farmers to join the union as a means of engaging with a system that was increasingly making demands of them. The Corn Production Act was seen as a huge gesture of goodwill from government through which farmers accepted the challenge of feeding the nation in return for a guaranteed fair price. It was seen as a proper partnership and not just as a series of top-down directives.

As the workload increased, the union needed to expand its work and offices at HQ. In 1918, under Nunneley's presidency, new offices were found, first at No. 39 Victoria Street and then at No. 45 Bedford Square, where the NFU remained until 1956. Also in that year the redoubtable H.W. Palmer resigned as

Bedford Square, home of the NFU from 1918 to 1956.

general secretary due to ill health and was replaced by G.T. Apps, a barrister from Chichester, who started with a £500 salary. Slowly, the NFU was moving away from being a rather loose and amateurish confederation of county unions to becoming a more sophisticated, professionally organised and centrally administered pressure group. At the same time, it should be remembered, the counties were their own dominions and any centralisation was only done with the acquiescence of the County Executives and at a pace they were happy with.

In 1917 the capitation fee was quadrupled to 4s. per member and the annual income received at HQ climbed from £1,350 to over £10,000. Counties were left to their own devices as to how the capitation fee was to be found. We can deduce from the escalating membership that this considerable rise did not put many off joining the union.

As the harvest of 1918 approached it became clear that the plough policy was working. The 1918 ploughed area was 12.02 million acres – the highest figure between 1886 and 1942 – and 60 per cent of the land lost to tillage since 1875 had been reinstated. The harvest of 1918 was a golden one with near-perfect weather. It was the largest UK harvest in living memory. Wheat production was up 58 per cent

31

on pre-war levels, oats 36 per cent and potatoes 59 per cent. While farmers brought in this golden harvest on the home front, the Allied troops on the Western Front, buoyed by the arrival of 10,000 fresh American troops every day, started the 100-day offensive. This attack, spearheaded by a new vehicle of war, the tank, punctured the German lines in key areas and, more importantly, punctured German morale. Three months later, on the eleventh day of the eleventh month, the German surrender was formally accepted in a railway carriage at Compeigne.

Amid the public rejoicing at the military triumph, others paid testimony to what had happened on the arable fields of England, as well as in the mud of Flanders.

In his war memoirs, published in 1934, Lloyd George indicated that without the extra millions of tons of food grown by British farmers, the nation would have gone hungry in 1918. He further concluded that 'the food question ultimately decided the issue of this war'.

With peace declared, the NFU realised that severe challenges still lay before them. Undoubtedly, the fortunes of farmers, particularly of large arable farmers, had changed for the better during the war, and with that came the accusation in the press of profiteering. This smarted with the likes of Nunneley, for he knew that, although profitability had improved, it had been from a cruelly low base. Furthermore, without profit farmers had no incentive to increase the production that was so important to national security in a time of war.

This factor triggered two lines of development in the union that are still key features of the NFU today. The first was the recognition of the need for good public relations. From 1918 onwards the NFU took the opinion of the non-farming public (or, as they are described in NFU journals, 'the townsfolk') increasingly seriously. Special statements repudiating the profiteering claims were sent to the press. The political fund, which was used to lobby MPs and to finance public relations work, was substantially increased.

Secondly, the NFU realised that these accusations of profiteering were easy to make when no one, not even the farmers themselves, had any clear idea how profitable farming actually was. At this time 90 per cent of farmers kept no proper accounts. Recognising that it would be next to impossible for the NFU to take a business case or a detailed economic analysis to government in this situation, the NFU started to offer free services in bookkeeping and farm accounts.

Another development that reared its head under Nunneley's reign was dissent from within. The NFU has always had members who think they know better than the leadership and are not afraid of speaking out. It was when the membership grew large enough to accommodate internal criticism that it first came to the fore. In the 10 February 1918 edition of the *Mark Lane Express* we find the following extract from the letters page:

The present proposition is to raise the subscription from a penny to two pence an acre. 'We must have more money', we are told for political propaganda, Press campaigns and official salaries. Now could anyone imagine three worse forms of investment for a farmer's money? Political propaganda is another word for intrigue, broken promises and party opposition. Press campaigns would entail a huge expenditure with no result. The farmer is the seller, whilst the public is a buyer, so each would still consider his own pocket. Official salaries – officials are easy to get, but rather difficult to get rid of. Like the poor, they are always with you. The first thing to be done is to get every farmer into the Union. You could do this, not by raising the subscription, but by showing the farmer that you can put some money into his pocket. At present, less than half the farmers are in the Union. Get the other half in and you will double your income and at the same time be able to put such pressure on every rural MP in the kingdom as they cannot ignore.

Throughout its history the NFU has always had a healthy open debate from within its ranks. Farmers are known for their strong opinions on a range of matters, and no president has ever escaped the benefit of hearing them. A personal account of the atmosphere of the 1919 AGM by Mr Ginger Burleigh, the Cambridgeshire delegate, is worth recounting:

No bear garden was equal to the noise and din of that meeting, when fiery speeches with threats of all sorts of blood-thirsty methods were shouted out from all over the room.

At that lively AGM Nunneley, having completed his one-year stint as president, stood down in accordance with the constitution. Although 12 months was a brief reign, to have led the union in such a momentous year as 1918 was an achievement in itself. Nunneley continued to serve on union committees and to give his sage advice on issues such as taxation until he died in 1929. The farm Nunneley took in 1905 on the outskirts of Wellingborough has since disappeared under a 1960s housing estate. It is part of the millions of acres of English farmland lost to development since 1908.

CHAPTER 4

F. Herbert Padwick, 1919

The key question after the war was: would government maintain its support for agriculture through the Corn Production Act, or would it revert to the laissez-faire free-trade philosophy that had characterised the late-Victorian and Edwardian eras? As we have seen, in its early years the union was ambivalent on the issue of tariff reform and protectionism. This ambivalence continued after the war and seemed to reflect the general attitude of farmers. When, in 1917, the NFU parliamentary committee was asked to include tariff reform in the NFU's programme it was refused.

On the one hand, farmers are proud, independent minded, self-reliant folk who instinctively do not like the interference of government in their affairs. On the other hand, the conundrum that has faced the industry through much of its history is the realisation that without some degree of protectionism agriculture can suffer cripplingly low prices. This has often led to a contradictory and schizophrenic attitude to protectionism and state intervention. The policy of the NFU has often reflected that.

When Edward Nunneley and Herbert Padwick gave evidence to the Royal Commission on Agriculture in 1919 on behalf of the NFU, they expressed a preference for a return to the open market so that farmers could attend to their business free of the fetters of state interference. But they made it very clear that they would accept continuance of control in the national interest, provided guaranteed prices were maintained.

President Padwick (right) *and an unnamed, smoke-exhaling friend.*

F.H. Padwick (known by his middle name, Herbert) succeeded Nunneley as president in 1919. A West Sussex man, he was born at Westborne in 1856 to a well-known Sussex farming family. He farmed 1,500 acres around the Chichester area, including Thorney Island. It was mixed farming, including arable, dairy, sheep and poultry. Unlike Campbell and Nunneley, who enjoyed the world of politics, Padwick was first and foremost an agriculturalist. He was a celebrated breeder of Jersey cattle and president of the Jersey Cattle Society in 1911. His Jersey herd was the largest in England, with over 140 milking cows, and included one cow which, for over ten years, yielded an average of over 1,000 gallons a year. Despite his eminence as a dairy farmer, Padwick's first love seemed to be his sheep. He had been president of the National Sheepbreeders' Association and was instrumental in setting up the South Down Sheep Society, of which he was president in 1909. Photos of him suggest he was much in demand as a stock judge. He had been involved in the NFU from its inception and was first chairman of the Sussex branch in 1910. The impressive 90 per cent NFU membership among West Sussex farmers by the end of the war was largely attributed to his popularity. In 1916 he had served as vice-president under Campbell.

We know little of his character other than that he is described as a man of 'a donnish bearing' who was also qualified as a barrister. His writings display a quiet intelligence and an understated delivery. Photos show he only had one arm – we can only guess at the circumstances whereby he lost the other. This, though, was an age of increasing mechanisation on farms, with very little regard for the dangers of working around moving machinery. Consequently, it was not uncommon to come across farmers and farm workers minus a limb or two.

As we are now in the company of a president who was a leading authority on sheep, it is appropriate to briefly consider the state of the British sheep industry in the early-twentieth century.

As we have seen, the main trend in British agriculture from 1870 through to 1910 had been a decline in the arable area from 13.8 to 10.5 million acres and an increase in permanent grass from 12.1 to 17.4 million acres. Cattle numbers over the same period increased from five million to seven million, but sheep stayed much the same, at around 27 million. This represented a little over half the mutton and lamb consumed by Britons.

Sheep farming in 1908, looking remarkably like a scene from a Thomas Hardy novel.

Pedigree sheep breeding was largely a Victorian introduction, and by the end of the nineteenth century had become a fine art, with 27 herd books. Fat lamb production had been brought close to perfection with breeds such as the Southdowns, Suffolks, border Leicesters and Lincoln Longwools. These breeds were folded onto the arable land of lowland Britain. Traditionally, sheep were an important part of the arable rotation, with roots every four years to be sheeped and cornfields to be trodden, grazed and manured.

Breeds such as Romney, with their big frames and long, lustrous wool, were fed on coastal marshes. The mountain breeds of the north and west had also seen much improvement, giving greater conformity and quality of breed. The Cheviots, the lakeland fells, the Welsh mountains and Exmoor all supported their own breeds of coarse-woolled sheep.

British sheep farmers thus had an extensive pedigree pool to use on their farms. Some crossed and re-crossed their animals with great precision and to great effect, producing animals which suited their farming, their topography and their markets. Others were less precise and could be found boasting that they had never spent more than a few pounds on a ram. The progeny often reflected this less than progressive approach to sheep genetics

From time immemorial the British trade in sheep had flowed from north to south, from west to east, from the hills to the lowland fields, pastures and marshes. Before the railway animals were literally walked to their final markets in the more populous south and east, and were fattened near to their desti-

nations. Transport by railway speeded and simplified the trade and also enabled some to be carried dead rather than alive. The sheep market remained a tangled web of dealers, live marts and geographically isolated farmers. Marketing was hopelessly opportunistic and localised, with sheep farmers at the mercy of the price they found when they took their animals to market. Before the war this price was undermined by the price of cheap imported meat that had been facilitated by freezing and shipping from South America and the colonies.

The impact on sheep farmers of the war was double edged. With imports subdued, there was some increase in prices in 1915, but from 1916 the food controller kept a check on this by ratcheting down the price of meat below that allowed by the free market. Meanwhile, better wheat prices and the scarcity of good shepherds caused many arable farmers to abandon their sheep flocks. The resulting fall in sheep numbers was then intensified by exceptionally severe weather in early 1919, which caused a high death rate among hill ewes and lambs. By June 1920 the British sheep population had fallen to less than 20 million, five million less than in 1916.

This decline in the British sheep industry was of great concern to Padwick, who was firmly of the opinion that a healthy sheep sector was fundamental to the welfare of British agriculture for two reasons. Not only did it represent the only farming option for many of the hard-pressed hill men in the west and the north, Padwick also felt sheep were essential to good arable husbandry in the south and the east, particularly on poorer soils.

Padwick suggested a two-fold policy to reverse this regrettable decline in sheep numbers. The first concerned the power of the press, which Padwick described as 'the greatest power in the world'. He felt that through the press three things could be achieved: foreign sheepmen could be reminded of the strengths of British pedigree stock; the arable farmers could be reminded of the importance of sheep to good crop husbandry and British consumers could be convinced that: 'There was no meat in the world equal to home-killed mutton, nor any so wholesome and digestable.'

Padwick's second proposal was to improve co-operative marketing in both lamb and wool and for producers to get closer to consumers by cutting out the middlemen. In 1920 there was little appetite for Padwick's ideas but, as we shall see in time, his proposals did come of age and in this respect he was a visionary.

Far away from the world of sheep another milestone in the history of the NFU was reached in 1919 with the launch of the NFU Mutual. As we have seen, in the earliest days of Harry Palmer and the LFU, there had been links between the business of the farmers' unions and the selling of insurance. There was a synergy between the two. Union secretaries could augment their meagre NFU remuneration by selling insurance to the farmers they met through union activities. Before 1919 this was operated at branch or county level, with a number of insurance companies offering franchises to NFU officials and discounts to union members. For instance,

the Crown insurance company (of whom Colin Campbell was a director) offered a 20 per cent discount to NFU members in several counties in the East Midlands. In the West Midlands it had a small rival – the Midland Farmers' Mutual Insurance Society, based in Stratford-upon-Avon. The latter had early links with the NFU in that, when the Mutual Society was formed by local farmers in a Stratford teashop in 1910, one key driver was to grow membership of the recently formed local farmers' union by offering members discounted insurance deals.

In the spring of 1918 the NFU insurance committee looked at the idea of forming a mutual insurance company and asked branches to pledge support. The response of the Warwickshire Farmers' Union was to suggest it would consider a liaison with the Midland Farmers which, despite being a small regional outfit, could offer something unusual – a service exclusive to NFU members and ownership by the policy holders themselves. It was also agreed by the Midland that all county or branch secretaries could act as agents and that premiums would be 20 per cent below those of tariff prices.

At the AGM in late February 1919 at which Padwick was elected president the proposal was put that there should be an agreement with the Midland Farmers' Mutual to form the NFU Mutual. One of the main objectors to the proposal was Colin Campbell, who doubted the wisdom of an alliance with this small, untried provincial organisation, which boasted an insurance staff of just one. Despite

James Black, one of the pioneers behind the NFU Mutual, outside his farmhouse in 1912.

The last harvest on Padwick's farm on Thorney Island before the arrival of the RAF.

these fierce objections the proposal was carried by a large majority, and on 21 June 1919 the NFU Mutual was born. It was managed by 16 directors, eight appointed by the NFU and eight by the Midland Farmers' Mutual. The plan at the time was to move the offices from Stratford to London to join the NFU at Bedford Square, but somehow the move was never opportune, and to this day the NFU Mutual's home has remained in Stratford. Within a year net premiums shot up from £9,790 to over £70,000. Despite this healthy start, the link between the NFU and the NFU Mutual was far from total. Under the 1919 agreement counties were still entitled to form agreements with other insurance companies if they so wished, and many did. Despite rapid growth across most of the country it wasn't until 1976 that all counties came on board and, as one might predict, it was the Cornish who were last to forgo their alliance with their own county insurance company.

With a membership of 76,000 at the end of 1919, branches in every county and representatives on several important government bodies, including a royal commission, the retiring president, F.H. Padwick, was justified in claiming that the 'status' of the NFU had improved considerably within the space of a mere two years. His assertion that it was widely recognised as an important organisation was

not an exaggerated indulgence in self congratulation.

Padwick continued to be a good servant of the NFU and agriculture generally through the 1920s. He died in 1945 at a good age. One brief postscript note should be made about his farm on Thorney Island. Thorney Island lies between two limbs of Chichester harbour. Flat land, it was reclaimed from the sea in the 1870s and made for productive farm land both for grazing and for crop production. Today it is an air-base and resounds to the noise of the jets and helicopters of the RAF, far removed from the marshland peace that Padwick would have known. The farm was taken by the MoD in 1935. As a public-spirited man, F. Herbert Padwick must have realised the importance of air defence in the 1930s, but one can also guess that the sight of the last harvest must have brought a tear to the eye of this wise old agriculuralist. He was a thoughtful man who had his roots in a more tranquil age.

Padwick's successor as president in 1920 was the redoubtable E.W. Langford of Hereford. At this juncture we shall skip the presidency of E.W. Langford in 1920 and move straight to 1921 and the presidency of Rowland R. Robbins. This is not out of any discourtesy to Langford, but rather that, as he was president again in 1926, we shall discuss him in detail at that point.

CHAPTER 5

Rowland R. Robbins, 1921

Rowland R. Robbins, a market-gardener from south-west London, was known as 'Cocker' to the men he worked with. Born in 1874 and originally from the West Country, Robbins found himself, as a very young man, sent to help out at his brother's greengrocery business in Chiswick, London. As the youngest of seven siblings he had a remarkable drive for self improvement. This led him to the market-gardening business of Wild & Sons, near Sipson. Mr Wild was not a well man and, as his sons were still at school, he needed a manager. He took a shine to the young Robbins, whom he had met at a local Baptist church. Wild offered the 20-year-old Robbins the post of manager. Robbins, in a display of business maturity beyond his young age, agreed on condition he had a half share in the business. Wild & Robbins of Sipson, Middlesex, was duly formed.

Sipson, 100 years ago, was a small Thames Valley village with three pubs and four farms that stood distinct from the sprawl of south-west London. Today it is swallowed up by the London suburb of Harmondsworth, the M4 and Heathrow Airport. If you drive from one of the link roads that joins Heathrow and the M4 you will drive over the farm Robbins managed. It seems a great irony that much of the concrete of London squats upon some of the nation's best farmland.

Wild & Robbins grew vegetables such as leeks, carrots and cabbages in the rich alluvial soils that followed the path of the Thames upstream out of London. Strawberries were also grown, as well as exotics such as peaches, grapes and tomatoes under glass. After a day's picking in the fields, horse-drawn vans would be loaded in the evening to arrive at Covent Garden by three in the morning. On being unloaded, the vans would visit cavalry stables in St James's to be filled with horse muck to be taken back to the farm. Today six or seven hours seems a long time to drive from Harmondsworth to central London, but it should be remembered that at the turn of the century roads still left much to be desired. Wild & Robbins drivers carried bales of straw to be slung into potholes on the way.

As a businessman R.R. Robbins was progressive.

Left: Rowland Robbins, who twice occupied the NFU presidency, in 1921 and 1925.

He paid above-average wages as he realised this secured a loyal, diligent workforce. He brought in steam engines and later vans to replace the horses.

At the turn of the century market-gardening was one of the few success stories in British agriculture. Increasing demand for a more varied diet from an increasing, wealthier population opened up new markets for the growers of fruit and vegetables. Fresh produce naturally favoured local production over imports, and in areas where the soils and climate were right – such as the Lea Valley, the Vale of Evesham, the Fens, the Lancashire Moss and the Thames Valley – prosperous market-gardening businesses were established. These businesses were characterised by an appetite to use the latest techniques and to grow the newest varieties. Usually they were run by shrewd marketeers who knew how to stay ahead of the burgeoning urban markets they supplied.

Market gardeners traditionally considered themselves in a different class from farmers. Accordingly, their participation in the NFU was always going to be a little awkward. They had their own associations but, for some reason, R.R. Robbins was attracted to the NFU and devoted a good deal of his life to it. His home county of Middlesex was one of the earlier counties to establish NFU branches, and Robbins was an activist in the early days. He was quickly

'Cocker' Robbins, with bike, oversees some steam-powered cabbages on the move.

earmarked by the NFU pioneers as a man of considerable ability that the infant union would do well to make the most of. The market gardener was clearly nervous about his rise in this farmers' organisation and, indeed, Robbins, was, on occasion, cheaply derided for not being a proper farmer. Sensibly, the NFU recognised both the value of representing market gardeners and of cultivating a potential leader such as R.R. Robbins.

As a man, Robbins was small and wiry and prone to ill health, but his strength of character gave him a robustness that made up for this frailty. He was a modest man, admired for his fierce intellect. With his clerkish demeanour, he was known as a master of facts and figures.

Robbins was a strict Baptist and was thus teetotal. In proposing him for president at the NFU AGM, a Kent delegate pointed out that Robbins was of completely unblemished character apart from two failings; 'he didn't drink and he didn't smoke'. As president and vice-president of the NFU he spent six days a week at Bedford Square, but the seventh day was devoted to the Lord and the Baptist Church in Harmondsworth. His first wife, Rosa, died of cancer at an early age when their children were young. Robbins was devastated by the loss of his first love but not so devastated as to stop him marrying her younger sister, Stella, some months later.

Having established Wild & Robbins as a successful business which gave him a comfortable living, he could afford to give time to more public matters. This led him to local government and then to the NFU. In politics he was a card-carrying member of the Liberal Party and with this came a belief in a free market of free-acting individuals rather than one which encouraged the interference of the state in the practise of business and enterprise. As we have already pointed out, the paradoxical attitude of the farmer to state interference in agriculture was an ideological dilemma the NFU struggled to come to terms with. In 1921 R.R. Robbins found himself on the cusp of developments.

As Britain emerged from the challenges of the First World War there was a political debate as to whether government should maintain its new-found role in proactively intervening in the economy of the nation or retreat to allow the 'laissez-faire' policies of the pre-war to re-occupy the throne. Agriculture was at the heart of this debate.

The royal commission that deliberated on these matters in the immediate postwar years came down in favour of continued guaranteed prices. The government remained hesitant, but the NFU pushed for an indication as to where policy might go. Delegations from the union were received by Prime Minister Lloyd George at No. 10. It would seem that union leaders such as Langford and Robbins had a good rapport with the fiery Welsh premier. It probably helped that they were both avowed Liberals. In late 1919, in a famous speech at Caxton Hall in front of a farming audience, Lloyd George intimated there would be no return to the pre-war refusal to protect and support agriculture. 'If you increase the agricultural production of this country,' said the premier, 'you will be rendering about a great service. Confidence,' he concluded, 'is the best fertiliser for the soil.'

The resulting Agriculture Act that became law in the last few days of 1920 retained the deficiency payments scheme that sought to guarantee prices for wheat and oats at 95s. a quarter. Crucially, it was agreed that this system would be guaranteed for four years. Along with this, the AWB was also retained and tenants were given better security of tenure. The latter had been a long-held demand of the NFU. There were also attempts to maintain some obligation to farm to a certain standard, but the relevant clauses were shredded by the landowning interests in the Lords to the point where they became meaningless. The NFU were happy to see this emasculation of state interference in what constituted good farming practice. To the practical farmers of the NFU the question as to how best to farm was best left in the hands of the individual farmer.

The 1920 Act was seen as a great victory for the NFU. A new sense of partnership between government and the farming industry was founded. With bigger and better harvests accompanied by guaranteed prices, there was a new-found confidence among NFU members, and a growing conviction that the locust years of the pre-war era would not return. The bitter irony was that within six short months all this was undone.

The harvest of 1920 was not only favourable in the UK but was also plentiful in the other corn-growing areas of the world. In the spring of 1921 there was much talk of a glut that would soon hang over the market. As the wheat price sank, the deficiency payments established in the 1920 Act suddenly looked worryingly over-generous in the eyes of the Treasury. To make matters worse, the UK economy started to creak. Industrial output was falling and unemployment rising. The government felt financial prudence was the order of the day and severe budgets were drawn up. Despite all the promises to the contrary, the deficiency payment scheme was scrapped and the promise of four years' notice was walked away from.

By August 1921 the Agriculture Act, passed just nine months before, was a dead letter. For the farming industry and for the NFU it was nothing short of treachery, and for a generation of farmers it was bitterly remembered as 'the great betrayal'. If confidence was the best fertiliser for the soil, then Lloyd George's volte-face seemed to have ushered in some very barren years.

To make matters doubly bad, a severe drought hit home in the summer of 1921. It was one of the driest, hottest years on record, with much of lowland Britain recording fewer than 20 inches of rain – and a good proportion of that fell in August, just when arable farmers wanted it least. Yields in 1921 were half those of 1920.

It fell to the president, R.R. Robbins, to pick up the pieces of the shattered confidence of the industry he led. Many members called for no more co-operation with a government as untrustworthy as 'a bunch of rogues'.

The sanguine Robbins realised cutting off relations with government would not help the situation. In fact, he had been made aware of the plans to walk away from the Agriculture Act as early as June 1921, two months before its actual repeal. In an act of damage limitation Robbins undertook frequent and detailed negotiation with Boscawen, the Minister of Agriculture (the old Board had been elevated to a Ministry in 1919). It was a classic case of exercising patient and skilled politicking to achieve the best result for farmers while facing a membership who wanted mindless tub-thumping and empty gestures.

Robbins hammered out a compensation package of £3 for an acre of wheat and £4 for oats for the 1921 harvest at a cost to the Treasury of £18 million. It was also agreed that the AWB would be scrapped. If the price of wheat was not to be guaranteed by the state, then nor would be the wage of farm workers. Both were to be thrown to the dogs of the free market. By 1922 the wheat price had fallen to 30s. a quarter from the high of 100s. in 1919. The locust years had returned.

Writing in the 1921 Year Book Robbins made it clear he felt this was not a matter of lack of government money but one of lack of government priority. In an intriguing parallel with today, Robbins wrote in the 1921 Year Book:

Surely it is a very humiliating and melancholy confession to make that we cannot afford to take steps to increase home food production [at a time when] *our resources enable us to discharge our obligations to the Jews of Palestine and the citizens of Baghdad.*

We do not know the exact circumstances, but it would seem this episode of high politics put a severe strain on R.R. Robbins's health. He spent the second half of his presidency in hospital following a serious operation and then convalesced in the south of France. The duties of the presidency were left to his vice-president, James Donaldson.

Mercifully, he made a complete recovery and returned to the presidency by unanimous acclaim in 1925. His second presidency, in 1925, was a good deal less traumatic and eventful. Throughout his time with the NFU Robbins had tried to steer a moderate course amidst a sometimes belligerent membership. As chairman of the Employment Committee he had tried to work with agricultural workers' unions to achieve agreed rates of pay amidst calls from the membership that the workers' unions should be smashed. He did, though, agree with members that attempts by government to impose a 48-hour week would be unworkable for the

Heathrow, another postwar blot on the rich alluvial farmland of south-west London.

Female staff pick onions in R.R. Robbins' fields while one laid back male looks on. Today these fields sit beneath the M4 motorway.

farming industry. Farms were more complicated than factories.

For many, R.R. Robbins was the most capable man of his generation in the NFU. Writing at the end of the 1920s, Colin Campbell described him as the union's greatest leader. Robbins's triumph was to positively lead the NFU during a dark and testing time. He was widely admired in NFU circles and at the end of his second presidency in 1925 was presented with a car as a large token of appreciation of the service he had given the organisation.

As we shall see, he fell out with union policy in the 1930s – in short, he did not approve of marketing boards with their powers of compulsion over the farmer in the way goods were marketed.

At heart he believed in the entrepreneurial spirit of the individual and disapproved of mandatory state collectivism. The irony was he led an industry that, in the main, had been badly served by the free market, the double irony being he came from one of the few sectors – horticulture – that had thrived in the face of free competition.

Despite his propensity to ill-health and despite being knocked off his bicycle by a car during a 1942 blackout, R.R. Robbins lived to a good age and died in 1960. He is buried in Harmondsworth cemetery, and, virtuous and pious man that he was, there he no doubt lies at peace with his maker amongst all the tumult of south-west London, with its motorways and the world's busiest airport. One suspects that if he could look out over the graveyard wall he would have mixed emotions.

As we saw with his enthusiasm to replace the horse with the machines on his farm, he would no doubt marvel at the speed and enormity of the planes and lorries that thundered about him. He might have been less enthusiastic about the concreting over of his productive farm. He might have been even more puzzled at the strawberries being air-freighted in from across the globe and landed where he once managed strawberry fields. And there may be one final insult for R.R. Robbins: there are proposals to put Heathrow's fifth runway through the cemetery in which he lies.

CHAPTER 6

James Donaldson, 1922

In our Hollywood-fuelled minds the 1920s are often referred to as 'the roaring twenties', a decade falsely remembered through black and white film as one associated with cocktail lounge glamour and all that jazz. But for much of rural Britain the period would best be described as 'dour'. It was a time of economic recession and austerity. The farming community did not escape this 'dourness'.

In his seminal work *Agriculture and Economic Progress*, E.J. Ojala gave the measure of the decline. The gross output of agriculture in the UK stood at the record level of £490 million for 1920–22. Net output for the same period was £333 million and the general agricultural price level (with 1912 being 100) stood at 233. But by the early 1930s gross output had fallen to £236 million and net to £140 million, the general price level being 126. Farmer bankruptcies grew from 44 in 1920 to 487 in 1928. If such a downturn had hit most other manufacturing industries it would probably have wiped them out. But farming tends to be in 'the long game', and in lean times belts are tightened.

As before, in times of hardship British farming turned from corn to horn. The decline in cultivation was such that before the decade had finished, all that had been gained in the expansion of arable farming during the war was lost.

In contrast, the 1920s for the NFU was a time of consolidation. The rapid building of membership over the previous decade was not continued, but at the same time it did not go backwards. Whereas the farm workers' unions lost more than 75 per cent of their membership in the 1920s (they peaked at around 250,000 in 1921 and had dropped to as low as 30,000 by 1930), the NFU largely retained its ranks of 100,000 farmers (99,000 in 1923 and 112,000 in 1930, to be precise). The fact that the membership did not decline through this trying decade says much for the robustness of the NFU structure and the leadership of its presidents.

The figure of 100,000 members was reckoned to represent a little under half the number of farmers in England and Wales. What proportion of English and Welsh farming is represented by the NFU begs the well-worn question as to what constitutes a farmer. At the time the NFU based this 50 per cent calculation on the fact there were 200,000 farmers listed in trade directories. Census returns and ministry assessments of the number of holdings suggested the figure was nearer 300,000. The simple fact is that in those days, just as today, it was very difficult to

The fifth NFU annual dinner in 1924.

distinguish in broad, statistical terms between commercial farmers, smallholders and life-stylers. As we have seen, the NFU, from the outset, focused recruitment on the larger commercial farmers. It can be assumed that it would have represented far more of British agriculture in terms of area and turnover than that suggested by a simple head count based on numbers of holdings on ministry censuses.

What was clear now was that the NFU was the pre-eminent farmer representative body in England and Wales. Its only rival in the early days, the Chamber of Agriculture, was now in sharp decline and was being dwarfed by the NFU. In 1925 the chamber organised a national conference on the future of agriculture. Rather pointedly, the union declined the invitation to attend. It was the last time the NFU would ever have to try to put the chamber in its place. From thereon the pecking order was undeniable. If government wanted to talk to the farming community then the NFU was the first port of call. Boscawen, the Minister of Agriculture in the early 1920s, praised the union for being 'a sectional organisation, devoted primarily to the interests of farmers for thinking and acting nationally'. One key characteristic of the NFU was its ability to provide government with a 'single desk' when it came to consultation with the farming industry. It was through the 1920s that this 'single desk' was cemented into place, and it remains there today.

At times in the 1920s the dialogue between government and the NFU was far from constructive, but it was a dialogue nonetheless. The decade was dominated by the Conservative administration of Stanley Baldwin, who was Prime Minister from 1924 to 1929. Baldwin seemed to have a personal aversion to the NFU and described their leaders as 'difficult, narrow minded and self-serving'.

Despite this political friction, the place of the NFU was further cemented into the establishment when Rowland Robbins, in October 1922, had the honour of being the first NFU president to be presented to the king, George V, on the occasion of his visit to NIAB headquarters in Cambridge. Similarly, in 1929, at the union's 21st annual dinner, the guest of honour was none other than HRH the Prince of Wales.

By the early 1920s the NFU had grown into a mature organisation with a well-oiled but sparsely manned machine working from No. 45 Bedford Square. There were now 11 national committees meeting regularly with the following designations: finance and general purposes (chaired by the president); parliamentary, press and publicity; land tenure and taxation; labour and costs; education; cereals; livestock and wool; milk and dairy produce; hops, fruit and vegetables; trades, advisory and transport; potatoes.

In 1922 two new departments were established – one dedicated to statistics under Mr Guild and a legal department under Mr Ellis. Through its legal fund, administered both at county and national levels, the union expanded the legal assistance given to farmers facing prosecution or being sued or needing to sue. From its inception, legal assistance for members had been one of the NFU's key selling points. 'How do you think you will stand if one of these big corporations comes up against you?' asked an NFU promotional leaflet in 1912.

The cases the NFU took on dealt with a wide range of issues, from tenants unfairly evicted to pig keepers sold poisonous feed. For instance, in the case of Ford v. Bucks County Council, a local council official used his powers under the 1919 Rats and Mice (Destruction) Act to lay poison on Mr Ford's farm. Some of the farm stock duly ate the poison and subsequently died. With NFU help the case was won and compensation paid. The judge, Mr Justice Sankey, ruled that the council rat man had acted in 'a Napoleonic manner' and had failed to give the farmer proper notice. This was but one of hundreds of legal cases in which the NFU assisted its membership. Some simply gave justice to an individual, others laid down precedents that were important to the whole industry. In Farnworth v. Manchester Corporation the NFU helped a member embroiled in an issue that affected many members. Farmer Farnworth was found entitled to compensation for damage done to his crops by sulphurous fumes emanating from the corporation's newly built electric power station. Remarkably, the judgement also involved an injunction to prevent future damage. The Farnworth case went all the way to the House of Lords and established important case law that led to changes in the design of power stations. It was a good example of how a union could empower the individual to take on mighty corporations and, in some cases, win court rulings that benefited thou-

sands of his peers. We might not readily think of the NFU as a pioneering environmental pressure group, but the Farnworth case proved it was exactly that.

Across the corridor from Mr Ellis's legal department, Mr Guild was in charge of statistics and intelligence. James Guild had been a lecturer in political economy at Edinburgh University. His office was in regular contact with the Ministry of Agriculture, helping compile statistics about the state of the industry as well as drawing up market reports. There were also joint projects with agricultural colleges, working on costings data to improve the business management skills of farmers, and give advice on income tax. It is from this office we can trace the NFU economics department of today. Throughout its history the NFU has been proactive in collecting and assimilating economic intelligence about English and Welsh agriculture to advise government and individual farmers, as well as many points in between. With its unique ability to reach out to tens of thousands of farmers, the NFU has always been strategically well placed to carry out this role in terms of both receiving and supplying information. In the 1923 Year Book there is a plea from the statistics department for prompt and full replies from county branches for local information upon which a case for the industry may be built up. It is amusing to note that today, over 80 years later, the chief economist can be found sending out the same chivvying messages to the regions as her department tries to prepare a dossier on a certain key topic.

In 1922 also came the launch of an NFU journal, the *Record*, which had a monthly circulation of 100,000 copies. It is from the *Record* we can trace the history of the NFU membership magazine which leads to the *British Farmer & Grower* today. The *Mark Lane Express*, which had given so much stalwart support to the NFU in its early years, was replaced with the *British Farmer & Stockbreeder* in the 1920s. The *BF&S* was as supportive of the NFU as the *MLE* had been and was always keen to cover union affairs.

The NFU also vastly increased the general literature it produced, including 60,000 copies of *What the NFU is Doing for You* and *Will You put the U in NFU?*

As we have said before, while this book concentrates on the men at the very pinnacle of the NFU, to understand the organisation properly one must remember that a pyramid only has a pinnacle because of the base beneath it. The strength of the NFU lay as much in the provinces as it did in the metropolis. To mix a metaphor, the branches of the NFU were its roots. By 1928 the union could boast over 975 branches, each with a branch secretary, in 59 counties, each county having its own individual structure. From Penzance in the far South West to Berwick in the North East, the market towns of England and Wales could all boast an office of the NFU. It was the work of the branch and county secretaries on the ground, along with farmer volunteers, that gave the NFU the ability to reach out to over 100,000 farmers and keep them loyal to their union. At this local level the union was about far more than just earnest politics. It was also about socialising with one's peers. Meetings were held in pubs and hotels so that the affairs of the day could be discussed over pints of ale. Ploughing matches, outings and 'best farm' competitions were organised. The NFU has always been about more than just a place to chew over the issues of the day. It is also about bonding with one's fellows in a spirit of unity and belonging.

The county branches, with their own county secretary, chairman and committees operating at a county level, were as important as the national organisation in London. This was an age when county councils were more powerful than they are today. Rates, roads and education were three important areas they dealt with. The NFU was key to representing the farming industry at this level, either through the direct representation of NFU men sitting on county councils or through representations made to councils. Similarly, county branches were key movers in the establishment and development of agricultural colleges and research centres, many of which originated from the work of the county war executives established after 1916. This period saw the flowering of new educational institutions and experimental stations devoted to the advancement of agriculture.

In 1922 a final piece of the national union jigsaw was put in place when the Northumberland Dairy and Tenant Farmers' Association and the Hexham Farmers' Protection Society agreed to merge with local farmers' unions to give Northumberland a comprehensive county branch. The merger and reconstruction were ratified at a crowded meeting in the County Hotel in Newcastle in the presence of president James Donaldson. The NFU now had an effective county structure in every English and Welsh county.

James Donaldson, a Scotsman by birth, was born at Ward Head Farm, Lanarkshire, in 1869. As a 20-year-old he arrived at Whitehouse Farm in Brightwell Baldwin, Oxfordshire. James was keen to take on the lease but, because he was under 21, was prevented by law from doing so. His father duly travelled down to Oxfordshire from Scotland to help his son take up the tenancy. A few years later his father returned to his homeland for fear he might be buried 'amidst the sassenachs'. James was left to plough his own furrow.

As a Scottish émigré taking on an English farm, James Donaldson was not alone. The late-nineteenth century and the 1920s are periods when many Scottish farmers' sons travelled south to find a farm. There were parallel movements of West-Country men who moved east. It was in the depressed arable areas that they found most opportunity. Today many eastern counties are heavily populated with third-

James Donaldson.

generation Scots who trace the history of their family farms back to the arrival of a grandfather born in Scotland a century before – give or take 20 years. These were times when many local English farmers were walking away from tenancies. Almost in desperation, landlords were known to offer farms rent free for fear they deteriorated into 'rack and ruin' ('rack' being the Scots term for couch grass, which proliferates as a pernicious weed on arable land that is not properly tended and managed). The Scots were a leaner, meaner race of farmers than the English. While English farmers indulged their daughters with tennis courts and riding paddocks, the Scots arrived with families of hard-working, poorly paid sons. Brought up in tough northern conditions, the Scots could survive in the exacting economic circumstances of the 1890s and 1920s where flabbier Englishmen failed. James Donaldson was such a man.

Known for his energy and wisdom, Donaldson made a success of Whitehouse Farm and its 'good wheat-growing' land. On his election it was noted from the floor that this was a man 'who had been through the mill, for as a young man he drove his own team in the fields'. Donaldson knew the meaning of hard manual work but also had a keen business mind. He founded a grain merchanting business at Hambleton Mill on the Thames. Unlike his father, James was keen to integrate into his new community. He married a local girl, Florence Bessie Weller, and they had two sons and a daughter. He was a keen churchgoer and at first would travel by pony and trap every Sunday to the nearest Presbyterian church, at Aston Tirrold. Eventually he assimilated into the Church of England and attended services at his local church in Brightwell Baldwin. In the mid-1900s, the first person in his locality to own a motor car, he would make a weekly trip to Oxford.

In his 30s he took to public life as a school governor, parish council chairman and county councillor. At first he joined the Chamber of Agriculture, but found the inclusion of landlords and farm workers blunted its focus, and so turned to the newly formed NFU. By 1919 he was chairman of Oxfordshire NFU and was involved at HQ with the improvement of the union's organisation as its membership grew rapidly in the late 1910s. He was one of the author's of a new constitution in 1922, at which time the executive committee was made up of the heads of the various sub-committees. Ultimate authority still lay with the Council, which comprised the delegates from each county.

Donaldson was president during the 1922 general election. From its early days the NFU had targeted Westminster to try to influence parliament, but with limited success. Donaldson's previous experience as chairman of the Parliamentary, Press and Publicity Committee meant he was well versed in the challenges of how best to gain political influence. In the 1918 election the union had sponsored seven independent candidates but all were defeated. Undeterred, when the 1922 election was called, Donaldson was keen to persevere with trying to get agriculturalist candidates returned as MPs. Seven of the prospective MPs running as independents or as Conservatives were NFU sponsored. There was also an attempt to put the two main parties under the farming spotlight. Party leaders were invited to make plain their policies for agriculture. A NFU parliamentary programme was drawn up and county branches were urged to put them before all candidates to see if they sympathised. Adverts along these lines were taken out in the national press. The campaign seemed to have an impact, and an awareness of farming's problems was raised in the country. The *Daily Mail* carried the comment: 'Farmers are

entering the Election campaign with a spirit never shown before.'

The expense and activity had some success. Four of the seven sponsored candidates were elected. All were nominally Conservative Unionists. The three Independent Agriculturalists failed. Furthermore, 63 MPs had signed up their support for the NFU parliamentary programme.

In the parliament elected in 1922 there were some victories for which NFU lobbying could claim some credit. The 1923 Agriculture Rates Act greatly reduced the 4s. an acre rating of agricultural land, giving agriculture a saving of £2.7 million a year.

But as time wore on it became clear that while the odd sop might be thrown by government to the farming industry and its NFU representatives, in the main the government were keen to side-step developing any comprehensive policy to expand or protect British agriculture. To try and bring matters to a head, James Donaldson's successor, Harry German, led an NFU delegation to Downing Street to take its demands to the Prime Minister. The union suggested the government had two alternatives in its policy for agriculture – it could continue and expand the system of subsidies which had proved effective in the war, or it could give agriculture protective duties in the same way other industries were safeguarded. But they returned with neither. It was reported back that Prime Minister Mr Bonar Law indicated 'honestly and bluntly' that the industry must in the main fend for itself in the economic gale that was now blowing. The PM was of the view that pubic opinion prevented the use of protection as a means of supporting agriculture. All that was offered was an enquiry into agricultural prosperity, which the union rightly condemned as pointless.

The 1922 election was a watershed moment in the history of the NFU. After this date it never really felt it could influence government policy by achieving representation at Westminster. The 1922 election was quickly followed by elections in 1923 and 1924. The NFU simply could not afford to campaign to the same level as it had in 1922. The rise of the Labour Party and the parallel fall of the Liberals in these elections also changed the dynamic of political lobbying. A Socialist party with land nationalisation at the top of its manifesto naturally alienated the farming vote. If the Tory Party, now under Stanley Baldwin, had come up with a comprehensive programme for agriculture it would have undoubtedly won the overt support of the NFU. The fact that it did not led the union to maintain its strictly non-political stance when it came to favouring any party. As we shall see, this policy of non-alignment echoed down the decades and still influences NFU policy today.

CHAPTER 7

Harry German, 1922

The forthright Harry German, first-class cricketer and one of the NFU's greatest servants.

The man who led the aforementioned delegation to Downing Street was Harry German, president in 1922. German prided himself on being the first 'northcountryman' to lead the union. He actually hailed from Measham in North Leicestershire, which some might think is actually the Midlands. But it may be that he felt being a 'northcountrymen' was a matter of culture and character rather than geography. He certainly prided himself on his 'plain speaking', which, as we know today, can be an honest virtue north of the Watford Gap and an uncouth vice south of it.

It would be neat to describe Harry German as 'a safe pair of hands', as he played wicket keeper for Leicestershire and rugby for Leicester Tigers in the 1890s. The fact is, Harry German had many admirable qualities which he brought to the NFU, but being a safe pair of hands was not one of them.

He was a stormy, forceful character, not always known for his delicate handling of sensitive issues. On more than one occasion in his 30 years' work for the union he resigned from his post on a matter of principle only to reappear almost immediately in another role. When he became president the sanguine Robbins wished 'discretion be granted to you in proportion to your energies'. In return, German promised Council that 'he would not lose his temper or say any unkind word so far as union matters were concerned'.

Born in 1865, he was part of the German family that founded John German & Co, land agents, whose business spread out from Ashby-de-la-Zouch to cover the East Midlands. The firm had its origins in the early-nineteenth century, when Harry's grandfather, John German, was employed by the Weston family to manage their extensive estates. It was customary for large landowners to employ agents (or 'factors', as they were known in the north). In the 1840s John German struck out on his own and formed his own company. Today the firm is still going strong as an estate agency, but there are no Germans involved any more. There is a neat bit of circularity in that, in 2004, the NFU signed up a membership service agreement with Fisher-German, who are still based in Ashby-de-la-Zouch and whose roots lie with John German & Co.

As a young man, when not playing sport, Harry German was an agricultural auctioneer and then, in 1907, started to work for John German & Co. In 1918, 'under doctors' orders', he left the family firm to manage farms on his own account. At one point in the early 1920s he was managing estates in 14 counties, where he gained a reputation as an energetic and successful farmer. By the time he was president he had reduced this vast management portfolio and merely managed farms in Essex, Hampshire, Yorkshire, Stafford and Nottinghamshire. In 1923 he lived at the Monks Barn in the grounds of Newstead Abbey near Nottingham, where he managed the farm for the abbey owners, the Webb family. Newstead Abbey is famous for the fact that in the early-nineteenth century it was the home of Lord Byron, who was far better at poetry than he was at running a country estate.

Harry German's apparent fluidity in taking on and relinquishing the management of farms in part reflects the period. The 15 years after 1910 saw great changes in land ownership and marked the beginning of the end of the predominance of the tenant farmer as the norm in UK farming.

By 1927 the proportion of farms occupied by their owners had risen to 37 per cent from 13 per cent in 1909. This transfer of land reached feverish levels between 1918 and 1922, when there were 57,000 transactions involving 12 million acres. Usually it was landlords selling to tenants. There were two factors driving this on. First was the break-up of many estates due to the demands of death duties. This had been accelerated in 1919 by changes in the way estates were assessed for the purpose of death duties. Secondly, there was the new confidence in returns from farming instilled by the increase in commodity prices during and immediately after the First World War.

This confidence had been backed by the Agriculture Act of 1920 and its four-year guarantees. This acted to push up the price of land as tenants were increasingly tempted to make an offer for the land they leased and landlords were increasingly pressurised and tempted to sell. The historian F.M.L. Thompson described this as the biggest change in land ownership since the Norman Conquest. It was a watershed period not only in the history of agriculture but also in that of the NFU. In its formative years the NFU had been exclusive to farmers, which

meant, by and large, it was an organisation of tenants rather than of owners of land. By the 1920s this distinction was becoming blurred.

The collapse in farming fortunes after 1921 caused tremendous problems for those who had taken the brave decision to borrow money and buy their farms. Even after the 1922 collapse, tenant farmers still found it difficult to resist the temptation to buy their farms when their landlords had a change of circumstances forcing a sale. For some it was the only way to stay on the farm. Usually a large mortgage was necessary and for most such a financial commitment, rather than being the key to a door to new independence, remained a millstone around the neck. The Agricultural Credits Act of 1923, hurriedly passed as a rescue operation with provision for state mortgages of up to 60 years, did little to alleviate the situation.

There is a common anecdote told by very old men of today about a time 80 years ago when their fathers appeared in the farmyard in a disconsolate mood. When the family asked what was the problem, the father replied: 'I've just bought the farm. It will keep us poor for the rest of our lives.'

For those who hung onto their tenancies in these exacting times, the NFU lobbied hard for greater security of tenure. Of the successes here, the most notable was the 1920 Agriculture Act, which fixed a year's rent as compensation for disturbance.

German's presidency in 1923 also witnessed 'the great strike' in Norfolk. Relations between farm employer and employee hit a rocky patch after the repeal of the 1920 Agriculture Act, which scrapped both guaranteed prices for farmers and guaranteed wages for farm workers. Farm workers' pay tumbled from 45s. a week to 30s. Things came to a head in Norfolk when the Norfolk FU refused to meet the demands of the National Union of Agricultural Workers (NUAW) for 30s. a week based on a 54-hour week, and wanted to pay 20s. for a 55-hour week. Some of the Norfolk FU felt this was a good way to make the point to government that without protection or subsidy farmers could not afford to pay a living wage. Others were less considered and expressed a wish to smash the workers' union. Either way, when some Norfolk farmers started to lock out NUAW members, a strike was called across the county involving 10,000 men. In places the strike turned violent when pickets met farmers and non-unionised men. At first German went to Norfolk to see if he could help mediate but had little success. Eventually, German and Robbins met with Britain's first Labour Prime Minister, Ramsay MacDonald, and NUAW leaders. An agreement was hammered out based on 25s. and 54 hours, which was accepted by both sides, and the strike was called off. One outcome of this low point between farmers and farm workers was the reinstatement of the Agricultural Wages Board in 1924 by the short-lived minority government of Ramsay MacDonald. The board was retained by the succeeding Baldwin government and still remains with us today. It continued to irk the NFU that while the state was prepared to interfere in the wage negotiation to protect workers' interests, it was not prepared to give the farmer protection from cripplingly low prices. All the same, the low point of 'the great Norfolk strike' was never repeated, and while other industries suffered from poor industrial relations in the inter-war years, farming seemed to avoid the worst of it.

No doubt the ability of the NFU to represent most farm employers on the AWB was one reason for this ability to set pay rates through negotiation rather than confrontation. Interestingly, in the 1920s and 1930s the AWB operated on a county basis and thus minimum wages varied from county to county. The record shows that wages were significantly better in the north (e.g. 42s. in Lancs compared to a miserly 30s. in Essex).

Another crisis point that marked the presidency of Harry German was an outbreak of foot and mouth disease. Although FMD was not unknown to British livestock farmers in 1922, this outbreak was the start of a run of severe and costly pandemics in the 1920s.

Cattle plagues had been about for as long as farming itself, and combinations of FMD and rinderpest stalked cattle farming in an uncontrolled and misunderstood manner well into the nineteenth century. In 1865–66 a particularly virulent dose of cattle plague, imported through a live shipment of cattle from the Baltic, affected 5.5 million animals in the UK and cost farming an estimated £83 million. In 1871 another outbreak affected three million animals. It was with this outbreak that the farming industry and the government recognised that national co-ordinated action was needed. Tighter controls were placed on the import of livestock from infected nations and veterinary officials gained the powers to close markets and fairs, as well as to impose general 'standstill' orders in certain areas in an attempt to isolate the disease. Under this regime FMD was no longer endemic in the UK by 1884 and the country was also cleared of the more deadly rinderpest.

To this day rinderpest has never returned, but, unfortunately, the same cannot be said of FMD. The government's open-door policy of importing meat from Europe and South America, where FMD remained endemic, meant British cattle, sheep and pigs were repeatedly infected. For 35 years, between 1885 and 1920, outbreaks were kept to an average of less than ten a year. When they did occur the slaughter policy with compensation that was implemented appeared to work well. In its early days the NFU lobbied for increased control of imports of live cattle from countries that had FMD outbreaks. For instance, in 1914 Campbell urged county councils, which oversaw much animal health regulation, to ban the imports of Irish store cattle until Ireland had

been seen to be clear of FMD for three months.

In 1922 things took a sudden turn for the worse, with by far the worst outbreak seen by a generation of farmers. Between 1922 and 1924 there were 5,000 outbreaks across 52 counties, affecting over a quarter of a million animals. Harry German led the NFU when the outbreak was at its zenith. No doubt his sporting days had taught him the ethic of teamwork, and he realised the importance of the NFU, the farming industry and the State Veterinary Service working together to control the disease. He urged farmers to inspect their stock and report any disease immediately. It was interesting to hear NFU president Peter Kendall repeat these words to farmers 85 years later in 2007.

On confirmation of FMD in a herd during the 1923–24 pandemic, farmers had the choice of compensated slaughter or isolation. German was in favour of slaughter for infected pig, sheep or beef herds and isolation for dairy herds. He was often to be found in FMD infected areas explaining the slaughter policy to doubtful farmers, many of whom still favoured isolation. Some stockmen still felt the disease could be treated by administering propriatary 'remedies' or home-brewed 'liquors' which, they believed, had secret powers of healing.

The slaughter-and-burn approach to FMD was also attracting public concerns in 1922-23. In Cheshire, where the disease was rampant amongst the thousands of short-horn dairy cows that dominated the county's verdant plain, footpaths were closed, hunting was stopped and social functions were cancelled. The smoke and smell of the pyres also caused consternation. In 1924 a committee of inquiry under a Captain Prettyman cross-questioned German and the government chief vet, Stockman, about this. The following transcript gives insight into the issue and into German's bullish, no-nonsense character.

German: *I went to some burnings during an outbreak; I did not think there was anything offensive about it at all.*

Stockman: *No there is not; but the people were suffering from nerves; they saw the fires blazing at night and it kept it all before them.*

Prettyman: *It was an additional horror. To see those continuous fires exercised a very depressing influence on the people generally and contributed very much to the antagonism to the policy of slaughtering.*

Stockman: *I think we should consider that sort of thing if human sentiment is involved and bury where we can.*

German: *It seems to me very weak-kneed, sir.*

Stockman: *You have had, as we have had, the letters of*

complaint that came in. It must be very real in the minds of these people.

German: *Their minds are not very strong.*

These same concerns over the slaughter-and-burn policy were to echo on down the century as FMD outbreaks continued to plague British livestock farmers. Ben Gill, NFU president during the 2001 FMD pandemic, might have sensed the ghost of Harry German on his shoulder as he, too, felt the heat of controversy the FMD pyres could generate.

The 1923 FMD outbreak was an early example of the NFU and the ministry tackling a farming problem in partnership. Later, ministry officials expressed their gratitude to German for this, as they realised farmers were far more likely to accept the advice of one of their own rather than of a government official.

German also called for investigations into the import of South American beef, which many thought might be responsible for the reinfection. In 1928 he led an NFU investigation to the Argentine and reported back that, while some action had been taken to prevent FMD being imported into Britain in chilled beef carcasses, there remained more that could be done.

It was after the 1922–24 outbreak that there were government-sponsored investigations into treatments for FMD in stock, including vaccination. A laboratory dedicated to investigation into the disease was set up at Pirbright in Surrey in 1926. This centre gained an international reputation for vaccination which did much to reduce or eradicate FMD in farm stock across the world. The irony was, vaccination was never used in the UK, where the stamp-out policy was persevered with. Throughout the pre-war period FMD outbreaks continued to hamper British livestock farmers at an average rate of 100 cases a year.

Harry German continued to lead the NFU on animal health after his 1922 presidency. His experience as an auctioneer made him well placed to negotiate with government over levels of compensation when slaughter was ordered for stock that succumbed to notifiable diseases. It was not just FMD that haunted British livestock farmers in the inter-war years. Swine fever and anthrax were also about. For instance, in 1927 there were 1,794 outbreaks of swine fever and 536 of anthrax.

German was still chairman of the NFU Animal Diseases Committee on his sudden death of a heart attack in 1945 at the good age of 80. He had been a good servant of the NFU and held positions within the organisation for over 25 years. He was also a director of the NFU Mutual for over 20 years. On his death the then president, James Tuner, wrote in the NFU *Record*:

Harry German was something more than a past President; he was an inspiration, particularly to we younger men. He it was who took the initiative some years ago in introducing a sound constitution for the NFU and we did not hesitate to consult him over its further development. Mr German's long NFU career is a real pattern of service and will always remain so.

✦ CHAPTER 8 ✦

T.H. Ryland, 1923

The clerkish but highly effective T.H. Ryland, NFU president in 1923.

Harry German was succeeded as president by T.H. Ryland. Thomas Howard Ryland was an Oxford University-educated lawyer who also farmed the family estate at Moxhull Hall, near Sutton Coldfield, north-east of Birmingham. Born in 1865, he was a contemporary of Winston Churchill at Harrow. The farm was 400 acres of mainly arable land but there was also an interest in some hill farming in Scotland, where sheep were run. The Rylands were a well-off family who had made money amidst the Victorian factories of Birmingham, manufacturing paint, fertiliser and wire. Ryland paint can still be found today. As a man, he was somewhat eccentric when it came to his health. In 1905 the Ryland family home, the Elizabethan manor house of Wishaw, was destroyed in an extensive fire. Officially, it was an accident, but the story was that, because both T.H. Ryland's father and grandfather had died in the previous two years, Ryland had the place torched because he thought the woodwork was harbouring disease. Ryland himself had his leg amputated when he thought he might have cancer.

With the family home destroyed, Ryland then built Moxhull Hall as their new home, a mile away. The only remnant of the grand manor of Wishaw is the stable block, which is now a night club at the Belfry golf complex. Today Ryland's farm is barely recognisable amidst the greens and fairways of the Belfry golf courses and the M6 toll road which thunders past it. International golfers have been known to blame missed putts and hooked drives on the ghosts of the Ryland family, which are reputed to haunt the place. Moxhull Hall is now a hotel and can be spied sitting on the motorway embankment just on the approach to the M6 toll heading north.

Under Ryland's presidency the NFU became more hard-headed in its dealings with Whitehall. Union representatives were withdrawn from the National Agricultural Council (NAC) when that body claimed to be the sole spokesman for agriculture. The NFU proclaimed in the *Record* that it stood alone 'as the representative organisation of farmers in England and Wales'. This assertion of its authority produced results; the NAC disappeared after the NFU withdrawal.

Home grown sugar, a pleasure the British public went without in World War 1 but not in Word War 2.

Relations with the Baldwin Government deteriorated as the union continued to lobby it to set a policy for agriculture. As a token of their frustration over Baldwn's inaction in 1925, the union ran a candidate against the Minister of Agriculture, Colonel Guinness, at the Bury-St-Edmunds by-election. The old union motto of 'Defence, not Defiance', which had marked the union's approach to government before the war, now seemed to have less of a conciliatory ring than in Campbell's day.

In the 1920s the NFU developed its position on tariff reform. As we have seen, from its inception it had refused to take a clear line on this key issue and refused to call for protection from imports for home agriculture. Point four of its 1924 programme evidenced a change in this position:

To support the imposition of countervailing measures to prevent the unfair competition of imported foodstuffs which reach this market with the assistance of export bounties, subsidised freight-rates.

The central principle for the union was that it was prepared to accept that farming must operate on purely economic lines without subsidy or protection from imports if, at the same time, it was not unduly regulated or expected to compete against foreign agricultures that were protected. Two key points of contention were, firstly, the reinstatement in 1924 by the MacDonald Government of the AWB, which artificially fixed farm wages. Second was the refusal of the Baldwin administration to include agriculture

in its 1921 Safeguarding of Industries Act (extended in 1926), which sought to protect other parts of British industry.

The Baldwin Government's refusal to protect or subsidise agricultural commodities had one notable exception – sugar beet. In the First World War, sugar was the first foodstuff in British history to be rationed. With 80 per cent of the crop grown in enemy territory, the price of sugar in 1914 quadrupled to 2d. per lb. Only 1 per cent of the UK's sugar was grown at home. Sugar beet was very much a minor crop, exclusively grown in Norfolk around a Dutch-owned factory built at Cantley in 1912. After the war sugar beet seemed an obvious crop for the government to promote as a mild panacea to the decline in incomes on arable farms due to the crash in cereal prices. At first the NFU lobbied and secured a reduction in the tax on home-produced sugar. In its 1924 parliamentary programme it urged MPs to 'promote the establishment in this country of the sugar beet industry'. The following year a subsidy for growing beet was implemented in the 1925 British Sugar (Subsidy) Act. The subsidy was on a sliding scale over ten years, starting at 19s.6d. per cwt and falling to 6s.6d. (By 1939 the government had paid out £42 million to beet sugar manufacturers.) One of the main purposes of the subsidy was to give manufacturers the confidence to invest in new factories. A bulky crop like sugar beet needed a processor within striking distance of the growers. The government policy was a success; by 1925 there were new factories at Newark and Bury, and by 1930 the number had increased to 18. The 20,000 ton harvest of 1912 had become 431,000 by 1926 and 3,060,000 by 1930. By 1939 Britain was producing a third of a million tons of sugar – 16 per cent of her requirements. Between the wars sugar consumption increased dramatically, largely due to confectionery. It was in the 1920s that such British staples as the Mars Bar and the ice lolly were introduced.

Under Ryland's presidency in 1923 a Sugar Beet Committee was set up under the chairmanship of one of the rising stars of the union, Tom Baxter. The committee, which quickly superseded the Sugar Beet Growers' Society as the pre-eminent representative voice of English sugar beet growers, negotiated the beet price with the factories.

The NFU also gave advice to growers on whether they should sign contracts with the investors looking to set up factories and secure local supply. Farmers were warned to keep away from some of these, as they were little more than speculators. One such disreputable outfit hawked around contracts to farmers in the Chichester area on the basis that they had a technique that could dry sugar beet, thus making it cheap enough to transport to factories over 100 miles away. The scheme was a non-starter, as the drying process inverted the sugar. Sussex arable farmers, on the good arable soils around Chichester, never did get the chance to grow sugar beet.

It was at the behest of the NFU that growers' representatives were appointed to work at each factory intake. These were paid for by a 1d. levy on each ton of beet.

These representatives, all trained chemists, checked both weighings and analysis. They then reported back to the Sugar Beet Committee.

The spring of 1925 proved to be the inaugural beet-growing season for many eastern region farmers and, sure enough, right on cue, the winter of 1926 was a late and a hard one. The NFU found itself caught between growers complaining they couldn't get the crop out of the ground and factories complaining they would have to shut down because of lack of supply. But a bit of testing weather never deterred a British farmer, and the crop was persevered with and proved to be one of the few success stories of the 1920s.

Today's sugar beet industry can be traced back to the 1925 Act. The system of supporting beet growing by paying the factories a support price per ton stayed in place until 1973, when it was superseded by the Common Agricultural Policy (CAP).

One of the less pleasant jobs for Ryland during his presidency was to oversee the winding up of the Agricultural Organisation Society (AOS), which, founded in 1901, was an early attempt at co-operative trading by English farmers. The AOS set up the Agricultural Wholesale Society (AWS), which bought in bulk for its members, but it was neither well run nor adequately financed. Caught out by the crash in prices in 1922, it went into liquidation. The AOS became insolvent soon after, not helped by the removal of the government grants it had enjoyed in the previous decade. The collapse of the AOS was a blow to the notion of self help by farmers through co-operative structures.

The NFU's response to the collapse was to set up a co-operative department at Bedford Square and a co-operative committee, which Ryland chaired throughout the 1920s. The department and committee gave help to local societies in terms of administration and sourcing grants when running co-operative ventures. It also sought to promote their use among NFU members, but only on the understanding it was: '... wherever it is that such societies could be started to the advantage of the farmers concerned and with a real prospect of success.' By 1927 there were 95 agricultural co-operative societies on the NFU's register which concerned themselves with bulk purchasing on behalf of their membership, which numbered 39,000 members with a turnover of 6.2 million. Furthermore, there were 67 co-ops group-selling on behalf of their members (half were dairy companies), turning over £4.5 million and with a membership of 25,000.

The co-operative philosophy has always had a chequered history in British farming. British farmers display a sturdy independence and instinctively dislike pooling themselves with other farmers when making purchases or sales. Having said that, over the years there has been some real success stories of co-ops working well to the advantage of their members. The NFU has always represented this dichotomy of views. In the 1927 Year Book the union pointed out that co-operative purchasing and marketing was no panacea to low commodity prices.

This ambivalence was in great contrast to the way farmers did business on the continent, where farmer co-ops were (and still are) the bedrock of agriculture. The reason for the contrast was largely a matter of farm size. For instance, in Belgium in the 1920s there were 720,000 farmers with an average farm size of 10 acres. For such peasants there was no choice but to co-operate. For the 200,000 British farmers with an average farm size of over 100 acres the imperative to join the local co-op was not so strong, and the opportunity to trade with independent merchants when buying or selling was greater. Again, in the 1927 Year Book the NFU pointed out that there was no evidence that farmers were doing any better in countries where co-operatism was far more commonplace than it was in the UK

Another area with which Ryland involved himself that merits mention was that of telephonic communication. It was in the 1920s that telephones became commonplace in UK businesses. In the isolation of the countryside it was inevitable that agriculture would be one of the last to benefit. Through his office at the NFU Ryland lobbied government for improve-

Mrs. Giles (ignorant of the latest form of stunt advertising). "COOM, JARGE, QUICK! ONE O' THEM WOIRELESS MESSAGES 'AS CAUGHT FOIRE."

Farmyards were some of the last places to receive or understand the revolutionary new communication technologies of the 1920s, namely, the radio and the telephone.

ments in the telephone network. In 1922 he lobbied for a 24-hour service rather than the usual nine to five service farmers received. In 1923 the union expressed its dislike of party lines in rural areas. Today, the thought of one farmer being able to listen in on his neighbour's private telephone conversations seems very strange, if not slightly humorous, but in the 1920s it was the norm.

Slowly but surely telephone posts marched out across the countryside of Britain, not only changing the landscape but also revolutionising the way farmers communicated with the outside world. The pioneering work by the union to give farmers access to telephones has neat parallels with the union's work today in pushing for better broadband access in the more remote areas.

Ryland was also the first president to have his AGM speech broadcast on the radio. The British Broadcasting Co., set up in 1922, first started broadcasting in November of that year from Marconi House in London. In 1927 it became the British

Broadcasting Corporation under Royal Charter. The NFU has always had a close relationship with the BBC. That relationship has usually been positive and fruitful, but at times it has been testy. In 1928 we get the first complaint at NFU Council about anti-farming bias in the BBC. It was over a broadcast that suggested farmers made poor employers and sweated their labour. This was not to be the last time farmers complained about what was broadcast on the BBC and expected the NFU to do something about it.

T.H. Ryland was one of a group known as 'the big four' in the NFU. They dominated much of the thinking in the union in the 1920s. The 'big four' was a playful reference to a term used to describe the four men – Clemenceau, Lloyd George, Wilson and Orlando – who had dominated peace negotiations after the First World War. Three of the big four – Robbins, Ryland and German – we have already discussed. The fourth was E.W. Langford, president twice, in 1920 and 1926.

CHAPTER 9

E.W. Langford, 1926

'The boss' – Langford of Hereford.

Ernest Wilfred Langford was born in 1870 in the small village of Wellington, just outside Hereford. Of all the NFU presidents he has some of the humblest origins. One of a family of nine, he grew up on a small farm and left school at the age of ten. Like Robbins, he displayed a sound business acumen at a young age. He borrowed money to set up a cider-making business in Hereford in the 1900s. Langford saw an opportunity to make cider on a large scale in a centralised factory and sell it to farmers who provided it for their workforce.

Edwardian farm workers expected substantial amounts of free alcoholic refreshment as part of their employment. It was not uncommon for farm labourers to drink a gallon of beer or cider during the working day – no doubt to anaesthetise against the drudgery of repetitive hand labour – but it must also have increased the accident rate. On today's HSE-inspected farms it does not seem possible that 100 years ago a semi-inebriated labour force worked around unguarded steam-driven machinery.

As a man, Langford, was proud of his 'self-made' origins. Physically he was a short man. 'Small in stature but big in brain power' was a phrase used to describe him. Nationally, as his reputation as a forward-thinking, dynamic farmer spread, he was known as 'Langford of Hereford'. More locally he is still remembered as 'the boss'. He was known as a racy and trenchant speaker with a pugnacious capacity to express his convictions, especially when his back was to the wall. He was a Liberal by conviction and believed in the free-trade ethic. He was well immersed in Hereford city politics and had the distinction of being mayor of the city twice, in 1927 and 1933. In 1918 and 1922 he had run as an NFU-sponsored candidate in the national elections. Both times he lost to the Conservatives.

Whereas in public life he was a larger-than-life character, closer to home he wasn't always so well regarded. Rumours of a dalliance with an NFU secretary probably didn't help his domestic reputation, and local disputes over grazing rights with commoners made him enemies in the Hereford area.

He may have been no saint, but his abilities attracted many admirers. Although his origins lay in fruit growing and cider, it is in the field of dairying that he made his main contribution to British agriculture. In 1913 he set up a dairy farm at Tupsley Court on the outskirts of Hereford.

Moving into dairying was a common response of many farmers to the decline in farm incomes after 1870. Increased demand for fresh milk and the ability to deliver it by rail had opened up new markets for British farmers. In the 50-year period either side of 1900 milk took over from wheat as the main product of British farms. By 1930 milk represented 27 per cent of farming's gross agricultural product, whereas in 1877 it had been just 12 per cent. In 1861 UK consumption of milk was 170 million gallons (nine gallons per person per year), and by 1930 it had reached 830 million gallons (22 gallons per head per year).

Traditional grass-growing counties in the South West saw most growth, but even counties such as Essex saw a doubling in milk production at this time.

The period also saw major technical advances in milk production. In the first half of the nineteenth century hygiene standards were poor, and before the growth of the railways in the second half of the nineteenth century dairy farming was usually to be found in scruffy sheds and yards in cities, where early dairy farmers kept stall-fed cows in less than sanitary conditions. In London one of the main dairying areas could be found amongst the Thames-side slums and gutting sheds of Deptford, where live cattle were unloaded from the river. These urban 'farm factories' were often fertile breeding ground for diseases such as FMD, murrain and rinderpest. Out in the geographically isolated countryside most milk was turned into cheese, usually by farmers' wives in farmhouse kitchens.

However, transport by rail via cooling depots, together with a better understanding of the microbiology of milk, transformed the dairy industry both in quantity and quality. As a dairy farmer, E.W. Langford was at the vanguard of technical development and by 1920 ran a dairy so modern it could be described as futuristic.

Despite starting with the ubiquitous Dairy Shorthorn he was soon buying Holstein Friesians – mainly progeny from Dutch imports. In 1920 less than two per cent of the national dairy herd was Friesian, by 1950 that had risen to 40 per cent. Langford's parlour at Tupsley Court milked 100 cows by machine rather than by hand. Milking machines had been developed over the previous 50 years – suction cups had evolved from devices designed to extract gunshot from wounds. By the 1900s the pulsating clusters that we know today were being used.

At Langford's farm standards of hygiene were exemplary. His herd and milk were tuberculin

A farmer loads his churns on the platform in the 1920s.

tested, churns and bottles were steam sterilised and the milk was pasteurised, filtered and then cooled. Langford would give group tours of his dairy and tell people with pride that his Grade A milk, bottled within five minutes of coming out the cow, was untouched by human hand.

But we must remember that in these respects Langford represented the future of dairy farming and was not typical of the times. Although most British dairy farms in the 1920s and '30s witnessed advances in combating TB and brucellosis (The Ministry and the NFU coordinated clean milk competitions throughout the 1920s), machine milking in modern parlours was unusual. In 1920 there were just 1,000 automated installations, and, although by 1939 their number had increased to 16,000, this figure still represented only a small minority. In 1939 90 per cent of the UK herd was still hand-milked.

Furthermore, milk was often sold out of churns on carts and ladled into whatever domestic containers the housewife had to hand. As one dairyman in 1920s Liverpool recollected, this receptacle was frequently the chamberpot that had only very recently been discharged from its bedtime duty.

One further nod to the future on Langford's farm was the use of electricity. He was a pioneer of what, at the time, was termed 'electro-farming'. He was one of the few farmers who enjoyed the delights of electric lights, motors and welders. There were even some misguided enough to believe that if they placed electrodes in their fields their crops would yield 10 per cent more, while others thought silage kept better in electrified silos. Langford was too intelligent to be taken in by some of the wackier claims, but still saw that the future lay in electrification.

Whereas nineteenth-century Britain had been transformed by steam power and the steam engine, in the early-twentieth century it was the internal combustion engine and electricity that were changing life beyond recognition. For most British manufacturing industries the uptake of these new technologies between 1900 and 1939 was dramatic, as were increases in efficiency. In farming the uptake was far more piecemeal. Although tractors were making an impact, the horse still reigned supreme. Similarly, most farms did not have the benefit of electricity. The main reason for this lack of progress was lack of money. The purchase of tractors or the electrification of farmyards involved significant investment and, while the returns from farming remained poor, there was little business incentive to spend money on new-fangled ideas. In the case of electricity there were other problems. Although the national grid was rolling out across rural Britain in the 1920s and bringing electricity to rural communities, it still remained out of the reach of most farms, whose remoteness could not justify the purchase of cables and transformers. Throughout the 1920s the NFU pushed for improved access to the national grid

for the farming industry. Even in 1930 the NFU were making the point:

So long as the cost of equipment and power remains at the high level of today it is utterly uneconomic to go in for electrical development on a large scale in agriculture. The Electricity Act of last year makes no provision for the development of the use of electricity in agriculture. The Commissioners seem to be chiefly concerned with the cost of transmitting current from one centre of the population to another.

By the mid-1930s farms with an electricity supply still numbered less than five per cent. It was a common complaint at union meetings in the 1930s and '40s that, although pylons and posts carrying electricity increasingly stamped across their farms, the farmers still could not get access to an affordable supply. Langford was an exception because his farm at Tupsley Court lay on the outskirts of the substantial city of Hereford, where an electricity supply was available.

Having served a year as president in 1921, the NFU sponsored Langford to take a study tour of the dairy industry in the US and Canada. He set sail out of Liverpool on 15 April on the White Star liner *Celtic*. On his return he reported back to Council as to what he had found. One of his key conclusions was that there was more milk drunk in the US per head because of publicity campaigns designed to promote its health benefits. Advertisements were commonplace, with medical experts encouraging consumers to drink at least a pint of milk a day.

He also noted that in the US and Canada milk was bought on the basis of butter fat. The seasonal gluts of milk which so often hung over the British market and undermined the price, were absorbed by dairy processors who made such delights as ice-cream and condensed milk. Langford noted how ice-cream was eaten routinely by American families and was not just as an occasional treat as it was in Britain. Four per cent of US milk production was turned into ice-cream and much of it was exported. Langford found American railways transported milk from farms more efficiently and with more care. Consumers paid the same as in the UK but processors took less, giving more back to the farmer. There was also more direct selling from farms.

Langford did not just sit on these findings. He tried to deploy them to benefit his union's dairy members. In the 1920s the lot of the 140,000 British dairy farmers was not a happy one, largely due to the fact that, as sellers, British dairy farmers were a disparate, fragmented bunch, whereas the processors and retailers were becoming increasingly organised.

The first attempts by the NFU to secure higher milk prices came during the First World War, when the Food Controller fixed the price of milk at levels farmers considered unjustly low. Farmers from

Devon, Cornwall, Somerset and Dorset were particularly aggrieved by the fact that the Food Controller had ruled that, as the South West area was well favoured im the production of milk they should get 2d. less than everyone else. The NFU made representations for higher prices and justified these suggestions by setting up a cost committee, which showed inflation was pushing up production costs.

When the powers of the Food Controller were suddenly removed in 1920 and a free market was restored, the weakness of the dairy farmers' position was quickly exposed. The price of milk fell from as much as 2s.6d. a gallon to as little as 4d. a gallon. One powerful dairy combine attracted the ire of Langford when it was found to be paying 2.5d. a pint for milk in Wales and retailing it in Guildford for 6d. a pint.

As chairman of the Milk and Dairy Produce Committee, Langford knew producers would struggle to negotiate with the increasingly well-organised milk retailers, and he sought to establish collective bargaining. In an attempt to give NFU dairy members some sort of national coordinated strength he was instrumental in setting up the Joint Milk Committee, made up of representatives of NFU producers and the dairy companies. The committee attempted to fix prices for fresh and processed milk and all NFU members were urged to join the scheme. The Joint Milk Committee had limited success but lacked the powers of compulsion. Neither farmers nor retailers were ever disciplined enough to abide by the board's deliberations when it didn't suit them. The NFU also organised producer groups at county level to negotiate on a more local basis. Central distribution agencies were set up for each county. As the price stabilised at 1s.4d. a gallon in 1923, the NFU took evidence to the retailers that farmers needed 1s.5d. to cover their costs. Prices never regained their pre-1922 levels but at least they stabilised for the rest of the 1920s. In the absence of other income streams, milk production remained attractive to British farmers in the 1920s, and the number of herds continued to increase. The dairymen on mixed farms through the middle of the country fared better in the hard times than their arable brethren in the east or the beef and sheep men in the hills.

Drawing from his American experience, Langford was also involved in setting up the Milk Publicity Council to initiate an advertising campaign to stimulate increased consumption. A sum of 50 guineas was taken from NFU funds to back the venture, and milk producers were asked to contribute a levy of 1d. for every gallon sold. The project was largely stillborn, however, as producers shunned the idea and remained suspicious of helping the retailers through advertising.

Despite the weaknesses of the Joint Milk Council and the failure of the Milk Publicity Committee, one should not underestimate the achievement of E.W. Langford. In many ways he was a visionary before his time and his work is key to the history of the NFU.

The idea of workable collective bargaining drawing NFU members together extended the NFU's influence at a time when the fortunes of British farming were on the rocks and the NFU was in danger of sinking with it. More importantly, Langford oversaw a watershed moment when solidarity and unity in marketing amongst farmers was placed firmly on the agenda. Through the NFU, farmers were coming to realise they were not just the victims of low prices for their commodities but were, to some extent, the authors of their own demise.

In the North West in the 1920s there were frequent outbreaks of what were known as the 'Milk Wars'. These were sparked when Manchester and Liverpool dairy companies refused to accept the price proposal of the Joint Milk Committee. In response, Cheshire dairy farmers united to sell their milk direct from carts in the city streets, thus directly taking on the dairy companies. Much of this was coordinated by the local NFU, and the farmer-owned dairy carts were bedecked with NFU banners. In 1928 Langford took up the chairmanship of a Cheshire farmer-owned dairy involved in one of these disputes and thus felt obliged to stand down as chairman of the Joint Milk Committee.

Eventually, through the NFU, dairy farmers would come to recognise the importance of collective bargaining and advertising. Many of Langford's ideas in the 1920s came to fruition in the 1930s. He remained a loyal and active Hereford branch member into his late 80s.

We cannot leave E.W. Langford without recording one ironic moment of ignominy. In 1941 he was gaoled for six months on being found guilty of defrauding the Milk Marketing Board (MMB) of £650. There were discrepancies in the Tupsley Court milk records where milk declared for cheese making, and thus eligible for a board payment, was fed to calves. One of the key prosecution witnesses was a disgruntled ex-employee who had been caught by Langford 'with a woman in the cheese room'. Despite this fact, and despite Langford's long, exemplary record in public life, the judge saw fit to gaol him at the age of 71 years and during a time of war. All that can be said about this is that, in the world of Hereford politics, local enmities between public figures can lead to injustices. It is an ill-fitting and sad postscript to the story of 'Langford of Hereford', who led the NFU twice and who proved a pugnacious fighter for British dairy farmers.

Langford's successor was a man of equal calibre whose career did not end in ignominy but rather in the celebration of a knighthood.

♦ CHAPTER 10 ♦

Sir Thomas Baxter, 1927

Born in 1877 on a 200-acre tenanted farm in Ashton Hayes, near Chester, Tom Baxter learnt much of his farming from his father, who was a renowned dairy man and known amongst his farming peers as Cheshire's 'Potato King'. As a small boy Baxter watched his mother making Cheshire cheese in the farmhouse kitchen, as well as gangs of itinerant Irish labourers, who arrived in the spring to hand plant potatoes with shovels and then hand-forked them out a few months later.

Unlike Robbins and Langford, Baxter grew up in a household that voted Conservative Unionist and disliked the politics of 'Manchester liberalism', which had its hot-house just 20 miles to the east of the home farm.

Baxter was privately educated at Turton Hall, near Leeds, and returned to work on the family farm at 14. Despite being the farmer's son, he was not spared long hours in the potato fields, digging and forking amidst the endless ridges. Later, he would recall with pride that, whereas Irish men always wielded a spade to the left of the potato ridge, with their left hand at the top of the spade, and English labourers worked to the right, with their right hands on the handle, he, the farmer's son, could happily and ambidextrously work from either side. Baxter was of a strong athletic build, and when the hundredweight baskets were filled with freshly harvested potatoes he would carry them to the farm pond to be washed. They were then ready to be sent to the markets in the industrial heartlands of the North West.

In early 1900, at the age of 22, he decided to heed the call from the Army for recruits to fight in South Africa against the Boers. For two years Trooper Baxter saw frequent action, as well as bouts of dysentry, across the veldt of the Orange Free State. It was an awkward conflict for the British Army, as the guerrilla Boer Army fought by way of ambushes and raids rather than in set-piece battles. When the Boer War came to an end in mid-1901 Baxter returned to Cheshire to resume his career as a farmer. Keen to branch out on his own, he borrowed money from his father and took a 300-acre farm at Freeford, near Lichfield in Staffordshire, for the rent of £400 a year. He also married Mabel Clare, a 'town girl' from Chester. His father had counselled his son against the match as:

Girls brought up in the town life aren't fitted to live in the country. She won't settle in. Her nose will be in the air and this'll smell and that'll smell and she won't be able to properly boil a potato.

Later, Baxter snr admitted his mistake, as young Mabel proved a hard-working farmer's wife and could indeed boil a potato to perfection. The marriage lasted over 50 years.

At Freeford Baxter milked 50 cows (averaging 2,600 litres a year), kept 550 Shropshire sheep, grew potatoes as well as some malting barley and was the first in the county to experiment with a new crop – sugar beet. He joined the Lichfield, Tamworth and Walsall branch of the Staffordshire Agricultural Society, whose main role was to put on the Staffordshire Show and to organise ploughing or hedging competitions. After attending a couple of meetings, Baxter was taken aback when the chairman, Edward Averill, announced it was time for him to stand down and proposed young Tom Baxter as a very good successor. Without bothering to consult with the newcomer, the meeting unanimously agreed and the proposed incumbent felt obliged to take on the post.

There is an old joke in farming circles that 'you can go a long way in the NFU – unless you are very

'If you want to get ahead, get a hat.' Tom Baxter (third from left) *leads the Staffordshire delegation into the NFU AGM in 1922.*

careful'. There is also the facetious wisdom that it is important to attend NFU meetings in case you get elected to do something. But for young Tom Baxter this early elevation to chairmanship was the first step on a ladder that took him to the very top of the agricultural establishment.

In 1919, after much heated debate amongst its members, the Staffordshire Agricultural Society decided to affiliate to the NFU. Staffordshire was one of the last counties to do so. Baxter was one of the main advocates of the affiliation and became Staffordshire county delegate, attending Council meetings in London. By 1922 he had been earmarked by E.W. Langford as a good man to join him in his pioneering negotiations with the milk buyers on the Joint Milk Committee.

In 1924 and 1925 he chaired the Sugar Beet Committee at a formative time for the industry. Keen to learn more about the cultivation of sugar beet, Baxter travelled to Germany, where the crop was far more established and technically advanced than in the UK. His report back to NFU Council gave an insight into the differences between German and English farming. In Germany two-thirds of the countryside was under the plough, whereas in England it was less than half. Furthermore, the German farmed landscape lacked the landscape features of its English counterpart. It was denuded of the hedges, walls and trees that delineated English fields, and instead the open landscape was populated with solitary 2ft stone pillars to mark boundaries. Similarly, in tribute to the German love of orderliness and efficiency, trees and weedy roadside verges were not allowed to interfere with a countryside dedicated to cultivation and production. Even streams were buried under precious farmed soil.

In 1925 the 'big four' – Robbins, Langford, Ryland and German – approached Baxter, urging him to consider standing as vice-president, and thus president-elect. Baxter agreed, but insisted on deferring for a year so he could sort out his affairs at home. Returning to Freeford, Baxter discussed his forthcoming responsibilities with Mrs Baxter, explaining that he would have to spend most of his time in London at meetings or addressing gatherings of farmers in various parts of the country. Mr and Mrs Baxter decided the best plan for the future was to leave the farm in the hands of their son and take residence in a town house in Sutton Coldfield, on the outskirts of Birmingham.

On hearing of his tenant's plans, Baxter's landlord gave him notice to quit. Thus, in 1927 Thomas Baxter became the first NFU president to take on the role while not actually being in the business of farming at the same time. In an organisation built on the strict understanding that it was for working farmers, and working farmers alone, Baxter's retirement from farming was a contentious factor in some quarters of the union. Others recog-

nised Tom Baxter was more entitled than most to the description 'working farmer', and his unquestionable talent made his withdrawal from everyday farming an irrelevance. It was also at this time that the NFU was starting to relax its rules on exclusivity, and retired farmers, along with 'Cow-keepers and Cow-renters' and those involved in agricultural research, were now also welcome.

It might also be worth mentioning here that the annals of the NFU never tell us how the term 'farmer' was defined for the purposes of eligibility to join. It was probably done on the basis that farmers know instinctively who is one of their own and who is not.

As a man, Tom Baxter was forthright but affable. If he thought people were speaking rubbish he would tell them so in his Cheshire burr. He was known as a skilled negotiator and his service on the Milk and Sugar Beet Committees saw him more than once secure good deals for various sectors of agriculture. His handsome, athletic demeanour portrayed a vital energy.

An adept sportsman, his time on horseback on the South African veldt pursuing and being pursued by the Boer enemy had made him a skilled horseman. On retiring from farming at the age of 48, he took up tennis as a hobby and promptly won the championship at the large, prestigious Goldislie Club in Sutton Coldfield. He won it several times more, even at the age of 56, beating men half his age.

Sometimes Baxter's forthright, no-nonsense manner could be disconcerting, but those who knew him realised that beneath the gruff exterior lay a well-meaning and courteous sensibility. One man who did not appreciate Baxter's directness, nor his unblinking defence of British farming, was Lord Beaverbrook.

As the recession of the '20s moved towards the major economic depression of the 1930s, Beaverbrook hatched a plan that he called 'Empire Free Trade'. The idea was to form a free-trade area across the Commonwealth whereby Britain and her dominions would protect themselves from imports from non-Commonwealth countries and show favour to exports from each other. Obviously, this caused concern at the NFU, as British farming was being bled dry by low commodity prices, often caused by the export of surpluses from the likes of Canada, southern Africa and the antipodes.

Beaverbrook was keen to win the support of the NFU for his ideas. In 1927 he was duly given an audience at No. 45 Bedford Square in front of past presidents Robbins, Langford and Ryland, with the current incumbent, Baxter, in the chair. As the somewhat haughty Beaverbrook outlined his Empire Free Trade plans to the four NFU heavyweights, Baxter could barely contain his frustration. Banging the table with his fist, Baxter exclaimed in his Cheshire burr:

Look here, Lord Beaverbrook, if home producers are going to be faced with a flood of imports it makes no difference to uz whether it's an Empire flood or a foreign flood. It's still a flood and the effect is the same. We'll go under and be drowned in either case.

Beaverbrook was taken aback at the outburst and it was no surprise that from then on Baxter usually received a carpingly bad press in the *Daily Express*. Such was the pettiness of the newspaper magnate. Baxter took it all on the chin and kept a scrapbook of all the negative headlines for his later amusement.

Beaverbrook's vision of Empire Free Trade saw some success five years later in the Ottawa Agreement of 1932. Baxter was part of the NFU delegation that attended the conference in the Canadian city which leant its name to the treaty's title. As Baxter had foreseen, the agreement was not good news for British agriculture. Apart from some protective quotas on meat imports, the farmers of the old colonies were given free access to British markets in exchange for British industrialists being given better export opportunities. Although, under the Ottawa Agreement, food imports from non-Empire countries fell by 32 per cent between 1931 and 1935, imports from Empire farms increased by 42 per cent.

Tom Baxter (left) *meets Lord Bledisloe, Governor General in New Zealand.*

The Empire now provided mother Britain with just over 50 per cent of her food.

One area of vociferous complaint by the NFU in the 1920s was over the apparent preferential treatment given to Dominion farmers over the ones at home. This took two forms. Firstly, the 1927 Empire Settlement Act gave grants for farmers or farm labourers to emigrate and take cheap farm land across the Empire. This was undoubtedly a state-subsidised drain on the life-blood of British agriculture. To rub salt in this bleeding wound, the government then gave millions in grants for Dominion producers to advertise their exported produce to British consumers.

In 1933 NFU concerns about dairy and lamb imports meant Baxter was on his travels again, this time to New Zealand. In the 1920s the NFU had cultivated good contacts with its counterpart unions in the dominions to the point where, in 1928, the NZFU had formally applied to affiliate with the NFU. Despite some enthusiasm for this from some NFU members, the leadership explained that it was not constitutionally possible, but assured the membership that it would continue to pursue regular and good liaison with farmers' unions in Canada, South Africa, Australia and New Zealand. Despite these familiar and friendly relations, there were concerns as to how exports from these countries could depress home prices. It was with that in mind that the NFU decided to send its Milk Committee chairman, Tom Baxter, to the other side of the world. Having spent six weeks on the White Star liner *Ionic*, steaming across the Atlantic and the Pacific via the Panama Canal, Baxter arrived in New Zealand in mid-September 1933. On his arrival Baxter was engaged in talks with farmers' leaders, the NZ Dairy Board and the deputy Prime Minister. While, as an honoured guest, Baxter had a very warm reception, his suggestion of a quota on his hosts' farm exports did not. His argument that quota restrictions would lead to better prices for both UK and NZ farmers was met with the counter-argument that it would be better to stimulate consumer demand for lamb, cheese and butter.

For once, the great negotiator Baxter came away with very little other than an agreement that a dialogue between the farmers of the two counties should continue. It is interesting to note that in the summer of 2007 another Thomas from the NFU, Thomas Binns, chairman of the Livestock Board, retraced Baxter's footsteps in New Zealand and had discussions about very similar export issues and their impact on UK prices. One significant difference between the experience of the two Thomases was that in 2007 Binns's journey was completed in 24 hours, a fortieth of the time it took Baxter.

It was on a ship from New Zealand, in mid-Pacific, that Baxter received news by telegram of a formal agreement to the setting up of the Milk

Baxter (far right) *at the BBC. The BBC was formed in 1926 and the NFU made its first complaint of anti-farming bias in 1928.*

Marketing Board (MMB) and his appointment as its first chairman. Having initially opposed the idea of the MMB because he disliked the principle of state-enforced compulsion, the enthusiasm for the idea amongst UK dairy farmers convinced him to change his mind.

The setting up of the MMB needed a two-thirds vote of acceptance from producers, and when the ship's telegram office passed the printout to Baxter, it read that the vote had been 66 per cent in favour, just 0.67 per cent short of the requirement. Realising the closeness of the figures, Baxter asked the operator to double check. This time the operator took a transmission from a different passing ship, which

disclosed a 96 per cent vote in favour. As we shall see, history records the second transmission as correct and Tom Baxter became the MMB's first chairman. He held the office until 1949, when he stood down at the age of 71. The initial years of the board were not easy ones and strong chairmanship was needed to see it through its teething troubles. Tom Baxter provided that strength. He was famed for being able to chair rowdy meetings and to quieten down the over-animated.

Many felt that it was Baxter's steadfastness and fixity of purpose that kept the organisation from early disintegration. In 1943 he was knighted for his services to agriculture. He died in 1951.

CHAPTER 11

Tom Williams, 1928

Tom Williams, who had a good eye for champion stock.

Tom Williams was the first Welshman to lead the NFU. As the retiring president, at the 1929 AGM at the Holborn Restaurant, he welcomed the 300 delegates in Welsh. It was a first for the NFU and was met with applause by the mainly non-Welsh audience, to which Williams replied in English: 'There was a great deal of meaning in that and I hope you have fully grasped it.'

As a character, Williams could be fiery and impetuous but, importantly, he recognised these traits in himself. Those around him appreciated his passion, vitality and Welsh spirit. Interestingly, his farm straddled the English–Welsh border and somehow he managed to represent English Shropshire in some instances and Welsh Montgomeryshire in others. As we shall see, he was not to be the first president who managed to have a foot on either side of the border.

But, in his heart, he was a Welshman. As we know, Wales is different from England to the point where some feel it is almost another country. Its topography and farming tend to be dominated by the

hill-grazing of livestock. This became more pronounced in the 1920s and '30s as the arable area shrank by 30 per cent to 571,000 acres, compared to nearly four million acres of permanent pasture and rough grazing. Over the same period sheep numbers grew from 3.3 million to 4.6 million. Welsh farming was dominated by the small farm. Between the wars two-thirds of recorded holdings were smaller than 50 acres .

As we have noted, unlike the Scots, the Welsh were active in the NFU from its inception, but it was also acknowledged in the union that Welsh agriculture was significantly different from the farming on the other size of Offa's Dyke in terms of size of holding and productivity per acre. As we have also noted, Colin Campbell discouraged very small farmers from joining the NFU by instituting a subscription system that insisted on a minimal capitation fee.

After Campbell's retirement from the presidency the leadership realised this capitation system might discourage expansion of the union in Wales and allowed for lower levels of individual subs for Welsh members. Welsh counties were also allowed to pay (in terms of members) proportionately less of the central fund collected from county branches for the running of Bedford Square. A Welsh Committee was also set up in 1922 under the chairmanship of Tom Williams.

Tom Williams was no small farmer. He was the tenant of a 500-acre farm, 'The Gaer', near Welshpool in Montgomeryshire. The farm was almost an island between rivers, with the Severn to the west, the Camlad to the east and an expanse of rich grazing pasture between. 'Gaer' means 'fort', and in Roman times the farm was the site of a Roman military settlement. Today 100 acres of the farm is a wet-land nature reserve.

Beef production, fattening 200 stores a year, was the main enterprise, but he also kept 200 pedigree Kerry Hill sheep and 50 non-pedigree pigs. Like other beef farmers at the time, Williams experimented with 'baby beef', such animals being slaughtered at 18 months. As British meat consumers became more affluent they developed a taste for smaller joints of meat from younger animals. Baby beef was the farmers' and butchers' response to this demand. While Williams considered himself no breeder of beef animals, it was a different matter with his sheep, and he often took prizes at the Royal Welsh.

The year 1928 was not an easy one to lead the farmers. As prices continued to weaken, the fortunes of farming worsened to the point where Williams decided to cancel the annual dinner. He did not think it appropriate for members to gather in their finery in the West End while so many of their fellows faced ruinously hard times.

Despite this austerity, 1928 was not without notable achievement for the NFU. Under the 1928 Agricultural Rates Act farmland was de-rated. thus saving the farmer an average of 2s.8¹/₂d. per acre per year. This was a tidy sum and a notable victory. The actual reform came in 1929 with the budget announced by the then Chancellor, Winston Churchill. The Baldwin Government estimated that it represented a tax reduction in the region of £5 million a year. As we have already noted, from its very beginnings in 1908 the NFU, at both national and county levels, had consistently pressed for rate relief on farmland and farm buildings on the grounds that local government expenditure mainly benefited built-up areas rather than the countryside. The union also sought to demonstrate through its statistical department that this was a tax the ailing industry could no longer bear.

As an industry we retain this rate exemption to this day, and it should be remembered that it can be traced back to NFU pressure in the first part of the twentieth century. It is a tax break that our continental counterparts do not enjoy in countries such as France and Germany. It is also interesting that in 2008 there are government plans to reintroduce the rating of farm buildings and thus reverse some of the victory gained all those years ago. Again, the NFU lobbying machine is on the move to try and save farmers from the burden.

In this chapter we have suggested that, in the 1920s, government showed little more than indifference to the decline in farming incomes, and the policy from Whitehall seemed to be that farmers would have to look to their own devices to see themselves through hard times. That is not to say, however, that government, or parliament, seldom concerned itself with the nation's greatest industry. For example looking at just the years between 1925 and 1927, the NFU gave submissions on over 20 pieces of legislation that impacted on farming businesses.

The following list gives a flavour of how the state was increasingly involving itself in the everyday lives and businesses of farmers: Auctions Act 1927; Destructive Insects and Pests Act 1927, Diseases of Animals Act 1925 and 1927; Fertiliser and Feeding stuffs Act 1926; Finance Act 1925, 1926, 1927; Horticultural Produce Act 1926; Housing Rural Workers Act 1926; Importation of Pedigree Animals Act 1925; Improvement of Land Act 1925; Land Drainage Act 1926; Markets and Fairs (Weighing of Cattle) Act 1926; Protection of Animals Act 1927; Seeds (Amendment) Act 1925; Summer Time Act 1925; Tithe Act 1925; Tuberculosis Order 1925; Workmen's Compensation Act 1925.

Some of these Acts increased the regulatory burden, while others improved the lot of the farmer. The key point was that it was increasingly important that the farming industry had a strong voice when it came to political lobbying. That voice was provided by the NFU.

In addition, there was legislation that did not appear to have any connection with agriculture but still impinged on the everyday life of the farmer. For instance, in 1928 legislation was passed forbidding the hunting of lapwings or the taking of eggs from their nests (the NFU had been to the Home Office in 1926 to seek full protection for the lapwing). There was also legislation, such as the Electricity Act, that failed to incorporate union proposals that 'special consideration be given to facilitate the provision of electrical power in rural areas'.

On top of this, adding to the workload, there was the lobbying on Bills in parliament that never actually made it into law. Some of these the union was keen to see argued out and others it was keen to see succeed. For instance, it had successfully resisted a proposed Sheep Dipping Bill that sought to ban the use of arsenic in the dip (when one considers it was not uncommon for farmers to dip their sheep in dammed steams one can appreciate why some might think arsenic was not a good thing to put into the

Sheep dipping in the 1920s.

The "Relay" event—Mr. John Garton carries on the N.F.U. president's baton handed to him by Mr. Thomas Williams. Our caricaturist's view of the continuity of N.F.U. activity.

President Williams hands over the baton to Garton in 1929.

watercourses of the countryside). On the other hand, the NFU supported the Reconstituted and Synthetic Cream Bill introduced by W.L. Everard MP, which intended to prevent synthetic cream being sold as the real thing.

There was also lobbying on matters that were dealt with through Orders and other administrative instruments. One such was railway rates. Throughout its first 50 years the NFU worked hard to secure better rates for farmers when they transported their goods by train, and for better facilities for loading or unloading. One member complained in Council in 1928 that he could travel from Exeter to Birmingham cheaper than could one of his pigs. In 1921 the Railways Act had rationalised the 200 separate railway companies into four and set up the Railway Rates Tribunal, whereby the state fixed freight charges. In 1924 the NFU had the good sense to appoint Frederick Sabatini as transport officer. Sabatini had previously been employed as chief goods manager for the Great Central Railway and thus knew the system inside out. By organising farmers and growers so they loaded their goods collectively onto trains rather as individuals, it was estimated that by 1927 Sabatini's work was saving the industry £200,000 a year. Sabatini was well regarded in Wales, not only for his skill in negotiating with the railways but also because he made the effort to learn sufficient Welsh to make himself understood in the Celtic tongue.

Like most presidents, Williams had a busy year of incumbency. He was in demand to talk to union members all over the country, as well as spending most days of the week at Bedford Square. A brief glimpse of his 1928 NFU diary for February shows the extent of his travels. On 26 January he was at Crediton in Devon, on 1 February at Newport, on 22 February at Epping in Essex, on 28 February back in Wales at Cardiff and on 7 March he was scheduled to visit the Sittingbourne branch in Kent.

One of the strengths of the NFU was the sense of unity and belonging it engendered in the farming community. This ethos is well illustrated by the example of a Welshman visiting farmers in Essex or Kent as their president and their political leader. In terms of his farming and accent, Williams was clearly very different from these eastern-region men, but he was still welcomed and respected as their leader. Farmers are notorious for exaggerating their differences according to region or sector. This can make them fractious and weak when it would clearly be better to negotiate from a position of unity and strength. But despite their differences, the president always had one common bond with his audience; he was a fellow farmer – a true-blooded man of the land. The fact that 100,000 farmers could unite under one banner and accept one man as their leader was a formidable achievement that gave them a strength they might not have individually possessed.

'Honest' John Garton, president in 1929. 'A man to go hunting tigers with.'

CHAPTER 12

John Garton, 1929

'Honest' John Garton, whose 'word was his bond', was a Lancastrian by birth who moved to the fair county of Essex in 1896 when in his 20s. He was a man who other men instinctively trusted. R.R. Robbins once said of John Garton that if he ever went tiger hunting it was Garton he would want by his side.

Garton farmed on the Essex-Herts border at Hatfield Broad Oak, four miles south-east of Bishops Stortford. The farm today is not much changed but for two notable additions to the countryside that sit just a couple of miles to the east – the M11 and Stansted Airport. The noise apart, the M11 and Stansted have not ravaged John Garton's farm to the extent that the M4 and Heathrow have decimated Rowland Robbins's stamping ground, but one suspects it is only a matter of time. As Stansted expands and the M11 corridor is developed, this patch of north-west Essex becomes ever less tranquil and less rural.

In 1929 Garton's farm was a patch of typical Essex clay far enough away from London to escape its intrusion. John Garton farmed 600 acres, a third of which was pasture. Essex clay was designed by the creator to grow wheat, and John Garton was of the view that if it didn't there was little else it could grow profitably. Although he ran 30 Short-horn dairy cows, along with some 120 Suffolk ewes, there was not enough rain, in what is one of the driest corners of Britain, to make grazing pay. The 200 acres of wheat was the main earner, along with some barley and clover for seed. Essex was always an important seed-growing county. The old four-course rotation typical of Victorian farming had been abandoned, and in the 1920s the land was occasionally fallowed with clover to build fertility. In terms of mechanisation Garton had not changed things much in a quarter of a century, and still relied on horses and steam. There were no tractors on the farm.

In this respect Garton was not unusual. In 1930 there were only 5,000 tractors in the UK, compared to 500,000 horses. Indeed, Garton was a great horseman. He bred shire horses and was a great point-to-point enthusiast.

For a farm dependent on wheat production, the collapse in the wheat price had left few farming alternatives to turn to. In 1928 the price of wheat fell to 47s. a quarter. As with most farmers in his position, Garton tightened his belt and soldiered on. There was little investment and little technical innovation. While some machinery enthusiasts wrote excitedly about the possibility of a 'horseless' farm in the 1929 *Farmer & Stockbreeder*, Garton continued with a 'tractor-less' farm and remained faithful to the horse, pointing out: 'I've yet to see a tractor win a ploughing match.'

Garton did not have a son, which made the demands of the presidency burdensome, but he did have a daughter, Mrs Burton, who helped run the farm in her father's absence.

The year 1929 was 'National Mark Year'. The National Mark was a mark put on foodstuffs to denote country of origin and a grade of quality. It had been introduced by the 1926 Merchandise Marks Act (backed up by the Agricultural Produce Act 1928) which was one of the Baldwin Government's 'palliatives' for agriculture in the absence of any serious attempt to formulate a comprehensive agricultural policy. In 1925 the NFU had lobbied the Baldwin Government to take action against dishonest retailers who passed imported produce off as home grown. The practice of butchers, in particular, in selling imported beef as British was widespread, and more than once caught the furious eye of the NFU Livestock Committee. The resulting legislation, however, failed to lay down the comprehensive labelling regime of imported and home-grown foodstuffs that the union had hoped. Instead, the ministry set up a committee of enquiry to which producers could apply if they wanted a government-sanctioned mark that denoted quality and country of origin.

For the ministry it was a flagship scheme that had great possibilities for home producers, but the NFU always viewed it with some disappointment, as it failed to insist on the labelling of all foodstuffs so that consumers knew their origin. The mark did, on the other hand, enable farmers to denote their produce as British and of a guaranteed grade.

The committee of enquiry accepted schemes to put the mark on home-produced, graded eggs, apples, pears, tomatoes, cucumbers, poultry, strawberries, cherries and even cider. There was also a scheme for National Mark flour that went to make the 'National Loaf'. The mark was successful for some products but not for others. In 1929, 200 million eggs were sold carrying the National Mark. Under the scheme there were four grades of egg. The statistics showed a resulting decrease in the number of imported eggs sold. The union and the ministry managed to bring together producers, packers and distributors to help make the scheme work, and the ministry estimated this had led to a £1.5 million cash gain for British egg producers.

Generally, the ministry backed the scheme with a publicity campaign based on 'strong support in the form of propaganda'. Advertising was placed in the press, on poster hoardings, in cinemas, on buses and trams and even in the Lord Mayor's Show in 1930. National Mark shopping weeks were organised in major towns and cities in collaboration with NFU branches. These promotion campaigns were limited, however, and the ministry clearly felt there should be more of a contribution to campaign funds from producers and packers. This was not forthcoming, and the NFU never expressed any enthusiasm to encourage farmers to provide any finance.

In the case of beef, a trial scheme was run in London and Birmingham whereby National Mark cuts were marked as select, prime or good. The ministry also provided butchers with material for shop-window displays complete with Union Jacks. Even so, it seems, most butchers were reluctant to give the scheme much prominence in their shops and it did not seem to catch the consumer's imagination.

The National Mark scheme limped on into the 1930s but was never given the funding it needed for the publicity properly to engage with the consumer, and was largely superseded by the marketing boards set up from 1933 onwards. Furthermore, it was resisted by some retailers, who had an interest in selling imported foodstuff to their customers. Nonetheless, it was an interesting experiment that has parallels with later initiatives to secure the home market for the home farmer through assured standards, labelling and promotion. It can be seen as a forerunner to various quality marks for British farm produce, most notably the Red Tractor we know today.

The conundrum as to how the British farmer best secures a healthy proportion of his home market has long puzzled the NFU and the wider industry. History suggests there are no easy answers, and it is a challenge that will continue to test the farmer's imagination, as farmers in the future. For a hundred years British farmers have recognised they have a huge market in the form of millions of increasingly affluent consumers on their own doorstep, but this opportunity tends to be effectively counteracted by Britain's historic tendency to import much of its food. The National Mark was the first attempt to correct this imbalance through labelling and by appealing to the average Brit's sense of loyalty to his local producer. It must be noted it largely failed through a

Left: *The National Mark.*

combination of insufficient funding, retailer obstruction and lack of consumer interest.

In 1929, which was an election year, the NFU finally abandoned its 20-year attempt to get direct representation in parliament through sponsored MPs either running as Tories, Liberals or Independent Agriculturalists. There was an agreement with the Tories that if the union did not field any candidates, the Baldwin administration would, if returned to power, do more to source food supplies for British troops from British farms. This was never tested, as Baldwin lost the election. Nonetheless, this deal with the Tories was tacit acknowledgement that, given the continued demise of the Liberals, the farming vote had largely become a Tory one. Despite this, the NFU remained strictly neutral under the 1929–31 Labour Government and remained true to the non-party principles established at its inception.

At the 1929 AGM the NFU Lancashire contingent, led by Colonel Sayce, urged Garton to get into the business of political horse-trading and make more of the £52,000 in the political fund. Sayce felt that an impending election was a chance to force politicians into policy positions. The sanguine and honourable Garton replied:

Let me give you one piece of advice. Do not grumble at HQ if election pledges are not kept. Some of us at headquarters are by no means popular in political circles because we have dared to compare Government's promise and performance. Let me speak quite plainly, the Conservative Party Agricultural Committee could at any time in the past four years have secured for you a square deal if they had meant business. Up to now members of that Committee have not given their whips a sleepless night and I strongly advise you to see what you can do to stiffen the Agricultural Committee's backbone. The problem the politicians have created for you – the gap between cost of production and market prices – remains unchanged, and political action alone can remedy what political action has done.

And so we come to the close of the 1920s on this rather disheartening note. For British farmers it had been a decade that had started brightly. Whereas the legacy of the First World War suggested that commodity prices had turned a corner and government was prepared to support and protect its home agriculture if necessary, by 1922 this hope seemed to evaporate like the morning mist and to prove as enduring as a politician's promise.

CHAPTER 13

Captain E.T. Morris, 1930

If the 1920s were austere for British agriculture, then the start of the new decade offered little relief. In fact the situation deteriorated even further. The Great Depression was ushered in by the Wall Street crash of 1929. Already depressed agricultural prices reached new lows, and an economic blizzard blew across the world following the catastrophic slump in the prices of farm products in the USA. In Britain the index of agricultural prices stood at just two-fifths of what it had been in 1920. The average 34 per cent fall in farm-gate prices between 1928 and 1931 was unparalleled in its severity.

For the British Government a balance of payments crisis grew rapidly. Slowly but surely they abandoned the two sacred cows of economic policy – free trade and the gold standard. France, Germany and Poland were now heavily subsidising their cereal production, some of which was landing at British ports, further driving down the unsustainable home price. German wheat was worth 67s. a quarter when

sold in Berlin, but was being landed at British ports at 23s. Even in the land of free enterprise the US Government was raising tariffs on farm imports and bringing in measures to support farmers.

In Britain the 1929 election, known as 'the flapper election' because it was the first time women under 30 were allowed to vote, returned a Labour administration under Ramsay MacDonald. MacDonald had a link with agriculture in that he was the illegitimate son of a Scottish farm labourer. As we shall see, despite his farm roots MacDonald seemed to be no more enamoured of the demands of the NFU than his Tory predecessor, Baldwin. MacDonald stayed in office as Prime Minister until 1935, but after the 1931 election he found himself leading a national government reliant on Tory support. Increased trade protectionism had been part of the Tory manifesto in 1931 and it was from this point that Britain finally abandoned her strict adherence to free trade in agricultural goods. It was a policy that had been in place

Moaning over a four-bar gate. Punch *magazine's 'Farmer' in the 1930s, with much to be miserable about.*

since the repeal of the Corn Laws some 80 years before. By 1938 every agricultural product was protected in one way or another.

In the 1930s No. 45 Bedford Square established itself as the nerve-centre of English and Welsh farming. The square, located just to the west of the British Museum, reflected the security and affluence of a bygone age. With its lawns and lofty plane trees, it was an oasis of quiet amid the roar and tumult of London. There was no other house in London quite like it. In it gathered farming men from the Lizard to the Lincolnshire Wolds, from the South Downs to the Northumberland hills, from the Midland grazing shires to the mountains of Wales, men whose birth, upbringing and circumstances differed as much as their accents, but they gathered under that roof as a band of brothers with one unifying purpose – the welfare of the land and the farmers who sought a living from it.

In January 1930 the newly elected Labour government convened an agricultural conference comprising the NFU, farm workers' unions and the Central Land Association (CLA, now The Country Land and Business Association). The NFU team comprised the president, Captain E.T. Morris, Harry German, R.R. Robbins and E.W.K. Slade. Prime Minister MacDonald opened the conference and then handed over to his Minister of Agriculture, Noel Buxton. In all, ten meetings were held over a period of six months. Among the various ideas discussed were a guaranteed price for wheat of 55s. a quarter and that His Majesty's Forces should use more British-grown food in their supplies.

After much dithering, the government finally announced, in August 1931, that: 'In view of the present general financial situation, it is impossible to make any announcement or, indeed, at the moment, any promise.' The NFU could but conclude that the conference would have been as well employed making corn dollies.

Later, Captain Morris recollected how, as the NFU delegation of farmers left No. 10, they were eyed suspiciously by a policeman. 'It's all right officer, we have not taken anything away,' said Morris. 'That's all right, sir,' responded the officer. 'Very few who come here do.'

Captain Edward Thomas Morris, known as Teddy to his friends, hailed from Buckland in Hertfordshire. At over six feet he was a tall, lanky, man of impressive stature. He is described as having 'a craggy presence'. His rank of captain came from service with the 69th Division as chief of transport in Lincolnshire during the First World War, when his main job was securing horses for the Army.

His forte was powerful oratory with a big voice that fitted his tall frame. The year 1930 was punctuated by a series of mass demonstrations by farmers and farm workers to draw attention to the

A Farmer & Stockbreeder *sketch of the NFU staff in the 1930s.*

Captain Teddy Morris – a 'man of craggy presence'.

Farmers on the march in 1930. The banner at the back reads: 'Wanted in 1918, neglected in 1930'.

plight of the industry and the iniquity of having to compete empty handed with imports from foreign producers defended by protection and subsidy. The most famous of these mass meetings was held in March on Parker's Piece in Cambridge, where 23,000 gathered to listen to speeches from the likes of Captain Morris.

Morris was essentially an arable man, born and bred in Hertfordshire. When the young Teddy was just three his father had taken a 500-acre farm in the village of Buckland that was part of Lord Mexborough's estate. Morris described the farm as part of that swathe of good arable land that cut across Northern Europe from the Urals in the east to the Vale of Evesham in the west. Just as had John Garton, he felt his farm was made to grow wheat. At 400 ft above sea-level, it was rolling clay that drained naturally if given very occasional mole drainage. Root crops were not grown due to the land's resistance to winter treading. Horses and steam cultivation provided the tillage for a five-course rotation (to which he was not enslaved) of dunged fallow, wheat, barley, seeds and wheat.

Until the mid-1920s Morris had known little other than cereal production on the farm, but by the 1930s the collapse in wheat prices was forcing him to rethink his farming. There were now 110 acres of pasture on which 140 head of Lincoln Red Shorthorns were grazed to slaughter weight and sold out at £30 a head. He felt cattle did better outside all year round rather than tied up in sheds. There were, however, increasing problems with moving cattle around the farm, as it was intersected by what Morris described as 'a quite a busy road which in these days adds difficulties to the movement of animals'.

The road referred to was the A10, the main road between London and Cambridge. Today, the thought of driving cattle along the A10 might seem ridicu-

lous, but in the 1920s that road, then better known as Ermine Street, for time immemorial had been used to drive farm stock from farm to farm if not all the way down to London's Smithfield Market. By the 1920s the demands of the motorist had finally superseded the demands of the cattle drover on the nation's main trunk roads.

In 1930 Captain Morris had recently taken on a vacant and derelict 350-acre farm, Tharbies, near Sawbridgeworth. As we have noted, in the 1920s and '30s it was quite common for tenants to walk away from farms, given the paucity of the return and the difficulties in finding the rent.

Land abandoned to scrub was a not uncommon sight in 1930, especially in the arable east. An estimated 600,000 acres of predominantly arable land was left to its own devices in the recession of the 1930s. It was said that at that time you could walk from Royston to Cambridge on good productive farmland that was neither cropped nor grazed but just left to dereliction. It was a situation that was not to be repeated again for 60 years, when the concept of set-aside was introduced.

As agriculture went further into recession, the NFU inevitably became increasingly fractious. There was always an old sore in the NFU between the 'grass' counties and the 'crop' counties, based around claims that one camp was disproportionately more powerful at HQ than the other. This was compounded by the fact that there were still those in the counties who saw the NFU as an informal alliance of county branches and saw no problem in counties taking their own policy lines. It was not unknown in the 1920s for county branches to make their own representations to government, irrespective of whether or not they were in accordance with the national line. Morris realised that such fractiousness was dangerous and that when times were tough it was important to hold the NFU together on policy issues. Otherwise it would be very easy for government to side-step union demands by playing the counties off against each other. As differing views were aired on government policy, in 1930 Council flexed its muscles by resolving:

It is not in the best interests of the union that any county branch should publicly associate the union with a policy which has not been endorsed by the Council of the Union .

In the face of a growing taste in the counties for the calling for heads to roll at Bedford Square, Morris could be found at meetings and in the pages of the agricultural press reminding the disaffected that:

The NFU is the most democratic organisation it is possible to have. If the members do not send the right men to the Council of the NFU then HQ are not to blame. The members are to blame if they send a mug instead of one of the cleverest men they have got. If you send your men there, give them whole-hearted backing and do not keep snarling and snapping.

As a good example of his sly humour and ability to twist back an accusation of poor representation at Council, Morris added: 'If Counties want Council of the NFU to be a sort of mental institution, then that is their business.'

Then, as now, it was easy to suggest from the provinces that the NFU was run by some sort of unaccountable London-based 'old guard', too far removed from the problems of the members at the coal-face. It was important for the top of the NFU to remind the membership of its democratic structure and the sacrosanct right of the counties to send whoever they liked to Council. Once assembled, these county representatives remained the supreme authority of the NFU, which no 'old guard' or individual president could defy.

Morris's desire to keep the union as a united front was complicated by his friendship with Lord Beaverbrook. They drank together in the same London club and there were rumours of Beaverbrook helping Morris financially when his farm business was struggling. Lord Beaverbrook, one of the most powerful men in inter-war Britain, was the Canadian-born son of a Scottish farmer who owned the Express Group of newspapers which, in 1930s Britain, commanded huge circulations. Politically

very astute, he had the ear of Prime Ministers and royalty. He also had very strong views as to how the plight of British farmers would be best served by his plan to set up a free trading bloc across what was the British Empire. As we have seen, he openly clashed with the likes of Baxter, Ryland and Robbins, who doubted British farmers' interests were best served by his Empire plan and openly encouraged NFU members not to trust the Canadian press baron.

Beaverbrook grew increasingly angry at what he called 'this sniping campaign carried out by the false leaders' of the NFU. Beaverbrook's ideas did find popularity with some NFU counties, particularly the arable men in the east. Beaverbrook sensed this disunity and set about stirring up disaffection with the leadership in the NFU ranks. Writing to Morris in 1929, when Morris was vice-president, Beaverbrook was adamant:

I am entitled to call for a declaration of opinion from the farmers. It would be along this line that I would fight our foes in the National Farmers' Union. I think we have nothing to lose and everything to gain if we can split up the farmers' forces into those who support and those who oppose.

This was too much for Morris, who then distanced himself from Beaverbrook. Generally, the NFU remained doubtful about Beaverbrook's 'one Empire' vision of English-speaking farmers freely trading across the dominions.

Morris gave the NFU the leadership it needed to stop it becoming increasingly factionalised in the early 1930s. After 1930 we find less unilateral behaviour in the counties and more observance of the nationally agreed line. Fundamental differences remained, but these were sorted out at Council which, in turn, became more rowdy.

One policy on which the NFU could easily unite was the iniquity of Britain opening her doors to dumping by foreign farms from countries such as Germany and Russia. In Germany there were subsidies and in Russia labour was used in a way that would be unacceptable in the UK. When a proposal to build a Channel tunnel was made in 1930, the NFU opposed the move on the grounds that it might suck in more food imports.

We shall come across Captain Morris again later, when he becomes the first chairman of the Pigs Marketing Board, but meanwhile we move on to his successor.

✦ CHAPTER 14 ✦

E.W.K. Slade, 1931

In August 1931 the wheat price dropped to less than 6s. per cwt, the lowest for 37 years. NFU president E.W.K. Slade announced to newspaper reporters:

It is impossible to exaggerate the seriousness of the situation. I fail to see what is going to happen to the British farmer unless some drastic remedial steps are taken. I don't very much mind what line is adopted – the quota, tariff reform or any other method – so long as the British farmer is given a fair chance to meet the cost of production and to live. The corn harvest is upon us and yet our products are practically valueless. I can see nothing but bankruptcy for hundreds of farmers.

When Slade said this he was speaking from the heart, his own farm being dependent on cereal production. Farming at New Farm in Compton, Berkshire, Slade had 800 acres of cereals with only 100 acres of downland pasture. Born at West Lavington in Wiltshire in 1876, Slade had taken New Farm at the turn of the century as a tenant on Lord Wantage's estate. When the estate was split up after the death of Lord Wantage, Slade had bought the farm to become an owner occupier. Dependent on cereals and having borrowed to buy his farm, Slade was at the front line when the cereal price fell during the 1920s and then crashed in the early '30s. He had joined the Berkshire

NFU county branch on its inception in 1916 and had quickly risen through the ranks to become chairman of the Cereals Committee in 1924. He was cereals chairman for 20 years apart from the time he was president.

Slade's Berkshire farm ran along a shallow valley that was the source of the River Pang between Compton and Hampstead Norrey. It also had the Didcot to Newbury railway running through it. As a valley farm it varied in soil and elevation, but despite this variation Slade's policy was to plough all the arable land every year and grow barley and wheat on the gently sloping fields, some of which were up to 100 acres in size. Slade was the first president of the NFU to use a tractor in earnest for cultivation. As we have said, tractors had first been used on farms at the very beginning of the twentieth century, but for 50 years the horse remained supreme. It was in the 1930s that the tractor became commonplace. In 1932 Henry Ford established his factory at Dagenham, where 20 Fordsons a day rolled off the production line. Though Fordsons were by far the most common tractor in the 1930s, it was at this time that other tractor brands, such as David Brown and Massey Ferguson, became established.

Today E.W. Slade's farm is an equestrian centre. In stark contrast to most of the farms of presidents

Slade's home, New Farm at Compton, on a bleak winter's day in 1931.

chronicled so far, New Farm is today a quieter place than it was in Slade's time, in that the Didcot to Newbury line was one of the victims of Dr Beeching's cuts in the 1960s. Trains no longer run though this part of the rolling arable Berkshire countryside that drains into the Thames Valley.

Given the seriousness of the arable situation, Slade requested an interview with the Prime Minister in October 1931. MacDonald was too busy, so instead a delegation of Slade, his predecessor Morris and the ageing Campbell went to see the minister, Addison, urging him to introduce measures to help maintain the acreage under cereals. Reporting back to Council, the delegation felt they had been amicably received and were hopeful something constructive would be forthcoming from the government. Such hopes were quickly dashed.

Prime Minister MacDonald might have been too busy to meet the NFU president, but he was not too busy to give an interview to the *Daily Herald* of 18 October. The PM's provocative words were directed straight at the NFU:

The Government will not yield an inch to the Farmers' Union agitation for protection or subsidy. It is a sorry revelation of the methods by which they [the NFU] carry on the business of agriculture. They show no sign of capacity or of willingness to think things out. With wonderful fidelity they follow the old, obvious will-o-the-wisp which has always led them into a bog, far from the only path to agricultural prosperity. What is the real dispute between the Farmers' Union and the Government? The Union maintains that the only way the Government can help is by giving them a free gift of public money. We are not even to ask them or to help them to set their house in order. The Government, on the other hand, think the right way to help is to create sound businesslike methods of dealing with agricultural produce, which will enable them to keep in their own pockets the money that should and could be theirs. This they now lose because in their unorganised condition... there can be no prosperity so long as the organised farmers want subsidies for inefficient agriculture and persist that everything in the world is wrong except their own methods of carrying on their business.

It was an extraordinary attack by government on the NFU, the like of which had not been seen before and which has not (yet!) been seen since.

President Slade gave a blunt response:

I call a spade a spade, and I call that a lie. To suggest that farming wants bolstering up at the expense of the nation and that it wants something for nothing is an absolute lie.

Without doubt this spat between the PM and the NFU was a low point in relations between the union and the government. Not even at the time of 'the great betrayal' in 1921 had relations been so strained. One explanation for MacDonald's inflammatory outburst might be that it was made during the run-up to the 1931 election, which was held on Tuesday, 28 October. Known as the 'rowdy election', it was the last British election not to be held on a Thursday. The Conservatives won a landslide 470 seats, and in a piece of extraordinary political horse-trading MacDonald was expelled from the Labour Party but kept in place as Prime Minister by the Tories, who took many of the government posts.

The 1931 election also saw the appearance of the Agricultural Party, which had grown out of the Norfolk Farmers' Union. It was bankrolled by Lord Beaverbrook and Lord Rothermere, both of whom had their own ideas as to the best way to save British agriculture. The Norfolk Farmers' Union, who backed the new party, not for the first time found themselves at odds with the rest of the union. Norfolk, along with Cornwall, prided itself on being one of the more wayward members of the family when it came to ignoring the HQ line. Norfolk men were always of independent thought as, indeed, they still are today.

The attitude of the NFU to the Agricultural Party was ambivalent. Just before the election it reminded the membership that the NFU 'has never sought to dictate to its members how they should use their vote'. It could not disagree that if the new party returned MPs then that would be good for farming, but the NFU also saw sense in not officially allying itself with any one party but instead seeking dialogue with the government of the day and trying to influence all MPs no matter what their political hue. It may also be that the NFU saw this new party as a possible threat in that it might detract from its own purpose. Either way, the Agriculture Party did not return any MPs in 1931. It put up candidates again in 1933, again headquarters discouraged counties and branches from getting involved and again it returned no MPs. After that it disbanded.

Meanwhile, the new national government returned to power in 1931 offered new hope for farmers. The Tories had accepted in their manifesto the need to take some measure to protect home farmers and the new Minister of Agriculture, Walter Elliot, proved an easier man for NFU leaders to deal with than his patronising predecessor, Addison. Elliot, the son of a Scottish farmer from Lanarkshire and seen as one of the rising stars of the Tories, was technically from the Scottish Unionist Party, which allied with, but was not part of, the Conservative Party. He was a 'corporatist' Tory and not in any way wedded to the free-trade philosophy that had dominated Tory agricultural policy in the 1920s. Generally, relations between him and NFU presidents were convivial and constructive. When, while Minister of Agriculture, Elliot had married, the NFU had presented him and his new wife with a silver

Thrashing at New Farm in the 1930s. While most industries were turning to electricity and internal combustion engines to provide their power, farming remained dependent on that Victorian staple – steam.

canteen of cutlery as a wedding gift. The new Mrs Elliot remarked that, although she knew very little about agriculture, every time she used the gift she would think of the farmer who put the food on her plate.

Almost immediately after the new government was formed in November 1931, heavy import duties were placed upon certain horticultural products. In 1932 the Import Duties Act imposed a system of import quotas on certain countries for commodities such as beef, mutton, lamb, bacon and ham. The quotas favoured Empire suppliers and restricted imports from the Continent.

The 1932 Wheat Act saw the extension of subsidies and price insurance which until then had only been applied to sugar beet. Producers of wheat received a deficiency payment equivalent to the difference between the average price realised in the open market and a standard price of 10s. per cwt. The fund from which this payment was made was raised by a levy on all milling wheat or flour imported into the country. The payment was reduced proportionately as sales of wheat increased beyond a specified quantity. The scheme was overseen by the Wheat Commission, on which Slade was an industry representative.

Wheat growers had to register details of their farm and the areas under wheat with the Wheat Commission to receive deficiency payments. The system was not without those modern-day banes of the farmer – paperwork and form-filling. After each sale of wheat a registered grower had to apply for a wheat certificate from an authorised merchant. This certificate, which had to show the quantity, quality, location, date grown, price and other details of sale and delivery, when presented to the correct ministry official at the correct time, entitled the farmer to a payment. The assistance of the NFU in the working of the Wheat Act proved invaluable.

When the Act was passed in Parliament, Lady Astor, the first female MP, commented: "Paying a subsidy for wheat might have the effect of encouraging farmers to grow wheat who have never grown it before and will never grow it economically." This was an early version of that rich vein of ill-informed criticism that haunts farmers the moment they are given a subsidy. It also demonstrates a readiness in some corners of parliament to oppose any attempt to protect farmers from cripplingly low prices on the grounds it is merely 'feather-bedding' the inefficient.

The levy system of finance meant that the wheat scheme did not involve public expenditure, which made it more politically acceptable. There is no doubt that the subsidy was a lifeline to wheat growers. In effect, the Wheat Act artificially doubled the price of wheat for British farmers from the world price of 5s. to the target price of 10s. per cwt. The annual subsidy bill for 1933/34 was £7.2 million. In 1933 wheat planting increased by 29 per cent. It was generally reckoned that the Wheat Act encouraged an additional 500,000 acres of wheat to be grown and, given that wheat at this time was yielding a little under a ton an acre, around an additional 500,000 tons of British wheat was produced.

As an aside, there is an interesting comment on the Wheat Act from Professor Lionel Robbins, who was an influential economist at the LSE:

Eventually equilibrium will be established with wheat farmers making no more than was being made elsewhere, a greater proportion of the food supply produced at home and a national income smaller than it would have been by the extra cost of raising that much more wheat at home rather than procuring it abroad

Professor Robbins was the son of Rowland Robbins, who we have met before.

The fact that, by 1932, the only two commodities to benefit from some sort of price insurance, sugar beet and wheat, were grown primarily on larger, eastern-region arable farms, did not go unnoticed by the western half of the NFU. Nonetheless, the Wheat Act proved a watershed moment for the arable farmers of Britain, and it is fitting that it has its origins at a time when the NFU was led by E.W.K. Slade, who chaired the NFU Cereals Committee for 20 years and whose farm was dependent on wheat production. Furthermore, it represented a change in government thinking with regard to protecting home agriculture that was soon to benefit livestock producers and dairymen. It is equally fitting that these latter developments came under the presidency of a Welsh livestock farmer

✦ CHAPTER 15 ✦

Mervyn T. Davies, 1932

Mervyn Davies farmed 250 acres of fertile red sandstone soil at Porthamel Farm, near Talgarth in Breconshire. Born in 1888, Davies was a first-generation farmer, his father being a colliery manager in Glynneath. He had sent his son for English education in Reading where the young Davies picked up a taste for farming. Having served as a farm pupil on a farm in Berkshire, Davies returned to his native Wales, where he bought a farm in 1907.

The farm was situated in a picturesque corner of Wales, with the Brecon Beacons to the south-west and the Black Mountains to the south-east and the River Llynfi running through it. Less charming was the railway that also ran through it, with the inconvenience of three level crossings. On the farm was grown 60 acres of hay and 30 acres of oats and roots, which were fed to beef cattle. Davies bred pedigree Hereford cattle and ran about 90 animals. There were also 150 Kerry hill ewes. In the 1930s a Scandinavian-style pig-fattening house was added.

President Davies – a natural orator both in the pulpit and on the NFU platform.

Davies, in 1908 one of the founder members of the Brecon and Radnor branch of the NFU, became branch chairman in 1916 and county chairman in the 1920s. He served as chairman of the Welsh Committee and of the Parliamentary Committee at Bedford Square before taking the presidency in 1932. As a man Davies was a gentle giant, 6ft 3ins, with a large frame to go with it. He was not only a proven orator in the world of farming politics, he was also a lay preacher in the Church of Wales and sat on the church governing body. He was known for his diplomacy and prided himself on having no enemies. His only failing, according to his son John, was his hopelessness with anything mechanical or practical. The family car was never driven more than a few miles from Porthamel in case it broke down or needed some sort of mechanical attention, in which case the Davies family would be forced to abandon it and return home on foot. The farmhouse was blessed with a telephone in the 1930s, which was unusual for the area. The phone had been installed by the railway company so farmers and signalmen could liaise over the use of the railway crossings. There was no electricity until after the war, and the Davies family were dependent on acetylene gas for their lighting from a gas house in the yard. Again, Davies's dislike of anything practical meant this was frequently breaking down and Aladdin lamps were used instead.

As an agriculturalist, however, he was well regarded, and served as chairman of Brecon Agricultural Executive Committee from 1939 to 1960. He was also Mayor of Brecon in 1946 and received the CBE for services to agriculture in 1950.

On his death in 1961, the standing NFU president, Harold Woolley, wrote in tribute to him:

> *Mr Mervyn Davies was one of the comparatively rare men who managed to combine qualities which are not usually found in combination. He was genial and relaxed whilst being capable and competent. He was full of fun and humour, whilst underneath there was a very serious and sober outlook on life .*

The 1932 AGM that saw the election of Davies to the presidency also witnessed a key turning-point in the union's policy position regarding the setting up of marketing boards under the 1931 Agricultural Marketing Act. It was an episode that must have tested all the diplomatic skills of the gentle Welsh giant.

Davies (far left) with the Brecon War Agriculural Committee, of which he was chairman. A gentle giant if ever there was one.

The 1931 Act was a flagship piece of legislation passed by the MacDonald Government designed to give better returns to farmers through pool marketing. The Act conferred upon producers the power – if two-thirds of them in terms of both numbers and productive capacity were in favour – to exercise compulsion over those prepared to sell at below the agreed price in the marketing of their products, but it made no attempt to set targets for home production and did not propose to regulate imports. Under the Act home producers could opt for the compulsory scheme but were still to be left to the cold discipline of global economic forces. The response of the union was to demand what was termed 'fiscal justice'– that agriculture be given a measure of protection equivalent to that enjoyed by the manufacturing industries. The union was also very suspicious of the Act, as it further introduced the spectre of state control of the farmer, with the prospect of government-paid bureaucrats meddling in the affairs of an industry made up of proud, independent men. Council ruled the Act was little more than an empty and useless gesture and refused the helping hand offered by government.

The union, however, was in a fractious mood and a schism was developing. Harry German, who had a big following in the north, led those who saw merit in the Marketing Act. They argued it offered the only promising alternative to chaotic marketing and was worthy of being given a trial. The extent of German's commitment was revealed in a statement he made

during a Council debate: 'I do not mind saying that I, more than the minister, was responsible for the inception of the Marketing Bill.' Those who supported German could also point to the weakness of the co-operative movement, which had not delivered the strength in numbers it had promised.

In 1931 this debate raged on at all levels of the NFU; in the parliamentary committee, in Council and in the county executives. The Act's principal architect, Minister Addison, further stoked the fire by bypassing HQ and writing to NFU county branches direct and offering to address meetings himself to explain his scheme. Only one branch, near Bristol, accepted the offer

At that meeting, in Bristol's Grand Hotel, the large audience of mainly Somerset milk producers, having listened to the minister, delegated their county chairman, Sidney Wear, to take a resolution to the 1932 AGM calling for a commission to be set up to explore the possible creation of a milk marketing board. Wear was a hero amongst the small dairy farmers of Somerset and had set up a co-op called the Bristol Area Milk Producers' Association, whereby producers were paid through a pool system. A dogged man, he was not afraid to defy the perceived wisdom of headquarters in the interests of his county.

The 1932 AGM in the Old Holborn Restaurant was attended by 78 members of Council and 213 delegates from the counties. Wear, backed by the likes of Harry German, led the attack on the Council's resolution against the principle of marketing boards and their powers of compulsion. Wear claimed the Joint Milk Council's inability to enforce contracts lay at the door of a small minority of producers who ignored its rulings and undercut everyone else's market. Therefore it was just and right that if a two-thirds majority of producers were in favour of a national scheme, then the majority should have power to bring the minority into line. In response to Wear's argument, the likes of Robbins, Ryland and Baxter maintained the Council line that the notion of compulsion was wrong in principle and, without import controls, would not assist prices paid to farmers while supply was in excess of demand. In a fever-pitch atmosphere a vote was taken and Wear's resolution won the day by the narrowest of margins – 97 voting for, 94 against and 100 abstaining. It was a watershed moment. It was this volte-face in union policy that led to marketing boards for commodities such as milk, pigs and potatoes. They were producer-controlled boards and the NFU was to sit at the very heart of them.

Consequent to this, Robbins and Ryland, who had done so much for the union throughout the 1920s, resigned their positions and, with good grace, walked away from the NFU. For a titan of integrity such as Rowland Robbins, it was incompatible with his old-style liberal, nonconformist principles of individual self-reliance – the hallmark of the yeoman farmer of his generation. He wanted no truck with a system that forced the individual producer to run with the herd, nor did he want anything to do with a scheme dreamt up by a socialist Labour Government that had state control and land nationalisation written into its manifesto. It should be remembered Robbins was not alone in these views, but increasingly the severity of the agricultural depression was forcing many to reconsider such long-held convictions.

Tom Baxter was one such who displayed a pragmatic attitude and was prepared to move his position in accordance with the wish of the membership as expressed by the AGM vote. As we have noted previously, he went considerably further than changing his view; he became the MMB's first chairman.

The events of February 1932 are testimony to the NFU's ability to maintain its unity together in the face of a potentially fatal schism. As Campbell had noted, a union of British farmers is by its very definition a fragile creation, given the diversity within the agricultural industry. The union's ability to face a divisive issue and change a previously held position without fracturing, shows its core strength. It is a strength that has served it well over the years.

But President Mervyn Davies was still faced with a potential constitutional problem, as an AGM vote could not constitutionally overturn a Council ruling. Fortunately, Council had the good sense to realise the danger of defying the AGM and the county branches in the west and the north. Davies accepted the proposal to approach government to investigate the setting up a Milk Marketing Board and the board officially came into existence in 1933, by which time B.J. Gates had been elected president of the NFU.

THE UNFAIRY GODFATHER.

Dr. Addison. "I AM HERE TO PROTECT YOU."
British Farmer. "PROTECT ME FROM WHAT? FOREIGN COMPETITION?"
Dr. Addison. "NO! NO! FROM YOUR OWN INCOMPETENCE."
British Farmer. "THANK YOU VERY MUCH."

Minister Addison shows a nonplussed farmer the solution to his ills, the Marketing Act, in this 1931 Punch *cartoon.*

1. The first meeting of the Milk Marketing Board held on 6 October 1933 at Thames House, the Board's first home. *L–R Standing*: C. T. Sproston, J. Trehane, J.P.; E. G. H. Maddy, J.P.; J. G. Searle; Capt. C. G. Y. Skipwith, J.P.; O. McBryde; Viscount Lymington, M.P.; M. Slade; B. Hinds; J. W. Rickeard, J.P.; M. Hely-Hutchinson, M.C.; H. B. Boden; P. R. M. Jaggard. *L–R Seated*: J. Joyce, J.P.; G. Fairbarn; Sidney Foster; J. L. Walton; Major R. H. Dorman-Smith, J.P.; Cleveland Fyfe; Miss G. E. Matterson

The board of the Milk Marketing Board – most were NFU men.

CHAPTER 16

B.J. Gates, 1933

Reporting on the previous year, the 1934 NFU Year Book noted that 1933 was the busiest year in the union's history and that, in connection with all the schemes, no man rendered more willing services than did the president, Mr Gates.

B.J. Gates was a tenant of the 370-acre Wing Park Farm in Buckinghamshire. We know very little about him other than that he retired from farming at an early age and devoted much of his life thereafter to the NFU, as well as serving on the council of the Royal Agricultural Society of England (RASE). Described as a true gentleman who was unassuming in his nature, he displayed remarkable patience in solving difficult problems. If there was ever a need for patience, it was in the setting up of the MMB.

There never was, and probably never will be again, a marketing project of such magnitude and complexity as that to which the union had to apply its resources after the 1933 vote in favour of the national compulsory pool marketing of milk. It involved bringing together on one side 140,000 dairy farmers and on the other 20,000 firms buying milk ex-farm. Both sides had been at each other's throats for longer than most cared to remember.

It was the job of the NFU to draw up a proposed scheme, which it did throughout 1933, consulting widely both at national and county level. The preparation of the marketing schemes imposed a huge burden on the union's resources.

A scheme was finally submitted to the Minister of Agriculture on 18 March. It was followed by a public enquiry at which, again, the union had to throw resources to ensure the best interests of its members were represented. Once the scheme was approved at this level it then had to be put to a poll of registered milk producers. Under the Act it needed two-thirds approval. Again, it was the job of the union to ensure dairy members were properly registered to vote and properly briefed as to the best way to vote. The poll was taken on 2 September and the result, declared on 6 September, showed 96 per cent of producers voting in favour of the scheme. Then came the task of agreeing prices and, again, the NFU was key to these negotiations.

On 11 September the board took up its new offices at Thames House, a massive building near Lambeth Bridge. With NFU heavyweight Tom Baxter in the chair, and with an office of the NFU legal department in the building, the influence of the NFU was writ large at Thames House. NFU men such as Maddy, Searle, Slade, Hinds, Boden, Fairbarn, Walton,

Dorman-Smith and Fyfe served on the first board. Their first act was the shrewd headhunting of Sidney Foster, at the time general manager of London Co-operative Society, to be the board's general manager on a salary of £5,000 a year. History suggests that without the abilities and personalities of both Foster and Baxter the MMB might have died at birth.

Later, Foster recollected in the *Farmers' Weekly*:

When I walked into Thames House on 16 September 1933 there were three girls on the staff. We had 20 days in which to fit the offices, engage staff, buy equipment, devise the system, make contracts. We wanted about £4,000,000 in the first month to pay producers. Where was it coming from?

Fortunately, Barclays and the National & Provincial Banks were persuaded to advance the money, and the first monthly cheques were sent out to producers in November for their October production, thus creating a precedent that was followed unfailingly for the next 60 years.

The board's achievement in the first year was immense. It had controlled 650 million gallons of milk for the liquid market and a further 200 million gallons for manufacturing. The board and the NFU

President Gates, 1933.

were not without their critics. It was not popular with some outspoken dairy farmers and, indeed, some did find themselves worse off. In 1934 the price arbitration panel (comprising a King's Counsel, a chartered accountant and a director of the Anglo-Persian Oil company) fixed a price of 1s. per gallon when the board had asked for 1s.2d. As a result, there was huge complaint from many producers, but memories of the milk wars of the 1920s were etched too deeply in the minds of most producers to induce any lasting desire to jettison the board, and when a poll for revocation was taken in 1935 it attracted only a small number of votes in favour. The MMB had become a fixture in the British dairy industry.

Throughout the 1930s the board went from strength to strength. It encouraged better management and improved hygiene. It increased milk consumption through well-funded promotion. Above all, it guaranteed the farmer a monthly cheque based on a pre-agreed pool price. The anarchy and misery of the 1920s were banished to history. Just as with the NFU, the greatest good of the greatest number was the bedrock principle on which the board was founded, and all but a few were ready to abide by it.

With the passing of the 1933 Marketing Act, government accepted the long-held NFU argument that marketing boards needed backing up with elements of state support. The Milk Act of 1934 introduced price insurance for milk made into butter and cheese. It also injected £750,000 into the MMB so it could pay a premium for high-quality milk. There was a further £100,000 to promote the health benefits of drinking milk, which led to cheap milk being supplied to schools.

The lot of the dairy farmer in the first half of the 1930s had not been made any easier by a series of droughts. In 1931, 1932 and 1933 there was lower than usual rainfall, which hit grass production. Writing in the 1935 *Farmer & Stockbreeder*, the Chief Meteorologist for the Greenwich Observatory (the forerunner of the Met Office) warned farmers that his calculations, based on weather patterns over many years, suggested that the British climate was becoming drier. He predicted farmers would have to adjust to this drier climate. Of course, in actual fact, by the end of the 1930s flooding was probably a bigger problem that drought, and 1950 proved the wettest year for 70 years. By then the Chief Meteorologist was safely retired.

While the MMB did not limit the production of milk nor its import, this was not true of the other marketing boards that were set up in 1933: the Hop Marketing Board, the Potato Marketing Board, the Pig Marketing Board and the Bacon Marketing Board. It also saw the Tomato and Cucumber Marketing Board and the Apple and Pear Marketing Board, both of which died soon after birth through apathy and disinterest.

The flowering of the marketing boards after 1933 further established the role of the NFU. When the Pig Marketing Board was set up the union proudly observed: 'No organisation other than the NFU possesses the requisite machinery for securing and focusing the opinion of the pig producers of England and Wales.' It was a proud boast but an honest one, and it equally applied to the other boards. The NFU was now firmly established as the mouthpiece of producers, and the Ministry clearly delegated certain responsibilities to the NFU to help with the implementation of policy. A ministry official openly admitted: 'In the absence of the NFU it is improbable that there would have been a Pig scheme or Milk scheme or Potato scheme.' In January 1933 the *Times* had noted: 'At every turn the Union is relied upon by Government for collaboration in the development of agricultural policy along new lines.' Predictably, a Labour MP had complained in the House in 1933: 'We have reached a stage where the present Ministry of Agriculture is synonymous with the NFU.'

This air of increasing alliance and co-operation was a two-way process. Inevitably, the NFU shifted from being a major critic of government policy to, on occasion, being an advocate of it. As NFU president Reginald Dorman-Smith pointed out in the House of Commons in 1936:

I and many of my colleagues in the NFU have spent many working days traipsing around the countryside trying to break down the opposition and give government plans a fair field for the agricultural policy.

The enthusiasm for marketing boards was not always reflected in the counties, where it was felt HQ was getting too close to government and there was not enough lobbying for protection from imports.

On a separate tack, in May 1933 there was a reminder that the NFU was capable of weakening at the seams as a national union of county organisations. As ever, Norfolk was the scene of the tension. The Norfolk County Wages Board had ordered a reduction in hours, at which point the Norfolk employers' delegation walked out, refusing to have anything more to do with it. Worried about the lack of NFU representation, headquarters appointed non-Norfolk men to take their place, men who subsequently negotiated an agreement with the workers' union. To rub salt into Norfolk's wound, one of these men, David Black, came from Suffolk. Norfolk lore decreed that Suffolk farmers were allowed to cross the Waveney but, once there, on no account were they to interfere with Norfolk affairs. Such was the hostility to these men's arrival in Norfolk they needed a police escort into and out of the offices where the negotiations took place. Jimmy Wright, the enigmatic but belligerent Norfolk county secretary vowed: 'Norfolk will remember the meddling of unwanted delegates from other counties.'

The Prince of Wales (centre) with President Gates at the 1933 NFU Dinner. Far right is Vice-president Ratcliff.

In a retaliatory measure the Norfolk Union executive decided it could no longer afford to send its £855 annual capitation fee to Bedford Square, and sent £110 instead. In response the National Council invoked Rule 20 of the constitution and suspended Norfolk from the NFU. All communications between Bedford Square and Norwich were cut off. The Norfolk Farmers' Union remained outside the NFU until the autumn, when a conciliatory B.J. Gates met with Jimmy Wright and persuaded him to pay the money owed in exchange for a promise they would leave Norfolk to its own wage negotiations in the future.

On a lighter note, 1933 saw the NFU, in conjunction with the NFU Mutual, commission a film about the work at No. 45 Bedford Square. It was intended that the film be played at branch meetings, with Council delegates giving a live running commentary. In this way members could better understand the goings on at Bedford Square. The film also promoted the work of the union to non-members, who were occasionally invited along to branch meetings. The *Record* (the union magazine) enthused about the 'Hollywood' qualities of the film and encouraged members to take their wives along as a treat. This episode is a little reminder of how different the 1930s were from today. In our screen-saturated age we forget that 70 years ago our farming forebears only seldom saw moving images. For some of the audiences in some of the more remote branches the NFU film would have been their first experience of film. In contrast, in the towns and cities, 1933 was the year that saw the first appearance of the cinema chains. Odeons, Gaumonts, Regals and Roxys, replete in their art deco splendour, started to become commonplace on the high streets of Britain. The box office hit of 1933 was the monster epic *King Kong*.

Back on the farm, one can only smirk at the thought of a male union member turning to his wife one early evening and saying: 'My dear, they are showing a little film about the NFU headquarters at our branch meeting this evening and, guess what, as a special treat you are allowed to come along as well.'

Pig farming at Ratcliff's Essex farm. Top and above: The past, in open strawed yards. Compare these images with the photograph of a modern pig farming unit on page 84.

CHAPTER 17

Stanley Ratcliff, 1934

Stanley Ratcliff was born in 1873 at Woodlands Farm near Woodham Walter, four miles outside the Essex estuarine town of Maldon. The Ratcliffs were well-heeled Essex landowners. When his mother died shortly after his birth, Stanley was brought up by that classic Dickensian combination of a distant father and an austere stepmother.

On leaving public school, Stanley borrowed £100 and purchased his own farm at nearby Great Beeleigh. On the death of his father he moved to Brick House Farm on the banks of the Blackwater estuary and took over the family farming enterprise. Brick House Farm is a famous spot in British history, for it was here in 991 that the warrior King Brythnoth bravely led a small Saxon force against 3,000 invading Vikings. Despite putting up brave resistance in what became known as the Battle of Maldon, the local boys took a whipping and the Danes scored yet another away victory.

Having paid off the debts his father had accumulated in the depression of the 1880s and 1890s, Ratcliff built up the family farming estate to the point it covered 3,000 acres, comprising 13 farms and 34 farmhouses or cottages and employing 126 people. These impressive figures make Ratcliff the largest farmer ever to lead the NFU. Conversely, physically he was quite a small man, with a pensive countenance, piercing eyes and a sharp mind. He was well regarded in farming circles for his pioneering attitude and his visionary solutions to farming problems. In debate he was a master of the issues under discussion and could more than hold his own when cross-questioned at length in parliamentary committee.

Ratcliff was a great servant of the NFU. He had been one of the Essex pioneers to sit on the original Essex County Committee in 1914, and after 1930 he travelled to Bedford Square almost daily until his death in 1958. The arduousness of this daily commute was somewhat tempered by the fact he made that journey in his Rolls-Royce, driven by his loyal chauffeur, Mr Punchard. While Ratcliff worked at Bedford Square on all manner of projects and issues, Punchard worked as a steward in the members' dining-room and then drove his boss back to East Essex in the evenings. Stanley Ratcliff was clearly one of the better-off members of the NFU.

The Ratcliff estate ran a good mix of agricultural enterprises. There were five dairy herds, all hand milked with the churns put on trains to London. There was extensive arable, with large acreages of

Stanley Ratcliff.

wheat and barley. One speciality was picking peas for the London vegetable market, but it was in the farming of sugar beet and pigs that Stanley Ratcliff made his greatest contributions to farming and the NFU.

Most of the presidents we have chronicled so far kept pigs on their farms. Indeed, Colin Campbell kept 60 Berkshire pigs in outhouses in the farmyard. This was typical of most early-twentieth-century farms, where somewhere in the farmyard a few pigs could be found, often in makeshift strawed yards. Pigs were a good way to use up waste and scraps. In 1934 there were a remarkable 250,000 registered pig producers in the UK. It should be remembered, though, when considering the enormity of this figure, that pig keeping went well beyond the commercial farm. Pigs were often to be found in rural gardens and even in urban back yards. It is in the 1930s we see the beginnings of the large dedicated pig units that typify the pig industry of today.

Pig numbers in England and Wales had seen significant rises in the 15 years after the First World

The future of pig farming at Ratcliff's Essex farm– the Scandanavian designed barns.

War, expanding from around two million in 1918 to over three million in 1934 and producing 300,000 tonnes of pig meat. The consumption of pork – particularly of bacon – was increasing rapidly during this period. By the mid-1930s Britain was importing two-thirds of her pig meat and half of this, 300,000 tonnes, came from Denmark. At this time the Danes produced a remarkable 60 per cent of the bacon consumed in the UK

In June 1936 Ratcliff led an NFU delegation to Denmark to look at grading and production methods. In the light of Ratcliff's connection with the site of the Battle of Maldon, it would be tempting to describe the delegation as an NFU raiding party seeking ways to stop the great Danish Bacon invasion – but such phrasing would be somewhat over-dramatic.

Ratcliff, though, did not leave Danish shores empty handed. Inspired by the Danish indoor rearing units, on his return Ratcliff set about constructing one of his own rearing sheds at Great Beeleigh. It was the start of what we know today as factory farming, with livestock reared intensively indoors in purpose-built barns. One suspects that Ratcliff would have had no problem with the phrase 'factory farming', as it would have suggested a rearing regime based on efficiency, order and control – qualities that were needed in the British pig industry if it was ever to compete with the Danes.

Ratcliff also brought in better genetics in the form of Large White boars, which he crossed with the local Essex sows. Ratcliff was particularly fond of one of his Large Whites, which he called Charles, and visitors to Beeleigh were obliged to pay a visit of adulation to see the boar. Charles was just part of a general movement amongst the more forward-thinking pig producers to improve genetic lines and produce better carcasses – particularly for bacon. The Ratcliff farms had large monthly bacon contracts with slaughterhouses and factories in Essex and Suffolk.

When the price of pork and bacon pigs collapsed

in the early '30s Ratcliff was one of the main architects of the pig and bacon marketing schemes, the basis of which was to limit the volume of pork and bacon imported through a quota system and to fix an agreed price for pigs based on the price of feed. When, in 1933, the scheme was put to the 250,000 registered pig keepers in a poll, an overwhelming 95.5 per cent agreed to it. During his presidency a trial contract period was run and in 1934 the first full trading year was begun. Also in 1933 the NFU set up a separate Pigs Committee, whereas before such matters had been taken up by the Livestock Committee. Ratcliff was an inaugural member of the new committee.

Of all the marketing boards set up in the early '30s the pig and bacon boards were least effective. Government was always reluctant to restrict the import of bacon through tariffs and, in the light of heavy competition from abroad, particularly from Denmark, the demand for bacon remained very sensitive to price. This factor, coupled with problems in bringing some of the many small producers into the system, meant that the board struggled to negotiate stable prices. The board was not revived after suspension in 1939.

The pig industry had to wait until 1938 before it saw any of the state support that had been given to the arable and milk sectors. The Bacon Industry Act brought in price insurance for pig producers by banning the selling of bacon pigs except under contract and by fixing the price. Curers were enabled to pay the contract price through a deficiency payment based on the target price set according to grade and the actual price paid. By 1939 over seven-million pigs had been put through the scheme.

Ratcliff was also a keen sugar beet grower and served on the union's Sugar Beet Committee. In 1934 a parliamentary committee had reviewed the sugar beet subsidy, which had been established in 1925 on the understanding that the subsidy was on a sliding scale for ten years. In 1934 the committee recommended that the scheme should not be continued. Although British farmers had made strides in the growing of beet, this was not as impressive as the progress of the cane producers abroad, who could produce sugar at less than half the price of beet production. Under Ratcliff's presidency the NFU then set about lobbying government not to accept this advice. Ratcliff made the point repeatedly in parliamentary committee that withdrawal of the subsidy would be a body blow to a crop that was an important lifeline for many arable farmers. The government accepted the union's arguments and the acreage subsidy was continued under the Sugar Industry (Re-Organisation Act) of 1936. The Act limited the quantity of crop that was eligible for support and amalgamated the various factories under the ownership of the British Sugar Corporation. This formed the model of a monopoly

An early crop sprayer, probably spraying an early insecticide, the highly toxic lead arsenate, on potatoes. There was little protection for man or beast in those days.

Scratching up and burning the roots – This was how farmers used to control the pernicious couch grass in the days before systemic herbicides.

processor which contracted an acreage with growers dictated by the support system. This is largely the model that is still in place today but which, as we know, is under fiercer attack today than at any time since 1936. Then, as now, the NFU remained the key intermediary between growers and processors.

In 1935 Ratcliff recognised the danger of a situation in which the sugar beet industry was dependent for its seed on Germany. Most sugar beet growers used a German variety called Klein. As Nazi Germany became increasingly belligerent and relations with Britain worsened, Ratcliff sought a partnership with a Polish seed house called Busczynski and set up a UK company, Bush, to produce UK varieties. Stanley's son, Len Ratcliff, can recall today his time as a teenager helping a Polish seed breeder called Mr Lutosloski find indigenous wild beet plants on the sea walls of Essex. These plants were then crossed with existing varieties to produce the UK's first home-grown beet varieties. By 1939 Stanley Ratcliff's vision had proved invaluable to the country's national security.

As a farmer Ratcliff had a natural curiosity in science, technology and progress. In 1938 we can find him in the press talking about the exciting possibilities of artificial insemination or, as he described it, the discovery of the means to produce fatherhood in a test-tube. In 1940 he was contacted by a Dr Ripper who, as a German national and therefore a security risk, had been held in a British detention camp. Dr Ripper was an agricultural scientist who had made important discoveries in the field of hormone weed control. Ratcliff realised the value of this work to British agriculture and helped secure the German doctor's release. Once released Ripper, together with Ratcliff, set up a company called Pest Control Ltd, based at Harston in Cambridgeshire.

It was in the 1930s that there were important developments in the commercial production of agro-chemicals. Insecticides designed for use in livestock farming and top fruit were becoming quite widely used. The use of chemicals was not widespread in broad-acre crops but it was at this time that research stations such as Jealotts Hill and companies such as ICI made advances in achieving weed, fungal and insect control by applying chemicals to a variety of crops.

In many ways Stanley Ratcliff was a visionary who foresaw problems and was interested in the technology that could counter them. He continued to serve the NFU for many years on various committees. In the 1940s and '50s he was union treasurer at a time when NFU finances needed serious reform. Again, his farsightedness put the union on a financial footing that saw it through several decades of growth.

CHAPTER 18

John H. Wain, 1935

John Wain was a dairy farmer who milked a herd of 100 Shorthorns in the Staffordshire hills five miles north of Stoke-on-Trent. His 200-acre farm, Rudyard Hall, was situated 700 ft above sea-level near the town of Leek. The sloping land, high rainfall and well-structured soil leant itself to good grass growing. The herd produced a daily output of 150–160 gallons of milk, which was mostly milked by hand. Grade A milk, bottled on the farm, and cream were sold direct and the rest was sold wholesale in bulk. The feeding regime was kept cheap and simple, with the cows turned out every day, even in winter, and the abundant pasture eked out as much as possible. Grazing was supplemented with 60 acres of hay and a few concentrates were fed.

Like his predecessor, Ratcliff, Wain had also recently erected a Scandinavian-type fattening house, where he fattened 240 bacon pigs. The pigs, fed on rations of ground barley, flaked maize, fish meal and skimmed milk from the cream enterprise, were sold at seven months into the Midland bacon trade.

Wain was a Methodist preacher, another example of the Nonconformist tradition in the NFU. During his presidency his patience was often called upon, as the NFU was in a rumbustious mood. This was well exemplified by the 1935 AGM that had a fair share of booing, shouting and walk-outs. The *Farmer & Stockbreeder* editorial noted darkly that, in the past, the NFU AGMs had been characterised by 'boisterous good humour' but now 'the atmosphere had become sullen, not in the sense of sulky but of the temper of men who were living in a deep gloom'.

By contrast, an extract from the 1936 AGM report suggests things weren't always over-earnest. Although the Norfolk County branch had tabled a resolution, the counter-attraction of the replayed cup-tie between Norwich and Chelsea proved too inviting and no one was there to move it.

One issue causing immense unrest in the South West was the regional pool price system of the MMB, which paid less in the grass-growing areas. As the MMB bedded in there were other areas of controversy. Where farmers refused to pay levies or penalties under the milk marketing scheme, the board decided it would have to pursue the debt through the courts and the bailiffs. This, in turn, led to gatherings of farmers at forced sales of stock to recover debts. It was the unseemly scenario of a board set up by farmers publicly pursuing individual farmers for money. Inevitably, tempers were often frayed. To show solidarity with the board, Wain and Baxter

President Wain outside his brooding neo-Gothic farmhouse – Rudyard Hall. It sat perched on the steep rolling hills that overlooked Rudyard Lake, near Leek.

attended one such sale near Tamworth in the hope of explaining the situation and calming bad feeling. Not surprisingly, a fight broke out. Wain was actually assaulted before the police managed to intervene. It was a rather ignominious way for a president of the NFU to be treated.

Another hotbed of discontent was tithes. Throughout the 1920s and '30s 'the tithe war' had caused huge unrest amongst the farming community, and the NFU had its part to pay in the debate. The tithe was basically a tax on the income from farmland paid to the church – 70 per cent of farmland was titheable. When the profit margin from farming became paper thin, this arcane tax became the straw that broke the backs of many farms. In Suffolk farmers were having to find £220,000 a year in ecclesiastical tithes, in return for which no special services were rendered to agriculture. Some of the iniquities of the system had been addressed in the Tithe Act of 1925, but many of the union's demands at the time had been ignored by a government reluctant to meddle in this most established area of the establishment. In 1931 a delegation of Slade, Davies and Robbins visited Minister Addison to state the case for tithe remission. They pointed out that, in many instances, there were tithes in excess of 20s. an acre, which was more than the rent. They also showed evidence, gathered by the NFU's statistical office, that the tithe was causing unemployment in the countryside as farmers sold cottages and laid off staff to pay tithes. Addison was dismissive of the complaint and, with his usual patronising haughtiness, told the delegation that if farmers bothered with improved marketing of their produce they could afford the tithe.

In the early 1930s, as farm incomes shrank even more, there were a number of flashpoints, usually sparked by the arrival of bailiffs at farms to force distraint sales of the farmer's stock where the tithe had not been paid. The tactic here was for local farmers to arrive in force and prevent the auctioneer from selling to anyone other than a neighbouring farmer, who would buy the stock for a very low price and then return it to the distressed owner. Such events bordered on civil unrest and riot and the police were usually involved to try to control the crowds and protect auctioneers and bailiffs. Often the crowd would bellow out the tithe hymn.

God save us from these raiding priests
Who seize our crops and steal our beasts,
Who pray 'Give us our daily bread'
And take it from our mouths instead.

In Suffolk one focal point was the farm of NFU Council member R.H. Rash, who, along with his wife, was an outspoken campaigner against the tithe. To press the issue Rash refused to pay the tithe demands in 1935. In expectation of the court bailiffs, trenches were dug around the farmyard and trees were felled across access roads. Neighbouring farmers agreed to send up rockets when they saw court officials approaching.

For the NFU it was a difficult issue. The iniquities of the situation were acknowledged in NFU policy and the union always lobbied for comprehensive reform, but it felt obliged to stop at the point of being involved with civil disorder or defiance of the courts. In contrast, many grass-roots members felt this sort of direct action was the only option. Inevitably, the NFU found itself accused of being weak in the face of injustice. To complicate matters even more, the tithe issue attracted the attention of the Mosley-led fascists. Blackshirt gangs would take part in the anti-tithe demonstrations to add a political element to the civil disorder. It must be said that Mosley was not without support in farming circles, where his policies of import controls were also popular. Without the moderating influence of the NFU one wonders how many more farmers would have been attracted into

FASCISM INFECTS THE FARM.

Left: *Possibly the moderating influence of the NFU stopped fascism infecting too much of the farmyard in the 1930s.*

Mosley's ranks. It was certainly true that in countries such as France and Germany, the fascists found ready support in country areas.

As it was, the NFU steered clear of political controversy or the endorsement of civil disorder but still kept up pressure for reform. This came to a head under Wain's presidency when a Royal Commission was set up. Again, the NFU was organised and persuasive in the evidence it gave. The result was the Tithe Act of 1936. This long-awaited measure reduced the capital obligations of the tithe-payers by £20 million, lowered annual payments by approximately 20 per cent and fixed a time limit of redemption well within the lifetime of most tithe payers.

It was a victory for the farmer over the establishment. Inevitably, for some, it still did not go far enough. It was not until the 1970s that the last tithes were paid. Today, NFU Council member Stephen Rash can show you the field just outside Wortham churchyard where his grandfather's ashes were spread. R.H. Rash left strict instructions he was not to be buried in a Church of England graveyard. It was one last gesture of protest and defiance by the doughty old campaigner.

Another victory of Wain's time in office was the introduction of the fat cattle subsidy in 1934 at a period of low prices. The subsidy was fixed at the rate of 5s. per cwt for live animals and 9s.4d. per cwt for carcasses. After three temporary extensions of the original Act the principle was made more permanent by the Livestock Industry Act of 1937, under which the actual rate of subsidy was determined by a new Livestock Commission; it was fixed in the light of market conditions and varied with quality, government liability being limited to £5 million a year.

When John Wain handed over to his vice president, Reginald Dorman-Smith, at the 1936 AGM, the new incumbent made light of the storminess Wain had encountered during his presidency by asking to say a few words in praise of Wain 'before the rough stuff began'.

After his presidency John Wain's life was cursed with tragedy. In 1937 his wife died of septicaemia from a broken leg, caused when their only daughter ran into her mother at speed round a corner. The daughter then died in 1938 during childbirth. Such events remind us today that not that long ago, in an age without antibiotics and good medical care, life was a good deal more fragile. Wain himself died in 1939, suffering a heart attack as he got out of a car.

CHAPTER 19

Colonel Sir Reginald Dorman-Smith, 1936–37

As his name might suggest, Colonel Sir Reginald Hugh Dorman-Smith was the quintessential English country gent of the kind readily associated with early-twentieth-century high society. His upper-class demeanor must have marked him out from some of the more earthy individuals in the committee rooms of Bedford Square. Whereas many of his associates were distinctly provincial, Dorman-Smith was more of a man about town. He was a member of the famous London gentlemen's club Whites, in St James's, where the likes of author Ian Fleming and Winston Churchill also took their afternoon tipple.

Despite his good breeding, he was in no way aloof or patronising to his fellow farmers, and proved to be one of the NFU's most popular and well-liked presidents. His easy manner and his passion for fighting the corner of the working farmer made him both friend and champion to those he represented. During his presidency, NFU membership rose to the unprecedented figure of over 130,000. Contemporaries remembered him fondly for his lack of self importance, and he was known for his personal touch, his playful wit and his inclination to offer his friendship. Invariably the friendship was returned. Informal, guided much by intuition, warm hearted and high spirited, he was the right man to lead agriculture at a critical time as it approached another world war. Another defining feature was his youth and vitality. Whereas most of his farmer associates would have been in their 50s, Dorman Smith was in his 30s and, at 37, became the youngest-ever president. The main drawback for the NFU was the fact that, given his abilities, it was inevitable he would move on to even greater things.

Like many quintessentially English men, he wasn't actually born in England. The Dorman-Smiths were an Anglo-Irish family from County Cavan. Their origins were humble but, having made their fortune in Victorian Liverpool, by the turn of the century they were a land-owning military family based at Bellamont Forest, Cootehill, in Ireland. Reginald was born in 1899, one of three brothers who all went on to make a big impression on the world. He was education at Harrow, won a history degree at Oxford and then went to Sandhurst, from where he was commissioned into the 15th (Ludhiana) Sikhs and served in the 1919 Afghan War. The young Dorman-Smith's blossoming military career was rather cruelly cut short when, at the age of 21, he was invalided out with acute back problems. It was a

President Dorman-Smith outside Bedford Square, looking every inch the 'man about town'.

disability that was to plague him throughout his life. Retiring from the Army, he married Doreen Hamilton and took up the life of a farmer at Dockenfield Manor in the rolling wooded Surrey hills, where he farmed beef cattle and poultry. His interest in the military was kept up through membership of the Queen's Surrey Regiment of the Territorial Army, in which he rose to the ranks of major and colonel.

Like pig farming, poultry farming was becoming more intensive in the 1930s. Most farmyards had a few hens scratching around to occupy the farmer's wife for a few hours a week, but in the 1930s prototype broiler houses and layer units with large numbers of birds were becoming more common. Consumption of eggs was increasing – in 1914 the average Briton ate 111 eggs a year; by 1930 that had risen to 123. Of these, 44 per cent came from British farms, compared to a pre-war figure of 32 per cent. Chicken was no longer the luxury meat it had been for the generation before. In the inter-war period poultry numbers on British farms increased by 54 per cent.

Dorman-Smith seems to have immediately involved himself in the NFU, joining the Farnham branch in 1922. He became Surrey county chair in

1928 and by 1930 was chairman of the Headquarters Organisation Committee, where he showed his flair for progressive thinking. In 1933 he was made vice-chairman of the Milk Committee, although he openly professed to have never milked a cow in his life. Later, Dorman-Smith recollected how, in his capacity as Milk Committee vice-president, he had addressed a crowded meeting of dairy farmers in Warwickshire and then spent the night as the guest at a local farm, where he found himself still discussing the pros and cons of the MMB into the small hours. Eventually he had to enquire where the toilet was. His host obligingly led him to a two-seater privy at the end of the garden and duly joined him in shared ablutions while continuing, with unabated zeal, what became a rather one-sided conversation.

While vice-president in 1935, at the age of 36, he decided to throw his hat into the party political ring and accept the nomination to stand as Conservative candidate for the seat of Petersfield. Wary of the union's strict non-party political stance when it came to party matters, he duly tendered his resignation. This was debated by the General Purposes Committee and by NFU Council. Both bodies over-whelmingly rejected the resignation – in fact they agreed that the NFU should sponsor him. Dorman-Smith went on to win the seat in 1936 with a 16,000 majority. Council duly recorded their congratulations. Thus, in 1936, for the first and only time, the president of the NFU was also an MP. Dorman-Smith sat on the Parliamentary Agricultural Committee, which gave the union a direct route into Westminster.

By 1936 No. 45 Bedford Square was becoming increasingly busy, and further office space was taken elsewhere to accommodate this activity. After a ten-year lull in growth, membership was starting to build again. Furthermore, with the new marketing boards and with schemes such as those brought in by the Wheat Act and the Fat Cattle Subsidy, more demands were being placed on NFU headquarters. The 11 committees of 1921 had increased to 16, each with around 20 farmer members meeting regularly in London. As in 1921, the committees were led by the General Purposes Committee, chaired by the president, which set general policy. Underneath there were committees on Cereals; Commerce; Co-operation; Education; Fruit, Veg and Flowers; Labour; Livestock; Dairy; Organisation; Parliamentary, Press and Publicity; Pigs; Potatoes; Poultry; Sugar Beet; Transport and Welsh. Some of these committees spawned a further nine sub-committees: for instance, the Poultry Committee had a Chick Sexing sub-committee under its wing. Out in the counties there were parallel structures of committees not only working on county matters but also feeding into the national level.

As can be imagined, these 16 committees delved into the minutiae of farming. There was such a range and depth of work being undertaken that a book such as this cannot possibly do it justice. It ranged from the grandness of delegations taken to No. 10 to the more mundane decision to make the second week of February 'National Pigeon-shooting Week'. The same committee that decided on National Pigeon-shooting Week also recommended the banning of imports of rabbit meat in the hope that this would drive up the depressed price of wild rabbits, which in turn would encourage the business of trapping, which in turn would act to reduce the increasing rabbit menace.

The committees at HQ dealt with the predictable issues that never went away, such as monitoring foot and mouth disease (59 outbreaks in 1936), sheep scab (221 outbreaks) and swine fever (1,812 outbreaks), but also unexpected one-off issues, such as the decrease in duty on imported Yugoslavian eggs resulting from government sanctions made against Italy as a result of their invasion of Abyssinia in 1935.

Invariably, these various committees would be chaired by past presidents, and these same men would dominate the General Purposes Committee. Past presidents Padwick, German, Ryland, Williams, Garton, Slade, Davies, Gates, Ratcliff and Wain all still occupied posts in the NFU in the late 1930s. Baxter and Morris were obliged to distance themselves from the union because of the chairmanship of the MMB and PMB, but they were still recognised unofficially as NFU men.

As ever, resolutions were received from many county branches urging the NFU to 'embark on extensive press advertising to present the case for agriculture to urban dwellers'. The relevant committee replied that much work had been undertaken, including publishing and distributing 13,000 copies of the pamphlet *Agriculture, the Home Market and National Security*, but, as ever, funds did not allow for the national advertising campaigns that the counties craved. When this issue was raised again at the 1936 AGM, president Dorman-Smith pointed out that farmers were already spending money on advertising through the medium of the marketing boards. He added that he would be pleased to spend money on a big advertising campaign, but headquarters had not the power to raise such money from the membership subs collected by the counties. He added that, if the counties were prepared to agree on a levy on their members for such matters, he would happily spend it.

In 1936 came the death of Alfred Ellis, who had been the union's legal adviser since 1920. Ellis's contribution to the NFU and agriculture generally had been immense. Under his guidance the NFU had become well respected for both its grasp of the detail of legislation and the way it assisted members under the union's legal scheme. By way of just one example from 1936; in that year the NFU had given assistance in the case of Forbes *v.* Paxton. Mr Forbes, a farmer near Durham, had recently installed an electric milking plant. One afternoon he found 16 cows lying dead in their stalls. Vets determined they had been electrocuted through the chains around their necks, which had come into contact with electrical fittings near the byre. The union supported the farmer in his action against the installer. On the eve of the trial the defendant agreed to pay the plaintiff his claim for £320. The union noted that the incident had not put Mr Forbes off using electricity but it was a reminder of the importance of proper installation.

In 1936 Dorman-Smith appointed Geoffrey Browne as the NFU's first Chief Economist. Browne was a graduate of the London School of Economics and realised that the union still lacked the necessary figures on the economic status of farm businesses. He duly wrote to all county secretaries and asked for the names of those farmers who kept audited accounts. With a promise of confidentiality, Browne used these accounts to build up accurate figures on farm profitability. This information was to prove invaluable in years to come, when the union took its case to government for the annual price review.

Having set the union one poser as to whether a sitting MP for a political party could also be the NFU president, in 1937 Dorman-Smith presented the union with another constitutional quandary. As his year of presidency came to a close, a number of the county branches petitioned Council that Rule 34, which prevented any president from serving more than one year, should be waived 'in order to enable the President to continue the work he had begun in connection with matters of long-term policy'. So strong was the feeling amongst the membership that Council felt bound to accede to this wish, and Rule 34 was duly suspended. Dorman-Smith warned Council that his additional parliamentary responsibilities would mean he would have less time to devote to his presidential role, especially in the counties. As far as Council were concerned, it was a sacrifice worth paying and he was duly elected for a second year. In 1937 he was knighted for services to agriculture, the first time a president had been so honoured.

The 'long-term policy' Dorman-Smith was working on was to remind Britain of the forgotten lessons of 1914–18, the main one being that a country that is dependent on imports for its food is vulnerable during a time of war. By 1936 the warning shots of a possible impending war were becoming louder, and Hitler was making clear his plans for extra 'Lebensraum'. Consequently, the state of Britain's farm production was becoming more apparent. Between 1918 and 1936 the cropped acreage of Britain had fallen by four million acres and the overall agricultural area had fallen by 2.5 million acres to 31.5 million. While most of this decline was due to industrial and urban development, a good proportion was due to abandonment and reversion to scrub. Since the First World War the number of

farm workers had fallen from 870,000 to 607,000, and their average age had become significantly higher. According to Sir Keith Murray:

In the three years preceding the Second World War British farmers supplied some 30 per cent, by wholesale value, of the country's annual peace-time food require-ments. About 70 per cent were derived from overseas – a heavy liability in the event of war .

Writing in the *Farmer & Stockbreeder* in March 1936, Lloyd George reminded its readers how:

... in 1917 Britain was within inches of defeat through the stranglehold of the submarine blockade upon our food supplies from overseas. Men in high office, civil and military, proclaimed disaster and foretold our imminent collapse... if there should ever be another war – which may God forbid – the food supply of this island will be in far graver danger peril than it was in the last. Not only are the world's submarine fleets far bigger and more powerful and more numerous than they were then, there is a new added danger of swarms of aircraft that can bomb and sink merchant shipping.

Lloyd George had conveniently forgotten that the depression and the poor output of British agriculture in the 1930s could be traced back to his great betrayal in 1921. Nonetheless, Dorman-Smith used Lloyd George's insight and dire warnings to lobby government to develop a comprehensive farm policy.

Against this there was still a free-trade lobby that had the ear of government and argued that strength in war would depend on the strength of manufac-turing industry rather than agriculture, which in turn meant trade, not protectionism. There was also a view that excessive cultivation would exhaust the soil. Consequently, government was increasingly influenced by suggestions to store more imported food in readiness for war rather than artificially raise home production.

Nonetheless, there was limited success for NFU demands for greater protection and subsidy. The 1937 Agriculture Act introduced a scheme of price insurance for barley and oats. Ever since the pioneering days of 1904, the LFU and then the NFU had called for assistance for British barley growers. After a 20-year wait, barley was supported by payment of £1 an acre. The 1937 Act also gave increased financial assistance to drainage boards, introduced subsidies for lime and basic slag fertiliser and gave a grant for the ploughing up of grassland.

Despite these victories, many county branches remained unimpressed. Both Northamptonshire and Suffolk sent resolutions that such action failed to address the continued problems of agriculture. At HQ, the Parliamentary Committee felt 'unable to endorse some opinions that the measure was of no use'.

In early 1938 Dorman-Smith, Wain and Fyfe were on the Orient liner *Orama* bound for Sydney, Australia, to attend a conference of Commonwealth farm organisations. Dorman-Smith opened the conference with a hard-hitting speech. He pointed out that the 'open door' policy for Commonwealth food exports into Britain established at Ottawa five years previously was no longer acceptable, as it undermined the British market to the detriment of British farmers. He demanded that Commonwealth exports be better regulated and suggested the setting up of Empire marketing boards based on the principle of voluntary co-operation. Some of the Dominion nations were at first hostile to the idea, but Dorman-Smith's persuasive eloquence won the day and his reforms were unanimously agreed. This was a considerable change in tenor from the 1932 Ottawa agreement, whereby Dominion producers had retained largely unrestricted access to British markets. We should remember, though, that this cannot all be put down to Dorman-Smith's charm. Governments across the world had moved to greater protectionism since 1933. Even the least protectionist of the Europeans, the British, had succumbed to NFU demands in 1937 for the regulation of imports on beef, wheat and sugar. Britain was no longer the open-door dumping ground for other nations' surpluses. The irony for British farmers was that these restrictions on imports did not lead to appreciable price increases for their own products, largely because demand remained elastic and sensitive to supply – i.e. if beef imports were reduced and the price subsequently rose, then demand from the British consumer fell, thus ratcheting back the price.

Even so, the idea that took root at Sydney, that farmers across the world should collectively look to control supply amongst themselves and thus try to influence price, was impressive in its novelty and ambition. It turned out that the outbreak of war in Europe in 1939 prevented the sentiment from being tested in practice, but an important precedent was set, namely that farmer organisations should attempt to work together for mutual advantage on an international basis. Furthermore, the NFU had staked its claim as a leading international player among farmer organisations. As we shall see, when the war ended in 1945, much of Dorman-Smith's international vision was taken up to great effect by the then NFU president, Jim Turner.

In early 1938 Dorman Smith stood down as NFU president to pursue his career in parliament. In January 1939 Prime Minister Chamberlain, in an attempt to address the increasing criticism of his agricultural policy, took the radical step of appointing Dorman-Smith as Minister of Agriculture. As we shall see, in October 1939 Dorman-Smith instigated the government's 'Dig for Victory' campaign. The appointment of an ex-president of the NFU as Minister of Agriculture was a key moment in the

history of the union. It improved lines of communication and further established the close relationship between executive power in Whitehall and farmer representation in Bedford Square. The NFU now occupied a privileged position of partnership with government from which it still benefits today. The man who probably gained most from this close relationship was Jim Turner, who was president in the immediate postwar years.

However, when Churchill took power in 1940, Dorman-Smith was moved from agriculture and put in charge of evacuations. In 1941 he was appointed Governor General of Burma and was subsequently in office at the time of the Japanese invasion. He was duly expelled from the country but remained Governor in Exile in India. He was removed from this post in 1946 by Mountbatten when the two men fell out over the policy for Burmese independence.

After this fall from grace Dorman-Smith seemed to withdraw from public life. Having been such a hero for the farming community, some joked unkindly that he went from Dorman-Smith to Dormant-Smith. There was a suggestion in 1944 that he would make a good ambassador for British agriculture, but it never came to be. By then the NFU was being dominated by younger men and there seemed little room for those from the pre-war era. It seems odd that someone who had achieved so much while in his 30s and 40s should spend the second half of his life in semi-retirement in Hampshire.

Even so, Colonel Sir Reginald Dorman-Smith remains one of the most charismatic men to lead the NFU. Widely admired, he led the union at a time when it seemed to turn the corner out of what had been a long, dark alley of falling farm incomes and stagnating membership. Today the NFU still benefits from his legacy of bringing union and government closer together. As a man who made it to the top of both the NFU and the MAF he should be remembered as a giant in our farming history.

The Dorman-Smith family at their farm in Surrey.

CHAPTER 20

George Gibbard, 1938

In contrast to the Irish-born aristocrat Dorman-Smith, George Gibbard was of solid farming stock from middle England.

As president and vice-president they must have made a good contrast, well reflecting the diversity of men within agriculture and the NFU. Where Dorman-Smith oozed panache and charm, Gibbard showed qualities of stout competence and under-stated wisdom. Despite their differences in background, they worked well as a team and enjoyed each other's company.

The Gibbards were tenant farmers who farmed the rich red ironstone soils around Banbury, in Oxfordshire. George's father took the tenancy of the 163-acre Crouch Farm in the year George was born – 1883 – and there George remained until he died in 1962, when it was handed on to his son, Ken. In George's time, Crouch Farm was typical of the area, with a mixture of crops and stock. Wheat, barley and oats were grown, along with roots such as potatoes and swedes. There were sheep, pigs and cattle. The cows were a 'flying herd', bought in the winter and kept in yards and then grazed through the summer to be sold in the autumn.

George was educated at a private day-school, Banbury Academy, and despite being a bright boy who was always top of the class, like most tenant farmers' sons he left school at 14 to work on the farm. George did not ignore his academic abilities, however, and in his young adult life took a postal course in Pelmanism, a system popular in Edwardian England based on memorising facts and figures by learning through patterns. George's ability with figures and his good memory served him well in life, especially at the NFU, and he was one of those at Bedford Square who recognised the future importance of sound and well-researched economic data when dealing with government.

He married Mary Bliss, a bank manager's daughter, in 1910 and they had two sons, Ken and Daniel. In 1918, when George took over the tenancy of Crouch Farm, there were seven men and seven horses working the 163 acres. Even in the late 1930s spreading fertiliser such as sulphate of ammonium was done by hand. In contrast to the mechanised precision of today, the fertiliser granules were thrown onto the field by a man carrying a sack. There were no tractors until 1942 and the first combine, an Allis Chambers, did not arrive until 1951, when George was at the end of his farming career.

George was involved in the NFU from its earliest days in Banbury and Oxfordshire. Both branch and county were founded in 1908 – Oxfordshire was among the initial ten counties that nailed their

A very young George Gibbard (centre) *poses for the camera at the turn of the century at Crouch Farm.*

George Gibbard (right) *and his son, Ken, inspecting cattle at Crouch Farm.*

colours to the NFU mast that year. George was one of those first activists who sought to expand the union's membership, and his son, Ken, remembers that, even as a 17-yearold fresh out of school, as a loyal son he was expected to help out as a local NFU organiser. Like many of the early NFU activists, George served on the County Council War Agricultural Committees in the First World War. On more than one occasion, when visiting a farm to offer firm but friendly advice on improving farm productivity, he was met by farmer armed with a loaded shotgun.

George worked his way up through the NFU ranks, becoming county chairman in the 1920s and undertaking HQ work in London by the early 1930s. He was chair of the Labour Committee and attended an international labour conference in Geneva in 1932. It was to be his first time abroad, and one can only guess what impact a visit to the splendid Swiss city of mountains, lakes and banks had on the humble Oxfordshire tenant farmer.

His son Ken recounts that in the 1930s his father was more often on NFU business than on the farm. He also recollects how times were tough and that, as a dutiful son, he was working all hours so that his father could afford time away to give the benefit of his ill-rewarded, but highly regarded, abilities to the NFU. In 1938 George was awarded the OBE.

The *Farmers' Weekly* of January 1938 described Gibbard as a 'shirt sleeved President'. It was an apt description of a man who had worked hard in the NFU at all levels. When he was Oxfordshire county chairman the county had the honour of being the only one to collect 100 per cent of subscriptions – largely achieved by Gibbard rolling up his sleeves and getting out amongst the membership to explain the importance of the union's work. In many ways the NFU was built on the backs of men such as George Gibbard.

In 1938, when the sheep price collapsed, the NFU pointed out to government that while it had brought in guaranteed prices in some form or another for the main products of British farming, namely milk, fat cattle, bacon pigs, wheat, barley, oats and sugar beet, the sheep sector was one glaring exception. Accordingly, the Agricultural Development Act, which became law in the spring of 1939, introduced price guarantees for sheep. A deficiency payment was to be paid based on 10d. per lb subject to grade and season. With the sheep scheme up and running, the total exchequer spend in the support of farm production rose to £9 million per annum.

In 1938 the NFU produced a major policy statement, 'British Agriculture in 1938'. This further awakened public opinion to the fact that agriculture was ill-prepared for the prospect of war, declaring that:

Many hundreds of millions of pounds are being spent on air-raid protection, food storage plans and the strengthening of defences on the sea, in the air and on land; but not a single penny has been voted under the re-armament plan for the maintenance, let alone the expansion, of the fourth line of defence. Not a single farmer throughout the length and breadth of the land of England and Wales knows what would be expected of him if war broke out tomorrow.

In late 1938 NFU Council, by formal resolution, placed the machinery of the NFU at the disposal of the government, should war break out, 'with a view to offering the closest co-operation in any question affecting the nation's food supplies'. In contrast with 1914, the offer was promptly accepted.

Today Crouch Farm is still tenanted and farmed by the Gibbard family. Roger Gibbard lives in the farmhouse from where his grandfather set out on so many mornings to catch the train up to London. Like

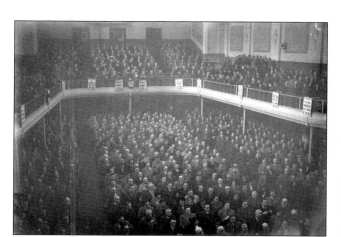

East Anglian farmers gather in Ipswich to protest about the state of agriculture in 1939.

many farmers, Roger has recognised that today a 163-acre tenanted farm would struggle to support a family and has rationalised things accordingly. The farm is all arable and contract farmed by others under Roger's direction, while he also holds down an academic job at Reading University.

And so we end this chapter, having reached 1939, a key date in the history of British farming. From 1939 onwards agriculture would never be the same again. For 20 years it had almost fossilised, but over the next 20 it would evolve almost out of recognition. The Gibbard home of Crouch Farm is a microcosm of this story and, as a 163-acre mixed farm in middle England, is about as typical as a farm can get. On the eve of the Second World War the overall output from Crouch Farm had altered very little since the First World War. Livestock numbers had been increased and the area of crops had been reduced. Yields in crops such as wheat and barley had, in the main, flat-lined for 20 years at around a little under a ton to the acre.

There were still no tractors and no electricity, and the use of fertilisers and pesticides was occasional rather than regular and their application imprecise. This was not due to any lack of enthusiasm for change on behalf of the Gibbards, but simply because the returns from farming did not encourage investment in new ideas.

For 20 years farming had been a matter of trying to survive by doing what you did the year before at the least possible cost. Government schemes had improved returns in some instances, but most farmers were still feeling under financial pressure. In real terms, agricultural prices were no better than they had been in the mid-1920s and were still worse than they had been at the end of the First World War. Just as the 1930s had kicked off with farmer rallies to draw attention to the seriousness of the situation, in 1939 similar rallies were still being held. Early in the year protest meetings in East Anglia culminated in a march in London of 5,000 farmers seeking to impress upon government that returns from farming, particularly arable farming, were cripplingly low.

Although the lack of change such as that experienced by the Gibbards at Crouch Farm was the norm, there were some farms where there had been significant change in the interwar years; where the tractor had taken over from the horse; where mechanisation and electrification had led to greater output with less labour; where pigs and poultry were being kept under new, intensive regimes to give greater efficiency; where new crops such as sugar beet and field vegetables were being grown; where the routine use of fertilisers and better genetics were increasing production; where milk production, backed up with better marketing, had taken over from the old staple of cereal production. The point is that these developments were the exception rather than the norm. As trends, they were more typical of the future than of the present.

As for the NFU in 1939, that too was on the brink of immense change. Just as with the First World War, the Second World War was to have a multiplier effect on the membership. In terms of its relationship with government, having started the '30s in a resentful and difficult mood, by 1939 the NFU was in the throes of cementing a real partnership. Through the 1930s it had learnt that it was best to concentrate its energies in Whitehall rather than Westminster – a lesson that is still relevant today. This sense of partnership with MAF would be accelerated over the next decade as the government moved from a piece-meal approach when addressing farming ills, through a series of sticking plaster measures to a more comprehensive agricultural policy.

Fordsons coming off the Dagenham production line in 1939. These were possibly as crucial to the war effort as the Spitfire.

A bevy of land girls and one lucky male instructor.

CHAPTER 21

Sir Tom Peacock, 1939–41

The man who led the NFU into the Second World War was Tom Peacock. At the beginning of his presidency he gave a battle cry: 'I will not be satisfied until every acre of the land which has gone out of cultivation and every ounce of soil is producing to its utmost capacity.'

Tom Peacock, a Cheshire man born in 1895, could trace his family back in the county for over 500 years. He farmed a 200-acre dairy farm at Cotton Edmunds, about four miles south of Chester, and was playfully known locally as 'the Squire of Cotton Edmunds Hall'. The farm was part of the Duke of Westminster's estate, which was then, and still is today, one of the UK's foremost landed estates. The farm was very heavily stocked with 84 milking cows, with 30 followers, 400 pigs and 200 sheep. The dairy herd was non-pedigree Shorthorn, typical of the area.

Accredited milk was produced, the milking done twice daily through a bucket plant installed in the early 1930s. Peacock was firmly of the view that:

If the machine is properly looked after and if every care is taken in such things as stripping, cleanliness and disinfection, you can get just as much milk with a good machine as you can get by hand.

As we have noted before, machine milking in 1939 was still the exception, with 90 per cent of farmers still hand milking. From March to October the milk was used for making farmhouse Cheshire cheese. It was graded through the National Mark Scheme.

Locally, Peacock had been chairman of the Cheshire Farmers' Trading Society, and under his chairmanship in the 1930s the turnover had jumped from £20,000 to £220,000. He had been involved with Cheshire NFU since its inception in 1918, and had worked with the then NFU president, Harry German, in controlling the foot and mouth pandemic in 1923. In 1933 he became a member of Council and chair of the Pigs Committee prior to becoming vice-president under George Gibbard. On becoming president he left the running of his farm to his son so he could concentrate his activities in London.

By 1939 Cotton Edmunds Hall was more or less all permanent grass, which grew well on the rich, red clay loam. In the previous 20 years the farm would have grown fodder crops such as oats, barley and roots, but now such feedstuffs were bought in. Under his stewardship the farm stock had doubled from his father's time through the application of increasing amounts of what farmers at the time called

Tom Peacock in his presidential office at Bedford Square in 1940.

'artificial manure'. We know it today as artificial fertiliser. In the interwar years British farmers were using increasing amounts of artificials such as basic slag, rock phosphate from North Africa and ammonium nitrate. While Peacock pushed the land harder, he also pushed his stock harder by feeding them more concentrates.

Peacock's farm policy of increasing stock numbers as well as the amount of bought-in food was typical of the trend in British livestock farming between the wars. Generally, in the interwar period the cropped area of the UK had fallen to the point that Britain had made herself vulnerable. From 1939 onwards she was going to need to dig – or plough – for victory. On the other hand, by 1939 the country's livestock numbers had increased. It was estimated that up to 25 per cent of the annual output of livestock products was dependent on the nine million tons of feedstuffs brought in from overseas. This increasing dependence of the livestock sector on cheap imported feedstuffs was an important dynamic, both for British agriculture and for the politics of the NFU. As we have seen, much of the policy drive of the NFU in the interwar years had been to increase commodity prices. This was not necessarily good news for those farmers who were increasingly looking to survive the downturn in farming fortunes by fattening stock on feedstuffs not produced on the farm. When farms were predominantly mixed, most farmers would agree that import controls designed to increase the value of both crops and livestock were worthy policies. As the mixed farm declined and specialised livestock units such as Peacock's became more common, then the 'horn or corn' distinction became more pronounced.

As men such as Peacock increasingly benefited from cheap imports, then import controls became an issue almost too complex for the NFU to have a clear policy position on. It was not always easy to steer a course between the two competing interests. This, of course, changed again with the prospect of war. Now the flood of imported feedstuffs would undoubtedly be curtailed by enemy action. By 1939 there was a clear need to encourage home production of feedstuffs by raising their price.

As war beckoned, the issue as to how much of Britain should be pasture and how much cropland was again brought into focus. It was the same question Tudor kings wrestled with when they recognised that too much farming based around wool risked famine and increased dependence on importing food from other realms. It was the same threat to food security that had faced Lloyd George's Government in 1916. History repeated itself when the effect of low prices in the period before the Second World War had

been to increase the livestock sector and to diminish the area under the plough, just as it had in the depression before the First World War some 40 years before. British agriculture became top heavy, with a disproportionate emphasis on livestock production. This, in turn, increased the country's dependence on imports and eroded self-sufficiency. Again, policy makers were aware that when it came to feeding the nation there were far more calories of food to be had from a cropped acre than from a grazed one. In early 1939 there was a mood amongst some members of government, most particularly the first Lord of the Admiralty, Winston Churchill, to greatly reduce livestock numbers through slaughter while stockpiling imported grain. The NFU urged caution and advised against de-stabilising the industry by moving too fast, too soon.

Dorman-Smith, the new Minister of Agriculture in January 1939, accepted the advice of his old colleagues at the NFU and resisted significant livestock reduction. Instead he inaugurated the 'plough up campaign' to encourage tillage and set a target of bringing two million extra acres under the plough. There were four initial drivers behind the plough policy. Firstly, acreage payments were made for the ploughing of grassland; secondly, price insurance schemes encouraged crop production; thirdly, propaganda campaigns were launched encouraging farmers to plough. The fourth element caused more heated cabinet discussion. Dorman-Smith demanded £2.75 million from the Treasury to place orders for 5,000 tractors. Again, the farmer minister won the argument. In April 1939, four months before the outbreak of hostilities, the order was placed. As there were only an estimated 50,000 tractors, in varying states of age and repair, working in British agriculture, Dorman-Smith's action was a visionary way to kick-start the plough campaign and ensured that British factories would tool up for increased tractor production. It was also a way around the conundrum that faced the policy makers in 1916 as to how to encourage more ploughing while depriving farmers of their staff and their horses through enlistment. In the six months from the outbreak of war the trade had sold 10,000 tractors and 11,000 tractor ploughs. In 1940 Fordson sold some 17,000 tractors, compared to 4,000 in 1938. By the end of the war British farms had an additional 170,000 tractors, three-quarters of which came from British factories. There was also the import of over 2,000 combine harvesters from abroad and 35,000 potato lifters, mainly home-produced. Before 1940 such machines were practically unknown. In addition, there were tens of thousands of implements to pull behind the tractors for the purposes of cultivating, planting and harvesting. Elsewhere on the farm, the installation of labour-saving devices was also the order of the day. By 1942 the number of milking machines had increased to 24,000 and in 1946 stood at 40,400. By

NEW FURROWS

"'Taint much, but it's a beginning."

[There has been an increase of 48,000 acres under plough in England and Wales since the returns of last June.]

How Punch *saw the start of the plough campaign in 1939.*

the end of the war, British farming, it was claimed, was the most highly mechanised in the world. It was an immense change and marked the beginning of the mechanisation revolution that was fundamentally to transform farms and farming in the latter half of the twentieth century. The wartime policy left a strong legacy of mechanisation. For instance, by 1950 the number of combine harvesters had increased to 24,000 and milking machines to 70,000.

More generally, the state took control of the buying and selling of food supplies. The Ministry of Food was set up as the sole buyer and importer of all major foodstuffs; existing stocks were requisitioned; price control was imposed at various stages of distribution and rationing was introduced. The immediate privation for farmers was the rationing of fertilisers and feedstuffs.

In the months before the war Dorman-Smith also laid down a network of county War Executive Agricultural Committees (WAECs) and subsidiary district committees whose members substantially came from the ranks of the NFU. There was also regular liaison between the WAECs and NFU county executives. Such plans had been discussed between the government and the NFU as early as 1936, when Dorman-Smith had been president. In the months before the war about 5,000 individuals were appointed to serve on these committees. This process clearly benefited from a strongly organised NFU, along with a ministry headed by a man who knew the NFU structure from first-hand experience over many years. Dorman-Smith also enjoyed the goodwill of much of the farming community, which enabled central government to execute policy at local level. The marketing boards were disbanded, apart from the Milk Marketing Board and the Hop Marketing Board, which continued under ministry supervision.

The powers of the WAECs were far reaching and, at times, controversial. They could enter farms to carry out inspections, then making directives on cultivation, cropping, stocking, pest control, drainage, general maintenance and all manner of everyday farm activities. Ultimately, the committees had the power to eject a farmer from his farm if he persistently failed to comply with directives. They also had powers to defer enlistment for farm workers, organise contracting operations and distribute machinery from the government's machinery reserve. A massive survey undertaken of every working farm duly classified them in three categories, A, B, and C, in order of efficiency and adequacy of equipment.

It was the power of dispossession that proved most controversial and most notorious. By the end of the war dispossession had been resorted to in more than 3,000 cases. Despite the seemingly draconian powers of these committees, it is generally agreed that the approach was based on sensible advice and

sensitive encouragement rather than dispassionate directives from the cold hand of faceless authority. Dispossession was a tool of last resort. In hindsight, seldom was the decision to turf a farmer out of his farm deemed unfair or unjust. Again, the presence and backing of an organisation such as the NFU, which had the majority of commercial farming in its ranks, must have considerably oiled the wheels of these local executive committees. They would have struggled to achieve their objectives if they had constantly been viewed with hostility by the men who worked the land. Farmers exercising discipline over fellow farmers and neighbours was a potential powder keg of bad feeling. There is no doubt that the presence of a strong NFU helped to keep the lid on that powder keg. In the main, farmers and NFU members recognised this was not a time for half measures.

Most farmers needed little persuasion or guidance to change their farming in accordance with government directives. From the day in 1939 when the network of county and district WAECs began to operate, farmers in general, and the NFU in particular, had to learn to live as full partners with the state. No longer could farmers follow their own impulse or assert their own will in planning production, unless the end accorded with the targets set. But the spirit in which this was done was clearly one of co-operation rather than direction. This sense of partnership between state and farmers was key to the mood that pervaded after 1945. The NFU was the main beneficiary of this new mood. In the words of Self and Storing in The State and the Farmer:

In hundreds of matters of detail, from the supply of binder twine to the acquisition of land for military purposes, and on dozens of official advisory committees, Whitehall and the Union's headquarters at Bedford Square were drawn together.

Just as with the setting up of the marketing boards in the 1930s, the NFU–ministry partnership was mutually beneficial. By way of practical example, throughout the war the NFU continued to distribute the *Record* and the NFU *News Sheet*. Both had monthly circulations of over 100,000, which grew substantially through the war. Throughout 1939–45 much space in these publications was devoted to disseminating information about government programmes and directives. Like most newspapers, they suffered the privations of paper rationing, but remained crucial sources of information for farmers.

At central government level Dorman-Smith instituted regular meetings between himself and NFU President Peacock, as well as between NFU General Secretary Fyfe and senior ministry officials.

In the month before the outbreak of war Dorman-Smith could be found inspecting the smiling ranks of the Women's Land Army (WLA) in Hyde Park. It was their first public appearance en masse, and their recruitment had proven a minor social revolution. By November 1939 25,000 had joined the WLA, which went some way to replacing the shortfall in workforce that faced the industry by 1940 – 14,000 workers had been lost to recruitment by the forces and, in total, agriculture was reckoned to be short 50,000 workers due to the decimation of the interwar years. At its height in 1943 the WLA numbered 87,000. At first the WLA was regarded by farmers with mixed feelings, but soon it was accepted as both necessary and well organised. Many of the young women were from cities and were unfamiliar with farm life or hard manual work outside in all weathers. Some struggled to meet the demands of farm work, while others proved adequate replacements for the men-folk who had left to enlist in the Forces. There was, of course, a more colourful side to this story of the meeting of city girls and country men. There are no figures to prove it, but the number WLA girls who married farmers is estimated to have run well into four figures. For the rural stock of Britain, the arrival of the WLA provided an unprecedented opportunity for the injection of new genetics.

Although the first months of war were known as 'the phoney war', in terms of curtailing imports it had been very real. Government estimates had proven widely optimistic, and by the October of 1939 imports were down by a third. Although they would not have dared describe it as such, it was good news for arable farmers. By January 1940 oat prices had increased by 100 per cent, barley by 67 per cent and wheat by 11 per cent. For livestock farmers it meant an increase in feedstuffs, and government accordingly increased the price of sheep by 2d. per lb to 1s. per lb and pigs to 15s. per score from 14s. The autumn and winter of 1939/40 proved wet and cold. There were concerns that farmers would struggle to meet the targets of the 'plough up' campaign, but by April 1940 it was clear that the ability of farmers to triumph in the face of adverse weather had been underestimated. Dorman-Smith's two million acre target had been reached, with 2,030,000 acres added to the arable area of Britain. There had been more achieved in the first year of the Second World War than had been achieved throughout the entire First World War.

In the early years of the war the plough was again transforming the British countryside. The introduction of the tractor accelerated the process. There was a wholesale reclamation of land that had suffered dereliction. Marshes were drained, the plough pushed back the moorland line, reeds gave way to sugar beet and bracken to wheat and potatoes. Acres of wilderness were now harnessed to contribute positively to a nation subject to the most rigorous rationing of food. In Wiltshire, 500 acres of common land, the grazing rights to which had been handed down from family to family since the days of King

Fertiliser trials at Jealotts Hill. The Second World War saw significant increases in the use of atificial fertilser on British farms.

Athelstan, were ploughed up. A sterile swamp of 2,000 acres between Ampthill and Bedford, which four centuries before had been made famous as the 'slough of despond' by Bunyan in *Pilgrim's Progress*, was drained and put down to wheat and potatoes. There were some dafter moments. For instance, one county war exec mistakenly ordered a Somerset farmer to plough up a section of the Great Western railway line. The farmer replied he would do his best, but the embankment was a bit steep.

One niggle in all this was the introduction of 'double summertime' in May 1941. Just as farmers and the NFU had complained in the First World War at the introduction of the annual habit of moving the clocks on an hour in April, so they now protested twice as much at the doubling of this process.

In May 1940 a metaphorical bomb was dropped on MAF and the NFU. Dorman-Smith was removed from his post. This was a result of politicking rather than a reflection of his record. Faced with increasing criticism in the House of Commons, the Chamberlain administration had lost the confidence of MPs, and the pugnacious Churchill had replaced Chamberlain as Prime Minister. In keeping with his dramatic style, Churchill duly dismissed most of the Cabinet and Dorman-Smith was a victim of the clear-out. Dorman-Smith had clashed with Churchill at the very beginning of the war when he resisted Churchill's proposal to Cabinet that there should be a mass slaughter of livestock to reduce their numbers. Dorman-Smith's removal was deplored by the NFU and the farming community generally. Had it happened in peacetime, no doubt, it would have rightly led to the strongest of protests, but at a time of war there was little choice for President Peacock than to offer his full backing and co-operation with the new Minister, R.S. Hudson.

As a man, Peacock was known for his good judgement and for 'getting things done'. He was not the most forceful of public speakers, but his quiet diligence and understated ability suited a time when wartime restrictions meant that important work had to be undertaken as a matter of duty, without fanfare or acknowledgement.

Preparation for war meant the activities of Bedford Square had to be curtailed. A large house, 'Wyclands', was purchased in High Wycombe so that an HQ could be established outside London as necessity demanded. The prospect of bombing by the Luftwaffe meant staff moved into the new wartime premises almost immediately war was declared, in early September 1939. The 'addressograph' and various records were sent to NFU Mutual headquarters in Stratford-upon-Avon. The president, the general secretary and a skeleton staff were kept in London to ensure their contact with Whitehall. Regular weekly meetings were maintained right through the war. Furthermore, such past presidents as Slade, Gibbard, Ratcliff, Langford, Davies and Williams served on ministry wartime committees.

In readiness for hostilities Council was suspended, and Peacock created a small War Committee comprising himself, his vice-president, Christopher Nevile, and seven previous presidents. The fact was that every time Council met, 35,000 miles would be travelled for it to assemble, and it was judged this could not be justified at a time of war. AGMs were also suspended, and the power to elect new office-holders was given to the Emergency War Committee. Under this system Peacock retained the presidency for three years. This was the first and only time the NFU abandoned its democratic structure of an electoral college elected through the counties. It does seem somewhat ironic that, at a time of war in defence of freedom and democracy, the NFU felt obliged to abandon those very ideals. Amongst the membership, however, these actions provoked very little complaint. Members recognised that, while there was a war on, the NFU would have to run along different lines.

Peacock's relations with the new Minister, Hudson, were not without tensions. By mid-1940 NFU county branches were inundating headquarters with protests over the new price levels that had been announced. The Ministry of Food was the focus of their complaint, and dissatisfaction was heightened by the fact that price settlements were being made without full consultation with the NFU. Under Peacock's chairmanship the NFU War Committee passed a resolution registering 'the complete mistrust which exists throughout the county in respect of the Ministry of Food in relation to the determination of price schedules'. The union called upon the Prime Minister to set up a new and independent body.

Churchill's reply to Peacock was characteristically blunt and unyielding:

The price structure reconciled just treatment for the producer with the wider requirements of the nation –

and even if this was not so, the call to duty would still go out to the farms, as it does to the factories.

This reference to the factories touched a nerve with Peacock, who replied:

We ask for nothing better than to be treated as the factories are treated. But none of us know of any manufacturing industry under state control which is compelled to accept for its products prices ordained, without prior consultation and agreement, by the Government department concerned.

Peacock's complaint did not lead to immediate improvement, but there was a change in tone from government. On 26 November 1940 Minister Hudson gave what became known as 'the pledge of 1940'.

The Government has, by ensuring a guaranteed market at guaranteed prices for the principal agricultural products for the year ahead, helped create more stable conditions up to the 1941 harvest. The Government has now decided to go further and to guarantee that the present system of fixed prices and an assured market will be maintained for the duration of the hostilities and for at least one year thereafter. Prices will be subject to adjustment to the extent of any substantial changes in the costs of production... The Government, representative as it is of all the major political parties, recognises the importance of maintaining after the war a healthy and well-balanced agriculture as an essential and permanent feature of national policy. The guarantee now given is meant to secure that stability shall be maintained, not only during hostilities, but during a length of time sufficient to put in action a permanent post-war policy for home agriculture.

For the older generation in the NFU the phrase 'for at least one year thereafter' had an ominous ring that cast their minds back to the events of 1921. But elsewhere within the union there was a generation of younger men emerging who thought talk of a permanent post-war policy for agriculture pointed to a new relationship between farming and the state. There was hope in union circles that after the war Britain would not go back to her traditional view that, as the workshop of the world, she was best and cheapest fed from abroad.

The pledge of 1940 marked a turning-point in the war, with government making greater effort to consult with the NFU in its price-fixing deliberations in an atmosphere of reasonableness. It was a tradition that was to continue well after the war. By 1941 the annual process of the NFU making representations on the suite of price-fixing proposals of the ministry was established.

On 11 November 1941, Prime Minister Churchill

acknowledged that in two years the area under crops had increased by 45 per cent and the cereal harvest of 1941 had been 50 per cent above that of 1939. In a statement he made reference to the fact that the recent defector Hess had made it clear to British intelligence that: 'Hitler relied upon the starvation attack more than upon invasion to bring us to our knees'.

In early 1942 Tom Peacock stood down from the presidency in favour of his vice-president, Christopher Nevile. The years of 1939, 1940 and 1941 are key ones in the history of British agriculture and the NFU. Accordingly, the contribution of Tom Peacock and Reginald Dorman-Smith cannot be overestimated. Nor should be forgotten the sheer physical danger to which Peacock exposed himself by staying in London at the height of the blitz to carry out his presidential responsibilities. Three times he was literally bombed out of his bed. The scale of the Blitz should not be forgotten. On one day alone – 11 May 1941 – 1,400 Londoners were killed by enemy bombs. It was in these times that Tom Peacock could be found, with General Secretary Fyfe and Chief Economist Browne, making his way around the smouldering rubble between Bedford Square and Whitehall.

Peacock continued to serve on various committees for the rest of the war, and in 1952 became chairman of the Milk Marketing Board, retiring in 1958. He was knighted in 1956 for services to agriculture. He died of a heart attack in 1959. Cotton Edmunds Hall, his old farm, is still a dairy farm and is now farmed by his grandson.

CHAPTER 22

Christopher Nevile, 1942

Christopher, known as Kit, Nevile, in Skellingthorpe, Lincolnshire, in 1893, could trace his ancestry back to Gilbert de Nevile, one of William the Conqueror's admirals. After a hard day's work at Hastings in 1066, the de Neviles were generously rewarded with vast tracts of land. Thus established as an important land-owning family, they continued as such for the rest of the millennium.

Educated at Winchester School, Kit Nevile became a farm pupil at Grove Farm, Wellingore, around the turn of the century. Grove Farm was owned by a wealthier branch of the Nevile family and was part of the original 1066 war spoils. While working at Grove Farm Kit Nevile took flying lessons and became a skilled pilot – in those days flying was very much a pioneering activity, the Wrights having made their first flight only a few years before, in 1903. In 1916 Nevile was keen to use his skill on behalf of king and country but failed the Flying Corps medical. Had he passed, it is most unlikely we would be writing about him now.

At Grove Farm he fell in love with Vera Burt, daughter of the the estate manager, W.B. Burt, who in August 1904 had been in the soggy tent among the pioneers who went on to form the LFU. On his marriage to Vera, Kit took on the tenancy of another Nevile farm at Haddington, but then borrowed money and in 1919 bought Whisby Hall, a 400-acre farm a few miles south-west of Lincoln, a stone's throw from Stapleford Hall, home of a certain Mr Colin Campbell.

In 1919 Whisby Hall had cost £10 an acre. If we recollect, the period after the First World War was a time when many tenants bought farms. For most this was a daring venture. Family members recount stories of Kit Nevile pacing the corridors at night at the time of the purchase. The worry of making such a financial commitment and doubts over the future prosperity of farming kept him from sleeping soundly.

As a young man Nevile had grown up surrounded by such NFU pioneers as Pat Hamilton, the Vicar of Skellingthorpe, his father-in-law, W.B. Burt, and his near neighbour, Colin Campbell. It is no surprise, then, that he joined the NFU in its earliest of days. In 1932 he was elected Lincolnshire delegate to Council.

Whisby Hall was predominantly light land. Nevile described it as 'hungry land that went foul with marigold, twitch and dodder if given half a chance to do so'. (In the 1960s a third of it was taken

for gravel extraction.) By the late 1930s the farm grazed beef, with 150 winter stores and 250 head summer grazing – mainly Lincoln Reds. The policy with the cattle was to feed them through the land rather than through the trough. Also kept were 200 breeding ewes and 200 pigs for fattening. Half the farm was down to arable; mainly barley with sugar beet, which was sent to the nearby Newark factory. Nevile had been one of the original suppliers of the Newark factory when it opened in 1927. Like most beet farmers, Nevile increased his acreage during the war. Nationally, the amount of sugar beet increased from 2.7 million tonnes before the war to 3.8 million in 1945. The price of beet over the same period increased 80 per cent.

The arable crops on Nevile's farm needed feeding on the hungry soils. Nevile gave his beet 3 cwt per acre of super phosphate, 2.5 cwt muriate of potash and 3–4 cwt of nitrate of soda. The cereals received 2 cwt of sulphate of ammonia. At first, in 1939, fertiliser was in short supply, as it was largely imported. Once supplies were plentiful, after 1943, then the amount used increased two-fold. One of the unlikely results of the Second World War was that it encouraged the use of artificial fertiliser.

In 1939, on the direction of the Lincolnshire WAEC, Nevile took over Skinnard Farm, a 380-acre block of poor, wet, low-lying grazing land. Indeed, Nevile served on the Kesteven War Agricultural Committee and, in accordance with his own committee's directives, dutifully set about ploughing Skinnard Farm. It was not a farm naturally given to ploughing and, despite it being made easier by the introduction of tractors, Nevile did not enjoy the

Nevile's farm, Whisby Hall, in the winter of 1943.

task. In 1943 he happily handed Skinnard Farm on to someone else.

Intriguingly, in 1941 he sold Whisby Hall for £16 an acre but kept the tenancy. His thinking was that wartime was a good time to sell. He remembered only too well the experience of the First World War, when farm land became more valuable as food became scarce due to wartime blockade. He also remembered the crash that followed 1921 as the sea lanes re-opened, causing Britain no longer to value its farm land or its produce. Nevile feared this pattern would repeat itself in the 1940s the moment hostilities ceased.

In terms of his character, Kit Nevile was an intelligent, plain-speaking man with an aptitude for organisation. As we shall see, he was also a man who could exercise great foresight for others but not necessarily for himself. Curiously, he stammered in social conversation but never when on a public platform. On one famous occasion, at an NFU county function, one after-dinner comedian included jokes about stammering, oblivious to the guest of honour's impediment. This did not go down well with the audience, and, after the comic's turn, to the great amusement of the audience, Nevile defused the situation by taking the microphone and announcing: Well, I c-c-could have d-d-done a lot b-b-bloody b-b-better than that!'

During the war, as both vice-president and president, Nevile spent the working week in London. His son recollects with some humour how, every Monday morning, his father would wander down to the level crossing a few hundred yards from Whisby Hall and, literally, 'request' the next train to stop and pick him up. Under an agreement he had negotiated with the Great Eastern Railway during railway work on Whisby Hall land, Nevile had secured the right to be picked up when he felt like it. Accordingly, he would arrive at the level crossing and a GER guard would be obliged to wander up the track with a flag and stop the train as it steamed through the Lincolnshire countryside. History does not record what the driver thought of having to slam on his brakes to pick up one single farmer just as he was achieving full speed five miles out of Lincoln Station. Appropriately, after the war Nevile served on the board of the newly nationalised British Rail.

As had Peacock, Nevile braved the worst of the blitz by lodging in central London at the Constitution Club. During his presidency he came under increasing pressure from the counties to negotiate higher prices with government. As ever, Norfolk made the loudest complaints and called for Nevile's resignation. In a famous exchange at a meeting in East Anglia, a Mr Bratley, from the floor, angrily urged the president to 'remember he was a farmer'. Nevile fixed his critic with a cold stare and replied: 'I am a farmer, but I am an Englishman, too.'

Nevile recognised, when in negotiation with ministers, that his was a difficult balancing act. His membership demanded of him that he negotiate the best deals possible and also that he take a more combative stance with the minister. Nevile refused, and stuck to his approach of working constructively with his opposite number, Hudson, to secure maximum farm output for least exchequer expense. The prices fixed in 1942 were tough, and the deal was worse for farmers than that of 1941, particularly in relation to milk. While Nevile privately protested the inadequacy of the deal with Hudson, publicly he knew demands for better prices by farmers would be viewed dimly by the wider public.

Nevile remembered only too well the accusations of profiteering against farmers made in 1918. He also remembered the counsel of his old neighbour and mentor, Colin Campbell, who had also led the NFU during a time of war. Campbell had told the young Nevile that one reason it was politically easy for government to walk away from agriculture after the First World War was because farmers had made themselves unpopular by allowing the 'profiteer' label to stick. With an eye on what would happen when hostilities ceased, Nevile took the view that the NFU should try to avoid repeating that mistake. Some short-term sacrifices made under his presidency improved the chances of his successors to secure a longer-term settlement that avoided a repeat of the 1920s crash.

To back up this concern over public opinion, £5,000 of new money was allocated to public relations work. The main outcome of this was the setting up of a press bureau. Initially, this work was contracted out, but in 1943 a Mr Wilfred Hill was appointed as the NFU's first publicity officer. Hill drew up campaigns that included 'the use of the Press, the cinema, broadcasts and speeches to present agriculture's case for a higher status after the war'. Press conferences were now also routinely arranged, and in 1944 a much-increased £30,000 was allocated to the further development of the public relations department.

It is from the initial initiatives under Nevile's presidency that we can trace the communications department of the NFU today. Before the war much of the PR work of the NFU had been somewhat ad hoc and amateurish. After the war it was approached in a more comprehensive, professional and better resourced manner. The union now recognised the importance of distinguishing between 'publicity mainly directed at the townsman and publicity on the Union's work'.

Writing in the *Farmers' Weekly* in late 1942, Nevile reminded farmers that, due to their wartime efforts they:

... have earned the good will of the population to an extent never attained before. This good will will be of

incalculable value when the war is over and the policy of postwar agriculture is decided.

By 1943 Nevile was feeling the strain of the job and decided to serve only for a year. He handed over to his vice-president, Jack Templeton. For two years afterwards he suffered a series of debilitating illnesses with no clear medical diagnosis. Today, his son Anthony, is convinced it was due to the nervous stress of his exertions in 1942. He eventually died in a car crash in 1961. Anthony then bought the farm back and expanded it to 900 acres. Today Whisby Hall is a typical light land Lincolnshire farm growing mainly wheat, rape and barley.

When we look back at the presidency of Kit Nevile we should remember that he not only weathered the flak of the Luftwaffe's bombs, he also shrugged off the flak from those he represented. He gave precedence to what he thought was right for the industry over any concern for his own popularity with the membership. Kit Nevile lacked the force of personality or speaking ability to barnstorm his way past his critics, but 1942 was no time for farmers to be led by the belligerence of self-interest or aggressive tub-thumping. These were the darkest days of the war for Britain. Militarily, there was little but bad news. Hitler had most of continental Europe firmly under the heel of his Nazi jackboot, while British troops were still on the retreat in such places as Singapore and Tobruk and, in the North Atlantic, German U-boats and dive bombers were still taking chunks out of the supply convoys. At home the Luftwaffe was extending the range of its deadly raids to the market towns. Everyday items such as clothes, electricity and confectionery were rationed for the first time and three years of grinding war was biting deep into the nation's morale. For farmers to have been seen to demand more at such a time might have turned a generation of Britons against them.

In the light of the government's continued postwar support for agriculture, we have a lot to admire Kit Nevile for. In selling his farm in 1941, we conclude, his own judgement was that the benign conditions for farmers wouldn't last. It seems ironic that by the time he died in 1961 he was proved wrong. The double irony is that he worked harder than anybody to make sure his own pessimistic forecast didn't happen.

President Templeton flanked by his deputy and vice, Deakin and Nevile.

Left: Maesllech Farmhouse

Carting hay at Maesllech Farm.

CHAPTER 23

Captain J. Templeton, 1943

The year 1943 is often viewed as a turning point in World War Two. The Yanks were 'over here' and reinforcing beleaguered British troops in huge numbers. Vast tracts of flat farmland were being turned into US air-bases, bringing the total area of farmland lost to wartime operations to 800,000 acres. In North Africa, Montgomery had turned the tide at El Alamein, while in the Atlantic the British and US Navies, armed with three new weapons – radar, more powerful depth charges and the Enigma code – had managed to clear the Atlantic of the U-boat menace. Under 'Bomber' Harris the RAF was starting to have an impact on both Germany's industrial might and the morale of the fatherland. In September the Italians surrendered as British and American troops swept into Europe's underbelly. The fear of an invasion of Britain was now gone as the German war machine became bogged down on the Eastern Front, having made the strategic mistake of attacking Mother Russia.

As the 1943 Year Book reported, a message of goodwill had been sent by the NFU to Soviet farmers on behalf of the farmers of England and Wales. The objections made ten years before to imported Russian wheat produced by collectivised slave labour were long forgotten.

Fittingly, the NFU president in 1943 was an old soldier, Captain Jack Templeton, who had the unusual distinction of being a Welsh Scot. Born in Ayrshire in 1875, he moved to Maesllech Farm, Radyr, near Cardiff, in 1909 with his parents. In 1914 he had joined the Royal Army Service Corps in charge of horse transport. At that time his farm business of direct retailing milk to the householders of nearby Cardiff was abandoned, but the dairy herd was expanded.

The changes witnessed on Maesllech Farm during the Second World War were a fair reflection of what was happening nationally. In general terms, government policy swung production away from livestock towards cropping, whereas milk production remained largely unchanged. By 1939 Templeton's 25 dairy cows were producing 1,500 gallons of accredited milk a year. This level of production was maintained during the war years. Nationally, British farms were producing 1,771,000 gallons of milk in 1939 and 1,789,000 in 1945. The arable proportion of Maesllech Farm was increased to 200 acres, with 100 acres of grassland ploughed out. Increased amounts of wheat, oats, barley, peas, potatoes and roots were grown. Nationally, the production of these crops doubled as part of the plough campaign, and the arable area increased from 13 million acres to 19 million acres.

Due to the reduction in grass, the number of Templeton's ewes was reduced from 125 to 50. Again, this was in keeping with national trends, with UK sheep numbers falling from 25 million to 20 million. Similarly, the modern, Danish-style pig-rearing units on Maesllech Farm lay empty during the war. Templeton had taken the decision that, with feedstuffs being rationed, it was best to downscale his pig enterprise. During the war the British pig-herd shrank from 4.5 million to just over two million.

Outside his NFU duties Templeton was a member of the Glamorgan WAEC and sat on the Agricultural Advisory Board of the University of Wales. At such times as he was called away by the NFU the farm was run by his wife.

He had joined the NFU in 1918 and had been Glamorgan county delegate since 1932, serving on the cereals, milk, commercial, labour, transport and organisation committees. He had been chairman of the Welsh Committee. He was a bluff, rubicund man with a homespun vision for an expanded agriculture and an improved countryside. At over 70 he was the oldest man to take on the presidency of the NFU.

In 1943 Minister Hudson called for the ploughing of another million acres, which was duly delivered by the farming community. The question remained as to postwar policy. Reporting in 1943, the Scott Committee on Land Utilisation in Rural Areas gave a striking vindication of the need to maintain a prosperous and thriving agriculture. In an agricultural debate in the Lords, Lord De La Warr observed that the British farmer and his workers were producing 2.5 times more per head than their German counterparts. Britain was on track to produce half the food provided by imports in 1939, and home production of food had risen by 70 per cent. In the same debate government minister Lord Woolton observed:

We have been learning that you cannot build an efficient industry on starvation prices and we have also learned that modern farming demands capital, enough financial security to take some risks, to make progress, to try out new methods, and to be able to face whatever the weather of the season is going to produce, without undue fears.

Such words would be equally relevant for any year of the NFUs 100-year history.

In contrast, towards the end of 1943, Minister Hudson announced in the Commons: 'There is to be no expansion of the home food production campaign beyond the limits of the present global total of our expenditure on home grown food'. In 1943 the government increased its spending on agriculture by only 3 per cent, from £21.6 million to £22.3 million. This immediately rang alarm bells with President Templeton and his NFU advisers, as it seemed to repudiate the pledge of 1940 that prices would be adjusted upwards if production costs continued to rise. These costs indeed were rising. In particular, the 1943 Agricultural Wages Board settlement had given farmworkers a 20 per cent increase, taking the weekly wage up to 60s. This amounted to an increase in the farm wage bill of £15 million.

There ensued a major public debate about the justice of the government's decision. For the first time ever the NFU were invited by the BBC to explain their position. The union also appealed to MPs on the grounds that the pledge of 1940 was not being kept. Their complaints were met with considerable sympathy. Even the Manchester Chamber of Commerce, which could trace their opposition to farm support payments and import control back to the Corn Laws, published a resolution calling on the government to draw up a comprehensive policy of agricultural support.

After 1943 the bald statistics were evidence that the government were now persuaded to stand by the pledge of 1940. In 1944 the exchequer spend had increased to £36 million. Most of the increase came in the form of new acreage payments for potatoes (£10 per acre) and wheat (£4 per acre).

When we consider that support payments for farm produce had risen from £9 million in 1938 to £28 million in 1944 (not including £7 million on ploughing grants and lime purchase), we can see how far government policy had developed during the war. Furthermore, these figures do not completely consider the market improvements farmers enjoyed during the war years. Cereal, potato and sugar beet prices had appreciated some 70–80 per cent and livestock some 40 per cent. Generally, agricultural prices rose by three times as much as the official cost of living but, as much of this was financed by government spending, there was not a pro rata increase in the price of food.

For the NFU these statistics represented no less than a victory for their lobbying. The 1944 Year Book emphasised that a new era seemed to be on the horizon:

In February of each year there will be a review by the Agricultural Departments in consultation with the NFU of the general financial position of agriculture in the United Kingdom, based on the above economic and financial data and any other relevant statistical material which is available.

The NFU was now thrust into an important new role in negotiating the fortunes for agriculture. Postwar farm policy was far from decided, but the position of the NFU in that debate was assured. Meanwhile the union needed to put its own house in order. The sad fact was that, as an organisation, it was not ready for this new pivotal role. In terms of structure and finance it was still hopelessly rooted in the past. It urgently needed to be radically modernised if it was to prepare the new demands of the postwar world. This job fell to Captain Jack Templeton's successor who, at 39, was some 30 years his junior. His name was Joshua Kenneth Knowles, known as Ken to those around him.

CHAPTER 24

J.K. Knowles, 1944

Ken Knowles took on the presidency of the NFU under a bit of a cloud. For a rather dull man whose only passion was fishing, this seems somehow appropriate. Jack Templeton's intended successor was his initial vice-president, Captain George Deakin. Deakin, a dairy farmer from Droitwich, was much admired in union circles and it was widely thought he would be just the man to lead the NFU towards postwar reconstruction. It was not to be. In late 1943 he was tragically killed in a car accident. Many in the NFU were in a state of shock at the loss.

Some felt now was the time to change the old system of appointing a union leader from within its farmer ranks. In early 1944 the Rutland County and Stamford branch requested Council should consider that some:

... really outstanding personality either from within or outside the industry should be invited to accept the Presidency of the Union to formulate and direct high policy, negotiate effectively with Ministers and others and take a leading place in the international discussions of the future.

The suggestion was not so much a feeling of no confidence in Knowles personally, but rather a growing belief that in the future the NFU would need to be led by a greater talent than could be found in the union's own ranks. There were doubts as to whether democracy among Union members could throw up the skill-set that was needed. Council rejected Rutland's submission with the observation that it was of the utmost importance that the union should appoint its leader from within.

Many still remained unconvinced, and the issue rumbled on throughout 1944. Several branches continued to suggest that a change in the way the top of the union was appointed was necessary. Others suggested a new position of NFU Director should be created, with a large salary of £30,000 to attract the right man to lead and guide the union. The Director idea would allow a farmer president to remain in place but, obviously, in a more honorary position. Commentators of the time described this plea from some branches in terms of the NFU grass-roots wanting a 'superman' at the helm. Others dismissed the idea asking, 'who wants a Nazi NFU?' Opponents of change suggested the 'superman' proposal was nothing short of wanting to put some sort of Hitleresque dictator in charge. The issue was finally put to bed at the 1945 AGM, when a resolution

Ken Knowles, a quiet man behind a desk, who rang the loudest of changes in the NFU.

from Norfolk proposing the creation of the professional post of 'NFU Director' was defeated. This was not to be the last time the wisdom of the union leader coming from the ranks of the membership was debated. Despite this, right or wrong, the NFU has stayed loyal to the notion of the 'farmer president'.

It was true that Ken Knowles was no large personality, but he was a sound administrator who recognised the NFU was in need of an overhaul. Although the war was not over in 1944, it was clear it was now not a matter of 'if' Germany and Japan would be defeated, but 'when'. In June 1944 the long-awaited D-Day arrived and Allied troops swept across North West Europe. The Nazis' days were numbered, and only the odd doodlebug endangered domestic lives in the British Isles. Although the union had been considering the postwar scenario for farming almost from the moment war broke out, it was largely Knowles who set about laying down a more professional union structure that would equip the NFU for its newly empowered peacetime role.

Ken Knowles was from a small dairy farm on the outskirts of Derby. His farm, Moor Farm, was a mere 150 acres. He had joined the NFU in 1922 because, in his own words, 'it was something one simply had to do'. By 1932 he had been Derbyshire council delegate and believed vehemently that the NFU should back the concept of the marketing boards. He was a quiet man, happiest when behind a desk, but at the same time he was brave enough to challenge the NFU establishment and push it in the direction it needed to go.

By 1942 Knowles had shown his aptitude for administration by chairing the Organisation Committee at Bedford Square. In this role he drew attention to the glaring weakness that, although membership had nearly doubled since 1921, the income sent to headquarters through capitation fees was more or less the same, at £29,000. The result was that staffing and offices at Bedford Square were hopelessly under-funded to cope with the increased demands of the wartime planning of agriculture. Knowles pressed for the raising of subscription rates and establishing a more realistic assessment for county contributions to central funds. Accordingly, Council agreed with his proposal to roughly double subs to 3d. an acre (with a minimum fee of 10s. and a maximum of £25), and county contributions were increased to 30 per cent of their income. This, in turn, increased the budget of headquarters to £45,000 and allowed for more staff to be taken on. These were the first significant increases in subscriptions since the First World War and were well overdue. It also represented a milestone in the route to centralised finance that characterises the NFU today. Despite some grumbling from the smaller members, there was no negative impact on numbers from the hike in subs. By 1944 membership had climbed to over 160,000. In 1944, under Knowles's direction, the sub was raised again to 6d., with a minimum of one guinea. The maximum was abolished. In 1945 membership was at 162,591. By 1946 headquarters income had risen to £127,941 and by 1950 nearly half of subscriptions collected were going to HQ in London.

In 1944 came the merger with the National Growers' Association (NGA). As we noted in Chapter 5, just as did market-gardening president Rowland Robbins, many horticulturalists saw themselves as growers rather than farmers. Although the NFU had always accommodated them, many horticulturalists saw their natural home as the NGA rather than the NFU. The merger of the NGA under the NFU banner was a key moment in NFU history, and from then on its representation of horticultural interests became far more pronounced. The NFU could now boast a plethora of new committees, such as Nurserymen; Horticultural Seeds; Vegetables; Flowers; Bulbs; Fruit; Glasshouse and Central Horticultural. Also in 1944, there were mergers with the Farm Crop Driers' Association, the Seed Growers' Association and the British Poultry Union. Yet more office space around Bedford Square was rented.

Knowles also applied his considerable vision and administrative skills to modernising the branches and their relationship with the NFU Mutual. From its humble beginnings in 1919, the Mutual had blossomed into a major insurance company. By 1940 it had over 400 staff in 12 regional offices, writing a million pounds worth of business to over 100,000 farmer customers. The war brought more business for the Mutual. Despite fierce lobbying from the NFU, the government had refused to extend its war damage compensation schemes to farmers. The Mutual assisted in setting up the Farmers' War Risks Association to provide cover for 12,000 members, mainly in the South East, who were at risk from bombs and falling aircraft. Although farms were never the target of the Luftwaffe, it should be remembered the Heinkels and Junkers had the nasty habit of randomly discharging any unused munitions as they flew back over open countryside to their bases on the Continent. Today many south-eastern farmers can point out the bomb craters on their farms.

In 1919 Colin Campbell had warned Council that the official alliance with just one insurance company would be the making or breaking of the NFU. By 1939, you could argue, the former scenario had triumphed over the latter. However, there were still counties that dealt with other insurers and, more generally, the level of integration between the union and the Mutual was failing to secure the many possible mutual advantages.

Along with its 12 regional offices, the Mutual worked through the thousand or so part-timers who ran the local NFU branches. The running of these branches was best described as 'home-spun' or, more accurately, 'ramshackle'. Many had rough and ready offices, with secretaries who approached union work as enthusiastic amateurs. There was a pervasive penny-pinching attitude to finances which only served to cheapen the NFU's ability properly to serve its members.

Under Knowles's direction, working in conjunction with Mutual managing director Ashley Clayton, the number of branches was halved through amalgamations. These were to be run by 450 full-time group secretaries on nominal union salaries plus the commission from insurance sales in their branch agencies. The NFU thereby gained a more professional branch network, with properly remunerated local officials acting as conduits for NFU business while at the same time selling farm insurance. Many of these new recruits into the NFU staff came from the officer stratum of the Services who were being demobbed post-1945.

Furthermore, the Mutual also agreed to pay a contribution to the counties. County Insurance sub-committees, composed of union and Mutual nominees, reported to the county executives and local Mutual directors.

This greater merging of the NFU structure with the Mutual was not without opposition. Some felt the tail was being allowed to wag the dog in that the Mutual was increasing its influence over the running of the union. Others felt the removal of many of the old branch secretaries was a shoddy way to treat those who had given the NFU good service over the years. Knowles had to spend many months patiently explaining to branches that the union and the Mutual, while separate legal entities, were in fact complementary, and that strong links were beneficial to both. It took some years for all local branches to be grouped under Knowles's reforms, but in general terms the structure he laid down in the final years of the war gave rise to the modern, professional NFU we know today.

By 1945 many realised that the organisational and administrative abilities of Ken Knowles were going to be key to the success of the NFU in its postwar role. To date, the union had lacked the overall business management it would need if it was to marshal and cater for a burgeoning membership fast heading toward 200,000. The NFU was outgrowing its strength. General Secretary Sir Cleveland Fyfe had proven a stalwart in his 25 years' service to the union, but he was primarily a political lobbyist rather than a manager or administrator. At the end of Knowles's presidency in February 1945 it was suggested that Fyfe should relinquish his role as general secretary in favour of Knowles and that a new policy role should be found for Fyfe. Fyfe was not keen and shortly afterwards he departed the NFU. At the age of 40 Knowles then took up the role of general secretary, which he carried on until 1970. Again, Knowles, who had a reputation for not letting the past stand in the way of the future, won the day. Fyfe's stature and reputation in the NFU were immense, but he was toppled by the quiet young moderniser from Derbyshire.

On taking over his new professional role at Bedford Square, Knowles retired from farming and relocated to Berkshire, allowing him to commute into Bedford Square every day. Today his old dairy farm, Moor Farm, now a training ground for Derby County Football Club.

In the decade between his first year as chairman of the Organisation Committee in 1940 to the time he was well ensconced behind his general secretary's desk in 1950, the NFU had been transformed from a largely provincial organisation run by enthusiastic amateurs on bare-bones budgets to an increasingly centralised one run by professionals with a system of finances that properly befitted its stature and its activities. Along the way Knowles undoubtedly ruffled a few feathers, but the increasing income stream from the ever-burgeoning membership was testimony to the validity of what he was doing. Knowles was not alone in pushing through the reforms; tribute should also be paid to men such as Stanley Ratcliffe, NFU treasurer in the 1950s. However, in the annals of the history of the NFU, Ken Knowles should be remembered as the principal architect of the postwar NFU.

And so we come to 1945, a date in British history that marks the closing of one chapter and the beginning of another. For the NFU, 1945 was the start of the reign of one of the largest personalities ever to be its president.

THE WIND FROM THE WEST

"And now get down to it!"

State intervention and the Marshall Plan were the order of the day in the 1940s, as Europe worried about its ability to feed itself.

✤ CHAPTER 25 ✤

Sir James Turner, Baron Netherthorpe, 1945–60

Jim Turner was president of the NFU from 1945 to 1960. Throughout his presidency he, the NFU and British agriculture grew in stature to unprecedented levels. We say this, partly tongue in cheek, in reference to the fact Turner weighed ten stone heavier at the end of his presidency than at the beginning, but mainly, and more respectfully, it is recognition of the his immense achievement as NFU president.

Like the NFU itself, he was born in 1908 at West Bank Farm, South Anston. South Anston was a small village a few miles east of the industrial city of Sheffield. This was South Yorkshire heartland, dedicated to business and manufacturing, alive with factories, quarries and farms. Turner could recollect the pinkish smog that at times enveloped Sheffield and its environs when he was a boy. As a family the Turners were quarrymen rather than farmers. The quarry they operated at South Anston was working a seam of magnesium limestone. The canal system of South Yorkshire allowed its stone to be ferried far and wide.

As a building material, magnesium limestone is most famous as the stone that gives the Houses of Parliament their golden hue. When the Luftwaffe laid waste to the House of Commons in 1941, several thousand tons of South Anston stone were needed for the repairs.

Quarrying at South Anston was closely allied to farming. Magnesium limestone was sometimes crushed to make a soil-improving liming material, and it was even sold as cattle licks. Furthermore, transporting heavy stone required large teams of horses that needed feeding. Consequently, it made sense for the Turner family to run a 440-acre farm alongside their quarrying business. Fed up with being overcharged for oats and hay to fuel his horses, Turner's grandfather had bought the farm in the 1840s, an early example of what is now called 'vertical integration'.

James was the fifth child of seven in a family typically Nonconformist, in that they were Methodist by creed and Liberal in politics. The Turners were

A trim and young Jim Turner sets off to visit America and Australasia. He brought back the vision of the International Federation of Agricultural Producers (IFAP).

113

imbued with the Protestant work ethic and with South Yorkshire pride in achievement. There was also a keen sense of public service. James's grandfather was Mayor of Sheffield in 1936, which half of Sheffield proudly remembers as the year Sheffield Wednesday won the cup.

James went to Knaresborough Grammar School and then to Leeds University, where he was one of a small group to graduate with a BSc in Agricultural Science. After graduating in 1929 he returned to the farm. He used his education to good effect by lecturing in agriculture to farmers taking evening classes. For him this was a good introduction to the farming communities of South Yorkshire and North Nottinghamshire. His father encouraged him to get involved with the NFU in the hope it would be a good way to absorb his son's youthful energies.

Turner was a large, powerful man, six feet tall and broad in the chest. For a party piece he would put two 16-stone sacks on his shoulders and climb a ladder. In the 1920s young James had achieved fame on the back page of the *Daily Mail* when he boxed in the final of the inter-university Christie Shield for Leeds. His father was not impressed and penned the following short missive to his son:

Dear James. Your Mother and I are deeply distressed to learn from this morning's Daily Mail *that you have been indulging in the degrading pursuit of boxing. Please desist forthwith.*

Turner's main passion was rugby, which he played for both Yorkshire and Derbyshire, notorious for his fierce scrummaging in the front row. He was surprisingly nimble for a large man and had small, size six, feet. In his 40s, as his weight approached 26 stone, he joked he could put down more pounds per square inch than the average elephant. In later life he kept up his passion for sport and was president of the RFU, a vice-president of the FA and a member of the MCC. He also enjoyed a game of golf, but noted that, given the size of his girth: 'If I can see the ball then it is too far away to hit and if I am close enough to hit it then I can't see it.'

In the tough years of the 1930s, James's brother ran the quarrying side of the Turner business and he ran the farm. It was light land, mainly sandstone and limestone. Wheat, barley, sugar beet and potatoes were grown in rotation, along with sheep folded onto roots. The small dairy herd was one of the first in the area to be tuberclin tested. Milk was directly retailed, but in 1939, in response to the strictures of war, the dairy was closed down. In his farming Turner's forté was buying and selling store cattle and pigs, which were fattened in strawed yards. In 1934 electricity arrived, as did a Fordson tractor. Tractors were first

Beef and pigs in strawed yards at Turner's farm in South Anston. Buying in and fattening stock was Turner's favourite part of farming.

used in earnest during the Second World War, by which time they were on rubber tyres.

Turner's first recollection of the NFU was in 1928, when he went to a large NFU rally organised by Harry German in Newstead Park. By 1932 he was acting as secretary for the Worksop branch, where he also ran the Mutual agency. This fact is a reminder that, before the reforms of the 1940s, NFU branches were often run more by amateurish enthusiasm than by professional administration. He became Nottinghamshire chairman in 1939 at the age of 30 and Council delegate in 1942. In Council he found a mentor in Harry German. Both were known for their no-nonsense eloquence and their love of sport. Furthermore, both hailed from that distinct part of England where the East Midlands meets the North. On Council Turner quickly gained a reputation for forceful advocacy of new ideas and a sound understanding of key issues. In 1944 he became Knowles's vice-president. As with Knowles, his elevation was rather opportunistic, owing to the untimely death of George Deakin. Compared to others he was young and inexperienced with a rather thin NFU record, but this was a time when new men and new ideas were firmly in the ascendancy. In 1945, at the age of 36, he was the youngest man ever to take on the presidency.

With Knowles as his general secretary, Turner was part of a young team at the top of the NFU, and both of them displayed the impetuous tendency of youth to break with tradition and sweep away established protocol when it stands in the way of progress. We should remember that in 1945 change was the order of the day, not only in the NFU but in farming and in society generally. There was a notable desire amidst the postwar generation to put the war years behind them and to look forward rather than back. This sentiment was most forcefully expressed by the 1945 election, in which victorious war leader Churchill was rejected and the reforming socialists of the Atlee Government were brought to power.

Although Turner was strong willed and headstrong, he was too clever to appear arrogant or dismissive. People always felt listened to when talking to Jim Turner, and he was careful to display a common touch. Those around him noted how he was careful to memorise people's names and their details. His nephew, David Naish, recollects how, if he walked into a room of farmers he barely knew, Turner would quickly take aside someone with local knowledge and find out who was who, where they came from and what form their farming took. Later in the proceedings he would then be sure to chat with everyone in turn on first-name terms, as if they were old acquaintances. Today we call this 'having people skills', and Turner had them in abundance.

Turner was an eloquent speaker, whose high-pitched, nasal Yorkshire brogue made him sound very similar to another famous Yorkshireman of the postwar era – Harold Wilson. Turner was not famed for his directness, and some complained he would use ten words where one would do. Others noted how he could hold an audience while saying very little of substance but could still send them away thinking they had heard something of note.

Similarly, the *Farmers' Weekly* noted how Turner could dominate NFU meetings, including Council and the AGM, and yet appear wholly democratic and accountable in the way he went about things. It was noted that Turner could *single-handedly squash a resolution from the counties*:

... with a charming disregard for common procedure... at general meetings... the President was careful to point out that the resolution being lost did not mean that headquarters would not act upon the spirit which inspired it.

By the same token, it might have been said that, had the resolution been passed, then Turner and Knowles were of the view that it did not follow they would necessarily act upon it.

But he was no bombast. Henry Plumb recollects how Turner encouraged him to pay everyone due regard, no matter how insignificant. One Yorkshire member on Council in the 1950s was a retired railway worker who ran a smallholding. Turner advised Plumb that, contrary to what one's instinct might tell him, he always found that member of Council one of the wisest.

As a negotiator, Turner was the master. John Cherrington, the farmer journalist, noted of Turner: 'I have seen him grasp the essentials of a case in a few minutes and then proceed to batter civil servants with it as though he had been familiar with it for years'.

Somewhat oddly, when the 1945 AGM conferred the presidency upon Turner he was on the high seas. In the winter of 1944 an NFU delegation of Turner, past president Ratcliff and chief economist Brown had been waved off from Bedford Square by President Knowles. For the following six months, while the war in Western Europe came to an end, they travelled extensively in the US, Canada, Australia and New Zealand, discussing international farm policy and trade issues. The idea was to pick up from where Dorman-Smith and his NFU delegation had left off in Sydney in 1938. In addition, there was now a change in perspective, a desire to broaden things out beyond the Commonwealth countries with a view to creating an International Federation of Agricultural Producers (IFAP).

The IFAP was formally founded in London the following year, when 17 nations came under one IFAP banner. Turner was initially elected chairman of the inaugural proceedings and then the first president. The London conference was an unparalleled bringing together of farmer organisations the like of which had not been seen before. The concluding resolution of the conference expressed a broad determination to secure co-operation between farmers in combating world hunger through promoting efficient production and marketing of agricultural commodities while fighting for the well-being of the international farming community. While the resolution was short on detailed policy, there was an expressed resolve for IFAP to work constructively with the newly founded Food and Agriculture Organisation of the United Nations. So the NFU had established itself as a world leader among farmer organisations, and Turner could rightly see himself as an international statesman. The 37-year-old Yorkshire farmer was starting to put his stamp on the world.

He was also putting his stamp on the NFU. In 1946 the question of his length of tenure was brought to the AGM. As we have seen with Dorman-Smith and Peacock, the prospect of a president serving for more than one year was not unknown, but it was the exception to the rule. Since the retirement of Campbell in 1917 the constitution was clear that there should ordinarily be an annual change in the presidency. By way of fundamental reform, Turner proposed to change this by allowing a president to serve indefinitely on condition he secured an 85 per cent majority from Council at the AGM. Under this system, Turner went on to hold the presidency for 15 years and thus is the longest serving president ever to lead the NFU. In one analysis the 85 per cent rule seems fair in that it requires an overwhelming vote of confidence from Council. Others have suggested it was a rather Machiavellian move by a power-hungry leader. By forcing Council to 'back him or sack him' each year, and by forcing any disloyal pretender to beard him in his presidential lair, Turner had seized the initiative which before had been with Council. Under the new system it was the president who decided when he would stand down, which he would do only if he was clearly becoming very unpopular. This led to longer presidencies. Between 1918 and 1945 there were 21 presidents; between 1945 and 2006 there were just ten. At the same time as this reform, Turner added another man to the leadership team by creating a new post, that of deputy president. It was clear the increasing work of the union necessitated another office holder, but again, Turner's determination to hold onto the throne for as long as he wanted it can be detected. When there was just one vice-president then there was always a man in waiting who might plot to secure a change in presidency. With two rival heir apparents beneath him the president shored up his own position. Throughout the 1940s and '50s a number of deputies and vices came and went, unable to budge the mighty Turner from his office.

Another fundamental change was the professionalisation of the presidency, with the granting of an annual salary of £5,000. This was very much in keeping with the spirit of the reforms Ken Knowles was masterminding. The NFU was becoming more professional from top to bottom. Turner also introduced the presidential Bentley, complete with NFU 1 number plate, to chauffer him about. There was little appetite in Council to stand in the way of Turner's demands, but when, in the 1950s, he suggested the union should purchase a presidential house in Hertfordshire – Hadley Hurst House – it proved rather controversial. Turner complained that all he had asked for was 'a little tied cottage' to go with the job. In fact it was a substantial property in extensive gardens designed by Christopher Wren. Turner envisaged that it would be like an NFU Chequers, where he could entertain the great and the good. After some negative comment about the idea in the press, the idea was withdrawn and Turner had to fund the purchase himself. Some wondered how he afforded it. Despite the doubters, it was clear Turner was determined to elevate the nature of the NFU presidency by surrounding it with the trappings of high office. In the 1950s the president was afforded a flat in Park Lane.

Meanwhile, at the outset of his tenure, there was still the question of what direction British farm policy would take in peace-time. The election of August 1945, in which the NFU maintained strict neutrality, returned a Labour Government with a large majority under the premiership of Clement Atlee. It was an administration fired with new, radical ideas on expanding the role of the state, but its programme was circumscribed by the dire economic conditions of an exhausted postwar Britain. The balance of payments in particular exercised the men around the Cabinet table. Dollar imports especially needed to be discouraged. The US had announced the end of the Lend-Lease agreement under which Britain received food imports from the US without down-payments in cash.

Rationing, particularly of food, was not to end with the armistice, indeed it was announced it was to be prolonged indefinitely. Further afield, the continent of Europe was hungry. Between 10,000 and 20,000 had died of malnutrition in the Netherlands in 1944. The end of the war was not marked by a return to plentiful food supplies. In the winter of 1947 German food rations were down to 1,400 calories a day and in Russia things were much worse. Over a million succumbed to famine in the USSR when a drought further weakened the war-ravaged country. At home in Britain the harvest of 1946 had been a bad one and the winter of 1947 was the severest for 80 years. There was no question of famine in Britain, but the spectre of food shortage was a real one. Turner was to be found in the newspaper headlines announcing: 'The era of cheap food is over'. A rather trivial but interesting footnote to all this was that in 1947 it was not possible to hold the annual NFU dinner, as dinners where more than 100 were gathered were forbidden.

At a reduced annual dinner in 1946 the guest of honour was Prime Minister Atlee, who reiterated the government's desire to continue 'close consultation between the Government and the industry'.

In 1945 the NFU published a 70-page booklet called *The Basis of Economic Security*, complete with tractor-drawn plough on the cover. It advocated a policy of stabilised and guaranteed markets through fixing prices in relation to costs. Furthermore, it made the case for rural regeneration through better housing and improved infrastructure of roads, mains water and electricity. Under Turner's wise guidance the document played down any talk of a national debt owed to farmers because of their wartime endeavors. Instead, it stressed the duty owed by the NFU and its members to the welfare of the country. In a remarkable spontaneous demonstration of unity, each of the 59 county branches sent messages to the president pledging their full support for the document. It proved to be highly influential at a time when the new Labour government was considering the basis of its postwar agricultural policy.

In the immediate postwar years the government kept most of agriculture on its wartime footing, but in 1947 the Agriculture Act gave the NFU the reassurance in statute it desperately sought. The Act stated the intention:

To promote a stable and efficient industry capable of producing such part of the nation's food as in the national interest it is desirable to produce in the United Kingdom and to produce it at minimum prices consistent with proper remuneration and living conditions for farmers and workers in agriculture and with an adequate return on capital invested .

The 1947 Act is the single most important piece of legislation in the long history of the NFU. It wiped away the 14 previous enactments that had resulted from the the hotch-potch approach by government to agricultural policy over the previous decade.

Under its provision the state retained its monopoly position as purchaser and allocator of food. Price levels were guaranteed for named commodities (which initially were cereals, potatoes, sugar beet and fatstock). The first part of the Act formalised the annual review that the NFU and the ministry had undertaken since 1943. The Act made reference to consultation with producers' representatives. It did not mention the NFU by name but, even so, that name was writ large between the lines. For such a key statute to tie in what was a non-governmental organisation was a ground-breaking moment. It was about as far removed as could be imagined from the 'laissez faire' policy the NFU had feuded over with government for much of its history. Small wonder the NFU abandoned its old motto, 'Defence not Defiance' for the grander 'Labore Agricolae Floreat Civitas'.

Part 2 of the Act continued the principle of

"FOR PETE'S SAKE RELAX — YOU'RE WORRYING THE STOCK!"

By the early 1950s the farming year had two key moments – the February price review and the summer harvest. A Farmer & Stockbreeder *cartoon takes a sideways look at how all the farmer could do in February was worry.*

117

wartime state management of farming through coercion and incentive. There was emphasis on state-sponsored encouragement of the individual to improve his farming. The county agricultural committees, with their powers of classification and direction, were retained, and they now worked alongside a new state advisory service, NAAS. This dovetailed with the provision of subsidies for fertilisers, as well as grants for drainage, liming and ploughing. There were also grants for new buildings. The AWB was kept in place under a 1948 statute but was given a more centralised role. The NFU retained its representation on the employers' side of the board.

The wartime powers of confiscation of privately owned land were not persevered with, but the power of eviction of tenants was retained. The power of direction was wielded with a light touch but, even so, the spectre of 'big brother' supervision remained. For instance, as late as 1952 1,000 supervision notices were issued demanding improved management, and there were 113 dispossessions.

At first glance it does not seem possible that the NFU, built on the shoulders of proud, independent, self-reliant yeoman farmers, should acquiesce to such peacetime interference with the farmer's liberty to farm as he saw fit. But this overlooks two factors. First, the county agricultural committees were dominated by farmers and NFU men rather than by civil servants and bureaucrats. Possibly, there was less of the 'them and us' attitude in the farming community than we have today between farmers and the various inspectorates that appear in farmyards. Second, many in the NFU thought such state interference would have to be accepted to secure the grants, subsidies and price guarantees that the 1947 Act also provided for. Again, one needs to cast one's mind back to the 1920 Agriculture Act, under which the proposed power of county ags was emasculated by the landowning lobby in the House of Lords. Once the 'stick' of state direction was gone it was politically easier also to take away the 'carrot' of state-guaranteed prices.

Nonetheless, the 1947 Act that Turner had so heartily endorsed was a triumph of state corporatism over individualism. At its heart was a notion that farmers should not be left to their own devices. Possibly, one should here think back to the time Turner spent lecturing farmers on agricultural improvement at evening classes in the 1930s. It might be a little strong to suggest the 1947 Act reflects in the NFU leadership a patriarchal attitude to its members, but just as the NFU was becoming a more managed, top-down organisation, then so too was farming not the individualist pursuit it had once been. What Turner's Nonconformist, liberal ancestors would have made of it all makes for an interesting thought. But one thing was for sure, few in the farming community saw the 1947 Act as an unacceptable threat to their liberty or entrepreneurship. If it saved them from the sorts of freedoms the inter-war years had afforded them, then it was an easy sacrifice to make, and if at the head of the NFU there was a youthful, benevolent despot, then it was the sort of vigourous leadership they were comfortable with. Turner's strong-willed, dictatorial style did not seem to put many off joining the NFU, and its numbers continued to climb. Although in the *Farmers Weekly* you could find letters complaining along the lines of 'just because Jim Turner says something, it doesn't mean to say it is right', this was not the majority view.

And so in 1948 began the first official February price annual review. It was an event that was to dominate the calendar of the NFU for the next 25 years, fading away only in the 1970s, when British farming fell under the auspices of Brussels rather than Whitehall. The new Minister of Agriculture in the Atlee government was Tom Williams, the son of a miner. One undoubted stroke of luck for the NFU was that he hailed from the same stamping-ground as President Turner – South Yorkshire. Thus both men shared an accent, a dry humour and a general Yorkshire sensibility. They were both tough bargainers, but there was a genuine warmth between the two men. Their rapport added to the partnership between union and government. There was an shared determination that 1921 would not be repeated and that British agriculture should expand its output with the help of state support.

Just as with the meeting between Hudson and the wartime NFU leaders, the February price review was officially about 'consultation' but in many ways was more akin to 'negotiation', with all the cards on the table. The 'cards' took the form of financial accounts relating to all types and sizes of farm. It was here that the Farm Accounts Scheme inaugurated by NFU Chief Economist Geoffrey Browne ten years previously proved invaluable to the NFU side of the negotiating table. Browne's work had grown to a comprehensive study of 4,000 farms.

There is an anecdote that gives an insight into Turner's approach to these high-level negotiations. When he first found himself in the Treasury, the Chancellor of the Exchequer, Stafford Cripps, asked Turner what he thought a reasonable budget would be for the first settlement. Turner pulled from his pocket a Player's No 3 cigarette packet on which he saw he had scribbled '£78 million'. Rounding it up, he gravely proposed that, given the intense research work he and his economic department had undertaken, then £80 million would be his considered target figure. Cripps duly agreed. The fact that a beef farmer in Northumberland might thereby have received another £1 a head for his steers and a Norfolk farmer another 5s. for a ton of wheat is an intriguing thought. It was always said that Turner preferred Player's No 3 because of the expanse of

The heavyweight 1948 NFU price review negotiating team limber up outside Bedford Square.

empty white space on the packets, on which he could scribble notes and reminders.

In 1947 the agreed target for expansion for British agriculture was an increase of 20 per cent over five years. The key driver in this was a 25 per cent increase in the price of wheat to encourage an extra half a million acres and an increase in the ploughing-up grant to £4 an acre. Linseed was given a price guarantee of £55 a ton in a bid to increase the acreage from 30,000 to 400,000 acres. Steer calves were to receive a grant of £4 a head and free artificial insemination centres were set up. In regard to rural infrastructure, agriculture was to be given the priority in new housing, and there was a substantial increase in the allocation of steel and other raw materials to aid the agricultural engineering industry.

This sense of the partnership between a farmers' union born of right-thinking countrymen in the shires and a socialist government born of the workers' unions in the industrial connurbations showed the NFU could live up to one of its oldest ideals – to lift agriculture out of party politics .

In 1948 the Agricultural Holdings Act provided security of tenure for tenants during their lifetime. Evictions could only take place if notices to quit had good grounds and were approved by the Agricultural Land Tribunal. Poor farming and the need for 'improved estate management', which was a euphemistic phrase for merging small farms, were valid grounds. In 1950 60 per cent of farmland was tenanted and 40 per cent owner occupied, but land was changing hands quite fast again. By 1960 the split was 50:50.

By the time of the 1951 election which saw the end of the Labour government's term of office, the 20 per cent expansion in agricultural output had been exceeded. In recognition of his services to this considerable achievement, Turner was knighted in 1949. At the young age of 41 he had secured a place in the establishment. As ever in farming circles, a facetious telegram from some fellow Yorkshire NFU men helped keep his feet on the ground. It read: 'Well done lad, but if t'king knew thee as we know thee, he wouldn't tap thee on t'shoulder, he'd knock thee head off.'

As the NFU entered the 1950s membership hit the 200,000 mark. In 1953 it peaked at 210,000. The NFU thus claimed to represent over 90 per cent of commercial farmers, of which it was estimated there were 220,000 across England and Wales. Some claimed the figure was nearer 250,000, but here we are back to the old chestnut of what constitutes a farmer. As ever, it is impossible to devise a rule of thumb that defines where commercial farming starts and hobby farming stops. It is even doubtful whether such terms as 'commercial farming' and 'hobby farming' stand up to any sensible analysis. There is also the fact that the usual pattern for the UK is for 25 per cent of the farmers to farm 75 per cent of the land. It was true that the NFU was probably weakest at recruiting at the smaller end of the spectrum when it came to membership. There were small farmer organisations to act as rivals in this regard. Even so, by the mid-1950s, in terms of numbers, the NFU was dominant and all-conquering. It was simply the only player when it came to farmer representation in England and Wales. As has been noted before, farmers are an eclectic bunch, and for any organisation to recruit 80–90 per cent of them is quite remarkable.

It was decided in 1950 to raise subscriptions to a basic figure of £1.1s. plus 6d. an acre. Expenditure at headquarters was now approaching £200,000 and an additional centralised fund was being accumulated 'in case of emergencies'. Since 1945 the number of committees had increased to 30 and many more staff had been taken on. Throughout Turner's reign the NFU built up in its staff a high-powered secretariat of administrators, economists and technical specialists who were able to match the men at the ministry – some were deliberately recruited from ministry ranks. The union's strict apolitical policy was reflected in the way it recruited staff. Whereas abroad some farmer unions preferred their staff to be card-carrying members of certain political parties, the NFU wisely showed no such political conformity.

To accommodate the burgeoning NFU staff more office space was rented out in and around Bedford Square, but things were becoming notably congested and fragmented. Knowles and Treasurer Ratcliff started to look for an alternative site to house a new HQ. Turner's only instructions were that it should be close to a tube station with a direct link to King's Cross. In 1950 a building site in Knightsbridge, close to Hyde Park Corner, was purchased for £5,000 and architects were commissioned to design a grand

The new edifice of the NFU emerges from a Knightsbridge bomb site. Though architecture critic Pevsner disliked its line and its false pretensions, nonetheless it was an impressive statement on the London skyline, befitting its representation of Britain's foremost industry.

building. Before the war the site had accommodated the Alexandra Hotel, which was a favourite with countrymen, but during the blitz it had suffered extensive bomb damage. Building was begun in 1954. When we consider that 50 years later this site was valued at well over £50 million, we appreciate that this was one of the shrewdest purchases the NFU ever made. Out in the provinces the county branches were also in the business of purchasing and establishing new town premises to provide NFU and NFU Mutual offices. Not only were such sites important to the effective running of the NFU, they also proved the wisest of investment decisions for the next generation. The post-war property portfolio has proven a very rich legacy.

The 1951 general election had returned a Conservative administration which, when it came to farm policy and the expansion of agricultural output, dropped a gear or two while maintaining direction. Food rationing was phased out over time as the government withdrew from the role of purchaser and provider. The new minister, Thomas Dugdale, was uneasy with some of the interventionist spirit of the 1947 Act and repealed Part 2 of the Act. It was a move the NFU opposed, again fearful that it would lead to the dismantling of the remaining support mechanisms. The powers and activities of the county ags were circumscribed, but guaranteed prices were maintained through a system of deficiency payments not unlike some of the pre-war measures. Guarantees were given for 11 main products: cattle, sheep, milk, eggs, barley, wheat, oats, rye, potatoes, sugar beet and wool. Horticulture took some protec-

tion from a variety of trade measures that limited imports. Generally, the Tory administration was keen to place less emphasis on market intervention and more on improvement grants such as those for drainage, fertilisers and new buildings.

With the encouragement of the NFU, the MMB (under the chairmanship of Tom Peacock) and the PMB were put back on a pre-war footing and additional boards were created, namely for Wool and Tomatoes & Cucumbers. An Egg Marketing Board eventually emerged in 1957.

In keeping with his enthusiasm for corporate management, Turner advocated the extension of the marketing board concept to cover areas such as seeds, top fruit, cereals and fatstock. The Conservative government was indifferent to many of the proposals and nervous of public criticism over too much control of food being placed in the hands of producers. The NFU grew tired of the shilly-shallying and, when meat rationing was ended in 1954, there was a real fear that without some sort of action the market for fatstock could descend into chaos. No doubt some could remember only too well what had happened to farm gate prices in the early 1920s, when the food controller had suddenly shed his powers. The union was also aware that meat wholesaling had fallen under the domination of large commercial concerns who had market power enough to drive down prices. The butchers had vigorously opposed NFU proposals to MAFF in 1953 to institute a public fatstock marketing agency.

In the absence of government action, the union solution was to set up the Fatstock Marketing

Corporation. This was done with great urgency, with Turner and Knowles acting both as parents and as emergency midwives. In a matter of weeks during the spring of 1954 a new trading organisation was set up. The charisma of Turner and the respect of the NFU meant it easily found the necessary finance in the City of London. Despite its lack of trading record and despite no formal backing from any producers, by the summer of 1954 it was doing business in excess of £1 million a week. With start-up capital of just £10,000, the co-operative handled fatstock worth £100 million in its first year of trading. One attraction for the farmer was that the FMC bought on a dead-weight basis. The stabilisation of meat prices and fat-stock marketing in the 1950s and 1960s owes much to the initiative of Turner in the spring of 1954. The

The NFU inner cabinet in 1957, including Deputy President Woolley (second left), *President Turner* (centre), *Vice-president Williams* (third from right) *and General Secretary Knowles* (far right).

FMC remained a considerable force for 30 years. In the early 1970s the FMC handled half the bacon pigs, a quarter of the porkers and about 12–15 per cent of the cattle and sheep slaughtered in the UK.

Meanwhile, the February price reviews continued apace. Vast amounts of time and resources at HQ were devoted to them. An economics department of 16 did little else but compile evidence on the financial performance of the various sectors of agriculture. From November to February economists from the NFU and MAFF would meet to discuss the state of the industry, sifting through a mass of information in order to achieve an agreed understanding. In February the more senior staff would be brought in to settle any remaining disagreements. When this was done the NFU negotiating team would be assembled to discuss the way forward for the next year. Increased costs, it would be argued, must be met with increased prices. Of major note here was the increase in agricultural wages as overseen by the AWB. Wages rose significantly after the war and doubled between 1950 and 1960 from £5 a week to £10. The final part of the price review was probably the most complex, that being the question of increasing agricultural productivity through increasing prices in real terms and providing improvement grants.

By the mid-1950s the atmosphere of the meetings was becoming more combative. In 1954 a new minister, Heathcoat Amery, was given responsibility for both farming and food, as the two ministries were merged into one – MAFF. With a broader remit and as the man who finally wiped away rationing, Heathcoat Amery was going to need the full force of the Turner lobbying machine to keep the expansionist policy on track. The world was no longer

A regular at the county show – the NFU tent – this time at the Bedford Show in the mid-1950s.

short of food and, indeed, surpluses were starting to appear again. The harvests of 1953 and 54 were good ones and the governments of the major exporting nations were reintroducing export subsidies to move their surpluses. Domestic output was also buoyant to the point that milk, pig meat and egg production was exceeding national needs. World market prices were falling and the gap between them and the agreed target prices was widening. With no import controls to back it up, the deficiency price system was becoming increasingly expensive. Total exchequer expenditure on agriculture rose from £200 million in 1953 to just under £300 million in 1957. The Treasury grew increasingly nervous of the unpredictable and open-ended nature of price support, especially in the face of falling world commodity prices. The response of government in 1954 and 1955 was to cut guaranteed prices in relation to milk and pig meat. Not surprisingly, the reaction from the branches and counties was one of uproar. In particular it was seen as an attack on the smaller farmer, who often relied on pigs and dairy to keep in business.

Turner led from the front foot and was not in the mood to acquiesce to any move to dismantle what he had achieved in the previous decade. The 1956 price review was the first where NFU and government were unable to agree. The final settlement was an imposed one rather than an agreed one. After a brief stand-off, differences between union and government were settled with the 1957 Agriculture Act. Under the Act it was guaranteed that commodity price guarantees would be not less than 96 per cent of that fixed the previous year and that livestock reduction would not exceed nine per cent in a three-year period. Furthermore, the 1957 Act brought in a scheme of capital grants for improvements, with a cost of £50 million spread over ten years.

The 1957 Act was a supreme example of effective NFU lobbying. It was a time when there could have been a significant steer back to the historic policy of sourcing cheap food abroad while home agriculture was left to fail. There were many ready to advise government that the idea of producing goods at home at a cost greater than that at which they could be sourced from abroad was not sound economics. The NFU had to be at its most persuasive in counter-arguing that the subsidy system maintained home production and thus greatly improved Britain's balance of payments.

In electoral terms, the farming vote was almost an irrelevance – particularly to a Tory administration with no significant Liberal or Labour opposition in their rural heartland to threaten their electoral margins. By the 1950s the Liberal Party was a politically spent force, returning only six MPs and securing less than three per cent of the vote. So the political influence of the farming voice was more than ever dependent on the NFU. To secure the promises of the 1956 Act was a triumph for the

Turner team and this time, unlike in 1921, they were promises the government felt obliged to keep. With a pressure group as heavyweight as the NFU on their case it would have been politically dangerous to repeat Lloyd George's act of 'great betrayal'.

In 1955 Churchill had resigned as Prime Minister, giving way to Anthony Eden, who went on to win the general election in the June of that year with an increased majority. The exit of Churchill from British political life is a contrived opportunity for us to make some mention of the curious way the career of the man who is recognised as 'the greatest Briton' is intertwined with the history of the NFU.

In 1906, as a young, aspiring politician cutting his teeth in the House of Commons, Churchill had crossed the floor from the Conservative to the Liberal benches over the issue of tariff reform. At that time Churchill was a great advocate of free trade which, as we have seen, was a policy with which the NFU also wrestled. In 1928, as Chancellor of the Exchequer, it was he who announced the derating of agricultural land. In 1940, as Prime Minister, it was he who sacked Dorman-Smith as Minister of Agriculture but maintained the 'plough-up' campaign. Whether we would have had a 1947 Agriculture Act if Churchill had won the 1945 election is an interesting point of debate. Given his intense dislike of state corporatism, it could be argued that the fate of British agriculture and the NFU could have been very different if it had been Churchill who had led the postwar administration. As it was, in 1951, under his government, the expansionist policy was tweaked but still maintained.

What is more, Churchill was not only a politician, author and statesman, he was also a farmer and an NFU member to boot. His farming career started in 1924, when he bought the house he lived in until his death in 1965 – Chartwell, in Kent. With the large house came 700 acres of farmland and woodland. From the word go Churchill took an interest in the farm and, when at home, would walk around the farm before breakfast and cast a knowledgeable eye over what he saw.

His NFU membership form (on which Churchill describes himself as a farmer) discloses about 350 acres comprising 107 acres of cereals, 2.25 acres of fruit, 128 head of cattle, 13 pigs and 300 poultry. Chartwell did not escape the tough financial climate of the 1920s and 1930s. Churchill's correspondence shows a letter in 1929 from his accountants concerning his farming losses of £1,788 in the four years ending Michaelmas 1929.

Churchill had a particular interest in cows. During the Second World War he made sure that a herd of English White park cattle was sent to the US to ensure the breed would survive if the worst happened as a result of the hostilities. At Chartwell there was a dairy herd of 50 Guernseys. One fine cow, a present from the grateful people of liberated

Churchill at Chartwell watching a Ferguson tractor demonstrate its three-point versatility with plough. Churchill's successor as Prime Minister, Anthony Eden, and his son-in-law and Minister of Agriculture, Christopher Soames, look on.

Guernsey in 1946, won many prizes at various shows, as did the Chartwell herd of pigs. Churchill's love of pigs is reflected in his immortal and oft quoted line: 'I like pigs. Dogs look up to us. Cats look down on us. Pigs treat us as equals.'

Churchill was guest of honour at the 1953 NFU annual dinner, where he uttered the memorable line: 'Thirty million people living on an island where we produce enough food for 15 million is a spectacle of majesty and insecurity this country can ill afford.' He also quipped, as he peered over his half-moon spectacles at the ranks of farmers in their dinner jackets: 'I see you are in your normal working clothes.' A recording of Churchill's after-dinner address was made available to members as a gramophone record.

On 18 October 1956 the NFU top table had another important guest in their midst. Her Majesty Queen Elizabeth, the Queen Mother, opened the new Knightsbridge headquarters on a bright and cloudless autumn day.

As she unveiled the commemorative plaque in the Council chamber she noted in her speech:

Perhaps it is significant – and a good augury for the future – that this new home of Britain's largest industry

should stand here – in the heart of London – constant reminder to townspeople that their daily bread depends on faithful work done in the fields.

It was a landmark day for the NFU. Bedford Square had been the London home of the NFU for 37 years but was no longer fit for purpose. By contrast, Knightsbridge sat as a statement of power overlooking Hyde Park Corner. With its five floors, its large, spacious rooms and brick-built edifice, the NFU now had a headquarters befitting its national role. There was proper office space to accommodate 150 staff and meeting-rooms where farmer delegates from across England and Wales could gather to discuss the increasing number of issues that confronted the farming industry. The building's pseudo-Georgian style had its critics, but perhaps it is well that it avoided the concrete cubism of the post-war modernist school that was all the rage in the 1950s. The president's office sat on the fifth floor at the right-hand corner. Elsewhere the rooms were dingy and utilitarian. Nowhere escaped the roar of the traffic outside

Meanwhile Knowles's centralisation strategy proceeded apace. In 1955 subscription levels were raised yet again and another method of assessment was introduced aimed at equalising services offered by county branches and relating them to each county's ability to pay. By the mid-1950s, it seems, membership growth (which had doubled in the previous decade) started to plateau. It was saturation point rather than a failure in recruitment. Income continued to rise, however, and by 1958 a third of a million pounds was rolling into the Knightsbridge HQ. Over a third of this was spent on staff salaries.

In 1955 there was a minor blow to this dominance. The Farmers' Union of Wales was founded. As we have seen, the Welsh were willing from the outset to form a national union with the English. The acknowledged differences between the two countries were reflected in the way the NFU collected subs, and there was special provision for Wales in the form of the Welsh Committee at HQ. Suggestions of a separate organisation for Welsh farmers had been mooted in the 1930s, but Welsh presidents such as Tom Williams and Mervyn Davies had done their best to quash such a breakaway. In the 1940s the small Welsh branch structure saw the greatest number of changes under Ken Knowles's determination to merge small branches together into more workable groups. By the mid-1950s the scaling back of the support system had hit small farmers the hardest. In 1955 disaffection, especially in the north and the west of the principality, grew. President Turner was invited by Carmarthenshire branch to discuss the increasing plight of the small man. We do not know why, but Turner didn't go. It proved a flashpoint for some of the Welsh and sparked the formation of the breakaway FUW. From that point on the NFU had a significant rival in Wales that it had never had in England. Turner can be criticised for not taking Welsh disaffection seriously enough to shore things up and prevent the splintering. On the other hand, it could be pointed out that nationalism was an emerging force across the political scene in postwar Wales, and this made the formation of a separate union for the Welsh farmer inevitable.

The extra space afforded by the new premises in Knightsbridge allowed the NFU the generosity of providing a roof for other national agricultural organisations. One such was ACCA, the Agricultural Central Co-operative Association. Since the war the NFU had had an uneasy relationship with the ACCA to the point where you could say there was a distinct lack of co-operation. Not for the first time the NFU found itself wrestling with the co-operative concept rather than mastering it. Where the union had supreme influence over the marketing boards, it failed to make this influence count in creating overlaps or joined-up thinking between the boards and the farmer-owned co-ops. The formation of the ACCA and its residence in Agriculture House represented a huge step forward in this respect. The union was also instrumental in setting up the Farmers' Central Trading Company Ltd, which sought to supply the farmer co-ops.

Another organisation set up by NFU initiative was the Association of Agriculture (AoA), whose objective was to bridge the gap in understanding between town and country. Its aim was largely educational, focusing on schools and teachers seeking to explain both how the countryside worked and how the townsman's food arrived on his plate. The NFU was careful not to go lumbering into the educational arena demanding classroom time for agriculture. Instead, it supported the AoA at arm's length, while in turn the AoA patiently built up relationships with directors of education and teacher organisations to encourage a better mutual understanding. Interestingly, the AoA managed to attract financial support from leading companies, not all of whom were connected with agriculture. The NFU gave it an annual grant of £2,500 a year.

More generally, the Turner years saw a major expansion in the NFU publicity department. As the HQ funding streams under the Knowles reforms flowed ever stronger, the finance to undertake extensive publicity work was secured. Where Dorman-Smith had complained to the counties in 1938 that there was not the money to fulfil their PR requests, Turner was not so curtailed.

In July 1948 The British Farmer was launched to replace the Record as the NFU's house magazine. The new magazine was produced monthly in a larger format. As paper rationing was relaxed, then more pages were added, and as membership increased then so did circulation. The weekly news-sheets continued to be posted out.

Building on the work started during the war, the press department increased its staff and its activity. In 1948 the Year Book proudly announced that more than a mile of newspaper column inches had emanated from NFU headquarters, which had issued 60 press releases. By 1958 this had grown to over 100. Regional publicity officers were appointed to coordinate local work. One element of their work was to identify articulate farmers, give them some media training and find them public platforms to get the farming message across. By 1951 there were 1,500 members on these speaker panels. Leaflet campaigns were initiated – It Pays to Buy British-grown Produce and Everyman's Guide to Farming Facts were two such examples.

Films such as United Harvest, created in conjunction with companies that produced newsreels, were distributed through cinema chains such as the Odeon. These were the days when the main feature would be preceded by informative short films of a factual nature. It was a good opportunity to get a positive image of farming in front of the burgeoning cinema audience. By the mid-1950s the NFU was in regular contact with the BBC to discuss its coverage of farming issues. Weather forecasts were always a contentious matter with members, and the NFU lobbied at the highest levels for improved forecasts for farmers. The 1950s was the decade which saw the introduction of the television set into the living-rooms of Britain. Turner was the first president to appear on TV. Interviews about the price review and the harvest were regularly broadcast by the mid-1950s. In 1956 Turner was featured in an edition of the 'Highlight' programme, broadcast live from the Royal Show. In 1957 both ITV and the BBC started broadcasting regular weekly features dedicated to farming – and it should be remembered in those days they were factual programmes about improved husbandry. ITV even broadcast one for children.

Just as new technology was fundamentally changing the everyday lives of the British public in the 1950s, so too was life on the farm being revolutionised.

As we have said previously, tractor technology had existed since the beginning of the century, but it wasn't until the Second World War that tractors became commonplace on British farms. The postwar years saw a continuation of this mechanisation renaissance that the war had kick-started. Where over 600,000 working horses could be counted on British farms in 1940, by 1960 the figure had dropped to just 60,000. By the mid-1960s the numbers had fallen to the point it was considered no longer worth-while to record them on ministry censuses. Meanwhile, tractor numbers exploded from 168,000 in 1944 to 512,000 in 1961. Where Fordsons had dominated the wartime ploughing campaign, it was the Little Grey Fergie (the TE20) that was most ubiquitous in the fields of Britain in the 1950s, with 500,000 built between 1946 and 1956. Combine harvesters, practically unknown before the war, numbered 55,000 by 1961. With these new machines came a multitude of new implements and other tractor-driven machinery that improved the efficiency of farm production. To reflect this, the NFU set up a new HQ committee – the Machinery Committee.

Not suprisingly, this increasing mechanisation led to a drop in the workforce. In the period up to 1960 it fell by 30 per cent to 450,600. The casual workforce decreased even further, by half, down to 72,600. This shrinkage was also put down to scarcity of labour and its increasing cost.

One curiosity was the fact that, in amongst the increasing efficiency and productivity in the 1950s, the number of UK farm holdings and the average size of farms did not alter as much as might have been expected. It is a tribute to the Turner years that farmers were kept on the land by being given a bigger share of a bigger cake. This obviously helped the NFU build and maintain membership.

With the machinery came the inevitable increase in field size and the much-discussed removal of hedgerows which, as we remember now with some irony, was encouraged through government grants. One consequence of the demise of the horse was the demise of the oat crop that fed it. The wheat acreage remained suprisingly stable through 1945-60 at two million acres, but the barley acreage nearly doubled, from two to four million acres. Having flatlined for much of the century, yields of cereals began to increase markedly, nearly doubling from just under one ton per acre in 1945 to over 1.5 per acre in 1960. This improvement was driven by new varieties with better resistance to rust and stiffer straw, so that more artificial nitrogen could be applied. Fertiliser use also doubled in the period, helped by grants to assist its purchase. Furthermore, the cereal grower had increasingly access to an armoury of weedkillers, which made him less dependent on rotation as a means of clearing a field of weeds, while insecticides were being more commonly used to protect against pests. Of course there was not the public sensitivity in these times over the use of pesticides by farmers, although it is interesting that we find in the 1950s NFU committees on more than one occasion asking whether more research should be done on the way pesticides interfere with the natural balance. In the 1948 court case of Bower-Roberts *v.* Ministry of Agriculture, the NFU successfully negotiated compensation for farmer Bower-Roberts against a WAEC who had been brought in to spray the char-lock out of a field of clover undersown with oats. The oats had been damaged as the acid mix was too strong and not mixed properly. The Agriculture (Poisonous Substances) Act 1952 was a response to the increasing number of accidents caused by handling pesticides without the proper protective clothing.

For the livestock farmer there was improved grassland management, with new strains of grass and better and increased use of fertiliser. Silage was starting to replace hay as the preferred method of conserving forage. In stock there were improvements in genetics through better breeding and AI. In 1945 there had been 16,000 first inseminations; by 1960 it was two million. There was increased use of antibiotics, vaccines and mineral supplements. Piggeries and broiler houses became ever larger and better designed. The animal welfare agitation over factory farming was still to come. Livestock numbers generally bounced back from their wartime decline. The sheep flock increased from 18 million to 28 million and beef cattle from nine million to 11 million. The pig herd trebled from 1.61 million to over five million, and poultry doubled from 43 million to 90 million.

The size of the milking herd was more stable, hovering around the 2.5 million mark. By 1960 hand milking was becoming rare, with 90 per cent of herds machine milked. Milk yields climbed 20 per cent, with the average cow in 1960 giving 630 gallons a

" She misses that personal touch ! "

The Staffordshire County NFU Journal gives a cow's view of the demise of hand milking.

year. By 1960 most British dairy cows were Friesians. In the 1950s the British public were being encouraged to 'Drinka Pinta Milka Day' by the MMB. Milk and cream consumption continued to rise.

More generally, the farmyard and the farmhouse caught up with town house and industrial factory by accessing electricity, mains water and telephone. In 1942 only 11 per cent of farms had electricity and 32 per cent mains water. By 1960 those farms without all three services were becoming a rarity – estimated at fewer than 10 per cent. The HQ Commercial Committee monitored with some approval the roll-out of the national grid to rural areas. The impact on the daily life of the farm was, of course, electrifying. Now there was a new complaint – the power cut – which brought everything to a standstill, leaving cows un-milked, barns unlit and egg hatcheries chilled.

As hedge removal and power lines started to change the look of the landscape, so too did more comprehensive developments leave their impact on the countryside. The 1950s saw the birth of the 'new towns' as metropolitan authorities sought to relieve the congestion of the cities by building new connurbations around market towns and on green farm land. Under the New Towns Act of 1946 sleepy country towns such as Peterborough and Runcorn were transformed out of all recognition. The most notorious of these, Milton Keynes, swallowed up 7,300 acres of good farmland and 96 farms. Turner's own farmhouse and farmyard in South Anston were lost to urban development in the early 1960s.

The 1950s also saw the birth of the motorway network. The intrusion of the motorcar into the tranquility of the farmed countryside, which President Campbell had complained about 50 years previously, reached yet another, higher, phase. Branches in the affected counties held meetings with planners and engineers to ensure affected farmers were appropri-

ately compensated and proper stock-proof fencing was provided. Britain's first ever motorway service station, at Watford Gap, was opened in 1959 on land once farmed by NFU President Nunneley.

With this rapacious change came a political demand for government to control and manage this pouring of concrete through planning legislation. The Town and Country Planning Acts of 1947 and 1954 were further advances in the power of the state to control what could and could not be done on privately owned land. One major escapee from this net of control was agriculture. There was considerable pressure to tie new farm buildings and other changes to the farmed landscape into this new government straitjacket. The NFU resisted such calls with considerable zeal, and farmers retained a crucial liberty to erect new structures and change land use as their businesses required and as they themselves thought fit. It was a freedom that few other commercial interests retained in this period and represented another key political victory for the NFU. By way of example, the Agriculture Silos (Subsidies) Act of 1956 not only allowed farmers to erect tall 'blots on the landscape', it gave them grants to encourage them to do so. The 15 years after 1945 saw the architecture of the farmyard change out of all recognition. With financial assistance from government, farmers were encouraged to replace the traditional wood and thatch with steel, concrete and asbestos. Corrugation became *de rigueur* in the farmyard. Buildings lost their old-world charm but became infinitely better suited for purpose. Only today, as farmers wonder how to dispose of all those asbestos roofs their fathers put up in the 1950s, do we doubt the wisdom of the farmyard building revolution of the 1950s.

Just as there were calls to control, through planning, the changes on the farm, similarly there were repeated calls at this time by the County Council Association to reintroduce rating on farm buildings. Again, the NFU was victorious in arguing out these proposals as injurious to the government's policy of expanding agricultural output. Yet again, agriculture was a 'special case' that required special consideration. Such truths were not self-evident but needed special lobbying by an especially adept national union that worked out of its London offices on behalf of the farming industry.

Of course, farming did not escape all of the constraints. This was an age of governments keen to legislate. The statutes affecting agriculture came ever thicker and faster. From the Artificial Insemination Act of 1946 to the Abandonment of Animals Act of 1960, farmers increasingly felt the eyes of the state on what they were doing. The Protection of Birds Act 1954 further restricted the freedom of the farmer to take a gun to whatever he considered an injurious pest. The Act allowed the worse pests to remain on the quarry list, but nonetheless it was indicative of the growing political muscle of the conservation

"Isn't it maddening!"

By the late 1950s the intrusion of the motor car on the tranquility of the countryside was almost complete.

lobby. In the same year the Pests Act had attempted to control the increasing rabbit pest but sought to prohibit the deliberate spreading of the myxomatosis virus. The virus had first arrived in Kent in 1953, having been deliberately introduced in France in 1950 by a French doctor who wanted to reduce the rabbit menace on his estate. The disease was first identified in South America in around 1900 and, when introduced to Australia in the 1930s, had stemmed the rabbit plague. In 1953 British opinion was divided as to whether it represented a valuable opportunity to rid farming of the rabbit menace or whether the virus should be contained, the consequences for human and animal health being unknown. What was more, its symptoms were particularly unpleasant for the rabbit and for the more squeamish humans who witnessed them. At first, attempts were made to contain the virus, but eventually it was clear containment was impossible. It was rumoured that farmers were deliberately spreading the virus by pushing diseased animals down uninfected burrows. Some accused the ministry of turning a blind eye to this illegal activity. Between 1953 and 1955 Britain's estimated rabbit population of over 60 million had been reduced by a remarkable 95 per cent. It was an interesting episode that would probably be treated very differently today. As for the rabbits, the population recovered,

though not to the levels of 1952. Today there are an estimated 37 million rabbits in Britain. Suggestions of introducing more virulent strains of myxomatosis have been firmly rebuffed.

As might be expected, new legislation, along with the bringing of town and country ever closer together, kept the NFU legal assistance scheme and its legal department busy. A few cases give a flavour of the times.

In 1954 the union's advisers gave their 10,000th opinion on a case, Hamps *v.* Derby, at the Court of Appeal. Unfortunately, it was not a success. The Court upheld the lower court's award of £200 in damages against farmer Hamps for shooting five racing pigeons feeding on his peas. The judge had ruled the farmer had not established that shooting was necessary or reasonable in the circumstances. The NFU wryly noted in the Year Book that if the farmer had bothered to put one shot over the top of the offenders rather than laying into them with both barrels, then he might have been more successful in engaging the sympathy of the judge. In 1955 the widow of a member who had been killed by a train as he drove his tractor and sprayer across a private crossing between field and farmyard was secured compensation irrespective of the farmer's negligence. In 1948, in Parry *v.* Anglesey Assessment Committee, farmer Parry lost his case when he

127

argued that because his shed was used for sheltering sheep as well as his car, it should be exempt from domestic rates.

The setting up of the National Parks in the 1950s, following the 1949 National Parks and Access to the Countryside Act, placed many farmers in special zones where farming was mildly curtailed and greater public access was allowed. This legislation was a forerunner of many of the schemes whereby access and landscape conservation were given precedence over the farmer's right to maximise production.

But major circumscription was still to come. For most farmers in the 1950s 'efficiency and increased output' were the watchwords of the day. They were the indexes by which agriculture and the NFU judged success. By such criteria it was a decade of success.

And so we come to the end of the 1950s and the conclusion of the presidency of Jim Turner. In 1959 he was awarded an hereditary peerage and became Lord Netherthorpe of Anston. Hereditary peerages were not handed out lightly, and it was a huge honour not just for Turner but for the NFU and agriculture generally. It was at this time he decided to stand down and move on. Although he now had the gravitas of an elder statesman of agriculture and the prestige of an established captain of industry, at 51 he was still relatively young. He went on to become chairman of Fisons, as well as a director of Lloyds Bank and Unigate. He served as a trustee of the Rank Foundation and as chairman of the RASE and became a freeman of the City of London. He did five years on the National Economic Development Council in the early '70s. Whereas in the past most presidents had continued to serve at NFU headquarters, Turner did not, preferring to leave his successors to get on with it. Given the enormity of his presence, this was probably only fair. He died on 8 November 1980 at the age of 72.

His obituary in the *Times* summed him up thus:

... he never forgot that he would be doing no service if he set the sectional interests of agriculture above the overall interests of the nation, or persisted in demands for price levels likely to arouse the opposition of the consumer. Although these considerations were not always apparent to the rank and file of farmers, he did not hesitate to take decisions because they might be unpopular. Confidence in his judgement grew with the years and both the union and agriculture benefited by his statesmanship.

It is true that Turner was not to everyone's taste. John Cherrington found him domineering to the point that he thought it unhealthy for the NFU in that such dominance subdued other talent from emerging. Cherrington had met Turner not only on the rugby pitch but also in NFU Council. In both arenas he found Turner's style not conducive to teamwork or team building. Nor did Cherrington appreciate Turner's tendency to subdue debate within the union. But not everyone agreed with Cherrington. Others enjoyed playing under Turner's captaincy and always gave of their best under the leadership of a man who could engender loyalty and trust.

There is an old saying in agriculture that 'a good farmer leaves his farm in better heart than he found it'. If this is the standard by which we should judge Jim Turner, then he was a truly great man and the NFU's most successful president. In 1960 he left both farming and the NFU in better heart than he found them in nearly every respect. Under his presidency the NFU was not just strengthened, it was transformed. Between them, Turner and Knowles overhauled the organisation to make it stronger and fitter for purpose. By 1960 the NFU was viewed as one of the most powerful lobby groups in the land, and other pressure groups sought to learn from it in order to emulate its success. Some MPs complained the NFU had become too powerful and too close to government. Other lobby groups complained they had been elbowed out of their place at the negotiating table by the ever-waxing presence of the NFU and its irrepressible leader.

Turner had inherited an established pattern of wartime liaison with the Ministry of Agriculture and turned it into something approaching a partnership. At times in annual review negotiations it was almost as if the NFU and the ministry closed ranks against the Treasury to secure a better deal for British farmers. It was without doubt a special relationship. Turner was also a master of avoiding political alignment and managed to build a rapport with both Tory and Labour ministers.

Turner clearly elevated the position and prestige of the NFU presidency. It was said that when Turner appeared in the visitor's gallery of the House of Commons, MPs turned to greet him. By 1960 the president of the NFU had become one of the most powerful men in the country and, through the media, one of the best known. It is true that Turner himself did profit personally from the NFU's new wealth and prestige, but it was a just reward.

Some might argue that the runes were in Turner's favour. The postwar world was short of food and he was lucky to be in the right place at the right time. He was the first president since Padwick in 1919 to benefit from a significant upturn in the fortunes of peacetime agriculture, but it should be remembered that the upturn of 1919 was nearly as short-lived as Padwick's short presidency. What Jim Turner oversaw was far more substantial and longer term. It was a 15-year period with a sustained growth rate of 2.8 per cent per annum – a greater rate than at any other time in the twentieth century.

In history there is always a debate as to whether it

'For he's a jolly good fellow' sung with utmost gusto. The jolly good fellow in question, Jim Turner, sits humbled and moved at the 1960 AGM.

was the man who made the moment or the moment that made the man. What we can say is that the future of British agriculture in 1945 was far from assured. Men such as ex-president Nevile were convinced the bad times would return. The fact they didn't must in some way pay testimony to the man who led the NFU and farming into the postwar era. In 1945 it was clear that postwar British economic policy was going to be radically different. The position of farming in that policy was not necessarily

secured, and farming interests had to be fought for. It was vital that at this time British agriculture had strong leadership. Jim Turner was a strong man who gave that leadership

When, in July 1957, Prime Minister Harold Macmillan told the nation that they 'had never had it so good', the average farmer and the average NFU member could but heartily agree. At the same time. most were grateful to Jim Turner, and they had much to be grateful for.

A countryman in the town. Harold Woolley taking his morning constitutional along Rotten Row in Hyde park.

CHAPTER 26

Sir Harold Woolley, Baron Woolley of Hatton, 1960–66

When Harold Woolley took on the presidency of the NFU in February 1960 he announced: 'I feel like a very small man walking in a big shadow.' Woolley had been at Turner's right hand as vice or deputy president, on and off as far back as 1948. With his premature shock of white hair, he made a striking visual contrast to the dark Turner. Behind their backs the irreverent referred to them as the 'black and white minstrel show'. By further way of contrast, while Turner was a mainly arable farmer in the east, Woolley was mainly livestock and from the west.

Strangely, the story of Harold Woolley's farming career starts with his father reading books to blind old ladies in Victorian Blackburn. It was largely done as of an act of kindness by a helpful working-class lad who had an aptitude for reading. In return the old ladies would give him their secret recipes for various homespun potions that cured a range of ailments. The young Woolley used the recipes to good effect and started a pharmaceutical business he called 'Q-Pal'. To cut a long story short, by the time Q-Pal was finally sold by the Woolley family in 1982 it was worth £35 million. (And the moral of this story is: always be nice to old ladies and never underestimate what they know.)

Harold was the youngest of three sons and, while his elder brothers took an interest in their father's burgeoning pharmaceutical business, Harold wanted to be a farmer from an early age. In 1915, at the age of ten, he could be found on a nearby farm milking cows. He was educated at a Methodist school. Thus we have yet another president who has a Nonconformist upbringing.

At the age of just 20, having been a farm pupil at a Lancashire dairy farm, the family business afforded him his first farm, Mersey Bank Farm, near Helsby, a 150-acre dairy farm. Woolley built up a milk retail business in nearby Runcorn, but in 1936 tragedy struck when his wife died of septicaemia, leaving him with four sons. This was the same condition that robbed President Wain of his wife in 1937, and again we are reminded that, before antibiotics, life was a good deal more fragile than it is today.

The emotional turmoil surrounding his wife's death caused Harold to move to Hatton House, a few miles south of Chester. He remarried and had two further daughters. Hatton House was 530 acres of fertile Cheshire clay created by the Lord for the purposes of grazing dairy cows. Woolley milked 150 Friesians, with a further 180 dairy and beef-crossed followers. In addition, there was a Landrace x Large White pig herd breeding 600 baconers a year.

In the war pasture had been ploughed up for cereals, but arable farming was not really to Harold Woolley's liking. In 1945 he quickly put Hatton Hall back to the traditional regime of grazing pasture and hay with a few acres of wheat.

As a farmer Harold Woolley was a bit of an enigma. While those around him in the '50s and '60s were moving towards silage and pushing their dairy cows to yield more and more, Woolley found all this rapacious change rather unseemly, preferring to stick with the tried and trusted way of farming he had learnt at a young age. While the pattern for most farms in the 1950s was to shed labour, Woolley kept his men on. Some joked he fancied himself the Squire of Hatton Hall, but no doubt his staff were grateful for his employ. When a journalist asked him in 1960 if he was, like many others, going to get out of pigs in response to the decline in pig prices, Woolley dismissively replied: 'You cannot be jumping in and out of everything. I do not think it sound farming and sound agricultural policy to be jumping around like a grasshopper.' It was a remark that neatly illustrated Woolley's preferred view of farming as a long-term game and his disdain for constant change.

In great contrast to Woolley's agricultural conservatism, the British farming industry he led continued its rapid postwar evolution. Woolley was not alone in being uneasy at the pace of change. It was in the early 1960s that the prospect of the concrete farm, which had no fields but was merely a huge fattening shed where feed went in one end and meat or eggs came out the other, reared its ugly head. In 1962 the *Daily Mail* carried stories of a single beef unit in the Midlands fattening 2,000 head of cattle a week – a figure that represented 8 per cent of the national production. The 1960s was the age of barley beef, whereby much of Britain's rapidly expanding barley crop was ground and fed to beef animals in sheds. Elsewhere there was an egg unit with six million birds producing 6 per cent of the national figure. The pig industry was a prime example of the way farming was changing in the 1960s. Over the decade the national pig herd rose from 5.2 million to 7.4 million while the number of holdings with pigs halved, and by 1970 half the pigs were managed in herds of 200 or more. The pre-war model of most farms keeping a few pigs in makeshift strawed yards was fast moving to the industry we know today of specialised larger units in purpose-built rearing sheds. In poultry things were becoming even more consolidated, with 200 holdings representing half the breeding stock and about a dozen companies controlling most of the output by the mid-1960s.

Some NFU branches suggested there should be limits on the size of some farms. It was an easy aspiration to voice but not so easy to translate into practical legislation. It should be noted, though, that on the Continent there were laws designed to limit the size of farms. This trend towards the concrete farm also presented a headache for the NFU in that members were quick to point out that these units would turn over millions but their lack of acres meant they paid very little in NFU subs.

Intriguingly, Woolley was planting hedges in the 1960s while most others were applying for grants to take them out (in the early 1960s hedge removal peaked at 16,000 km a year). It remains a matter of conjecture as to whether this made Harold Woolley a stick-in-the-mud or a throwback, or whether it made him a visionary who could see the future. Either way, Woolley was a good countryman who took pleasure from the traditional rich green Cheshire countryside around him. For him there was no better way to start the day than to exercise one of his hunters. When up in London during the week on NFU business, Woolley would exercise a horse along Rotten Row in Hyde Park early each morning, and on his return to the office his secretary, Elizabeth Campbell, would be expected to pull off his riding boots. With his pipe, his bowler hat and his traditionally cut tweed suits, Woolley preferred the traditional patterns of life rather than the immense social, technical and cultural changes that Britain was undergoing in the 1960s.

As a man, Woolley was first and foremost solid and assured, with a good analytical mind. 'If you have a problem, make a decision', was one of his adages. He had a quick intellect that made his public speaking lucid, penetrating and, on occasion, caustic. Farmers liked him for his no-nonsense, barnstorming style of address and his honest commitment to their cause. He would speak at branch and county meetings, banging his fists on the table, and then falsely apologise saying: 'I forgot myself, banging the table here. It's the sort of treatment I always save for Whitehall.' Physically, Woolley looked older than he was, which gave him an air of gravitas and sagacity but could also make him look old and 'past it'. He was 55 when he took the presidency.

Woolley was known for his shrewdness in negotiation but also for an impatience that could make him sharp with people. Where Turner was affable and easy mannered with NFU staff, Woolley could be a little cool and disapproving, yet he still inspired loyalty and respect. . He was what you would have called in a more genteel age, a decent man who had 'standards' and expected standards of others.

As president, Woolley was less domineering than Turner and keen to be more inclusive of those around him. One of his first acts was to set up a President's Council comprising the main office holders and two of the 30 committee chairmen. This acted as an NFU Cabinet. One virtue Woolley had that Turner sometimes lacked was the ability to admit he might be wrong.

In the 1930s Woolley had become Chester branch chairman and in 1943 county delegate. In 1948 he was vice-president and deputy in 1952. By the late '50s, waiting for Turner to vacate the presidency, his patience snapped and he walked away from office to concentrate on farming and hunting at home in Cheshire (Mrs Woolley noted how much his health improved). But in 1960 he returned to fill the vacancy that Turner had decided to create.

His abilities were immediately put to the test. By 1960 Turner's predilection for spending more and more at HQ had crashed headlong into a declining revenue caused by a declining membership. Losses and budgetary deficit were the inevitable outcome. One of the union's first acts under Woolley's presidency was to increase subs substantially to a basic of £3 and 1s. for every acre. The Turner years had sucked money into Agriculture House with relative ease on the back of a rising membership and an increasingly prosperous agriculture. For the presidents who followed Turner, balancing the books was not to be so easy. By the time Woolley left office in 1966 NFU membership had fallen to 168,000. It was a reflection of what was happening to the wider farming industry.

By the 1960s the policy of guaranteed prices was starting to creak even more. Put in simple terms, both globally and nationally agricultural supply was starting to exceed demand. Technical improvements were leading to greater efficiencies, causing increased output which was not being matched by increased consumption. The harsh fact was that the world, and Britain, no longer needed so many farmers. At this time Britain was losing 3 per cent of its farmers annually. Some economists took the view it should be nearer 5 per cent. It was an unpalatable issue for the NFU and its members to the point that it could not be sensibly discussed. The job of the NFU was to work to minimise the shake-out in its own backyard and to cry foul at any policy that sucked in more imports. To make the problem even more pronounced, elsewhere in the economy living standards were starting to rise quite dramatically. Understandably, farmers objected to being left behind their increasingly affluent non-farming neighbours. One response was for individual farmers to take on more arable land with their ever-larger tractors, or to graze more stock on better fertilised pastures and to erect more fattening sheds with ever-ready grants. New technology and new genetics were allowing the individual farmer to produce significantly more.

"Gentlemen will please deposit all tanks, bazookas, limited atomic weapons and small-arms in the cloakroom..."

NFU Woolley leads a belligerent NFU price review team. A Farmer & Stockbreeder *cartoon notes how in the early 1960s negotiations became bit more intense.*

Through the 1960s the prospect of significantly increasing production was a financial solution for many farmers. The problem was, as government reined in the expansion policy of the 1950s, there would be less room for the 250,000 full-time English and Welsh farmers. Many were forced to leave the industry. With land prices on the increase, selling up was increasingly attractive for owner-occupiers who for the first time now represented more than half the NFU membership. While average farms made less than £30 an acre in 1939, by 1960 the price was nearer £150 and continued to rise through the 1960s to 1970, when it hit £500. With many of its members, especially the smaller men, permanently looking over their shoulders at the prospect of quitting the industry, these were never going to be easy times for the leaders of the NFU.

The start of the 1960s saw inflation jump to four per cent and wages rise even more. The price reviews under Woolley's presidency usually took the form of the NFU team calculating the increase in the farmer's costs for the year and then demanding that figure plus 10 or 20 per cent more to stimulate an increase in production. The outcome would usually be something below the initial demand. How much below the initial demand would determine how successful the NFU had been in fighting the farmer's

corner. One problem for the NFU and its president was it was increasingly judged just on the annual price review. Woolley often pointed out that the NFU was far more than just 'some sort of boat race team' who prepared all year for just one event. Despite this, the February price review was fast becoming more important than the August harvest in the farmer's year.

The price review for 1960 was announced on 10 March. The farming press christened it 'Black Thursday'. Prime Minister Macmillan had appointed John Hare as Minister of Agriculture in 1958. Although Hare was a Suffolk farmer. the NFU had found him a difficult minister to get on with. In 1959 Hare's first price review had attempted to reduce bacon production by reducing the price guarantee on pigs. The result was a huge increase in Danish bacon imports in 1959. Some in the NFU commented that Hare made an effective agricultural minister for Denmark but a poor one for Britain. The 1960 review was even worse. Price guarantees were cut by £9 million to £257 million in the face of NFU claims that costs had increased by £13 million. Only beef, pigs and potatoes escaped reductions, while sheep, milk, eggs, wheat, barley, sugar beet and wool were reduced by 1–3 per cent. Woolley had emphatically rejected the review, and in a telegram

Woolley and two of the Hatton Hall staff help launch NFU Seeds with the help of that ubiquitous 1960s farm phenomenon – the one hundredweight paper sack.

to Prime Minister Macmillan accused his government of 'a clear determination to restrict home agricultural production and make way for more imported food-stuffs'.

To make matters worse, foot and mouth reared its ugly head again in 1960, and the autumn proved one of the wettest on record. Winter wheat plantings were down 900,000 acres on the previous year.

Woolley sought an interview with the Prime Minister which resulted in a White Paper which laid out new government policy. Minister Hare was replaced by Christopher Soames – Churchill's son-in-law. The changes seemed to place agriculture on a better footing, but the Treasury remained determined to rein in the farm support budget, which in 1961 had shot up to £342 million. Lamb and beef prices had fallen well below the agreed target prices. The milk situation was little better, and the 1961 settlement introduced a dual pricing system which, in effect, acted as a quota system. Soames also introduced a system of 'standard quantities', which set expenditure limits on the level of deficiency payments the Treasury were prepared to pay. This was backed up by securing voluntary agreements with exporters abroad as to how much food Britain would import.

There was 'the butter agreement' with New Zealand, the 'bacon-sharing understanding' with the Danes and minimum import price agreements with the world's main cereal exporters. The idea of further control of expenditure through production quotas was explored but never implemented. The following price reviews with Soames were hard-fought affairs, and many farmers wondered if they might be better off with a return to a Labour government.

The 1960s saw the reheating of the old debate as to whether British farmers could find salvation through co-operation and collectivised marketing. Ever since the bankruptcies of the 1920s, these concepts had remained something of an anathema to British farmers, who remained probably the most independent minded of all nations' farmers when it came to collective marketing and the pooling of resources. The reasons for this, no doubt, stretch back to an ancient British psyche that, in part, inspired the enclosures. One is reminded of the words of Horace Plunkett, the great advocate of co-operative structures, who called the English: '... essentially an independent self-helping group of people who are inclined to carry their self-help a little too far '. What also stifled this group mentality in agriculture was probably the marketing boards and the price review system. Another hindrance in the early 1960s was the personal animosity between Woolley and Sir Frederick Brundrett, chairman of the ACCA. Both were strong characters who were prepared to defend their own empires at the expense of the farming community. Woolley supported initiatives such as the setting up of ACT and NFU Seeds, both of which antagonised the co-ops as they acted as commercial rivals. NFU Seeds was an example of a number of ventures made by the NFU into the commercial world. None was particularly successful – NFU Seeds lost money throughout the 1960s. Some members expressed the view that the NFU should get back to the basics of representing agriculture politically.

Meanwhile, in mid-1962, the talk of a possible application to join the EEC exercised the minds of Harold Woolley and his NFU colleagues. Under the 1957 Treaty of Rome, six countries – France, Germany, Italy, Holland, Belgium and Luxemburg – had come together to form a free-trade area with pretensions of becoming a loose political union. In the early 1960s a Common Agricultural Policy was in the making between the six. It was during this process that the British made their application in an initiative led by Lord of the Privy Seal Edward Heath, who was to gain notoriety for his pro-European enthusiasm.

At this time the debate as to whether Britain should join the newly formed EEC was embroiled in party politics, with the Conservatives keen to make overtures to join while the Labour Party was antagonistic to the idea. Woolley was conscious that the NFU must be wary of taking sides, but, even so, his personal antagonism to the idea of entry could barely be disguised. There were constant rumours that Woolley was a card-carrying member of the Labour Party, but even if that were true, he would have been too clever to let it be proved. Consequently, it remains a matter of conjecture only. It is also a matter of conjecture whether, in his opposition to joining the EEC, Woolley was faithfully representing the views of his members or whether he was actually following the personal 'little Englander' tendencies that he sometimes displayed.

Either way, when the application to join the six was made, Woolley was quick to spell out why it would be problematic for British farmers. Above all, he expressed his unease at British agricultural policy being moved from Westminster to Brussels. Clearly, such a move would subsume British farming interests and weaken the influence of the NFU, who were well ensconced in the Whitehall scene. Despite the recent tensions with ministers Hare and Soames, Woolley felt British agriculture was well served with the annual review and its deficiency payments system, which he described as 'the best-designed method of agricultural support in the world'.

The agricultural arrangements of the six were such that the Continentals were 90 per cent self-sufficient compared to the figure of 65 per cent in the UK.

" LOOK WEST, YOUNG MAN. LOOK WEST! "

A Farmer & Stockbreeder *cartoon illustrates Woolley's EEC scepticism.*

Woolley warned of production soon exceeding demand in the six, and of Britain, as part of the EEC, having to cope with the surpluses with no possibility of import controls. The Common Agricultural Policy (CAP), which was still at its early, embryonic stage in 1962, was not based on deficiency payments but rather on tariffs on imports and guaranteed prices through intervention schemes. This meant the burden of farm support would primarily fall on the consumer rather than on the Treasury. Woolley was quick to point out that this would lead to higher retail prices for consumers and thus was not in accordance with traditional British food and farm policy, which placed the burden of farm support on the exchequer. Furthermore, although the EEC system offered British cereal growers the prospect of higher prices, Woolley argued that this would lead to higher feed prices for livestock producers. Similarly, Woolley warned that an open door into British markets for continental horticulturalists would clearly threaten home producers, as continental producers had the benefit of better weather and lower labour costs (or, in the case of Dutch glasshouse-men, cheaper fuel, better organisation and better marketing). British milk production, thought Woolley, was fundamentally different on the Continent, where it was dominated by milk manufacturing in contrast to the British tradition of high-quality fresh milk sales. As for the marketing boards, which the NFU had fought

so hard to put in place and which had dominated much of British agriculture, there were question-marks over their future in the EEC.

Finally, Woolley reminded the pro-marketeers of Britain's historic links with the Commonwealth, and the country's historic pledge to take a proportion of its food needs from its colonial cousins. When we remember the heated exchanges between President Baxter and the pro-Empire Beaverbrook in the 1920s, and when we recollect Dorman-Smith's hard line on the Ottawa agreement in the 1930s, it does seem extraordinary that in 1962 we have an NFU president singing the praises of the historic obligation to accept food imports from the Commonwealth.

It was clear that, although the NFU's concerns and doubts did not derail the British negotiating team, they did complicate matters as they were, under NFU insistence, brought to the negotiating table. A long-drawn-out 'phasing-in' period of up to 12 years for British agriculture was insisted upon.

Despite such problems, by the New Year of 1963 Britain's entry negotiations seemed roughly on track, but then in late January they hit the road block that was Charles de Gaulle. The French President suddenly said 'non' to the idea of British membership, and Britain's application form was thus ripped to shreds. The main substance of de Gaulle's objections was Britain's historic ties to the US and the Commonwealth, but he also claimed some of the

" Those against entry? ... "

The Farmer & Stockbreeder *imagines... what if another President turned up at the NFU AGM?*

Above and overleaf: *The Tug Tractor campaign.*

Take the brake off British farming

says Tug Tractor

Published by the N.F.U. Printed by Gothic Press Limited London.

negotiations for Britain's entry had become overly protracted. There is no doubt that agriculture was one of the sticking points between the British and EEC delegations. The reservations and qualifications demanded by the NFU would have contributed to the protraction alluded to by de Gaulle .

The place of Harold Woolley in Britain's failure to join the infant EEC is of historic interest. Obviously, it was the French President who scuppered the plan and not the NFU president, but had Woolley and the NFU been more enthusiastic about the prospect of British agriculture falling under the auspices of the CAP, then negotiations might have been less problematic and de Gaulle might not have found his pretext to object to British membership. The suspicion was that de Gaulle was keen to establish a French-orientated CAP majoring on artificially high cereal prices, and de Gaulle did not want the heavily pastoral Britain in the design team.

Some argue today that if Britain had been more involved in the moulding of the CAP at its inception in the early 1960s, then the CAP might have proven a better fit for British farmers. Britain eventually joined the EEC in the 1970s, but by this time the fundamentals of the CAP had been decided and Britain's opportunity to determine them was gone. The other question that the events of 1962 raises is, to

what extent was the NFU policy on EEC entry being driven by the prejudices of Woolley, or was the president quite properly voicing what most farmers thought was best for British agriculture at the time?

With one dragon slain, Woolley had another to deal with at home – the myth of the 'feather-bedded farmer'. The phrase 'feather-bedded farmers', which has haunted British agriculture and the NFU for much of its history, can be traced back to 1950 and Labour MP Stanley Evans. Evans was a Birmingham industrialist who held office in the Ministry of Food in the postwar Atlee government. In 1950 he held a press conference at which he criticised the policy of providing farmers with guaranteed prices at the taxpayers' expense and questioned how long it could continue. He went on to claim that subsidies concealed inefficiency and inertia, and commented that 'no other nation feather-beds its agriculture like Britain'. The NFU, through President Turner, responded by expressing amazement and giving detailed figures to refute Evans's claims. Evans was forced to resign, commenting wryly that: 'The National Farmers' Union have my scalp under their belt,' and later adding: 'Farmers are lying on feather beds and carrying their money to the bank in pillow cases.'

This damning sound bite did not go away. As

Sussex farmer Richard Denny gives his chickens away in 1965 as they are not worth selling. One wonders if such an act would draw such an enthusiastic crowd today.

price reviews in the 1960s were costing the taxpayer more and more money, the media increasingly took a liking to the throwaway insult. The leading newspaper columnist and broadcaster of the day, Bernard Levin, would write ferocious articles on the theme. In December 1962 Levin was presenting his usual slot on the pioneering and highly satirical TV show 'That Was The Week That Was'. Some farmers had joined the audience with the intention of heckling him. Live on air, Levin responded to their boos with the immortal line, 'Well, good evening, peasants'.

We should remember here that in the 1960s Britain was becoming a less deferential society and journalists were given more liberty to have a cheap swipe at whatever came across their paths. Reporting became less restrained and 'feather-bedded farmers' inevitably attracted increasing media comment. This was not limited to journalists. When Woolley demanded an increase of $^1/_2$d. on a pint of milk, a letter to the *Daily Express* responded: 'Let him advise his members to get up a little earlier; do a little work themselves; sell with a fair return and not imagine they can equal the Beatles.'

The NFU recognised the need to respond to this general sentiment about 'feather-bedding'. Negative media comment, combined with tougher February reviews, meant the NFU needed to champion the farming cause more proactively. In 1964 it doubled the budget spent on public relations (this was net of publicity staff salaries), which was double what had been spent in the previous year. It also called on the counties to raise money for a new national campaign.

At this time the Publicity Committee became increasingly important under the chairmanship of Dorset farmer Bob Saunders. Saunders was an interesting character in that, in the 1930s he had become known as the 'black shirt farmer'. Later, writing in the book *Mosley's Blackshirts*, he noted:

We were proud to be British in the 1930s and yet... her position as a world power was being undermined by largely unilateral disarmament which left her without adequate defences. Her agriculture was being depressed by imports of cheap food which ruined her farmers and left them to face bankruptcy.

By 1935 he was a district organiser for Mosley's British Union of Fascists and held blackshirt training camps at his farm in Dorset. During the war he was interned as a security threat. After the war he kept links with Mosley but understandably became somewhat quieter about his political views in public. By the 1960s he was exercising much of his considerable energy in the NFU. His role on the Publicity Committee fitted well with his passionate belief in protecting British agriculture from the ruin of cheap imports.

It should be pointed out that he was a generally liked individual, although some did wonder why he always carried with him a locked briefcase that no one ever saw him open. In 1964 he got within one vote of becoming NFU vice-president and was eventually awarded the OBE for services to agriculture. Bob Saunders continued to serve as chair of publicity and information committees into the 1980s. It should also be pointed out that Saunders was not part of some right-wing undercurrent in the NFU. For instance, another key figure in the NFU in the 1960s and 1970s was Asher Winegarten, the chief economist. Winegarten was the son of Jewish émigrés and a member of the Reform Club. He was highly influential in forming NFU policy and the presidents were dependent on his advice and analysis. Unlike their counterparts in Germany, the DBV, who tended to recruit only Christian Democrats from farming backgrounds, the NFU was far less strictured, and people rose through its ranks because of their abilities. It gave the tea rooms of Agriculture House a free-thinking atmosphere.

Under Woolley's presidency the NFU launched a number of campaigns aimed at the non-farming public with the intent of convincing them that, far from being 'feather-bedded', British farming was an efficient provider of highly affordable food and, as Britain's biggest industry, was a vital part of the economy. One key point to be made was the contribution agricultural output made to the balance of payments. Some 20,000 copies of the booklet *Britain's Biggest Industry* were sent out to industrial and financial leaders, while 300,000 copies of the pamphlet *Talking about Agriculture* were handed out to 'townspeople' attending NFU-sponsored meetings. In 1964/65 the union launched one of its most famous campaigns, the Fair Deal campaign, and its logo, 'Tug Tractor'. This time 360,000 posters, 1,250,000 leaflets, 2 million handbills and car stickers were printed. Some 2,900 billboards in 111 towns and cities were rented and 172 newspaper advertisement spaces in 17 national and regional newspapers, reaching out to 38.5 million readers, were booked. The key message in all of this was that, while in the ten years between 1955 and 1965 workers' earnings had risen 78 per cent, retail food prices had risen just 31 per cent, and furthermore, while national productivity had increased by 3 per cent per annum, in agriculture it was 6 per cent. Literature was handed out to the branches so that members might distribute it to the public. President Woolley made a national tour, speaking to audiences on the theme of a fair deal for farmers. Most notably, in December 1965 he addressed an invited audience of 2,000 housewives in Newcastle City Hall. Such was the pulling power of the NFU president in 1965!

The Fair Deal campaign was very much a response to the 1965 price review. It was the first under the new Labour government, which had won the 1964 general election under the leadership of Harold Wilson. Wilson was the first Labour Prime

Mayfield farmers make their voices heard in 1965.

Minister since Atlee in 1950. During the 1964 election campaign Shadow Farm Minister Fred Peart had written:

In the last nine years, the Conservative Government has imposed five price reviews on the industry, despite opposition from the farming community. The Labour Party is acutely aware there has been, in real terms, a drop in farm income since the Tories took office. Such a situation cannot possibly continue.

Peart had been private secretary to Tom Williams in the Atlee government and so, given his track record and given his encouraging words, it was no surprise that farmers and the NFU entered the 1965 price review with new heart.

The NFU economics department reckoned farmers' costs had risen by £29 million since the previous year, and so Woolley entered negotiations looking for an increase of £31 million above the 1964 settlement. Milk prices were a particularly hot topic for dairy farmers. A.G. Street wrote in the *Farmers' Weekly* of 5 February 1965: 'Nothing less than a rise of 6d. a gallon will halt the drift from milk' In the early '60s thousands of small dairymen were going out of business every year.

After protracted wrangling, Peart agreed to a figure of £23 million and retired to get cabinet ratification. The Cabinet, heavily under the influence of Chancellor Callaghan, who was overseeing an increasingly rocky economy, were in a tight-fisted mood and sent Peart back with a measly £10.5 million. Milk was given a desultory 1d., taking the price to 3s.6d. a gallon. The price of pigs, wheat and barley was reduced. Such was the consternation

amongst MAFF officials and the shell-shocked NFU that there was a three-week delay in making the announcement.

Not surprisingly, when the announcement was made in mid-March the reaction of farmers was one of outrage. A few days later the BBC flagship current affairs programme 'Panorama' put Peart in front of ten farmers. Millions of viewers enjoyed the sight of Sussex farmer Richard Denny pulling a live chicken from his coat pocket and handing it to Peart as a neat symbol of what the farming community thought of the minister – give him the bird, indeed!

The following day, as Peart arrived to give an address to a Labour Party meeting in Saffron Walden, 600 farmers turned out to burn effigies of him in the market-place and then gate-crashed the meeting. An unseemly slanging match ensued between the minister and the farmers. Peart made the mistake of suggesting their contempt for him was not because of the price review but because they were Tories.

On 25 March, when the House of Commons held a debate on the price review, county branches from across the land arranged for thousands of farmers to descend on Westminster to make loud their protest. For the first time since the 1930s farmers were in militant mood and taking to the streets. Tractors adorned with placards formed processions through a number of county towns. At Caxton Gibbet in Cambridgeshire an effigy of Peart was hung from the ancient gallows with the message 'Now cut this down, brother Peart' around its neck. In Uckfield in Sussex a cow draped in black was led through the town. For some reason the village of Mayfield was a particular hotbed of unrest. The main road from London to Brighton was blocked with tractors. Many

NFU branches met and passed resolutions of no confidence in Minister Peart and called for his resignation. In Dorset 1,500 of the county's 3,100 members rallied in the Dorchester Corn Exchange and collected a £2,500 fighting fund. But at the end of the day the protests made little impact on parliament, which approved the mean settlement.

As farmers' anger grew, Harold Woolley was not to be seen. He had suffered a disabling slipped disc and needed an operation followed by several months of recuperation. That this was an unfortunate time for it to happen has remarkable parallels with the times of presidents Robbins and Nevile, who also took ill just as the NFU membership reached a crescendo of dissatisfaction in 1921 and 1942.

As a new year dawned in 1966, the prospect of re-election at the AGM stood before a recovered Woolley. He knew there was a significant level of complaint about his leadership out in the counties, but it was difficult to second guess how much. Woolley was the first president to face the real possibility of standing for re-election without being sure he had the necessary support of Council. Out in the regions NFU members were still in a bad-tempered, militant mood. An NFU questionnaire sent out in January 1966 asked farmers if they would take 'direct action' to press for a better price review. The vast majority said they would. One particular question – 'Would you be prepared to support action to reduce supplies of a commodity' – roused the ire of Minister Peart, who personally warned Woolley that the government took a dim view of the NFU issuing threats of industrial action causing food shortages. He also added a dark remark along the lines that if Britain couldn't get its food from her own farmers they would secure it elsewhere. Woolley dismissed Peart's remonstrations as 'a storm in a teacup', claiming the NFU were only asking their members their views. The NFU was learning that the line

between, on the one hand, showing solidarity with its aggrieved, increasingly militant membership while, on the other, distancing itself from the accusation of orchestrating public disorder, could, at times, be a fine one to tread.

Woolley also equivocated over his determination to carry on as president. For once he failed to live up to his own favourite adage – if you have a problem, then make a decision. First he announced in January he would stand down, then in mid-February, as the AGM got nearer, he decided he would stand again. Changing his mind proved a mistake. Harold Woolley suffered the ignominy of being the first president to be voted out of office by Council. Under the demanding rules that Turner had brought in 20 years before, he needed 85 per cent of the vote but failed to secure it. In the end he felt forced out by an ungrateful NFU and it left a bitter after-taste with him. In this he was not alone; there were many in the NFU who felt he had been badly treated.

Harold Woolley was a genuine, sincere man with a good intellect and strong leadership qualities, but the crisis of 1965, combined with his spell of disability, proved too challenging for his abilities. The mid-1960s were a time that demanded vitality, and maybe a president who looked old and had suffered ill health was seen as ill-fitted to lead the NFU in its time of challenge.

Woolley was the first president, but by no means the last, to be forced from the presidency by events largely not of his making. Having been knighted in 1964, he was made Baron Woolley of Hatton in the County Palatine of Cheshire in January 1967. It was an appropriate reward for a man who honestly and earnestly served agriculture, and an appropriate title for a man who was most at home on his Cheshire farm. In 1966 he returned full time to Hatton Hall, where he died in the 1980s. Today his grandson, David, can still be found farming in Harold's old stamping-ground.

CHAPTER 27

Sir Gwilym Williams, 1966–70

Despite a bid for the presidency at the 1966 AGM by a young, ambitious and well-regarded Warwickshire farmer called Henry Plumb, Council observed traditional protocol and chose Woolley's deputy, Gwilym Williams, as his successor. Gwilym Tecwin Williams, a Welshman by birth, but somewhat anglicised, and everyone new him as 'Bill'.

Born in 1913 in Llanrhaeadr-ym-Mochnant in Powys on the Welsh borders, Bill Williams was the son of an agricultural auctioneer and one of seven children. Befitting a borders man, he grew up bilingual, but his English had very little Welsh intonation. We should remember that in times past, heavy regional accents were not the badges of honour they are today, and some saw them as a sign of a poor provincial education. Not long ago, those who wanted to get on in life took the trouble to receive proper pronunciation of standard English, and 'boyos' from the valleys were not necessarily linguistic role models. Bill came from a solid Presbyterian, middle-class family that placed an emphasis on a good education. Most of the seven Williams children went into the professions. Bill chose farming. After doing well at the local school he went on to study poultry management at Harper Adams Agricultural College in Shropshire.

Williams was the first president to graduate from an agricultural college. As we have seen, most of the presidents learnt their farming as boys in the footsteps of their fathers. Some, such as Campbell and Woolley, followed the very traditional path of becoming a 'farm pupil', whereby they left school to be posted onto a farm, sometimes a long way from home, to learn the art of farming as an apprentice. The limitations of such a system are obvious, especially at a time when new ideas in food production and new technologies were characterising the age. The concept of 'the agricultural college' was a development that was to professionalise farmers and better equip them for the changing demands of the twentieth century.

The story of Harper Adams is typical of many British agricultural colleges. Set up in the 1890s through private benefaction, it suffered an inauspicious start but saw a flowering between the wars, when it attracted public funding as the state took more of a role in providing a better education for the nation's future farmers. One specialisation that Harper Adams established in the 1920s was a course majoring in poultry husbandry. The college became a recognised leader in the field. The inter-war years

Gwilym Williams.

saw considerable advancement in the British poultry industry, where self-sufficiency in chicken and eggs rose from less than 50 per cent to around 75 per cent. It was a trend that was to continue into modern times, as self-sufficiency today is just under 90 per cent for both.

It should be noted that Harper Adams was quite radical in that it admitted women, but only to study poultry management. No doubt the other courses, such as those involving heavy machinery, were not considered 'becoming' for young women. We cannot be sure which 'birds' most occupied the young Bill Williams at Harper Adams, but we do know he not only graduated in poultry management but also found his future wife, Cathleen Edwards-Adeney, who was from a well-heeled farming family in nearby Market Drayton.

After a brief spell working as a manager for Streetly Eggs in Surrey, Williams returned to Shropshire to marry Cathleen. Using family money, they bought Longford Grange Farm, which was added to in the 1930s by the purchase of Mill Farm. These were the days when farms in Shropshire were making as little as £25 an acre. With land at that time comparatively plentiful and cheap, it was far more common than it is today for sons from non-farming but related professions to enter the farming industry. By the 1950s Longford Grange was an unusually large 600-acre farm but typical of Shropshire in that it ran a good mix of enterprises. There was an Ayrshire dairy herd, pigs and poultry in the yard. If there was a spare shed something would be put in it. Out in the fields, on the coarse, sandy loam, there were onions,

Lifting spuds on Williams's farm. The 1960s saw huge advances in the mechanisation of potato and sugar beet production.

Bill Williams in his new packing shed, which was previously the farm dairy.

potatoes, sugar beet and cereals. Traditionally, Shropshire was a county of mixed farms which found an important niche in supplying the greengrocers and chip shops of the West Midlands and Wales.

Typical of many sugar beet and potato farmers in the 1950 and '60s, Williams transformed the growing of these crops through increasing mechanisation. Before the war both beet and potatoes were highly labour-intensive, with planting, singling, weeding and harvesting of the bulky crops all done by hand, hoe and fork. By the 1960s hand labour had more or less been ousted by machines pulled by tractors. It is not suprising that the number of full-time workers in agriculture nearly halved in the 1960s (400,000 in 1959, 200,000 in 1971), and the number of casuals dropped even lower. In contrast, the UK sugar beet crop increased from four million tons in 1946 to 6.3 million in 1961 to 8 million in 1984. It was all part of the long success story of the NFU: Britain was completely dependent on imports of sugar when it was founded and is 70 per cent self-sufficient today.

Another area where Williams was typical in his husbandry of roots and vegetables was his increasing use of irrigation. In the '60s irrigation licences were handed out quite freely by the relevant authorities, and large dirt movers started to appear on many farms, enlarging ponds or creating new ones. Suddenly, the farmscape was populated with a new feature – the reservoir. Again typical of the time, Bill Williams converted the old dairy into a potato pack-house. Williams was also instrumental in setting up

'Longford Packers', a farmers' co-op that supplied the potato trade.

Williams had first joined the ranks of Newport NFU in the 1930s and by the 1950s was vice-chairman under Jim Turner. Turner and Williams enjoyed each other's company and were good friends. In 1956 Williams was elected chairman of the Potato Marketing Board, one of the boards reconstituted in the 1950s by the Churchill administration. As we have seen, the Tories were doubtful about setting up too many of these producer-controlled boards. As chairman of the NFU Potatoes Committee in the early '50s Williams had been a key advocate for its reintroduction. He argued that the potato market swung too often from over- to under-supply and needed an acreage regulation. One of the main functions of the PMB under Williams's chairmanship was controlling production through quotas. One character who was a permanent thorn in Williams's side here was Jack Merricks, who farmed a large acreage on the Romney Marsh. Merricks was an arch-opponent of the quota system and saw the PMB as a 'Stalinist' institution. In the '60s he even spent a few days in Wormwood Scrubs because of his continued refusal to declare how many spuds he was growing. The intriguing thing about Merricks was that he was often popularly elected by his fellow growers to the very boards to which he vehemently objected. It was a good example of the ambiguous attitude of British farmers to state control and market regulation.

Like that of Woolley, Williams's presidency also

Members have always pled poverty whenever NFU subs were raised.

saw a decrease in members, from 182,000 in 1966 to 150,000 in 1970. Again, it was a reflection of what was happening in agriculture generally as the industry continued to shed both labour and farmers through increasing efficiency. The average farm size grew from 200 to 300 acres. In 1966 there were about 210,000 holdings, according to ministry censuses, and, as farmers were merging farms but keeping holding numbers, it probably exaggerated the number of farmers. It was clear the NFU was retaining its market share and continuing to represent 80–90 per cent of the industry.

As a man, Williams was affable, capable and considered. He could not match the enormity of Turner or the imperiousness of Woolley, but people warmed to the well-mannered, well-spoken Welshman and found him open, assured and welcoming.

In the metropolis, Williams enjoyed the London scene. These were the Swinging Sixties and London was enjoying a heyday. With his well-cut Italian-style suits, Williams was better dressed for the times than his tweedy predecessors. We should remember that the climbing of the NFU ladder was quite a journey for this quiet Shropshire lad. To come from the humdrum world of sleepy Market Drayton to the dazzling lights of the West End was to step into another, far more glamourous world, a world Williams enjoyed even if he was slightly starry-eyed about it. Achieving high status in the NFU meant this humble son of the soil from the shires was suddenly mixing with the great and the good in fashionable, cosmopolitan society. There was the presidential flat on the Brompton Road opposite Harrods, as well as a taste of the jet-set lifestyle, as the president frequently travelled the world, representing his industry in such far-flung places as Japan and South America, meeting with foreign presidents and royalty. The president of the NFU was 'a face' seen around, a creature of high politics, an attendee of glitzy receptions and a target of media curiosity. Bill Williams enjoyed being part of that scene. He also enjoyed a drink. In this respect, his sober Presbyterian upbringing was well behind him. However, we should be careful not to overstate this. Williams's boozing was nothing out of the ordinary in a world where it was the norm for business and politics to be conducted over a surfeit of cigarettes, gin and whisky.

Today, Bill's youngest son, David, still vividly recollects the events of 30 July 1966. Treated as if he was part of the aristocracy, he was driven, with his father and mother, by the NFU chauffer, Duffin, in the Humber Super Snipe with its NFU 1 plates, to be a guest of honour at the World Cup Final at Wembley. When watching rugby, Bill Williams was always true to the red shirts of his Welsh birthplace, but you can be sure that, as Geoff Hurst and the heroes of '66 booted their way into English sporting history, Bill

Williams would have been cheering along with the rest of the delirious home crowd.

The presidency of the NFU was not all fun and games, however, and the president carried the expectations and frustrations of 180,000 farmers on his shoulders. In 1967 Bill Williams had to lead British farming through one of its more miserable chapters. Ironically, it all started close to his home in the Welsh Borders.

On 25 October 1967 a dairy farmer at Bryn Farm, Llanyblodwel, near Oswestry, noticed one of his cows was lame. The vet confirmed it had foot and mouth disease. This was a setback for the farmer but, at that stage, not too much out of the ordinary in the larger scheme of things. As we have seen from the presidency of Harry German in 1922, FMD had largely been eradicated in Britain in the late 1880s and Britain had secured a 'foot and mouth free' status thereafter whereby the disease was no longer endemic. But the government's open-door policy for imported meat, particularly from South America, where FMD was endemic, meant British farmers were always going to have the spectre of the virus hanging over them. From 1922 to 1962 there was not one year when there were not at least ten outbreaks of FMD somewhere in the UK. Usually they were sporadic and duly stamped out through isolation and slaughter. The actual source was seldom traced, but imported beef bones that ended up in swill fed to pigs was usually reckoned to be the most likely explanation. In two notable years, 1942 and 1952, outbreaks were in the hundreds rather than the tens, but generally the UK remained on top of its occasional FMD and was noticeably in advance of the Continent, where FMD remained virulent until vaccination programmes were introduced in the 1950s.

When Bill Williams became president in early 1966 there was a hope that, given the very low level of incidence over the preceding three years, the disease was slowly disappearing. Within a week of the October outbreak in Shropshire, it was clear such hopes were cruelly dashed. Before FMD had been officially diagnosed at Bryn Farm, two cows from the originally infected farm had been through Oswestry market, along with 7,000 other animals. Throughout November 1967 the disease swept across the Cheshire plain and into Lancashire. By the middle of the month MAFF vets were diagnosing 80 new cases a day. It was as serious as, and geographically similar to, the 1922/24 outbreak, and it was not long before the civil servants of MAFF and the vets of the state veterinary service were overwhelmed and the Army was called in to help.

Although Cheshire remained the epicentre of the outbreak, by the end of November it had spread across 11 counties, from the South West to the Scottish borders, and the whole of the British mainland had become a 'controlled area'. Live marts were banned and all animal movements were stopped

A foot and mouth pyre in the early '50s. It was an unpleasant sight witnessed all too often from the 1920s until 1968.

unless under licence. The 'diagnose, isolate, slaughter' policy was persevered with and there were few calls for vaccination. Those who could remember the 1922/24 pandemic in Cheshire, remarked that the control methods were much the same 40 years later, the main differences being that bolt guns were used rather than poleaxes to slaughter and JCBs, rather than navvies with spades, to inter.

The disease was not completely stamped out until June 1968, by which time the number of outbreaks had reached 2,228 and 442,000 cows, pigs and sheep had been slaughtered. (By contrast the 1922/24 epidemic had seen 2,691 outbreaks and 300,000 animals slaughtered.) The dairy herd took the brunt of the losses in the biggest loss of stock since 1884. The cost to the exchequer in compensation was £26 million, while the cost to the farming industry was estimated at between £150 and £200 million.

It was Shropshire and Cheshire, Williams's and Woolley's home counties, that felt the most pain, with 75 per cent of all the outbreaks. Williams's farm, which by 1968 only had pigs, did not directly succumb to the virus, but in Cheshire, Harold Woolley's dairy herd did. Williams could not return home and was obliged to stay in London.

The devastation in the two counties was immense. Farms and fields were cleared of animals and, on the urging of the NFU, government took measures to close footpaths and restrict country sports such as hunting and shooting. Villages and towns developed the eerie sense of being ghost towns, while farmers found themselves isolated in their farms, frightened

of the outside world and the viruses it might bring. How the virus was spreading remained the subject of speculation. Some blamed its spread on the movement of birds, while others thought it due to the movement of milk tankers. Others felt the virus travelled on the wind or, at the least, that the smoke from the ubiquitous pyres moved the virus on the wind. As ever, there were the wackier theories put about – such as the possibility it was spread by international jet aircraft, which were increasingly common in the sky in the 1960s. Others wondered if the preponderance of the Friesian was to blame now that the dairy herd and the Cheshire plain were dominated by this one breed. The fact was that there was no evidence for this and the minority Shorthorn, Ayrshire or Channel Islands breeds that were still about succumbed in proportionate numbers.

For those culled out it was a traumatic time, suddenly facing a morgue-like farmyard which just days before had been filled with noise and movement. It was at such a time that an organisation such as the NFU came into its own. No one else had the ability to reach out to so many farmers, many of whom were growing more desperate by the day. The NFU could not only provide vital information but also was able to play a key therapeutic role for members in distress. Cheshire NFU in particular, under the chairmanship of John Richardson, deserved a mention in dispatches. To its credit the union made no distinction between members and non-members. Cheshire was a county under siege and every farmer would be helped by the only organ-

" *It's been a disastrous year for pop festival bookings.* "

Punch *takes a sideways look at the fortunes of farming in the late 1960s*

isation that could coordinate and liaise across the farming community, both with MAFF and the vets.

Back in London President Williams lobbied government hard to ban imports of beef from Argentina, as the most likely source of the outbreak, while Argentina itself suspended exports before the Wilson government belatedly got round to taking action. Incredibly, in March 1968, while sporadic outbreaks were still occurring, the government lifted the ban. The NFU was incensed, and Williams was quick with the castigation: 'It amounts to no less than a deliberate decision to expose our livestock to the gravest risk of mass suffering and wholesale slaughter.' Back in Cheshire, Harold Woolley described the resumption of imports from countries where FMD was endemic as 'near criminal'.

One macabre development in the 1967/68 pandemic was the appearance of sightseers in the worst affected areas. Up to 100 'day tripper' cars could at times be counted near culled farms. John Richardson described them as 'ghouls'. At a more remote level, media interest was intense and the NFU set up regular press conferences, recognising the need to keep the press or TV properly informed and

steer them away from alarmist reporting and some of the more outlandish stories that were circulating. Just as in 1922, the enormous pyres of burning dead beasts were a sensitive issue. Generally, it was felt that media coverage was sober and responsible.

As the number of outbreaks started to subside in the spring of 1968, the NFU recognised it had another important role to play. Registers of members with cows for sale, particularly in-calf heifers, were circulated among those known to have been culled out. This was a key way in which devastated farms could be helped back to their feet again.

One positive result of the pandemic was an inquiry by a committee headed by Lord Northumberland and on which deputy-president Plumb represented the NFU. The committee spent one day a week for over a year taking evidence on the issue. One of the main conclusions was that the slaughter policy was the correct one and that vaccination would be problematic. One of the recommendations was a restriction on imports of meat on the bone from countries where FMD was endemic. This was duly implemented. The NFU had been calling for this for over 60 years. These new restrictions, along with progress in combating the disease through vaccination across the world, kept the UK almost completely free of FMD for a further 32 happy years.

A far happier event in 1967 was the twentieth anniversary conference of IFAP in London. The conference included addresses from NFU President Williams, Lord Netherthorpe and Prime Minister Harold Wilson. It was appropriate that, after 20 years, it should return to the home city of the NFU, the union having been so instrumental in its founding. If it had not been for the largesse of the NFU and the Americans it would have struggled for funds. By 1967 it had grown into an umbrella organisation of over 50 farmer unions from 50 countries across the world and had extended its membership to include countries from Africa and South America. To sharpen the minds of the many who gathered in London, one of its delegate countries, India, was experiencing a serious famine which was causing starvation and misery to thousands. It is difficult to evaluate the role of IFAP within the pages of this book. As a body it tended to issue broadly worded aspirational statements about ending world hunger and providing a living return for farmers. It did, on occasion, issue clear position statements – for instance in 1967 it resolved that the International Wheat Agreement should be extended to cover coarse grains.

Although it lacked teeth when influencing the positions of respective governments, it would be wrong to dismiss IFAP as a talking shop. It represented the bringing together of the world's farmers under one roof and thus acted as a sounding-board through which the different organisations could better understand the position and views of others. For the leaders of the NFU it was a forum where they could meet with their counterparts from abroad to engender dialogue and understanding. Farming issues are often global issues that need global perspectives. IFAP facilitated such perspectives. In 1967 came the conclusion of the Kennedy round of the General Agreement on Tariffs and Trade (GATT), which had been set up in 1945 to allow countries to come together and agree to the mutual removal of tariffs and other restrictions to trade. Agriculture was always one of the toughest bones of contention. IFAP always had an input into GATT negotiations, and it made submissions to the FAO and OECD. FAO Director-General Dr Sen attended the conference. In 1967 the NFU rightly took pride in the fact that the child to which it had acted as both midwife and sugar-daddy had now grown into a creature of substance.

Meanwhile, back in the domestic sphere, the February price review continued to punctuate the farming calendar. Williams's first price review in 1967 was reasonably successful, with the government agreeing to a £25.5 million increase against increased costs of £10.5 million. But 1968 and '69 were not so

convivial, with awards of £16 million and then £6 million below increased costs, which were escalating with higher inflation towards the end of the 1960s.

Farmer anger was mounting and, again, calls were for the NFU to become more militant. One man who personified this growing discontent within union ranks was Devon Council delegate Wallace Day. Day was a small dairy farmer on a heavily mortgaged farm. The declining returns for milk production in the 1960s were pushing many small dairymen like Day out of business. The number of registered milk producers shrank from 131,000 in 1960 to 86,000 in 1970. The total number of dairy cows was quite stable, increasing only a few per cent, but the average herd nearly doubled in size, from 25 to 45.

The price reviews were largely unsympathetic to the plight of the small dairyman, as successive governments in the 1960s were reluctant to increase the milk price for fear of over-supply. The 1969 review had given a derisory 4d. increase per gallon and, to add insult to injury, had cancelled the effect of the rise by including a reduction in the standard quantity. As Williams tried to pick the positives out of the 1969 price review and thus defend his negotiating record, out in the regions the farmers, up to their eyes in debt and with nowhere to turn, became more impatient with the leadership.

The South West was characterised by its numerous small dairy farmers, and Day was a typical West-Country firebrand whose tub-thumping oratory was popular with members and very much in contrast with President Williams's more reserved, diplomatic style. It was easy for Day to talk up the 'that lot in the London HQ have lost touch with us lot on the ground' line. It was a cheap shot but one which normally hit the target. After the 1969 announcement, the South West called for a protest march on Whitehall to demand the resignation of the new MAFF Minister, Cledwyn Hughes. Council rejected the call.

Privately, Williams deplored Day's bloodymindedness but found it too difficult, publicly, to effectively counter or deal with Day's rabble-rousing style. There was no good evidence that Day's call to arms would be any more effective than Williams's quiet negotiation behind the scenes, but farmers were increasingly desperate for someone to be seen to be taking radical action. Within the county ranks an action group, the Farmers' Action Committee, was formed. Direct action such as withholding food supplies, refusing to pay taxes, traffic disruption and creating blockades was planned out. Although this activity was being undertaken on union premises and in action committees elected within the organisation, NFU HQ had to be careful it did not condone lawlessness or expose itself to prosecution or other sorts of litigation. It was a delicate balancing act that was easy to get wrong.

The temper of farmers was not improved by poor weather in 1968 and 1969, with indifferent springs and harvests. When, in 1969, the government justified its penny-pinching price review on the grounds that farmers should remedy the shortfall themselves by increasing productivity through greater efficiency, the inclement weather reminded farmers that Mother Nature did not always allow such policies, no matter how technically improved farming was becoming.

Finally, to add insult to injury, there was the little matter of 69,000 farmers in 1969 being threatened with court action for non-payment of Agricultural Training Board levies. The arrears mounted to nearly £500,000. The ATB had been set up in the mid-1960s under the Industrial Training Act, financed though a compulsory levy of £3 per worker per year to be paid by the farmer/employer. Farmers saw it as a state-imposed bureaucratic nonsense, wastefully overlapping what the agricultural colleges were successfully providing. Furthermore, the training offered was often irrelevant to the needs of the farm. It was an added burden on employers, particularly when the Agricultural Wages Board was awarding higher and higher wage increases. In 1968, the biggest ever award, 7.3 per cent, was imposed, bringing the minimum weekly wage to 12s.8d.

Farmers' refusal to pay the ATB levy rumbled on, and many swore they would go to prison rather than pay. The NFU was divided on the issue and Bill Williams struggled to give a clear line. In August 1969 Employment Minister Barbara Castle found a solution by making it part of the award of grants given in the price review.

In 1970, as the new year of the new decade dawned, Bill Williams was under pressure. Farmers were on the streets on foot and on tractor in many provincial towns protesting the need for an improved price review. Wallace Day was corralling the discontent by addressing large, angry NFU audiences in town halls across the land with his message on 'direct action'. Williams was torn between keeping integrity by patiently negotiating with government and playing to the cheaper seats by making threats about public disruption. What didn't help his predicament was the fact he was knighted in the New Year Honours. At another time it would have been a congratulatory moment for a man who richly deserved such recognition given his long service to agriculture, but in early 1970 many in the farming community were in a cynical mood, and it just added weight to the 'us and them' sentiment and gave validity to the accusation that the leadership were too cosy with government for their own good. At the AGM in late January a large banner was unfurled with the cutting message 'We want more Days and less Knights'. On the top platform during the AGM the president was clearly unnerved by the hostility of some of the assembly. Unsure how to react, at times he struggled to find his words. 'For

God's sake say something, even if it's just good-bye,' shouted a heckler from the audience. The perfectly mannered Williams did not deserve such rudeness, but the writing was on the wall. He failed to secure the 85 per cent vote he needed at Council and, like Woolley before him, suffered the ignominy of being pushed out of the job before he wanted to go.

Bill Williams was one of the nicest men to lead the NFU, but by the late '60s he lacked the pugnacity that the times demanded both in terms of standing up to the militants and of being seen to stand up to government. The *Farmer & Stockbreeder* commented at the time that he was 'too fair minded, quiet and patient an operator for these thrusting, strident and impatient times'. In one analysis he was a victim of the NFU's success. Since the war the NFU had worked in partnership with government for the benefit of the farming industry. Many outside agriculture had claimed it was too powerful and too close to government. At the same time, many within agriculture also complained it was too weak and too close to government. In the 1960s Joseph Heller wrote a book that perfectly captured the zeitgeist, *Catch 22*. 'Catch 22', as a concept, neatly summed up the dilemma in which presidents of the NFU could find themselves.

Meanwhile, back in Shropshire, the farm had not benefited from Williams's continual absence and was sold to the Prudential and leased back. It was good evidence of the sacrifice that sometimes had to be made by those farmers who aspired to be president of the NFU. Since 1945 the presidential salary had increased from £5,000 to only £8,000.

Williams's deal with the Pru was a sign of the times. As we have seen, the great estates of the private landowner had diminished at the beginning of the century, but some 60 years later a new type of large landowner had emerged, the city institution, usually in the form of pension funds and insurance companies. In the early 1970s these institutions were buying as much as 20 per cent of the land for sale. By the mid-1970s the Prudential owned 20,000 acres and, compared to the Eagle Star Group and Barclays Bank Trust Co., which both held over 70,000 acres, was only a minor player. It was an interesting development in the complex story of who owned British farmland and how much it was worth.

The good news for the Williams family is that Bill's son, David, still runs the family farm at Longford. As with many modern farms, the livestock has gone, but the range of crops Bill would have known is still there, long after his death in 1989. There is, however, one new crop – oilseed rape. Although this crop can be traced back to Roman times, it was during Williams's presidency that its yellow flowers started making an big impact on the farmscape of the southern counties. In 1968 4,000 acres were grown.

And so we come to the end of the 1960s, in many ways the end of the postwar era and the beginning of a radically new chapter. The 'price review' era was also coming to an end, soon to be replaced by life under the CAP. For 25 years farmers had had their prices guaranteed by government at levels fixed in negotiation with the NFU. Although Britain clearly didn't want, or need, as many farmers as it had had in the past, there was a general consensus throughout this 25-year period that the goal of increased agricultural production on UK farms was a good thing. It was an age when the phrase 'intensive agriculture', leading to greater levels of production, did not have the negative connotations it was later to attract. Two of the brakes on agricultural production that farmers know only too well today, animal welfare concerns and environmental constraints, were of little consequence in this postwar era. The publishing of the Brambell Report of 1965, which looked at animal welfare on farms, was a ground-breaking moment in that it put the issue firmly on the government agenda but was equivocal as to whether factory farming was cruel or not. It established codes of conduct and set minimum standards in the keeping of livestock. This had little dramatic impact on the way farm animals were kept, largely because British livestock standards were internationally high. The NFU was keen to make the point that if British farmer livestock practices were to be regulated, then imported meat should have the same protocols applied.

It terms of the environment there were a couple of signs of things to come. In 1970 the NFU held a conference with the RSPB which looked at hedgerow removal, and there was some early regulation of the use of fertilisers and muck near water authority boreholes. In the main, though, transforming the countryside to facilitate increased production through hedgerow removal and drainage was not just allowed, it was encouraged through grants. As we shall see, the next 25 years were to be a good deal more complicated when it came to shaping the countryside around increased agricultural production. The 25 years after the war had seen the removal of 232,800 km of Britain's 980,000 km of hedges, mainly, but not exclusively, through agriculture. In 1972 MAFF removed the grubbing-out grants, and since then a further 109,800 km have disappeared. The practice died out in the early '90s.

The year 1970 also represented a watershed moment for the NFU as an organisation. Ken Knowles, who had quietly sat behind the general secretary's desk for 25 years, retired. Under his guidance HQ income had risen from £30,000 in 1940 to a cool million in 1970. The changes he had overseen in terms of income, premises and staffing had transformed the headquarters of the NFU out of all recognition.

His reforms had also transformed life out in the counties – by the time of his retirement they were enjoying £1.5 million of income. As we have said before, although this book concentrates on the men at the top of the NFU, to understand that role you have to appreciate what was going on beneath him. Out on the ground there were 150,000 members across 49 county branches. Although Knowles had done much to centralise the NFU, it was still essentially a federation of county branches, each with its own income, its own staff, its own committees, its own headquarters, its own magazines, its own endless meetings, its own dinners and, above all, its own county secretaries. In the larger counties, such as Somerset, Devon, Essex, Norfolk and Lancashire, these county secretaries lorded it over serious fiefdoms. As the recipient of a percentage cut of the entire insurance business done by the NFU Mutual in the county, the county secretary was handsomely paid. There is the story of a county secretary who, having boarded the train with the rest of the county delegates on their way to the NFU AGM, would make his way to first class, leaving the farmers in second class, saying, 'Enjoy the journey and see you all at Paddington'. In those days the average member of the NFU knew two names – those of the man who was president and the man who was county secretary. We recollect here Harry Palmer, the first-ever county secretary who, in the 1910s, was obliged to travel third class, 'unless there was a fourth'.

Although the ill-discipline of the 1920s was gone, there was still very much a spirit of independence in the counties. Just because HQ said something, it didn't mean it had to be observed. There was room enough, and large enough audiences, for such mavericks as Wallace Day, who delighted in bearding the leadership in their Knightsbridge lair.

It was through the counties and branches that the NFU reached out to the individual on the farm. There was a myriad of ways in which this local nexus worked to help the farmer member; from guidance on obtaining one of the endless improvement grants available through to liaison with the relevant council on a new road; from setting up technical talks by NAAS on the latest ideas on good husbandry to giving advice on the latest set of regulations. While Knightsbridge was constantly in touch with Whitehall at all levels, so, too, the counties built up parallel local relationships. A book like this cannot possibly pay proper testament to the work the NFU did for the benefit of its members on the ground, but to understand the role of the president one must also understand how it was that he presided over so many thousands of rugged individuals who, every year, coughed up a not insignificant sub to be members of the united organisation that was the NFU. One also has to remember how the NFU, literally, brought farmers together under one roof. The meetings, the conferences, the dinners, the NFU show marquées, the rallies – all acting to sustain a camaraderie among farmers. One should not underestimate the therapeutic benefit of this. After all, 'a problem shared is a problem halved'.

*Henry Plumb dressed for a chat on the farm. Note the 1960s 'farmer uniform' –
tweed cap and jacket, not forgetting the collar and tie.*

Plumb joins a tractorcade in 1975.

CHAPTER 28

Sir Henry Plumb, Lord Plumb of Coleshill, 1970–79

Another factor in the demise of Bill Williams was the presence of his deputy, Henry Plumb. At the 1970 AGM, which sealed the fate of Williams, a member had shouted from the floor: 'If you won't fight for us, there's a young man at your side who will!' It was a portentous moment.

Unlike his two predecessors, Henry Plumb was a farmer's son, born in 1925 in the Warwickshire coalmining town of Anstley. The Plumbs had been farmers for generations in Warwickshire and Cheshire. In 1939 his father took two farms around the village of Maxstoke, near Coleshill in Warwickshire. Coleshill lies in a busy part of the world between Coventry and Birmingham. Today, the farm lies a few hundred yards north of the point where the M6 and the M6 toll divide. Like T.H. Ryland, his predecessor, Henry Plumb once farmed the good Warwickshire soil that now lies beneath the M6.

The farm was a typical mixed Midlands affair, milking cows and growing a range of crops such as potatoes and cereals on 300 acres. Henry was a bright lad, attending the King Edward VI School in Nuneaton, but one day in 1940 his education was brought to a sudden end before he could gain any academic qualifications. There was a war on and his father had lost much of his labour, and so the young Plumb was needed back home on the farm. As Luftwaffe bombs rained down on the nearby industrial conurbations and the night sky burned red, Henry spent his teenage years milking cows and riddling potatoes by hand. The only relief to all the drudgery was the arrival of three land girls in 1942.

In 1943 the 18-year-old showed his first signs of leadership potential when he was elected chairman of Coleshill YFC. By this time he had gained a reputation as a good speaker. Indeed, some of the older generation found it difficult to shut him up. Shortly afterwards he became chairman of Warwickshire North District YFC, where he became acquainted with vivacious secretary Marjorie. They were married in 1947. Through the 1940s and '50s the Plumbs built up a high-performing 200-strong Ayrshire herd, complete with automated milking. Young Henry showed early business acumen, building up direct sales for his Ayrshire milk, which he proudly marketed in waxed cartons, claiming his milk was 'more easily digested'. Aware that Trading Standards regulations prohibited unsubstantiated claims for consumables, he wisely did not mention what, exactly, he was claiming it was 'more easily

digested' than. In 1952 his father died at the young age of 58 and Henry was grateful for the help given by the Warwickshire county secretary in his moment of grief. Henry's father had been Warwickshire county chairman and eventually, sometimes despite his better judgement, Henry moved on from the YFC to become involved in union work. By 1959 he was sitting on Council to witness the last year of Jim Turner's leadership.

Plumb's talents were soon recognised and, in 1960, he became chairman of the Animal Health Committee. The postwar years had seen considerable advances in the health of British livestock, in particular the eradication of TB. One of Plumb's great achievements was to convince government to make brucellosis vaccine both free and compulsory. The early 1960s were possibly the last time that the combination of good farming husbandry and a comprehensive state veterinary service gave British farm animals a health status that was the envy of the world.

Henry found his NFU work rewarding, but not in the financial sense, and so, in 1963, he resolved to quit his HQ commitments. Only 38, he had a young family back home, as well as a dairy herd of 200 pedigree Ayrshires with a tidy direct-sales milk business. However, Warwickshire delegate David Darbishire had better plans for the young Plumb and proposed him as vice-president at the 1964 AGM, which he duly won by a narrow margin. Darbishire likened it to 'the Kennedy effect', whereby youth and vitality were given precedence over age and wisdom. Mercifully for Plumb, none of the NFU dissidents were to suffer a 'Lee Harvey Oswald' effect.

In 1968 he sat on the post-FMD enquiry and spent time in South America looking at the way the disease was handled. He came to much the same conclusion as had Harry German in 1928: that there were signs of progress when it came to controlling the disease, but there was still much left to be desired. It was clear that beef exports from the subcontinent, when combined with the swill feeding of pigs in the UK, clearly created an FMD risk in Britain, and further controls in South America were necessary. The NFU reached a similar view in 2008. Plumb also clashed with the British butchers' organisations over this. The butchers had called for his resignation from the Northumberland committee. Clashing with the butchers over measures to improve farm animal health, particularly in cows, is another NFU habit that goes back a long way.

By 1969 Plumb was deputy president and, with Williams' noticeably weakening grip on the presidency, was faced with the dilemma of whether he should remain the loyal deputy or openly run against his superior. In the end, Council sealed Williams's fate by not giving him the 85 per cent approval he needed, and in February 1970 the ambitious Plumb eagerly walked through the door that had been opened for him.

When summing up Henry Plumb as a man, one has to be careful. This is partly because he is still alive, but mainly because, such is the character of the man, one easily slips into seeming sycophancy. Avuncular is a word often used to describe Henry Plumb. Apt as it is, one must remember Henry has not always been the well-regarded and much-loved elder statesman he is now. There was a time in the NFU when he was a good deal younger than most around him. The impressive fact is that the young Plumb easily gained the confidence, trust and support of his elders.

To meet Henry Plumb now is to sense a self-assurance which, one guesses, he has always had. It is a self-assurance that is in no way self-regarding or pompous. He is confident of his own abilities while appreciative and encouraging of the abilities of others. Henry will be the first to admit he was never the brainiest man in the NFU, but his judgement was instinctive and usually right. He wisely looked to the counsel of those around him, particularly his revered Chief Economist, Asher Winegarten.

'Friendly' is another good word to describe Henry Plumb, but with, it is sensed, a ruthless streak. He is bluff and pugnacious, but in no way bullying or vindictive. He is good humoured and, although easy in his company, you would never dare take undue advantage of his good nature. He exudes energy and, even now, in his 80s, he seldom falters, and displays a stamina that would outpace a man half his age. He is known for the common touch whereby he is relaxed and welcoming in the company of all he meets, from factory workers and farmers to popes and princes. He has the stature of a stout yeoman and speaks with a light rural burr. Everyone knows him as 'the farmers' man'.

Unlike his mentor, Turner, Plumb always kept his feet firmly on the soil. Throughout his long career as NFU president and beyond, he remained a hands-on farmer. This undoubtedly made him a credible spokesman for the farming industry in the eyes of the public. As the viewing public of the '70s switched on their new colour TVs, it was often the articulate Henry Plumb, 'the farmers' leader', beaming out persuasively, putting over the farmers' case. At a reception at No. 10 in the late 1980s, Margaret Thatcher, introduced Plumb, then leader of the European Parliament, to the King of Spain as, simply, 'Our farmers' leader'. The King of Spain, who knew Henry well, replied: 'I think he is a good deal more than that.' The farmers of Britain would have agreed with the king but would have liked Mrs T's one-line resumé of the man. Down on the farm, Henry Plumb was, and for many still is, 'Our 'Enry'.

Plumb sees his remarkable life as a sequence of

"Hey!—How about waiting for the Plumb Line!"

Waiting for the Plumb Line in 1970.

events that 'threw him in at the deep end'. His sudden transformation from schoolboy to farmer's boy in 1940, the sudden death of his father in 1952, the sudden elevation to the NFU vice-presidency in 1964, have all moulded Plumb's strong character. In February 1970 came another 'sink or swim' moment. Just four days into his presidency he had to lead the price review negotiations.

The review that year was accompanied by a mass demonstration of more than 10,000 farmers, who marched through London and descended on Whitehall. As Plumb arrived to go into the MAFF buildings, he was carried in on the shoulders of the crowd. Farmers were desperate for a generous price review and, as Plumb, literally, sat on the shoulders of the farming community, he knew that their expectations and their frustrations, metaphorically, sat on his own.

The NFU position was that the industry's deficiency income should be brought up to £650 million, which meant an increase of £141 million. After a month of protracted stand-offs, when there was considerable pressure on Plumb to walk out, a final figure of £75 million was offered by the government. Plumb wouldn't accept it and, in a culmination of the review, he requested an interview with Prime Minister Wilson. Plumb later recollected the conversation at No.10 like this.

Wilson: *What makes you think that by coming to see me we can increase the offer.*
Plumb: *Because you wouldn't otherwise have agreed to see me at all*
Wilson: *If we can manage an increase, where would you want to put it?*
Plumb: *£5 million on milk and £5 million on potatoes*
Wilson: *Hmm, and if we do this, will you agree the package?*
Plumb: *No. We are still way off the £140 million income objective. But I will behave responsibly.*

There are two important points that this exchange illustrates. Firstly, as we freeze a moment in time, we witness one man, all alone, fighting for a better deal for 200,000 UK farmers, as he sits face to face with the most powerful man in the UK, the Prime Minister. It was a position in which Turner, Woolley and Williams had also found themselves over the preceding 25 years. Williams described it as 'the time when a President walks alone'. It is a vivid illustration of the key role the NFU president had in leading the farming industry during the price review era. Also, Plumb's rejection of Wilson's offer, along with his promise to 'behave responsibly', was a manifestation of the dilemma of Plumb's position and his genius in handling the predicament. Plumb knew that if he stormed out of negotiations, as many NFU members had demanded he do if the government didn't come up with £140 million, then the

outcome would probably be worse, as the government imposed a low settlement. On the other hand, if he agreed the package he would engage the wrath of many in the membership and possibly damage the NFU.

Convinced he had got the best deal he could from Wilson, Plumb set about publicly rejecting it. A resolution of protest as to the total inadequacy of the price review offer in ensuring industry needs was duly drawn up at Knightsbridge HQ and delivered to the House of Commons by Plumb in person, accompanied by the rest of Council.

At the post-review press conference the NFU rejected the settlement but warned the militants that they would disapprove of any illegal action and urged farmers not to block roads that would inconvenience or alienate the public. Plumb would have no truck with some of the stunts that Wallace Day and his action committee were advocating, but the NFU did draw up some contingency ideas as to what direct action might be taken to articulate their frustration with the settlement. Day had now been suspended from the NFU, and his newly formed Farmer Action Group was working outside the union structure. Plumb came head to head with Wallace Day, live on BBC1 television, with an audience of millions. The pugnacious Plumb managed to dampen down the West-Country firebrand by putting him on the spot as to exactly what the NFU strategy should be beyond spouting emotive rhetoric and threatening the public with disruption.

In May that year the NFU organised a week-long boycott of meat markets whereby farmers refused to take stock to market. This was widely observed and made a point in the media, but achieved little else. As spring sprung farmers' anger died down as land work took their attention.

Generally, it is accepted that one of Henry Plumb's achievements in the 1970s was the way in which he managed the disaffected and the militants. In 1970 the union was in a fractious mood, with a schism developing between those who wanted to take direct action and those who felt patient negotiation with government was the best approach. Under Plumb's leadership the rift never fully fractured and in 1980 he handed on a more united union than the one he had inherited. Where Williams had more or less ignored the militants, Plumb engaged with them. Plumb never side-stepped any confrontation with those members who thought he was taking a weak line. Once, at a branch meeting, a heckler had shouted out at him: 'We've heard all this tripe before. We want some action!' Plumb's response was, as ever, unyielding, pugnacious and blunt: 'So you've heard it all before, have you? Then suppose you tell me what action we should take!' Once off the podium, Henry would always make sure he talked genially and reasonably to his fiercest critics face to face. The president of the NFU is always going to be a whipping-boy for whatever ails its members. Plumb had the temperament not to take umbrage at this unfairness but rather dealt with it head on. His charm and approachability often softened the ire of the NFU's most critical members.

With the election of Ted Heath as Prime Minister in June 1970, entry into the EEC was firmly back on the agenda. With de Gaulle replaced by Pompidou in France and the Labour Party now prepared to back entry, it seemed there was little to stop Heath fulfilling the plan he had hatched ten years before. Many in the NFU were still sceptical, and shared the concerns Harold Woolley had had in the early '60s that the CAP would be a bad fit for the UK. In 1970 Woolley could still be found speaking up for the continuation of the deficiency payments scheme, which 'all envy and would copy if they could'.

Plumb was convinced the NFU should back entry and secure the best deal for its members. For him this was no time for fence sitting or acting in denial of inevitable change. Some sceptics on NFU Council wanted a vote to establish union policy. Worried that the vote would be against entry, Plumb refused to let a motion be brought and warned the proponents that if they forced the matter he would resign the presidency. Accordingly, the NFU line was not to oppose or campaign against EEC membership but help government prepare for entry by getting the best deal for UK farmers.

Henry Plumb will tell you he is not the euro-fanatic that many have painted him. His line is that he simply recognised the reality of the situation and sought to do what was best for British farming, given that, one way or the other, British farmers would soon fall under the auspices of the CAP. There was a lively political campaign against entry in 1971, but whether it would have succeeded if the NFU had put its weight behind it is doubtful. Nonetheless, Plumb

"There, in essence, is the story of EEC."

The British public have long been sceptical of the merits of the Common Agricultural Policy.

will be remembered as one of those who helped take Britain into the EEC, possibly in the face of what his membership wanted. What British agriculture would look like today if Britain had remained outside the EU is an interesting 'what if?' question, but not one we are going to explore in this book.

Ted Heath put Britain's name to the Treaty of Accession in January 1972 and Britain formally became a member a year later. A key victory for the NFU here was that agriculture was given five years to wean itself off the price review system and become one of the nine countries operating under the CAP. In March 1972 the NFU opened its Brussels office at No. 53 Rue Ducale, just down the road from the commission. Cumbrian farmer Tom Cowens, the NFU's new EEC Director, held the office with one secretary, one policy staffer and one interpreter. The NFU also affiliated to the pan-EEC farmer organisation COPA, and Plumb became its president in 1975. For its entire history the NFU had targeted Whitehall and Westminster with its lobbying. Now there would be a third front – Brussells.

EEC membership represented a fundamental shift in UK agricultural and food policy in the UK. In essence, under the old system consumers benefited from food at world prices and the taxpayer supported farmers through direct subsidies. The CAP was more about managing markets through imposing restrictions on the prices of competing imports. Farm support came through the increased price paid by the consumer and government expenditure in intervention buying and disposing of surpluses through subsidised exports.

With only a few price reviews left, Plumb recognised that it would be very important to keep British farm production as high as possible through higher guaranteed prices in order to give his members the best chance to thrive when they became full subjects of the CAP. The CAP most benefited those in the EEC who had the larger agricultural sectors, particularly in those areas where the CAP concentrated its subsidies – beef, sheep, dairy, sugar and cereals. Therefore, it made sense for Plumb to urge the government to maximise output in these areas through generous price reviews. The problem here was that in the 1970s the British economy was floundering. Out-of-control inflation, which in 1975 touched the high point of 22 per cent, was driving up farm costs. Also, the pound was on the ropes and devaluing fast. Not surprisingly, governments were mighty reluctant to give farmers the increased treasury expenditure needed to keep prices in line with costs and thus maintain 1970 production levels. The NFU also repeatedly made the case to government that, while the British economy was hard pressed, it made sense to reduce its balance of payments by maximising the output from one of its most efficient industries – agriculture.

Under the Tories, the price reviews of '71, '72 and

'73 partly reflected the need to keep farm production high. It probably helped that the minister at the time, Jim Prior, was a Suffolk farmer. Between 1971 and '74 the Tories introduced a levy system that put controls on imports. In 1975 this was disbanded as British farming moved under the protective umbrella of the CAP, with its fortress-like tariff system to keep out imports.

The 1971 price review was the first to list the deficiency payments in the new decimal currency, which many Britons were struggling to get their heads around. In the live marts farmers wondered if the new bidding increment of 5p really gave them as good a deal as when they bid in good old shillings. It doesn't seem possible now that there were farmers then who preferred it when there were 12d. in a shilling and 20s. in a pound. But, then, there are still farmers today who prefer to do their farming by reference to acres, yards, gallons and hundredweights rather than simpler metric units.

The last full price review, in 1972, was satisfactory to the NFU. They had asked for £100 million and settled at £72 million when increased costs had been £48 million. Cereals were given the largest increases in an attempt to move them towards the high CAP levels. Suffolk cereal farmer and MAFF Minister Jim Prior could be found urging farmers to grow more cereals and to improve their yields.

In 1974 Harold Wilson returned with his Labour administration and Minister Fred Peart returned to MAFF. So 1974 can be summed up as 'up corn, down horn', and livestock farmers were back out on the streets in protest. It was a grim year in general for Britain, remembered for strikes, power cuts and the three-day week. In contrast, for cereal farmers it was a golden year, as prices of wheat and barley doubled when a poor Soviet harvest forced the Russians to grab the world's meagre stocks. In contrast, British farmers had enjoyed a record harvest of 16 million tonnes. For livestock farmers the situation was not so rosy. In the early '70s the beef herd in Britain had increased by 2–3 million beasts. It was the heyday of barley beef. In 1974 a poor hay crop had left livestock farmers short of fodder, and escalating cereal feed prices added insult to injury. Fertiliser prices were also painfully expensive on the back of high OPEC-controlled oil prices and the Flixborough disaster, which saw the Fisons plant blow up. More than ever livestock farmers needed price support. The opposite happened. Having promised support for the beef sector, the Labour government found that the new EEC system of 'intervention buying' of beef was suddenly unsustainable, as the system had built up huge stocks. Minister Peart opted out of the intervention-buying level and the price of meat went into free fall. For the first time in 25 years there was no market support for beef. Live cattle prices were halved. Young calves dropped to 50p each and many were slaughtered on farm and buried. The milk, pig

and poultrymen were also in trouble, as prices were not even closely keeping up with costs. In May angry cattle farmers demonstrated through London and released steers onto the streets of Whitehall. The following week the pig farmers arrived and released a 133k sow from a van.

As ever, Plumb had a balancing act to achieve. Fortunately for the NFU, he was predominantly a dairy and beef farmer and experienced the pain of low prices personally, at his own farm. (In unguarded moments Henry will sheepishly admit that sometimes, when he returned home to Maxstoke after a week in London, he would check his cows before checking his wife and children.) This gave him credibility with the hard-pressed livestock sector. Throughout the summer of 1974 Plumb made trips down to the West Country and Wales to try to calm the militants, who were threatening breakaway groups as well as unlawful direct action. Plumb was keen on 'shirt-sleeves' meetings, face to face with members. In September he led a 100-strong tractorcade through Birmingham city centre. There were over 200 similar events elsewhere, involving 50,000 farmers and 5,000 vehicles. On the forecourt of Sheffield Cathedral NFU members gave away milk, bacon, eggs and chicken to passing shoppers.

As ever, some farmers hatched plots that, for Plumb, were such that it was better he appeared to know nothing about them. There was, though, an extremely cavalier attempt by three Westcountry farmers to kidnap Prime Minister Wilson from his summer retreat in the Scilly Isles. The outrageous plot was subverted by fog, which made it impossible to land their light aircraft. At Holyhead farmers blockaded the port to stop Irish beef being unloaded. The NFU was quick to distance itself from the Holyhead blockade, particularly as it could find itself in breach of the Restrictive Trade Practices Act. Instead, Plumb sent well-publicised telegrams to Prime Minister Wilson and his Irish counterpart, Cosgrave, demanding reductions in Irish beef imports. Through negotiation the NFU did secure some improved headage payments, but livestock returns remained very low and 1975 saw more demonstrations and farmer blockades. The mid-1970s were a bruising time for livestock farmers, but Henry Plumb remained their champion – just.

On a more technical front, throughout the 1970s the NFU had to work hard at minimising the tax burden as governments brought in new regimes. In 1972 VAT was kept off food and farm produce generally. Relief from the new Wealth Tax and Capital Transfer Tax was achieved in 1975. This was particularly relevant to farmers because of the land boom of the early 1970s, when farmland prices doubled from £500 an acre to over £1,000. Again, Plumb led with the argument that, as Britain's balance of payments deficit escalated and as Britain entered the EEC, then it was important to maximise farm output and give farmers confidence to invest in the future. Left-wing MPs and journalists could be found complaining that farmers, led by the NFU, somehow always managed to slip much of the taxation net with their spurious argument that they were somehow a 'special case'. A more fundamental disagreement the NFU had with the left wing of the Labour Party was the fact it still had land nationalisation written into its constitution. Throughout the 1970s the NFU resisted any proposals that smacked of compulsory public owner-ship of land. The irony in the late 1970s was that the Labour leader, James Callaghan, owned his own farm in Sussex. History doesn't record whether he was a member of the NFU.

One area where the NFU found itself in agree-ment with the socialists was that of tenant rights. In 1976 the Miscellaneous Provisions Act further extended the protection of tenants by giving succes-sion rights to two succeeding generations. With the large increase in land prices in the early '70s, a number of landlords had become keen to oust tenants and take occupation. There were many instances of farmers in their 40s and 50s being uncer-emoniously removed from the farms they had spent their lives improving. The 1976 Act sought to redress such injustices, and represents another chapter in the twentieth-century story of the swing of the balance of power from landlord to tenant. Throughout its 70-year history the NFU had fought for increased secu-rity for tenants. It turned out that the 1976 Act repre-sented a watershed moment. At first the NFU had welcomed the Bill as a gesture that protected the family farm and encouraged tenant farmer invest-ment, but afterwards, as the number of new tenancies fell, the NFU realised that the Act might have gone too far. The YFC had opposed the measure, as they felt it would stifle the opportunities for new entrants trying to get a foot on the farming ladder. With time, the NFU came round to their view. The 1976 Act represents the zenith of sitting-tenant power in their long struggle to lobby government for greater secu-rity. Not suprisingly, the period also represents a nadir in farm tenancies. By 1980 the NFU was 75 per cent an owner-occupier organisation. This was a turnaround from the time of the NFU's inception, when it was primarily a tenant farmer organisation in a country where 80–90 per cent of farms were tenanted. You could argue that this was a triumph of farmer power and reflects well on the history of the NFU, but the ghost of the union's founder, Colin Campbell, who was a tenant farmer and an advocate of landlordism, would remind you that there were significant advantages for agriculture if land owner-ship and farming did not always go hand in hand.

Throughout the 1970s the NFU as an organisation went through a period of slow restructuring under the new director-general, George Cattell. Cattell's background was not in farming, but rather he had worked for car makers Rootes and then for the Ministry of Labour under Barbara Castle. Just like his predecessor Knowles in 1945, Cattell arrived at Agriculture House in 1970 determined to shake up the county structure and centralise the organisation. As he asked President Plumb in 1971: 'Are we a national union or not?'

As agriculture had lost farmers through the '60s and '70s so, inevitably, had the NFU. From the high point of 210,000 in the mid-1950s, membership had fallen to 150,000 in 1970 and by 1980 would fall to 140,000. For some of the smaller counties it meant numbers were getting perilously low. It also meant income was under pressure, and, by the late 1960s, the NFU was often running an annual budget deficit. Cattell's solution was amalgamation and direct finance. Under the latter, the counties no longer collected subs but rather it was done centrally. The counties thus no longer employed staff directly, HQ was now the employer. This was an important reform, as it struck at the heart of county independ-ence. Generally, centralised finance met little resist-ance in the counties, but the second plank of Cattell's reform, amalgamation, certainly did. The idea was for counties to merge with neighbours until, eventu-ally, there would be just ten regions in the NFU rather than 49 counties. Some of the smaller counties, such as Surrey, Sussex, Middlesex, Cumbria and Westmorland, Leicestershire, Northamptonshire and Rutland, Berkshire, Buckinghamshire and Oxfordshire did merge, but the majority flatly refused. Predictably, Norfolk was the first to announce it would not be merging with anyone, least of all with Suffolk. Cornwall, aware that the only bedfellow on offer was the dreaded Devon, would have no truck with Cattell's plans. Devon agreed wholeheartedly with Cornwall's isolationist position. Henry Plumb's home county, Warwickshire, now home of the Royal Show at Stoneleigh, considered itself far too important to share with any of its seven neighbours. Somerset and Dorset looked at each other, flirted a bit, and decided not to bother. Even Yorkshire, which was divided into four convoluted segments, couldn't bring itself to unite as one county. It was not until the late 1980s that regionalisation was set up. Until then the county structure of the NFU stayed more or less intact.

One minor reform Plumb introduced was the reduction of the number of council meetings from 12 to eight a year. There was little complaint from Council apart from one member, who told Plumb he would accept the scrapping of four of the London meetings on condition no one told his wife.

In terms of services to members, under Plumb's leadership the NFU withdrew from the commercial field it had wandered into over the preceding 15 years. NFU Seeds was folded up after years of indif-ferent performance. NFU Services, which was basi-cally a secretarial agency run by the NFU for the benefit of its members, was also terminated. With

500 clients, the service was not without its success. The problem was that many members thought it was a free service already paid for by their sub, and so were reluctant to pay the bills.

Plumb was always an advocate of the co-operative concept and was convinced British farmers would have to move in this direction if they were to compete with their fellow Europeans in the EEC. As ever, the Continentals were far in advance of anything that had been established in the UK. Early on in his presidency Plumb had gathered together the marketing boards, the FMC and the co-operatives under a body called BAMDO, the British Marketing Development Organisation. It largely failed to achieve its objectives of improving collective marketing by British farmers. To this day Plumb worries about the British farmer's failure effectively to co-operate with his fellows.

The late '70s were characterised by some testing weather. In the first six months of 1976, the year of the great drought, much of southern England received only 30 per cent of the rain that could normally be expected. With cereal crops dying on their feet, harvest was very early and yields were low, but there were some bonanza potato prices around for anyone with good irrigation. In the winter of 1978 heavy snow, gales and floods had caused havoc in the West County. As ever, Plumb was quickly on the scene to see the problems for himself. He realised it was a crisis point for the many livestock men who had lost stock to the weather. Frustrated at apparent government indifference, Plumb personally initiated an appeal which quickly raised a £1 million relief fund. With Plumb's lead the British Government added £3 million, sourced from the EEC disaster fund that the NFU had helped establish. This enabled the farmers in trouble to be compensated £20 a sheep and £70 a beast. It was a good example of the NFU working to relieve members in a crisis.

Throughout his presidency, Plumb recognised that to understand British agriculture it was necessary to see it in its global perspective. He travelled more extensively than any previous NFU leader. In 1973, at the 19th World Conference of IFAP, Plumb made clear the NFU's aim to strengthen world commodity agreements on wheat and sugar and to conclude an agreement on dairy products. As president of IFAP in 1975, he ensured it was the only agricultural NGO that enjoyed consultative status with the UN in the GATT and WTO rounds. He thought it vitally important that, through IFAP, the world's farmer organisations presented a united policy position to politicians in the WTO arena. At the same conference Plumb established a dialogue between the European and the American farmer delegations, which he felt was important as Britain entered the EU. In his role as president of COPA after 1975, he pursued these same goals of the farmers of the world presenting a united front. In the Tokyo round of the GATT, 1973/79, beef and milk were kept out of the multilateral commitments, which was to the benefit of UK farmers.

Plumb's increasing roles in Europe and further afield gave him an appetite for spreading his wings beyond the confines of the NFU. As with Dorman-Smith before him, it was inevitable that, given his undeniable talents, he would eventually resign from the presidency of the NFU of his own accord and move onto greater things. It was clear that the NFU was happy under his leadership and, unlike his two predecessors, there was never any serious attempt to unseat him. In 1978 his long-serving deputy, Richard Butler, had said to Plumb: 'Henry, you know one day soon I will have to think about challenging you.' Plumb replied: 'Quite right, Richard, you certainly should challenge me. Your problem is that you will lose.' It was a comment typical of Plumb – playful but ruthless, as well as being a correct analysis. Mercifully for Butler, in 1978 Plumb decided to move on to different pastures and stood down at the 1979 AGM. He calculated that he had travelled over a million miles and consumed three tonnes of food at official functions as president of the NFU.

In 1980 he was elected as an MEP for the Cotswolds in the first ever elections to the European Parliament. He took the Tory whip, although one suspects that if Plumb thought he had a chance of winning the seat as an independent then that is what he would have done. In 1987 he became president of the European Parliament and, as such, was a leading world statesmen who strode the world stage amongst world leaders – from Pope Paul to President Reagan. He also got heavily involved with providing development for third-world agriculture. Knighted in 1973 and ennobled in 1987, today Lord Plumb of Coleshill sits in the House of Lords and contributes more than most, especially on agricultural matters. Every weekend he returns home to his farm at Maxstoke and to that vivacious secretary he met all those years ago at Young Farmers. We don't know if he still checks his stock before he goes in to say hello to Marjorie, but we suspect he still might.

Henry Plumb's life merits a book all of its own, and indeed it has one, his autobiography, *The Plumb Line*.

For the generation of farmers born after the Second World War, Henry Plumb is the greatest NFU president. When they were running for the 2006 presidency, both NFU President Bennett and challenger Kendall listed Plumb as their greatest inspiration. In fairness to Plumb's predecessors, such comments suffer from the fact that such men as Campbell, Robbins, Baxter, Dorman-Smith and Turner are dead and overlooked. Either way, Henry Plumb is undoubtedly one of the greatest men to have led the NFU and British agriculture. His crowning achievement was that he took over a frac-

Top and above: *Mrs Thatcher and the Pope get to meet an icon of the age.*

decade made positive reading for the farming industry. During the decade self-sufficiency in food had risen 10–15 per cent. Output per man had doubled and British agriculture was the most efficient and most mechanised in Europe. Yields in eggs, pigs, sugar beet, potatoes and cereals had all seen 13 per cent improvements in the decade. Sugar beet had seen an increase of 460,000 acres to 560,000. Even in the beef and dairy sector, which had been the source of most of the farmer angst in the '70s, there had been expansion. UK cattle numbers increased from 12.5 million in 1970 to 13.5 million in 1980, though this was a million short of the peak of 15 million in the middle of the decade. Sheep numbers had increased 15 per cent.

Annual public expenditure on agriculture by the UK Treasury rose from 250 million in 1970 to 800 million in 1980 which, in light of the chronic inflation that characterised the decade, was about the same in real terms. Most farmers in the 1970s were more productive and better rewarded than in any other decade in the twentieth century. For large lowland farmers in particular, it had been a rich decade, with prices running ahead of inflation. The downside was that the number of farmers had fallen 20 per cent, and it had been tough for many of the small men. Even so, in short, Plumb's goal in 1970 to increase UK farm production so that it could make the most of EU membership had, by and large, been achieved.

Henry Plumb will always be known as the man who took British farming into Europe. One thing we should remember about Henry Plumb is that, as a teenager, from his farmstead vantage-point a few miles to the north, he witnessed the bombing of Coventry and all the death and destruction it entailed. In his lifetime he has seen the European nations at each other's bloody throats and has also seen the continent of Europe enjoy the longest peace it has ever known, along with the undeniable prosperity that that peace has facilitated. Although the postwar generation may quibble about the inadequacies of the EU, men like Henry Plumb have a deeper, more profound understanding of what the fundamental achievement of the European Union of Nations really is. Peace and harmony are only truly appreciated by those who know what it is like to be without them. Lord Plumb of Coleshill is one such.

tious union and led it united through a testing time which saw the slow, painful disappearance of thousands of small farmers. He also kept the union together at a time when the arable men had enjoyed an appreciably better decade than their livestock brethren.

Although the 1970s will be remembered for farmer anger on the streets, some statistics about the

CHAPTER 29

Sir Richard Butler, 1979–86

Richard Butler had been at Henry Plumb's side as his vice or deputy throughout his ten-year presidency. With Plumb's 'up-front' style, Butler was the man in the background. It was said that between them they made a very effective partnership of brawn and brains. Where Plumb was bluff, boisterous and instinctive, Butler was modest, diplomatic and considered. Unlike the bear-pit atmosphere of the 1970 AGM that saw Plumb take the presidency, the 1979 AGM was a far more sedate affair, as befitted the man who calmly took the reins. No one challenged Plumb as he stood down of his own accord, and no one challenged his deputy for the role that was vacated.

Of all the presidents of the NFU, Richard Butler probably has the best pedigree. Just as Harold Woolley's farming could be traced back to Victorian medicinal potions, Butler's farm had its origins in silk and underwear. His mother was one of the Courtauld family. The Courtaulds were self-made Victorian silk magnates with extensive mills in North Essex. The wealth they generated from silk turned them into landowners and benefactors of the arts. In the twentieth century the Courtaulds moved into synthetic fibres and became world leaders in their production. Richard will tell you proudly that he still has a pair of pyjamas made from Rayon.

Richard's father was the famous 'Rab' Butler, who served in the Tory cabinets in the late '50s and early '60s. Although he was variously Home Secretary, Foreign Secretary and Chancellor of the Exchequer, politics conspired against him and he never made it to the top job. Consequently, he is remembered as the best Prime Minister Britain never had. The Tory grandee was known for his integrity, his humility and his sense of public service. They were virtues he passed on to his son.

Rab Butler had met one of the Courtauld daughters as an undergraduate at Cambridge. They married and Rab was selected for the safe Conservative seat of Saffron Walden in North Essex. He was duly elected in 1929, the year Richard was born. Eventually the family moved to one of the Courtauld farms, Gledfen Hall, near Greensted Green, where Richard grew up. With Courtauld land and Butler politics in his genes, it was only logical that Richard should turn out to be a consummate farming politician.

Educated at Eton and Cambridge followed by a short spell in the Guards – these were the days of compulsory National Service – he returned home to start farming the family estate of 1,100 acres in the early 1950s. He joined the NFU in 1953 and became a council member in the 1960s, then chairman of the Peas Committee. In 1970 he became deputy under Plumb and finally, when Plumb stepped down at the end of the decade, president.

Richard Butler – hands-on Essex farmer.

Although most postwar NFU presidents were hardly smallholders, Butler was probably the first perceived 'large landowner' to take the presidency since Stanley Ratcliff, also from Essex, in 1934. Moreover, Butler was clearly from the corn side of the 'up corn, down horn' equation that had become more pronounced during the 1970s. The moniker that was cheaply bandied about in the 1960s – Barley Baron – would have applied to men such as Butler. Inevitably, some suggested he would struggle to appeal to the small livestock men in the hills, or understand their position. Butler's response was that 20 years of working at NFU headquarters had not passed unnoticed. He was only too well aware that British agriculture was a wide spectrum of different sorts of farmers, all of whom had a right to be represented by the NFU. While Butler did not have Plumb's gift for the common touch, he knew the importance of getting out to the regions and meeting farmers face to face. He could often be found standing on trailers, megaphone in hand, speaking in all corners of his constituency.

Through the 1950s Butler acquired more land by taking tenanted farms in hand. By the 1960s he was farming over 2,000 acres as a single operation. The soils were mixed, as they gently undulated across the picturesque shallow river valleys of North Essex. In the 1960s it was typical mixed eastern counties farming. There were two milking herds, barley beef, strawed pigs and poultry lofts, as well as large acreages of wheat, barley, peas, and sugar beet run by a small army of men and machines. In the '60s Butler jointly formed a grower group, Essex Peas Ltd, with five other large Essex farms, in order to secure a grant from the Central Council for Agricultural and Horticultural Co-operation (CCAHC) for a mobile viner. When the grants were withdrawn in the early 1970s the small co-op stayed together jointly to market their peas and beans for canning and freezing.

By the time he took the presidency of the NFU in 1979, apart for a few residual beef animals, all the livestock had gone, the pigs and poultry in the '50s and the dairies in the '60s. Barley beef, which for many lowland cereal farms had seen a boom in the 1960s, was severely scaled back in the 1970s as the price of barley and other concentrates rose quicker than the price of beef.

By 1980 Butler's farming concentrated on cereals, oilseed rape, vining peas and sugar beet. It was a story of gradual arable specialisation over the 20 years after the war that was typical of eastern-region farming. Cereals, which had represented 50 per cent of the land in tillage in 1950 had reached 60 per cent by 1980. The introduction of oilseed rape was also typical. In the early '80s it covered over 400,000 acres in the UK. The late '70s and early '80s, with good harvests and good prices, had been successful times for the combinable crops men. One is reminded of the tired old joke that did the rounds at the time that the East Anglian four-year rotation had now become 'wheat: barley: wheat: bahamas'.

This increasing specialisation was intrinsically linked to mechanisation, efficiency, increased inputs and increased output. The other side of the coin was the decline of the dairy and livestock sector in the South and East. In 1945 these regions still represented 25 per cent of dairy production, but by 1970 this had fallen to less than 10 per cent, and fallen quite rapidly. Rotational grass that before the war had accounted for a third of the arable acreage was now less than a fifth.

When he first embarked on his farming career in the early 1950s, Butler still used carthorses alongside the small tractors. Cereal crops were still harvested with reaper and binder, stacked and then, in the winter, thrashed in a static threshing machine, all labour-intensive work. Within 20 short years all this had changed out of all recognition. A handful of men armed with a few large tractors and a couple of combines could now cover a couple of thousand acres. In 1950 the UK boasted just 10,000 combines; by 1971 it was 57,000.

Cereal yields tripled from than 1 tonne/acre in 1945 to over 3 tonnes/ha in 1980. Better varieties, greatly increased fertiliser use (a four-fold increase between 1945 and 1980) and the introduction of herbicides, insecticides and fungicides had all led to a revolution in cereal husbandry. The wheat and barley hectarage in Britain had expanded from 1.5 million in 1945 to 3.7 million in 1980, with barley seeing the larger threefold increase. It was in the late '70s, with a run of good wheat harvests, that wheat production started to dominate the flat eastern counties. It was even creeping into the traditional grass downland of such counties as Hampshire and Wiltshire. Although the grant for ploughing up grassland had been stopped in 1972, good combinable crop prices, coupled with indifferent returns in the livestock sector, continued to push the plough and the cereal drill ever westwards. Prices had encouraged this expansion, rising from £10 a tonne in 1945 to over £100 in 1980, the latter being the price at which 'intervention' buying by the EU was triggered, thus putting an artificial floor in the market. It was in around 1980 that Britain changed from being a net importer of cereals to being a net exporter. It also became far more self-sufficient in milling wheat for bread, which before the war had been 30 per cent but which had risen to 75 per cent by 1990. The only combinable crop to decline was oats. With the demise of the horse, the acreage down to equine fuel in the form of the oat crop plummeted from 1,400,000 acres in 1940 to just 100,000 in 1980.

It was a golden year for cereal farmers in 1984. Many farmers were making it into the ICI 'ten tonne club', which, in old parlance, meant they were achieving crops of over 4 tonne/acre. The year was a pinnacle of achievement but, in another analysis, the pudding was possibly getting over-egged. Europe was producing huge surpluses of cereals which were costly to store and had to be exported to third-world countries at discounted prices achieved through export restitutions. EU cereals were fetching prices at as much as twice the level the free world market was dictating. Also, environmentalists were becoming increasingly noisy about what they saw as the degradation of the countryside through the rapacious expansion of the cereal crop and the accompanying pesticide use. The increased efficiency and productivity had come at a cost. Hedges had been taken out to create larger fields to accommodate the new large machinery and the average farm size in the arable east had more than doubled. For the NFU one of the fallouts from all this was a loss of farms and farmers. Another consequence was the demise of the mixed farm. The membership of the NFU was becoming increasingly polarised by sector and by region, which obviously made effective representation more challenging. The gap between horn and corn was widening as the 'up corn: down horn' dynamic became more pronounced through the 1970s. It is a remarkable testimony to the NFU that in the face of this polarisation it managed to retain 80–90 per cent of commercial agriculture under its broad umbrella.

The start of Butler's presidency witnessed a change in government. In 1979 Margaret Thatcher had been elected Britain's first lady Prime Minister. Curiously, her brother-in-law was an Essex farmer like Butler, and some of Thatcher's Saatchi & Saatchi-groomed photos had been taken on the Essex farm. The Thatcher administration was to prove very different from the previous Conservative one led by europhile Ted Heath. The 'one nation' Toryism of Butler's father was also now a distant memory. Fired by the economic philosophy of monetarism, Mrs Thatcher was keen to take her handbag to any industry that looked to the public purse for support, and she displayed an icy single-mindedness that made her indifferent to political lobbying. There was also a hefty dose of EU scepticism and a determination to reduce the EU budget, 70 per cent of which was consumed by the CAP. One saving grace was that Thatcher's first agricultural minister was Peter Walker, one of the so-called 'wets' in the cabinet.

Intriguingly, one possibility that was discussed in 1979 was that Richard Butler's younger brother, Adam, who was a Tory MP, might be given the MAFF job. Some joked it could result in the biggest falling-out between brothers since Cain and Abel. In the end Walker's appointment, rather than that of Butler jnr, avoided any possible family difficulty.

It is not easy to sum up Richard Butler as a man because of his complexity. 'Benign indifference', 'inscrutable', 'detached' and 'aloof' have all been bandied about by others in describing him. They are superficial impressions that don't get beneath the surface of the man or do him justice. He has an alert, analytical mind and in his company you feel you are being read like a book. There is no pulling the wool over his eyes. As an NFU office-holder he had a reputation for being easily able to pick up a brief and grasp the key points. He was a good listener. Generally, he exercised good judgement and was never prone to rashness. He oozed a quiet competence and, if he sometimes could appear a little severe, was never unpleasant or unkind. Some referred to him as 'the dining-room diplomat'. He had a mental toughness that proved a worthy attribute in the bear-pit of politics. In his time as president, those around him respected his grasp of issues to the point that it was said council members were frightened to publicly challenge him for fear the president would expose their ignorance. There was a cool aura of patrician authority surrounding Richard Butler that put people on their guard and commanded their respect. What Butler sometimes lacked, though, was the appreciation that most farmers were not as intelligent as he himself.

In his manners, as well as in his measured diction and in his physique, he reflected the good breeding of his pedigree. He was unhurried and unflappable. 'I need to speak to you about something rather urgently,' his deputy, Tom Boden, once requested. 'I can give you 15 minutes some time in the week after next,' was Butler's calm reply.

To meet him today you get the feeling there is something pleasantly old-fashioned about Richard Butler which you can't help but warm to. It comes as little surprise that he lists horse riding and hunting as his hobbies. It makes you think he comes from a different, more noble age, when men were in some way more civilised than they are today.

Butler was the first NFU president to spend his entire presidency immersed in EU politics. One convenient development for him was the expansion of Stansted Airport, just ten miles from his home in Essex. It made his journey to Brussels or Strasbourg a good deal easier. The irony was that the NFU had largely opposed the expansion of Stansted as London's third airport on the grounds of its deleterious impact on the local agriculture. In the 1980s Britain was losing 20,000 ha of farmland a year to development. It was a time when the NFU tried to fight a rearguard action against the loss of good agricultural land to the ever-expanding towns, cities and roads.

As Britain became a full member of the EU, British farmers were having to learn a new euro-language with acronyms such as EMU, EMS and MLAs. There was also a new public figure in their lives, the EU Agricultural Commissioner, who was like a European über-Minister of Agriculture. To make life more complicated, these men didn't have proper names like Prior, Peart and Silkin; this lot were called names like Gundelach, Dalsager and Andriessen.

One of Butler's first political battles was the 'green pound' gap. At the time, EEC farm prices were set in European currency units, which represented an average of a basket of the main EEC currencies. These ECU rates were then converted into national currencies at the so-called 'green' rates of exchange, which were fixed in order to prevent prices fluctuating on a daily basis. The lower one's green rate of exchange, the higher the national equivalent of the ECU price, with the result that 'we must have a devaluation of the green pound' became the NFU's chief rallying cry (hardly an inspiring one) throughout the late '70s and early '80s. The issue was made complicated by the British refusal to join the EMU. Because of the weakness of sterling by 1980, the green pound was overvalued by 15 per cent, which meant lower support payments for British farmers compared to their continental counterparts. The government was loath to devalue the green pound, as it would raise inflation by increasing food prices for consumers. Although the NFU argued that a 15 per cent devaluation of the green pound would

Dumping tomatoes outside the Dutch embassy to make the point that Dutch producers were given unfair an advantage over British growers.

lead to less than a 1 per cent impact on inflation, the government were steadfast, and it wasn't until the pound strengthened in 1981 that some sort of parity was achieved. By the early '80s it had become clear that government policy was concentrating on reducing inflation and public expenditure. It was proving largely impervious to NFU complaints about the plight of the farming industry, which was suffering decreasing returns (real farm income fell 50 per cent in the period 1978–82) and increasing debt. Union calls to reduce high interest rates were also ignored.

In 1979 the French refused to accept imports of British lamb, while they were happy to take from the other eight in the community. The dispute stemmed from the British insistence in the entry negotiation in the early 1970s on continuing freely to import dairy and lamb products from New Zealand according to the quota arrangements they had with their old colonial cousins. This had complicated the establishment of an EU Sheep Meat Regime, which rankled with the French. To make their point the French banned British lamb, which reached a critical point when British farmers completed their EU transition in 1979. At the time lamb was fetching 60p/lb in Britain and 90p in France. Not surprisingly, the British lamb producers were keen to have access to the French market and the French were keen to keep them out. Despite a ruling from the European Court of Justice against them, the French kept the ban in place. It proved the European Court rather toothless and led to demands from farmers that the British Government follow the French example of breaking the rules when it suited. One hot issue at the time was the import of French apples, which was decimating the British apple industry. Rather than encourage this 'tit for tat' mentality, in November '79 President Butler and a motley bunch of fellow NFU men were aboard the good ship *Viking Valiant* bound for Cherbourg armed with 2 tonnes of British lamb determined to make the French play by the rules. On

their arrival at Cherbourg, the cunning French avoided a publicity-fuelled stand-off by allowing the lamb and accompanying party through but then promptly continued the embargo. The dispute rumbled on until October 1980, when the British secured a higher lamb price from the community budget. It was not the first time, because of their slightly detached membership, that British farmers found themselves being treated differently from farmers in the other eight members.

Butler's presidency was marked with a number of efforts to ensure fair play for British farmers on the supposedly 'level playing-fields' of the CAP. Another cause of vociferous complaint from the glasshouse men was the practice in Holland of providing their growers with cheap subsidised gas.

There was more EU grief in 1980, when Prime Minister Thatcher blocked a much-anticipated and improved farm price agreement because of her dispute over UK budget contributions. Eventually, rebates were agreed as demanded by the Iron Lady and the new CAP package was agreed. In 1982 the British Government tried the tactic of blocking farm price reviews again to press for a budgetary rebate. This caused considerable frustration for Butler, as the two issues were technically not related, but it was clear the government were happy to compromise British agricultural interests in the pursuit of their budget agenda. Eventually, in May 1982, the issue was solved by the rare use of majority voting. The episode was a neat illustration of how Mrs Thatcher's 'non-communitaire' attitude to Europe made the NFU feel they were sometimes the step-children around the CAP family table. More than once in the early '80s, Butler and the NFU found themselves considering the possibility that Mrs Thatcher might actually take Britain out of the EU.

In July 1982, with Britain celebrating the victories in the South Atlantic as the British taskforce successfully evicted the Argentinians, who had invaded the Falklands four months earlier, a little bit of paramilitary conflict blew into Agriculture House in Knightsbridge. A Semtex bomb in a blue Austin car was detonated a few yards away on the corner of Hyde Park, breaking windows and sending glass flying over NFU staff. The target was not the NFU but the Household Cavalry, who were making their way back to barracks having changed the guard at Buckingham Palace. Two soldiers and several horses were killed. Mercifully for the NFU, it was Royal Show week. Ordinarily at 11 in the morning, when the bomb went off, the first-floor committee rooms, which took the main force of the explosion, would have been busy with farmers and staff and the casualty list would have been much higher. Richard Macdonald, who was then an NFU parliamentary adviser, had the misfortune to be walking back to Agriculture House when the bomb went off and was literally blown through a carpet-shop window. Mercifully, he only suffered a few cuts and lived to tell the tale. Claus Hubrecht, who was working at Agriculture House as an NFU translator, ran from his office to see if he could help amidst all the carnage. Hubrecht had served in the Dutch resistance and knew how to shoot horses. Borrowing a pistol from a dazed soldier, he dispatched some of the animals that were badly injured and in distress.

It wasn't the first time the NFU had been caught up in the campaigns of the IRA. Both Williams and Plumb had been threatened by the IRA that the terrorists would unleash germ warfare onto the British livestock industry unless the president of the NFU put pressure on the government of the day to withdraw from Northern Ireland. Generally, the early 1980s were punctuated by a number of IRA bomb outrages on the British mainland, the most notorious being the attack on the Tory Party during their stay at the Grand Hotel in Brighton for their annual conference.

The 1983 election returned the Thatcher government with a thumping 144-seat majority and Peter Walker was replaced by Michael Jopling. In the words of one MAFF official, speaking about Jopling: 'Unlike Walker, he will do what Maggie tells him. Maggie has given him an axe and told him to cut us down to size.' To add more salt to the NFU wound, Jopling was a Cumbrian farmer who had sat on NFU Council. Jopling's time at the ministry was characterised by EU budgetary strain, resulting in the first significant cuts in support prices the CAP had ever seen.

One key factor putting a strain on the EU budget was the over-production of milk. By 1980 the CAP dairy regime was costing £3,000 million annually, which was nearly half the total CAP budget. For the first time the CAP was going to have to introduce serious supply management and curtail production. Quotas seemed to be the preferred solution for most of the EU farm lobby and the commission. The prospect of quotas was particularly sensitive to

British dairymen because Britain was not self-sufficient in dairy produce. In 1980 Britain still imported a large proportion of its butter and cheese. Furthermore, British dairy farmers were among the most efficient in Europe and did not need the structural reform that was needed by the small producers on the Continent. British milk producers, who had numbered 131,000 in 1960, had streamlined down to 50,000 in 1980. When, in 1982, the commission had proposed a system of co-responsibility that favoured smaller producers, the NFU was successful in backing the UK Government in resisting the idea, which clearly discriminated against Britain's larger farm structure. With co-responsibility measures clearly failing to curtail over-production, it then became clear to many in 1983 that quotas were inevitable. The NFU, on the other hand, over-influenced by the chairman of the MMB, Steve Roberts, who was apoplectically adamant that quotas would only be introduced 'over his dead body', failed to take a clear line. Some feel this attitude was a form of denial which failed to prepare the membership for what was about to happen. When quotas came in on 2 April there was considerable anger and confusion amongst British producers. It did not help that the quotas were based on 1983 production, and for many UK producers 1983 had been a difficult wet season with lower than normal production. Whereas the Irish were given 3,187 pints of milk quota per head of population, the British received just 545. Butler had to spend a good deal of time in 1984 and '85 reassuring some very disillusioned dairy farmers that quotas were probably the least worst of the solutions to an intractable problem. Further testing their tempers were rumours in the press at the time that the Italians would find it impossible to apply quotas because no one there had much idea which farmers produced what. Nor did it please farmers or the NFU that the quota attached to the land and not the producer. The NFU and the CLA remained at loggerheads for some years about who was entitled to the quota, owner or occupier. Eventually, the NFU got the upper hand as quota became transferable

A key blow for the NFU and the red meat industry in the early 1980s was the demise of the FMC. From its origins under President Turner in the 1950s, the FMC had, by the 1970s, grown into the largest meat-handling organisation, with 120 slaughterhouses and employing 1,1000 people. It handled half the bacon pigs in the UK and 15 per cent of the cattle and sheep. In the early 1980s it suffered a sudden deterioration and eventually collapsed in 1983. It had made the mistake of expanding fast into the notoriously unstable bacon market just as the market declined and suffered vigorous overseas competition. Also after 1975, its aim of stabilising producer prices became impossible in the face of increasing fresh meat surpluses. The NFU had attempted to prop up the FMC by purchasing it, but, unable to operate it at a profit, sold it on to Hillsdown Holdings, who duly sold it off bit by bit.

The 1980s saw the political road map change with the emergence of 'pressure group' politics. Friends of the Earth, Greenpeace, Compassion in World Farming (not to mention the splendidly named 'Chickens' Lib') were all founded in the 1970s. Existing organisations such as the RSPB, the National Trust and the CPRE grew in size, turnover and political importance. By the 1980s these new players were mastering the fine art of media relations or, as others called it, the dark art of 'spin'. All too often it was 'intensive agriculture' that was the focus of their campaigns.

Amongst the media and the opinion-formers, high input–high output farming was becoming very unfashionable. Marion Shoard's book *The Theft of the Countryside*, and the writings of Tory Lincolnshire MP Richard Body were key parts of an accumulating body of evidence suggesting that the expansion of agricultural production was damaging the environment and would have to stop.

For 30 years agri-politics had been run largely between the two agendas of the NFU/MAFF matrix and the Treasury. Agricultural expansion had been the order of the day, and if the necessary expenditure plans could be wound out of the exchequer, then the state would underwrite this expansion through guaranteed prices and improvement grants. Suddenly, in the 1980s, the world of agri-politics was becoming more crowded with more agendas, particularly those that aimed to put conservation above production.

A flagship piece of environmental legislation was the Wildlife and Countryside Act of 1981. It was concerned with the preservation of wildlife, countryside protection and access. Prior to the legislation there had been some very heated exchanges between farmers and conservationists in areas such as Exmoor, where, in the late 1970s, there had been some ploughing of heather moorland. Lord Porchester had been called in to lead an enquiry and a truce was secured as farmers were offered generous compensation for keeping the land as it was – largely thanks to lobbying by the NFU.

The feud between conservationists and farmers then spilled out onto the Somerset levels – the second Battle of Sedgemoor, as it was then christened. Again it was farmers wanting to improve the land through drainage or ploughing against the Nature Conservancy Council trying to stop them. Local farmers publicly burned effigies of NCC men. There was a similar row going on in Norfolk, where a farmer ploughed an enormous V sign across some of the grazing marshes on the Norfolk Broads. The nub of the argument was whether the farmer had a right to farm the land to his best economic advantage, or whether the state should have the power to force the farmer to preserve the landscape in some sort of statutory aspic.

Such was the interest in the Bill from a multitude of different groups, including the NFU, that a staggering 2,300 amendments were tabled as it made its way through parliament. The key point of principle on which the NFU lobbied hard was that the Act should not oblige farmers to protect designated areas of the countryside for conservation purposes, but rather voluntary schemes should be put in place with proper funding that gave farmers financial incentives to manage their land according to agreed conservation protocols. When the Act was eventually passed, apart from the obligation to give advance notification of certain farming operations on SSSIs, the NFU lobbying position had been successful. The original generous provision the NFU had secured on Exmoor provided the basis for the compensation schemes. Some conservationists were appalled that the farm lobby had got their way, and made known their disgust. Charles Secrett from Friends of the Earth described it as 'a wretched and disheveled piece of legislation'. It was a key victory, but the NFU were under no illusion that, given the intense level of lobbying over the bill, if the voluntary nature of the new schemes did not attract farmers into the management agreements, then new compulsory measures would be difficult to resist. Having established the key principle of trusting the individual farmer to steward his land and for the state to compensate for income voluntarily forgone, the NFU realised the membership would have to fulfil its side of the bargain and make the schemes work. The value of the 1981 victory was witnessed again when similar schemes based on individuals volunteering their land for compensated management agreements were rolled out by setting up ESAs under the 1986 Agriculture Act.

As the voice of the conservation lobby got louder, so did the concerns of the NFU membership that the NFU was not doing enough to counter the claims that farmers were in the process of 'spoiling the countryside'. The early 1980s had seen greater media focus on the claims of degradation. It was clear that, whereas the NFU had considered such issues as fringe matters in the past, they were now moving centre stage. Furthermore, the discussion was being coloured by an anti-farming agenda. The 1980 Year Book described it as a 'latent antagonism to agriculture which has not been so obvious in the past'.

The BBC documentary 'Butterflies or Barley?', broadcast in February 1981, was a good example of the many programmes and press articles appearing at the time which got members exasperated. Complaints about the biased nature of the reporting were made by the union, but it was doubtful what impact such protests made. The NFU had been complaining to the BBC about programmes that reflected an anti-farming sentiment since 1928. Before 1970 this was usually over programmes that suggested farmers were poor employers and that the lot of the farm labourer was not a happy one. After 1970 the nature of the complaints changed as the media picked up on growing concerns about the welfare of farm animals and the impact of farming on the countryside. The irony was that, just as these issues received more air-time, the corner had actually been turned in terms of conservation awareness in the farming community. Farmers had largely stopped grubbing out hedges, and many were undertaking positive conservation management, taking up local authority grants to plant trees and hedges and create new ponds. Indeed, at this local level the NFU worked to liaise with local council officers and farmers in administering these conservation schemes. The ravages of Dutch Elm disease and the great gale of October 1987 convinced many farmers of the need to plant trees. The trick was to get all this good work reflected in the media. That was easier said than done. What certainly didn't help were the activities of farmers such as Hughie Batchelor in Kent, who seemed to revel in the media spotlight as he continued to rip out hedges. Eventually, Batchelor's local branch threw him out of the NFU.

But the NFU wasn't silent. President Butler made around 80 broadcasts every year of his presidency. He had argued against the author of *The Theft of the Countryside*, Marion Shoard, in a debate at the Oxford Union. Shoard had gone on so long with her diatribe against modern agriculture that the debate overran and she missed her train back to London. Like the perfect gentleman he was, Butler gave her a lift back in the chauffer-driven, NFU 1-plated Rover.

Booklets and such pamphlets as *Sense or Sentiment?* were issued. Media training was offered to members. In 1982 a new campaign, 'Farming – the Backbone of Britain', was launched, aimed at improving public understanding of farming.

Another image problem was the increasing media-driven perception that the EU was primarily in the business of creating butter and wheat mountains surrounded by milk and wine lakes, while the taxpayer increasingly had to pay for the privilege.

In terms of communications within the NFU membership, the 1980s were also changing times. Computers and the wonders of electronic communication were becoming commonplace. The NFU set up its own Prestel communication service whereby members could have up-to-date information beamed into their computer monitors or even their television sets. By July 1983 all county branches had installed Prestel equipment and two-way communication links were beginning to grow. Access to the database grew from 7,000 a month in early 1981 to 62,000 in autumn 1983. It was a new departure, possibly as revolutionary as the gradual spread of the telephone network during the NFU's first 50 years. With thousands of members far flung across the rural outposts of Britain, the NFU had always found internal communication a challenge and a considerable

expense. Electronic communication opened up exciting new possibilities. The problem was, as ever, to what extent the membership would take up the new technology. For many the idea of reading their correspondence 'on the telly' was a step too far, and most still much preferred a nice letter in the post.

Magazines remained a key source of NFU information for the membership. In 1970 the NFU in-house magazine, *British Farmer*, was merged with the old stalwart *Farmer & Stockbreeder* to become the *British Farmer & Stockbreeder*, which went out fortnightly to NFU members. This was added to in the 1970s by the NFU *Insight* magazine.

A key change in the organisation of the NFU in 1984 was withdrawal of the NFU Mutual commission paid to county secretaries as part of their remuneration package. For those in the larger counties, this was a substantial sum of money. This commission was now paid to the NFU centrally. This was a key dent in the autonomy and power of the counties and the final step towards centralised finance that President Knowles had started to further 30 years previously.

Another key piece of legislation that absorbed union time under Butler's presidency was the Agricultural Holdings Act of 1984. In the early 1980s the union had canvassed the views of the branches on tenants' rights. The view that came back was that protection had gone too far, and consequently the tenanted sector had lacked necessary fluidity. In particular it was stifling opportunities for new entrants. There was, though, one vital codicil in all of this; that existing tenants should not lose their rights of succession gained under the 1976 Miscellaneous Provision Act. Subsequently, from 1981 onwards, the NFU worked with the CLA to present a package of measures to form the basis of a new bill which, after extensive lobbying of government and resistance from Labour opposition, eventually entered parliament in the autumn of 1983. The Act, which became law in the following year, laid down new rent formulas and abolished statutory succession on new agreements. It was important legislation that was to allow for restructuring in the industry at a time when falling returns meant it was imperative that there was more flexibility in the system. It also represents a key point in NFU and farming history in that it put into reverse 100 years of providing extra security of protection for sitting tenants. Subsequent legislation in 1986 and 1995 was probably to have more impact on farmers, but the 1984 Act is important as it marks the watershed.

One related development in all of this was the establishment of the Tenant Farmers' Association (TFA) in 1981. It was not actually born out of concerns over impending new legislation that weakened the tenant position, but rather from the increase in rents that had been witnessed over the preceding decade, combined with declining farm incomes.

Butler contacted the proponents of the new organisation in early 1981 to try to dissuade them from their plans, arguing that there would be no significant policy position differences with the NFU, who already comprehensively covered tenants' issues as one united voice. His words went unheeded, and for the first time since the formation of the FUW in 1955 there was a new dent, albeit a small one, in the hegemony of the NFU and its representation of English and Welsh agriculture. By the mid-1980s the tenanted sector had fallen to cover about a third of farmland. Having initially been in the vast majority, tenants were now very much in the minority in the NFU, and it may be that this was a key factor in the forming of the TFA. Just as with the FUW, the TFA clearly took membership from the NFU, but the fact remained that the vast majority of tenant farmers stuck with the national union just as the majority of Welsh farmers had since 1955. Although NFU membership continued to fall to 120,000 under Butler's presidency, it still dwarfed any rivals and remained the main spokesman for all sectors and regions of the NFU. In terms of resources, it clearly remained the main player. Although the NFU was constantly tightening its belt through the 1980s, it was still well resourcedl. With £8 million worth of income and nearly £10 million worth of assets in 1986, it remained the envy of many alternative organisations.

In 1984, while UK cereal farmers enjoyed an enormous harvest and the *Daily Mail* was full of pictures of mountains of grain in intervention stores, out of the Horn of Africa came a very different story. It was one of famine. Thousands were starving while the EU was wondering what to do with its surpluses. One South Cambridgeshire farmer, Oliver Walston, realised there was an obvious solution. Working with the charity War on Want, he asked his fellow arable farmers to 'Send a Tonne to Africa', which, to their credit, they duly did in their thousands. The first load of 10,000 tonnes left Hull in October 1984 bound for the Ethiopian port of Assab. In 1985 the NFU took over Walston's initiative and used remaining reserves to finance agricultural development in the famine-stricken area. It was a good example of farmers taking a charitable lead well before the rock musicians of Band Aid got their act together in 1986. It is also a good, positive note on which to conclude the presidency of Richard Butler.

The Butler years had been something of a culture shock for the farming community. They saw the final death throes of the idea that expansion of the farm sector was a worthwhile goal for Britain to pursue. The notion of 'food from our own resources' that had characterised much of postwar agricultural policy had seen its last flowering. In 1984 the NFU had published a new policy document, *The Way Forward*, which was groundbreaking in that it signalled the end of the NFU's support for expansion of produc-

tion and an acceptance of the need to take more account of environmental pressures.

During Butler's time the political scene had changed quite dramatically. The new Thatcher administration probably reflected more enthusiasm for the sensibilities and discipline of the free market than any government since the days of Baldwin in the early 1930s. Whether Thatcher would have worried if farming had returned to the 'dog and stick' days of the 1930s is another matter. While many farmers liked Mrs Thatcher's anti-corporate message that sang the praises of the individual entrepreneur, the irony was that, with the advent of production quotas, farmers as businessmen were being told by the state how much they could produce and how much they would get for it.

The fact was that British farming had fallen under the auspices of the CAP rather than the free market. The bad news for British farmers was that, just as they came under the full jurisdiction of the EU, it suddenly had to wrestle with major budgetary constraints at a time when farm incomes were falling quite rapidly. Inevitably, tensions spilled out into a number of squabbles between the members. There was one certainty in all of this; the need for farmers to have effective political representation and the need for a safe pair of hands on the rudder. The NFU gave that representation and Sir Richard Butler was that safe pair of hands.

In 1985 he decided he would stand down at the next AGM in 1986. This was partly because he wanted to pursue other things. His twin sons, Michael and Christopher, were growing up, and Richard needed to think about the future of the farm back home. After he stood down he became a director of National Westminster Bank and, controversially, later accepted a position on the board of Feruzzi, which had designs on the British sugar beet industry. Another reason why he decided to stand down was because he knew that at his right hand there was an ambitious young man called Simon Gourlay, who was growing itchier by the day to have a shot at the presidency.

Sir Richard Butler leaves the stage to the applause of his successor, Simon Gourlay, and Minister Jopling.

✦ CHAPTER 30 ✦

Sir Simon Gourlay, 1986–91

Simon Gourlay was yet another NFU president to come out of the Welsh Borders, and could claim to have a foot on both side of Offa's Dyke. His farm literally straddled the border, being partly in Hereford and partly in Brecon. The late Ben Boot, long-time chairman of the NFU Dairy Committee, once playfully said of him: 'The thing about Simon is the Welsh think he is English and the English think he is Welsh.'

Simon was born in 1934 near Gloucester, his father a professional soldier who left the forces to work for John Halls in Bristol. The young Gourlay took an interest in farming from an early age and even at the tender age of nine could be found organising a farming club at his prep school. After an education at Winchester College followed by a spell of National Service during which he was an officer in a cavalry regiment, he attended the Royal Agricultural College, Cirencester but left after the first term. He had fallen out with the college principal over the practice of increasing milk output from dairy cows by feeding them ever-greater rations of concentrates. The young Gourlay thought it was the wrong way to go about things and instinctively felt that a less intensive regime, with less emphasis on high input–high output was a more sensible way to farm.

Disillusioned with college, he promptly spent two years working as a foreman on a Cheshire dairy farm. In 1958, in partnership with his father-in-law, he bought a 260-acre farm in Brecon, near the town of Knighton, for £16,600. In the 1960s he was forced to borrow money to buy out his in-laws when they suddenly wanted out of the business. Helped by land prices that were yet to escalate, he also bought more land. By 1970 he was farming 850 acres (200 acres tenanted) of mixed soils that overlay the Devonian red sandstone 1,000 feet up in the hills. The land was a typical borders combination of some flattish land interspersed with steep hills, only usable for grazing. There was a beef suckler herd of 200 Herefords, 500 Lleyn ewes, 300 acres of cereals and 50 acres of seed potatoes. In the mid-1970s, when the beef price collapsed, the beef herd was wound down and Gourlay went into dairying, building up a herd of 230 Holstein Friesians. In keeping with his principled falling-out 20 years before at Cirencester, the dairy herd was mainly fed on grass. Elsewhere across British agriculture feeding cows on grass and silage rather than on cereals and other concentrates had seen a resurgence in the 1970s, when the price of

high-protein feeds had increased faster than the price of milk or meat.

The postwar years had seen an increase in the national sheep flock from 23 million in 1945 to 25 million in 1970, and a sharper rise to 30 million by 1980. Over the same period Britain's self-sufficiency in lamb and mutton increased from under 40 per cent to over 80 per cent. There had also been a concentration of sheep in the hills, where cattle and sheep farming was the only option. In the arable lowlands the practice of close-folding of sheep to de-pasture break crops had largely disappeared in the 1950s. Even the Downs and the Wolds, where huge numbers of sheep had thrived 50 years before, were now being ploughed, and there was little room for traditional sheep grazing. In the hills sheep numbers and stocking rates were increasing, partly in response to healthy fat lamb prices but largely due to hill farm subsidies which, in the 1970s and 1980s, were providing the majority of hill farm income.

One distinctive feature of Gourlay's farming was his light-footedness, which enabled him to succeed where other hill farmers were struggling. It could be argued that this skill, in part, came from being a self-made first-generation farmer. Apart from some help from his father-in-law in the 1950s, Gourlay was one of those rare farmers who built up a substantial farm largely due to his own business ability, with little help from inheritance. This aspect of his background came out in his attitude to farming and to his fellow farmers which, at times, could be harsh.

As a man, Gourlay was a challenging character in agricultural circles. With a willowy frame, Winchester-schooled manners and a high, cerebral forehead, he did not come across as a typical farmer, least of all as the 'Welsh cattle farmer', as the press sometimes described. (But then few farmers live up to the gum-booted, ruddy-faced, straw-chewing yokel image they are meant to have.)

When you meet Simon Gourlay today you appreciate he must have made quite an impact on the NFU and the farming community in the 1980s. True to the tradition of Army service in his blood, he has an officer-corps demeanour that makes you slightly uneasy in his presence. He was known for his unblinking cold eyes and a slight aloofness. While some found him overly dismissive and sardonic, others appreciated his no-nonsense, matter-of-fact style. He has a sinewy directness and can be abrasive, but, in all of this, there is certainly nothing snooty, affected or superior about him. Being brisk but not brusque, he expects you to take him as you find him and he returns the compliment. He is dry but has an amusing wit that comes from a very sharp mind. In conversation he is agile and articulate.

At times Gourlay displayed a certain intensity. It was said that when in the chauffered NFU 1 he would insist on taking the wheel if he thought his driver was not making fast enough progress. There was also a story how, on one occasion, he offered to drive EU Commissioner Andriesson from Heathrow to a meeting in the West Country to give them both an opportunity to discuss CAP policy while they drove. By the time Andriesson arrived at their destination he was in a state of nervous exhaustion brought on by the speeds he had just experienced.

At home, Gourlay was a modern man a generation on from his predecessors, Plumb and Butler. Whereas previously the tradition had been for the president's wife to be at the president's side as a sort of 'first lady' of the NFU and to entertain accordingly, Gourlay expected no such duty from Caroline, his wife of 19 years. He was a modern man and these were post-liberation times. Caroline Gourlay was her own woman and not some sort of a female 'bolt-on' to the presidential arm. Eyebrows were raised among some of the NFU branches when it transpired Caroline had been involved in the Greenham Common peace camp that protested at the presence of the American Airforce and their nuclear weaponry in the early '80s. Some in the membership were suspicious that if this was the sort of company Gourlay liked to keep, then he was probably 'a bit of a lefty'. Even more worryingly, he could speak half-decent French, not to mention being well read and having an interest in the arts. To cap it all, he was an authority on Alpine plants.

On becoming President, Gourlay was quick to point out:

I am not a traditionalist. I do not think we should do things just because we have always done them that way. I suppose you could say I am a bit radical, but only when I feel it is necessary for the industry.

Despite this taste for radicalism, it must be pointed out that, under Gourlay's leadership, the NFU continued to abide by its strict political neutrality. It steadfastly refused to show any favour to any political party but merely got on with the government of the day.

Gourlay's time in the NFU can be traced back to a wet, miserable day in 1958 when, as a new English immigrant, sheltering in an outbuilding of the farmyard, he spied the soggy figure of Verney Pugh trudging up the lane towards him. Pugh, the local NFU branch chairman, duly wagged his finger in Gourlay's face, explaining why it was important that all farmers should join the NFU. The new boy, not of a mind to disagree, duly succumbed to Pugh's direct

sales pitch. In time Gourlay became Brecon and Radnor county chairman, Council delegate and, in the late 1970s, chairman of the Employment Committee, leading the employers' AWB team. He cut a reputation as a tough negotiator.

Just as it had done since 1947, the NFU AWB team would meet with the representatives of the farm worker union and the independents on the board to negotiate the size of that year's award. In the 1970s negotiations had become particularly complicated as wage inflation escalated and economic returns for farmers were starting to fall. Things came to a head in 1979, when no agreement could be found between the three parties. The employee's side wanted a minimum weekly rate of pay of £100, some £40 more than the current £60. Gourlay's team proposed an increase around the inflation rate of 10 per cent. Eventually, the independents decided to enforce a 21 per cent increase to take the average weekly wage packet to around £70. With an echo of Norfolk 60 years before, Gourlay's team took the unprecedented step of walking out of the meeting to register the strongest possible protest. The settlement was duly imposed.

Despite this hiccup, it should generally be noted that while many industries were dogged with strikes and poor labour relations in the '70s and early '80s, farming was not. There were some half-hearted attempts at industrial action in the 1970s, but they had little serious impact. Henry Plumb recollects his chief cowman telling him one evening that, in accordance with a NUAAW ruling, he was going on strike the following afternoon, but then added that Henry wasn't to worry as he was going to get in early in the morning to make sure he got all his jobs done. The relative harmony between farmers and farm workers can partly be put down to the way the NFU and the workers' unions negotiated through the AWB over pay.

Having spent three years as Employment Committee chairman, Gourlay moved to vice president in 1982, deputy in 1984 and took the presidency when Butler stood down in 1986. As president, Gourlay saw himself as a moderniser. He came into the office determined to move the NFU on in terms of policy and in terms of administration. In this task he was joined by a new chief executive, David Evans. Evans was an ex-senior civil servant known for his administrative skills. Under the auspices of Gourlay and Evans the NFU entered a new era that markedly broke from the previous 16 years under Plumb and Butler.

By 1987 the NFU was an organisation of 827 local branches in 49 county branches. There were 356 group offices serving the branches. The membership was now around the 100,000 mark, which was reckoned to represent 75 per cent of full-time farmers in England and Wales. The basic annual sub had risen to £34 plus 52p per acre. (There were additional rates for areas of glass or buildings for intensive livestock.) Although annual income was now approaching £10 million, expenditure was regularly exceeding income, giving worrying budget deficits. Gourlay's view, and he was not alone, was that the counties would finally have to accept the regionalisation that had been proposed over 15 years before. Director-General Evans was to mastermind the operation.

A report was commissioned and, after due debate and consultation, a proposal was put before Council in 1989 to regroup county staff into nine regional centres. NFU staffing was thus reduced by 10 per cent and annual costs of £300,000 were saved. Council approved the plan and on 1 May it was implemented. It was a key date in NFU history in that the county structure of the NFU was thus fatally undermined. It was a culmination of the centralisation Knowles had started 40 years previously. Many of the county unions had proud histories older than the NFU itself, but now that was the past and not the future. The county unions still existed as legal entities; some pooled their assets centrally, some didn't, but their *raison d'être* was cut to the core. They were now administered externally by the regions and, although they retained their own structures, these structures now inevitably started to wain as they became more cut off from the mother ship. In a shrinking world it was a reform Gourlay felt he had to push through. There was little room for romance or tradition in Gourlay's modernising zeal whereby he was determined to make the NFU fit for purpose and face the realities of the changes the last two decades had seen. The old county structure was failing to meet the needs of the individual members and was inefficient and ineffective in the way it deployed staff and resources. To a certain extent, Plumb and Butler had side-stepped the need to reform the county structure, largely because of local intransigence. Gourlay had the vision and the determination to realise the NFU could no longer shrink from the task.

The efficacy of the reformed regional structure was almost immediately tested when livestock producers in the West and Midlands were supplied with lead-contaminated feed. A boat carrying coconut husk had been unloaded at Torquay and raw lead from the previous shipment had not been properly cleaned out. Over the next few months it transpired that hundreds of farmers had been supplied with the feed by six different feed merchants, and subsequently their milk and meat were unsaleable because of high levels of lead contamination. Through its legal scheme the NFU coordinated a class action to secure damages for members against the feed suppliers, who agreed to settle out of court. It was an extremely successful action made easier by the fact that it was handled regionally rather than through a large number of county offices.

There was also a fundamental change in the relationship between the NFU and the Mutual. With a declining number of farmers and an increasingly competitive insurance market, the Mutual was struggling with its old, confined market remit of only insuring NFU members. It was clear that to survive they would need to tap into the increasingly lucrative countryside market that went beyond the farm gate. The answer was for the NFU to create a 'countryside' membership at a much reduced subscription for those who owned 'more than a garden but less than a farm'. This opened up a whole new market for the Mutual to sell into. In terms of administration, with the county secretaries now gone, the emphasis was now more on the group secretaries and their relationship with the Mutual HQ at Stratford. Although the NFU still received a tidy sum of money each year based on the Mutual's sales, and although the branch secretaries retained their dual NFU and NFU Mutual roles, the sense of close partnership that had been set up 70 years before and cemented into place in the 1940s was now eroding. The positive news was that the NFU was now extending its umbrella and its good name out beyond just full-time farmers. Just as importantly, the Mutual now had a sales strategy that would ensure its survival and allow it to flourish.

Gourlay's knife was also taken to Knightsbridge. Agriculture House, which for 30 years had stood as an symbol of NFU power in its grand West End location, was now exceeding the NFU's requirements. With its huge rooms and endless corridors it was more suited to housing an imperial civil service from a previous age than it was to accommodating the needs of a modern organisation. Also, given its location, it was a piece of prime real estate that could earn the NFU a great deal more money if it was used for other things in addition to housing the NFU. In 1990 it was agreed to redevelop the site and for the NFU to move out to alternative temporary accommodation in central London. The plan was to redevelop the whole site with a new NFU HQ on 40 per cent of it, this to be financed by letting out the remainder on a 150-year lease with a 10 per cent rental clawback. As it happened, the NFU, while retaining the freehold, never did return to Knightsbridge, and Gourlay was the last man to occupy the presidential office overlooking Hyde Park Corner that had seen so much agricultural history unfold under its high ceiling. The move out of Knightsbridge was a key moment in the NFU's history. With its large committee rooms and bar, its dining-rooms and spacious offices, not to mention the library, the tearooms and the wine cellar, the Knightsbridge HQ had been the physical manifestation of agriculture in a properous and expansive age. It housed an enormous staff of over 200 to mirror and match a ministry. It had drawn to its doors thousands of farmer representatives, who descended on this London hub from the four corners of England and Wales. Some farmers, possibly with not enough to do back home, practically lived there

A cartoon in the British Farmer *plays on Gourlay's military past and his battle with Europe in controlling over-production.*

to over-imbibe on the 'country comes to town' bonhomie the place exuded. Some fondly remembered the Spanish barman, Rudolph, who had a good nose for the best Riojas. But now, for better and for worse, all this was to change. Just like the British agriculture it represented, the NFU had to become a leaner and meaner body more focused on its key purposes.

There were other reforms. Council was reduced from 140 to 100 and now only met four times a year. There was also some slimming down of the committee structure. By the mid-1980s there were 31 committees meeting at Knightsbridge on a regular basis, some with up to 50 members. They covered all fields, from economics and taxation to marketing, and they covered all sectors, from fish farming to apples and pears. By the end of the '80s their number had been reduced to 24 through mergers.

In all of this we should remember that, although by the mid-1980s, the NFU may have become overweight, it was no slouch. A quick glance at the year 1988 shows how the NFU was as busy as it ever was. Although Mrs Thatcher's motto was a promise to lift the burden of the state off the back of the individual, the farmer didn't seem to feel much lightening of the load under her administration. In 1988 there were no fewer than 13 statutes and 33 regulatory orders that impacted on the business of farming. The NFU lobbied at Westminster and Whitehall on all aspects to ensure the legislators and regulators were aware of the farmer's position. For instance, under the Water Act, which privatised the water industry, it successfully improved terms for farmers affected by pipelines. Similarly, while the Finance Bill was going through parliament the NFU persuaded government to allow CGT gift relief where a retired farmer had let his land to a member of the family. In the same year it gave evidence to ten parliamentary committees and made 25 formal submissions on subjects from lead contamination in feed to future road planning.

Furthermore, there were 37 responses on government consultation papers, from 'Action on Litter' to 'A Review of Summertime'. And that was just Westminster in 1988. In Brussels there were 45 formal submissions on subjects as diverse as glucosinolate standards for oilseed rape and EC zoonoses regs. All this fed into and impacted on the design of the welter of regulation under which the average farmer increasingly found himself. As the regulatory burden on agriculture increased, the NFU found itself busier than ever ensuring the farming voice was heard loud and clear where, and when, the laws and measures were being unhatched.

With the task of getting the information out, again the single snapshot of 1988 finds the NFU distributing 43 leaflets and booklets. By way of examples there was the mainstream *The single European Market: Agricultural Implications* and *Farm Visits in Britain,* and then publications such as the more eclectic *Brent Goose News* and *Who's Who in the Turkey Industry.* It was all designed to assist the individual member when he went about the increasingly complicated and ever more regulated business of farming. As ever, the union kept an eye on the future. In 1988 the Asher Winegarten memorial lecture, given by Professor Martin Parry, was entitled 'The greenhouse effect and agriculture in the future'.

And, it should be remembered, this was just 1988. Every year under Gourlay's presidency was just as busy. In terms of lobbying and the detailed assessment of the impact of policy on the economy of farming, the NFU stood unrivalled.

Gourlay's presidency was punctuated by a number of key events. The first occurred on 26 April 1986, when the fourth reactor of the Chernobyl nuclear power plant in the Ukraine exploded at 1.23a.m. local time. Further explosions and the resulting fire sent a plume of highly radioactive material into the atmosphere and over an extensive geographical area, extending as far as the eastern seaboard of North America. In North Wales, the Lake District and the South West NFU members had their pastures contaminated by radioactivity. Under the recently passed Food and Environment Protection Act, restrictions were initially placed on over 5,000 holdings and their 2 million sheep for fear contamination levels in the meat could present a risk to public health. Eventually, this was reduced to 359 holdings and 180,000 sheep. The accident had caught the authorities by surprise, which led to difficulties for farmers in the affected areas. The NFU was active from the outset, firstly in securing proper information and then in pressing for full compensation for those sheep farmers whose livelihoods were at risk. Remarkably, some 20 years later there were still some sheep farmers under market restrictions and who were still being paid compensation.

Gourlay's view on environmental issues generally was that farmers would have to recognise the agenda had moved on and face up to their responsibilities. The days of ever-increased production were over and now farmers everywhere, not just in the SSSIs and ESAs, would have to respect that non-productive conservation was written into their job description. He tried to build bridges with some of the environmental groups, such as Friends of the Earth and the Ramblers, believing that a common agenda would be better than a permanent Punch and Judy show. For instance, when the Countryside Commission and the Ramblers were demanding better observance of footpaths in the late 1980s, Gourlay's response was to draw up codes of good practice on footpath maintenance and urge farmers to observe them. It was not always the farmer's instinct to do so, but Gourlay was determined to show leadership where he thought his members were failing to move with the times. Similarly, with straw-burning, Gourlay realised that unless farmers put their own houses in order they risked legislation banning the practice.

On the broader political scene, Gourlay was determined to wage war on the policy of continued support price reduction in Brussels. He was convinced that such policies would not tackle the problem of over-production and would squeeze out the smaller farmer. His analysis was that falling farm prices led to fewer farmers producing more, whereas the EU should seek policies that kept farmers on the land and stabilised EU supply and demand. Gourlay's alternative was to advocate production control through concepts such as quotas and set-aside. It was a complete volte-face from the policies of the previous 80 years. The NFU was now calling for the restraint of farm production rather than its increase.

Another policy mooted through the 1980s by the Commission was direct income support for farmers. The NFU opposed this because it clearly was intended to target small farmers and thus bypassed most UK farmers. It was a thought-provoking statistic for UK farmers that, while the average farm size in the UK in the 1980s was about 200 acres, for their new EU neighbour, Greece, the average was less than ten. At the time the average farm size across the EU was less than 40 acres.

In Europe a new commissioner, Frans Andriesson, had taken office and brought with him a determination to bring CAP spending under control. Between 1980 and 1986 CAP spending had doubled from around 10 million euros to over 20,000 million. Andriesson's favoured policy was price adjustment rather than management measures such as quotas. In 1987 there was 12 million tonnes of cereals in intervention storage, half a million tonnes of beef and over a million tonnes of butter.

In 1988 Andriesson introduced stabilisers whereby, when production of any given commodity rose above an agreed threshold, price cuts were automatically triggered. Co-responsibility levies

Gourlay (centre) *and Naish* (right) *try to explain the Green pound to a quizzical Minister John McGregor.*

were also increased. Through such measures the runaway CAP budget was checked but certainly not reduced.

Pressure on the CAP was not made any easier by the accession of Spain, Portugal and Greece in 1986. And just to add one final additional pressure, 1986 saw the start of the Uruguay round of the GATT, where farm support policies were for the first time explicitly included in negotiations. The US and the Cairns Group, all major exporters of farm commodities, were pushing hard for a 75 per cent cut in EU farm support. Sir Michael Franklin, who had been British deputy director-general of the Agriculture Directorate of the commission, but who was then permanent secretary at MAFF, described the GATT negotiations as 'part of a multilateral exercise giving equality of misery'. Although he didn't mention them by name, it was clear most of the misery would be felt by primary producers such as farmers.

While the EU's common prices showed annual increments through the '70s and early '80s in line with, if not in excess of, inflation, by 1985 they started to flatline, which meant, in real terms for the farmer, they were falling year on year. The impact of all this was felt in Britain as much as elsewhere in the EU. Although the NFU was no longer in the business of undergoing annual price reviews, once a year it sat down with MAFF and assessed the state of the industry. Now, under the lead of Chief Economist

Sean Rickard, the NFU economics team kept its pre-eminent place in the NFU structure. Through its work it was clear that in real terms farm incomes in the 1980s were falling dramatically at an average of 9 per cent a year and by 1987 were at their lowest level since the war. A total of 60,000 jobs had been lost and investment had halved.

From the start of his presidency Gourlay had stepped up the NFU attack on the Thatcher government and its rather nonplussed minister, Jopling, for their lack of vision in the way they led CAP reform by continually calling for cuts in farm prices. He also condemned government for their shortsightedness in cutting the R&D and advisory budgets for agriculture. At his first AGM as president in 1987, with a captive Jopling in his midst, he laid into the minister with a bit of blood and thunder. The farmers lapped it up with whooping and cheering. They hadn't seen this sort of thing since Plumb was in his prime. Gourlay's attack culminated in a vote of no confidence in Jopling. In a good example of his dry, trenchant wit, Gourlay famously said:

Farmers are used to cuts in their professional life. We prune trees and we castrate animals. The purpose of these two operations is different. The thing about Mrs Thatcher is that she thinks if she cuts our balls off, they'll grow back stronger.

A week later it was clear that the NFU's new president was testing Mrs Thatcher's patience with his ankle-biting. In a curt public letter she said she found the vote of no confidence 'astonishing' in the light of the £2,500 million the government had budgeted to spend on agriculture and food support in 1987, adding: 'It helps no one for resources to be wasted in producing unsaleable surpluses which then have to be stored and disposed of at huge expense to the taxpayer.' During the same week the Prime Minister had reprimanded the NFU in the

Simon Gourlay waits to pounce as Michael Jopling fails to impress the 1987 NFU AGM.

House of Commons for taking 'a very short view' on agricultural policy. In one analysis, relations between government and the NFU had reached their lowest ebb since Ramsay MacDonald's war of words with President Slade in 1931. It is probably no surprise that they were both times when farm incomes were at their lowest for a generation. The key difference was the vastly different amounts Macdonald's and Thatcher's governments were spending in agricultural support.

Such fierce rebukes by the Iron Lady herself did temper Gourlay's tone, as he realised he may have dangerously distanced himself from government, but, even so, he maintained his attack on the policy of grinding down farm-gate prices. In 1988 the NFU renewed its campaign to secure a devaluation of the green pound which, it maintained, was set by government at too high a level, so holding down farm prices. The NFU efforts were not without limited success, and a 3.2 per cent devaluation was achieved. In 1990 all the UK's negative MCAs were cut in half.

Gourlay's enthusiasm for set-aside saw some result when Minister Jopling put it on the EEC's agenda in September 1986. The idea of deliberately taking land out of production was novel in Europe and had recently been rejected as a policy by the Commission. In the US there was a long history of land retirement programmes, with mixed results. Whereas Gourlay was in favour of compulsory set-aside and maintenance of cereal support levels, Jopling's suggestion was that it should be a voluntary measure, compensated to make it barely attractive to most farmers and accompanied by further price cuts. The measure was targeted at the cereals sector, where EU production was still causing huge budgetary problems in terms of intervention storage and export restitutions. To the surprise of the Commission, the Germans backed the British suggestion, but without the decrease in support prices. In 1988 a scheme whereby farmers could voluntarily take out a minimum of 20 per cent of their land for five years for £80 an acre per year was introduced. For the first time since the 1930s, significant tracts of British arable land were now to be left abandoned and uncultivated. The sad fact was, though, that these measures had little significant effect on the problem of over-production. Another downside was that, in the eyes of the British public, farmers 'were now paid to do nothing'.

It was under Gourlay's presidency that the NFU, for the first time, found itself wrestling with a relatively new phenomenon – the food scare. As an organisation it had primarily concerned itself with food production rather than food safety, but on 3 December 1988 that was to change forever. On that day, the outspoken Junior Health Minister, Edwina Currie, live on ITN, announced to the world: 'Most of the egg production in this country, sadly, is now infected with salmonella' The impact on both consumers and egg farmers was extreme and long lasting. Before her statement, Britons were consuming 30 million eggs a day. Almost overnight sales dropped a massive 60 per cent and British egg farmers were accumulating millions of excess eggs every day. MAFF were quick to try and undo the damage by explaining there had only been 26 cases of salmonella poisoning in 1988, and that the chance of catching it from an egg was two million to one. The egg industry and the NFU duly demanded Currie's resignation, which was delivered a fortnight later. At the same time Mrs Thatcher reassured the nation that she always had eggs for breakfast. Egg consumption did not revive significantly and the following year remained at 50 per cent of what it had been before Mrs Currie opened her mouth. In 1989 the NFU worked hard to restore confidence in British eggs, and 19 new measures to eliminate salmonella in eggs and poultry were implemented. A £19 million package was agreed with government to reduce laying flocks and remove the surplus eggs from the market to help balance supply with reduced demand.

Meanwhile, another food scare was brewing, this time in cattle. In November 1986 a farmer in Surrey had noticed some of his cows trembling when they were milked. Over the next few days he noticed the condition getting worse as they started to stagger and finally couldn't get up. The six affected animals were slaughtered and screens of the brains showed a spongiform encephalopathy similar to that found in sheep suffering from scrapie. In 1987 the new condition was officially acknowledged by MAFF and became known as BSE or, more colloquially, 'mad cow disease'. In 1987 it became clear that this was not an isolated or minor problem, as a further 413 cases were recorded in all four corners of Britain. Working with the NFU, government hammered out a compensation package of about £654 for animals confirmed with the disease. It represented about half the price of a healthy animal. With 2,235 cases in 1988 and 6,420 cases in 1989, and with a compensation bill now running into millions, the issue started to get air-play in the media. Professor Richard Lacey, a microbiologist from Leeds University, who had a long track record when it came to doubting the wholesomeness of modern agriculture, could frequently be found in the press wondering what the consequences might be for human health if the British public had been eating the meat of cows that had succumbed to this nasty brain-wasting disease, which always led to death. MAFF and its ministers went public with assurances that the beef was safe and represented no more a health risk than scrapie in sheep, which had been around for centuries. Agricultural Minister Gummer was pictured on television force-feeding his small daughter a beefburger.

Epidemiological evidence suggested a link with animal feed and a ban was put on feeding bovine

Gourlay juggles with the salamonella issue following the intervention of Mrs Curry.

material in bovine food. One speculation was that changes in the rendering of MBM were at the core of the problem, but this was never proved and, as time went on, seemed increasingly unlikely. The NFU had been calling for greater transparency on what was being put into animal feed for a number of years and this was now, at last, agreed to. The downside to this transparency was that the public showed revulsion to the news that dead cows were being fed to live ones. The media treated it as yet more evidence there was something increasingly unwholesome about modern farming. Few journalists bothered to spoil this story by pointing out that this had been common practice for over 100 years. As the media spotlight intensified on this new plague of cattle that might compromise human health, the NFU found itself in a state of permanent rebuttal. President Gourlay was doing scores of interviews on the subject and becoming increasingly uneasy.

Despite further measures to remove offal from the food chain and further government reassurances about the safety of beef, Gourlay took the view that not enough was being done to satisfy consumers on food safety. By 1990 the BSE confirmation rate was topping 350 a week, and in May 1990 there was a media storm when it became clear the disease could jump species when a Siamese cat from Bristol, which for some reason had lived off beef steak, died from a spongiform encephalopathy. Almost immediately schools started to take beef off the menu and beef prices came under pressure. France, Germany and Italy pushed for bans on imports of British beef. The NFU and MAFF negotiated a compromise position in Europe whereby the bans on boned beef were overturned and exports from herds certified free of BSE were continued.

Despite these successes with government, Gourlay started to doubt that the government were doing enough to eradicate the disease or maintain consumer confidence. One of his key contentions was that it was not appropriate that MAFF, the body that was regulating agriculture, should also have responsibility for food hygiene. This roused the ire of the new Minister of Agriculture, John Gummer, and led to a heated conversation with Gourlay at the Royal Show in 1990. Gummer felt that Gourlay was undermining public confidence in his ministry and sharply reminded the NFU president that union and ministry must be seen to be as one on the issue. There was also pressure on Gourlay from within the union to play down consumer fears as unwarranted.

But Gourlay's pressure proved worthwhile, as government brought in a ban on all offals in animal feedstuffs. Slaughtering and rendering methods were also improved. In time, Gourlay's far-sighted views on the need for an independent body to oversee food hygiene saw success with the establishment of an independent Food Standards Agency in the 1990s.

And so we come to the end of Gourlay's presidency under the cloud of BSE. Hindsight shows that the measures put in place under Gourlay's presidency had successfully checked its spread as a disease. The real consumer fallout and subsequent damage to the beef industry were still to come.

Gourlay (by now Sir Simon Gourlay, following knighthood in 1989) had always said, from when he took the presidency in 1986, that he would serve for five years and five years only. During that time his domineering intellect had ensured no one had come out of the woods to challenge him. True to his matter-of-fact nature, he stood down in 1991 and returned to his farm in Brecon. Light-footed as ever in the way he ran his farm business, he closed down

his dairy in 1991 and increased his stock of sheep and beef animals. Since then, disillusioned by the fact that over 60 per cent of his beef income was coming from headage payments rather than from the sale of the animals, he has moved out of beef into the unsupported sector of eggs. He now runs 22,000 free-range hens and is converting to organic. He is no organic zealot and, with his usual lack of sentiment, he simply sees it as a business decision that secures him a worthwhile premium. Having said this, it is no surprise that such a system should appeal to a man who thought the solution to agriculture's problems in the late 1980s was for farmers to produce less and get paid more for it.

In his time, Gourlay was a radical man with a radical mind. Possibly he ran too far ahead of those around him and sometimes showed a lack of sympathy with those who struggled with the present. History may yet show that, had his ideas been given more credence and attention, then farming may have found itself on a better footing. Gourlay's problem was that he struggled to grasp why farmers instinctively believed the way out of a problem was to produce more of what they had produced in the past.

As a first-generation farmer, he possibly lacked some of the emotional bond that fellow farmers can instinctively enjoy, but in another analysis he managed to shake farmers out of their own nauseating communal self-pity. He also had no time for the delusional assumption that farmers were in some way more deserving than other sectors of society. When you ask Simon Gourlay what his main challenge was as president, he will tell you that it was to convince farmers that they were no longer the 'chosen race' or the 'special case'. It was time they faced up to some harsh realities.

Farmers desperately need men like Simon Gourlay in their ranks, but only in small doses. Too many officers mixing with the regulars can spoil the atmosphere in the mess and undermine the instinctive camaraderie that makes farmers feel good about themselves. But there is no doubting Simon Gourlay was, and still is, a genuine farmer. He can be found today, now in his 70s, on his farm which straddles the English–Welsh border, still enjoying the challenge of hands-on farming.

CHAPTER 31

Sir David Naish, 1991–98

When David Naish succeeded Gourlay as president at the 1991 AGM, there was a sense of destiny in the air. Naish was the nephew of Jim Turner and held the memory of his uncle in revered esteem. Turner had led British agriculture and the NFU through a time of abundance. History had smiled on Turner and, so too, did it smile on his nephew. Like all good dramas, however, there was one very cruel twist in the tail.

Naish hailed from North Nottinghamshire, where Turner had first cut his NFU teeth. His grandfather had been a hotelier, owning the Hop Pole Hotel in Ollerton, and Naish's father rented a 300-acre farm at nearby Edwinstowe. Born in 1941, the young Naish grew up on the typical mixed farm, where sugar beet, potatoes and cereals were grown alongside a dairy and beef herd. After studying at the RAC at Cirencester, David returned home to help build the business up to 600 acres – concentrating on broad-acre root production, namely potatoes and beet rotated with cereals. As with many eastern-region

farms at the time, the stock was discontinued and crop irrigation was introduced.

The soils were typical Nottinghamshire sand-land in a landscape interspersed with the remnants of Sherwood Forest. The village of Edwinstowe is where, according to legend, Robin Hood married Maid Marian. Sherwood Forest is where it is largely because, in times past, the soils were considered too poor to farm. It was an area of infertile rough heaths and oak woods. After the war a combination of fertilisers and irrigation transformed the area from one characterised by unimproved grassland to one dominated by productive arable farming. The easy-working sandy soils were an especially good medium for root crops. Mechanisation also enabled farm units to grow in size. Naish vividly recollects how tasks such as the hand-singling of beet severely limited how many acres of roots a farmer could manage. Improvements in seeds and precision drilling introduced in the 1960s ended the need for this back-breaking hoeing operation and greatly

David Naish amidst one of his first loves – sugar beet.

reduced the labour requirement. It was a similar story with potatoes. It was in this postwar period that the number of farmers growing potatoes fell by 75 per cent while the tonnage produced remained the same. The area halved while the yields doubled.

The 1980s had seen a large increase on these Nottinghamshire sands of broad-acre vegetable crops such as carrots and onions, as traditional areas for these crops, such as the fens, started to suffer from diseases and pests such as eel-worm. These were unsupported crops which forced growers to improve their integration with those they supplied.

North Nottinghamshire is also characterised by mining, and Naish farmed land that backed onto collieries and pits. In the early 1980s the North Nottingham area had witnessed pitched battles between pickets and police in the year-long miners' strike of 1984–85. The Yorkshire–Nottingham border was known for its flashpoints, as the Yorkshire miners strongly backed the strike while their Nottinghamshire counterparts did not.

At this point in this century-long narrative, it is worth remembering that farming was not the only primary British industry in decline. When the NFU was formed in 1908, both farming and mining each employed roughly a million people. A century on, the British mining industry employs just 23,000 people and the amount of coal produced has fallen by 90 per cent. In contrast, agriculture still employs over 350,000 and production has gone up. One could argue that agriculture has fared relatively well, particularly in the 1980s and 1990s, when mining saw its biggest decline under the Thatcher administration. One might also suggest that farmers' reluctance in the 1980s to take to the streets as they had in the 1960s and '70s did not actually harm their cause. For all its bluster and show of strength through direct action, Scargillism did not achieve much for the miners. Then again, the NFU and the NUM were very different sorts of unions.

By the time he was in his mid-20s Naish had established a reputation as a competent farmer and an ambitious businessman. As such, he caught the eye of local poultry magnate John Eastwood, who invited the young Naish to come and work at his side in his burgeoning business.

Eastwood's career merits mention in any book that looks at the history of twentieth-century British agriculture. Originally trained as an engineer, Eastwood ran a successful civil engineering business before the war, but in the 1950s was inspired by the broiler industry in the United States. He saw it as an opportunity to turn home-grown cereal into higher-value chicken meat. Using his engineering skills, he designed and built large broiler units complete with the first automatic feeder systems in Britain. Through these methods and by using new poultry genetics, Eastwood could achieve remarkably fast growth rates, with birds achieving 4lb in just 11

weeks. He rapidly built more broiler units, adding a 3,000 ton a week mill at Belle Eau Park. By 1960, running 11,000 acres of poultry units, the company went public. Egg units added in the early 1960s also incorporated Eastwood-engineered purpose-built factory farming techniques. By the mid-1960s Eastwood was supplying an astonishing 10 per cent of the national market for chickens and eggs. His remarkable success was based on three qualities that had not seen much pre-eminence in pre-war agriculture – engineering, vertical integration and business marketing. There were also new techniques, such as keeping thousands of animals in very close confinement and using antibiotics in the feed to suppress disease. It was 'agri-business' and 'factory farming' writ large. Eastwood pioneered a revolutionary model of farming that transformed the British egg and chicken industry out of all recognition. He started with nothing and grew a business he sold for £40 million 30 years later. Whereas before 1939 chicken farming had been the occupation of thousands of farmers running medium-sized outdoor units, the postwar period saw changes that concentrated production into a few powerful hands. Today it is fashionable to regret these developments on all sorts of grounds, such as animal welfare and loss of farmers. In amongst all this middle-class angst, we forget that Eastwood's real achievement was to put affordable chicken and eggs on the dining-table of the working man. He also helped build an efficient, resilient part of British agriculture that could easily have lost out to imports just as the bacon industry had lost out to the better-organised Danes.

And so it was that into this burgeoning and pioneering agri-business environment the young Naish was thrust in the 1960s. He became Eastwood's trusted right-hand man at a time when Eastwood's health was faltering through badly failing eyesight. For seven years Naish was managing director of Eastwood's mighty empire and learnt, first-hand, the importance of skills such as finance and marketing. While other young farmers his age were drenching cows or sitting on tractors, Naish was in the city raising millions in venture capital through debentures, or securing huge deals with the major supermarket buyers. It was at this time that a handful of grocers such as Asda, Sainsbury and Tesco were starting to dominate the UK grocery market through their all-conquering supermarket chains. These changes, in the late '60s and early '70s, must have created a heady atmosphere which did not pass the young Naish by. It gave him the conviction that agriculture's challenges must be addressed through modern business skills as much as through traditional farming skills. Naish was emphatic from the outset of his presidency that, in the modern world, farmers should find their returns in the marketplace rather than rely on the taxpayer for their income. He built on Gourlay's view that the dependency culture within farming was hindering both marketing and business skills

As a man, David Naish very much reflects his background. Like his Uncle, Jim Turner, he hails from a busy, industrious part of the world and possesses those same qualities. The area where North Nottinghamshire meets South Yorkshire is a scarred landscape populated by factories, farms, mines and roads. Its culture is imbued with business, trade, manufacture and the pursuit of money. The people are energetic and like to be 'on the make'. Naish was known for his hard work; he would get into his presidential office at five in the morning, well before anyone else. He saw the NFU as a business and would delegate or organise accordingly.

Along with his earnest sense of professionalism he had an infectious sense of humour. NFU staff would delight in trying to 'corpse' him before he was about to speak at conferences. At one NFU Council meeting some fractious beef farmers from Devon insisted that Naish write a letter, in French, to the French Embassy on an issue concerning beef exports. Policy adviser Martin Haworth whispered to Naish that the obvious thing to do would be to send the ambassador a French letter. Naish took several minutes to regain his composure and proper control of the meeting.

Naish talks with a fast rat-a-tat patter that reflects a busy mind. He has a barrel-chested bluster that clearly takes an old-fashioned pride in a sense of achievement. At the same time, he has his uncle's humility, which keeps him from boorishness or arrogance. Naish is a man of business who enjoys the company of his fellows, but is also happy pursuing his own ends. He is polite and decorous, welcoming and considerate. As president he displayed a strong sense of public service and duty, another characteristic he inherited from his uncle. When in Brussels, the Continentals liked his rotund English charm and his diplomacy as well as virtues they themselves struggled with, such as starting meetings on time. But in amongst Naish's self-assurance and smooth competence, others detected occasional self-doubt and insecurity. He could also be remarkably emotional when speaking. South-West regional director and wry wordsmith Anthony Gibson once wrote of him: 'He wore his heart not so much on his sleeve, as nailed to his forehead.' The question that comes to mind when you consider Naish in the long narrative that is the history of the NFU is: 'Was he inspired by the memory of his uncle, or was he haunted by it?

Naish's belief in improved marketing is reflected in his NFU career. In the 1980s he spent seven years sitting on the board of Food From Britain (FFB), a government-backed quango set up by Peter Walker in the early 1980s. Although it did not radically transform the lot of the farmer on the ground, it did help Britain move away from its reputation for

having the worst food in the world. It promoted exports of products such as Scotch whisky, and there can be no doubt that a healthy UK distilling industry helps both British cereal and British livestock farmers. Similarly, as president, Naish was a keen member of the Institute of Grocery Distribution (IGD) and always tried to break down the 'us and them' attitude of farmers when it came to dealing with food processors and the retailers. He had learnt from his Eastwood days that, while it was not always easy for producers to deal with the ever more powerful players in the ever more consolidated grocery chain, it was far better for farmers to work with these people than work against them. In Naish's words: 'Farmers must realise nobody wants to do business on the basis of mutual distrust and personal abuse.' He felt his presence as a farmer was vital for his industry in the working of IGD. He had similar views when he chaired the Prime Minister's Food Marketing Initiative

The irony for him was that, as fast as he ran to try to play catch up with the grocery chain, the more it consolidated and the greater the gap became between the farmer and the rest of the chain. It was through the 1980s and early '90s that the big five (Tesco, Sainsbury, Asda, Safeway and Somerfield) increased their share of the grocery market from 30 per cent to 75 per cent. They were acquiring the ability to control the market and squeeze down prices. Many in the farming industry castigated Naish for being in bed with the supermarkets while farmers were going under because they were no longer being given a just share of the food pound. Naish wanted no truck with such bloodymindedness and felt it better to be a supplier in a bed rather than a dog in a manger. It was a classic dilemma many presidents before him had faced: either to thump the populist tub for the amusement of his membership or to try to devise a strategy that actually improved the bargaining position of the farmer in the face of a growing imbalance of power.

One such idea that established itself in Naish's time was farm produce assurance. In the early 1990s the supermarkets were making moves to establish their own assurance schemes to be imposed on suppliers. The NFU view was that it would be better to have a few general schemes which everyone could operate under. The idea was to give UK farm produce a marketing edge by demonstrating to the consumer it was assured as safe and wholesome in the way it was grown. The idea also had the other objective of self-policing the food chain in the face of the prospect of greater inspection and regulation by an over-assiduous British civil service. It is from these times that we trace the assurance schemes that were set up in the '90s. Again, they were never popular with farmers, who struggled to see what the extra self-imposed costs of production were returning to them. One reason for this is that the retailers only showed piecemeal loyalty to the schemes and felt little moral compulsion to fulfil their side of the bargain, namely to give preference to UK-assured produce and to promote it to their customers as such. History records that farmers had been let down like this before, particularly by the butchers in the 1930s, who had failed preferentially to buy British meat under the National Mark scheme, preferring instead to keep their options open to buy from where they liked, most notably from FMD-riddled South America where, not suprisingly, production costs were lower and meat was cheap.

We also recollect that in 1908 there was another row between the NFU and the butchers over the control of TB. We also recollect that a call for the government to take action to control the spread of TB in cattle was the first ever resolution of the NFU. In the first half of the century TB had been a serious disease in both humans and cattle. Through tuber-clin testing and inoculation in both species the disease had been eradicated completely in humans and largely stamped out in cattle.

Work by the NFU and MAFF to improve milk hygiene was also part of this victory. Past NFU presidents such as Langford and Turner, with their TT herds and milk, were all part of that process whereby milk became a more wholesome and healthier product. But in the 1990s TB was making a comeback in the British cattle population. By 1996 there were over 3,500 animals slaughtered in the DEFRA eradication programme.

The other thing that was increasing in the British countryside was badgers. Counting badgers has always been problematic, but the best evidence suggested badger numbers doubled from 200,000 to 400,000 in the 20 years before 1995. They were one of the beneficiaries of the general postwar movement to protect wildlife. The 1992 Protection of Badgers Act consolidated previous legislation that sought to stop badger-baiting and all interference with badger sets. Meanwhile, there was evidence from 1971 onwards that badgers harboured and spread TB. Under Naish's presidency there were increasingly angry calls, mainly from the South-West bovine TB hotspots, for the government to take action against TB spread by badgers.

The 1990s saw various initiatives on the environmental front, placing the concept of farmers being paid 'to look after the countryside' firmly on the agenda. The 1992 Rio-Earth summit introduced two new words into the farming vocabulary that would be heard again and again. One was 'sustainability' and the other 'bio-diversity'. The Countryside Stewardship scheme, introduced in 1992, rolled out conservation management agreements beyond those areas designated in SSSIs or ESAs. Under these schemes farmers were paid for income forgone if they undertook measures such as creating uncropped margins or reducing stocking levels. By 1999 over 4,800 agreements covering 100,000 hectares had been established. The 1991 EU Nitrates Directive led to designated areas restricting the use of fertilisers and manures in order to achieve the nitrate target of 50 ppm in drinking water. This was particularly pertinent to Naish, who farmed near a Severn Trent bore-hole that in the late 1980s had struggled to achieve these levels. The nitrate policy led to the establishment of NVZs in 1997 which substantially expanded those areas which monitored and curtailed fertiliser use. In 1997 came the Hedgerow Regulation Order that protected 65–70 per cent of the nation's hedgerows from removal without good reason.

In terms of organisation in the NFU, the start of Naish's presidency saw the completion of the reforms decided during Gourlay's watch. The Knightsbridge leviathan was evacuated and more modest, more modern premises were found in an office block in Long Acre in Covent Garden. Headquarters staff was downsized to 150 and the membership department was moved to Stamford and the IT department to Devizes. In 1994 Council decided not to move back to Knightsbridge but rather rent it out and keep the site as an appreciating asset. It appreciated enormously in the property boom of the early '90s. Whereas in 1974 it was valued at £6.1 million, in 1996, after extensive redevelopment, the NFU-retained share was worth £15 million. Ten years later it was to be worth a healthy £39 million. When the temporary lease at Long Acre expired in 1996, the NFU moved its headquarters to Shaftesbury Avenue. Out in the regions, brand new purpose-built centres were built to service the new regional structures. The first was opened by Prince Charles in Exeter in 1991, followed by further offices in Skelmersdale, Swansea, York, Newmarket, Telford and Uppingham.

Top of the NFU policy agenda in 1991 was CAP reform. A new commissioner, an Irishman called Ray MacSharry, was in place in Brussels and he was determined to control the CAP budget and make it more GATT-compliant. There was also the need to consider the possibility of the EU pushing eastwards to take in members of the old Warsaw Pact countries. The end of the 1980s had seen the redrawing of the map of Europe with the demise of the Soviet Union under the Gorbachev era. Newly liberalised countries such as Poland, with its vast backward agriculture, were knocking on the door of the EU requesting entry. All this meant the CAP would, as ever, have to be reformed.

Despite the lack of agreement during the six years of the GATT Uruguay round, the EU accepted that it would have to continue to lower its protective barriers on farm imports and move its commodity prices closer to the world market. At the same time it agreed with the US that direct payments to farmers were largely acceptable in the new GATT/WTO framework.

The original reform proposals that MacSharry produced in July 1991 proposed: cuts in support prices; compulsory set-aside; cuts in milk quota and, finally, compensation targeted at small producers through capping. It was the latter that was potentially most damaging to the above-average sized British farmers. The NFU lobbying machine duly swung into action. Working closely alongside MAFF, it argued strongly in Brussels that the proposals threatened the existence of the typical medium-sized family farm that was the very lifeblood of British agriculture and the British countryside. British Minister John Gummer said he would not stand by and witness the proposed 'Sligo-isation' ruin his farmers. The British argument was won and most of MacSharry's modulation proposals were removed or watered down. It was a key victory for the NFU that must have secured many millions for its members. Generally, the British came out of the MacSharry reforms very well, largely because the new direct payments were based on compensation for what was lost. Due to their historic high yields, British farmers ended up with some of the highest payments in the EU.

Despite this undoubted victory, the compulsory set-aside aspect of the MacSharry reforms wrankled with many farmers and, possibly, lost the NFU members, as they thought the union too compliant with the idea. By the early 1990s many British farmers had spent a lifetime since the Second World War getting their farms into good productive order. For this postwar generation the prospect of 15 per cent of their land standing idle went against the grain. In passing, we should note that another grumble farmers had in 1992 was the banning of straw burning. Again, some farmers vented their frustration by blaming the blameless NFU, who had fought harder than anyone in the 1980s to keep the farmers' right to burn in the face of immense public hostility.

What also caused umbrage was the welter of new paperwork. Suddenly farmers no longer secured their CAP money indirectly through supported prices but now had to apply for direct aid according to hectares grown and numbers of sheep and cows kept. In 1992 farmers and NFU advisers scrabbled around with maps, forms and field numbers. Whereas on the Continent there was a tradition for farmers and the state to have accurate mapping because of the tax system of rating land, in Britain this did not exist. From the 1990s onwards form-filling was the new bugbear that farmers couldn't afford to neglect or get wrong. Often it was the NFU they turned to for hand-holding and advice. The NFU responded by providing the help that was needed.

Just as British farmers were heaving a sigh of relief that the MacSharry proposals were not as draconian as they had originally feared, along came another fortunate event. It occurred on 16 September 1992. It was known amongst the yuppies of the city as 'Black Wednesday'. For others, including farmers, it was 'Golden Wednesday'. The April 1992 general election had seen the surprise return of the Conservatives under Prime Minister John Major on a small majority. It was a politically weak administration, riven with splits over Europe. It should be said, though, that the NFU found a government with a small majority in the Commons more approachable. It also helped that Major represented the reasonably rural constituency of Huntingdon.

One of Major's key finance policies was membership of the ERM. This led to an over-valuing of the pound, which collapsed in mid-September, forcing it to withdraw from the ERM. For farmers the fallout from this saw increases in both their new CAP support payments through green pound adjustment and an appreciation in commodity markets as exports became more competitive against foreign currencies. Although in 1991 farm income had fallen again to a new postwar low, the period 1992–95 saw a reversal of fortunes that brought welcome relief from the privations of the previous ten years. Suddenly, UK farmers were at the top of the EU income league. It was the larger arable farmers who saw the best improvement in prices, but livestock, horticulture and milk were not far behind. It was only in the egg and pig sectors that the improvement was not so evident. Overall, total income from farming per head in the UK nearly doubled from 1990 to 1995. In terms of productivity, UK agriculture was close to its postwar peak and was 86 per cent self-sufficient in indigenous foods. It had only ever been higher than this for a short period in the early 1980s.

For a farmer such as David Naish, it meant his wheat prices climbed 30 per cent during the first four years of his presidency and potato prices improved three-fold. For Naish this was a golden period. The market was delivering for most farmers, and there was even talk that British farmers could survive without CAP payments. As an advocate of the free market, Naish was in his element. He was even welcome at the USDA, where Commissioner Glickman shared with Naish his thoughts on a radically reduced US Farm Programme in exchange for ideas on how the CAP could be downsized and its support payments de-coupled.

For the NFU this same period saw an improvement in membership and income. With countryside members (paying an average of £30 a year and not receiving voting rights) now included in the membership figure, it was now more difficult to compare NFU membership with that of the past. Suffice to say that by 1995 membership was 121,454, 33,668 of whom were in the countryside category. The NFU still claimed to include over 70 per cent of full-time farmers and growers in its membership.

Subscription income improved to £16.6 million, with a total income now at £23.2 million.

Naish was always of the view that the structural fetters that stopped agriculture responding to market forces should be minimised. The Agricultural Tenancies Act of 1995 is quite in keeping with his presidency. It further freed up the rented sector by allowing short-term farm business tenancies. These yearly agreements were particularly useful to potato growers such as Naish, who only wanted to rent a field for one year and then move on. By removing tenancy rights in such situations it gave landowners confidence to make more land available for such a purpose without fear it might tie the land up for generations. It was a good example of the NFU moving from protecting sitting tenants and the status quo to allowing the industry to restructure in response to changes in the market.

With prices for most commodities improving, the scrapping of the marketing boards under the 1993 Agriculture Act was not met with the level of regret one might have expected, either in the NFU or in the farming community generally. By 1993 there were three boards left, for milk, potatoes and wool, and by 1994 they were no more. With the Milk Marketing Board it was the end of a proud 60-year history, a history that was closely intertwined with that of the NFU. It was the greatest marketing co-operative venture ever undertaken by British farmers, and those farmers had, by and large, always given it their overwhelming support. When Britain entered the EEC in 1973 there was a question as to whether the marketing boards could legally be allowed to survive as they struggled to comply with EU competition law. In the 1980s the MMB had been challenged by dairy farmers who wanted to process and sell milk direct without paying the MMB levy. By the late 1980s it was clearly past its sell-by date and, with a government who instinctively preferred unregulated markets, it soon received its *coup de grace*. At the same time, with milk prices on the up, there was little fight amongst the dairymen to retain the MMB. There was also a belief among many that if farmers stayed loyal to Milk Marque, the MMB's successor,, then life under the newly deregulated market would not be very different. Having said that, no ballot of milk producers was ever offered by government or pushed for by the NFU. The government had rejected the MMB/NFU proposal of a national integrated co-op with a processing capacity and so, instead, Milk Marque was set up without any processing facilities. Its weakness was that, without processing, it could not add value to its milk. Many think today that had regional co-ops with processing been set up in 1994 rather than a national co-op without them, then the milk industry would have survived the late 1990s much better than it did.

As we recollect, the marketing boards were set up because of NFU membership pressure in the face of

opposition by the NFU leadership in 1933. Men such as former president Rowland Robbins had argued in favour of not forcing the individual to run with the herd. It could be argued that, 60 years later, Naish led the NFU back to that position, but it would be wrong to suggest he acted alone or without the pressure of EU competition law. Whether or not, like Robbins, his views were not those of his members is something we will never know for sure. It was clear that Naish thought the marketing boards, of which his uncle had been a passionate advocate, had had their day. When at Eastwoods he was keen to see the Egg Marketing Board disappear, which it did in 1971. As a potato grower, he, like many other potato growers, felt the PMB had a negative effect on the market and was abused by growers as a market of last resort.

Whether or not the demise of the MMB was a good thing or not is a matter for debate. Maybe it is best just to leave the matter with a few bald statistics. When the NFU helped set up the ballot required by statute to set up the MMB it had to consult with the 140,000 dairy farmers producing milk at the time in England and Wales. By the time the board was abolished in 1993 this was down to 28,000. Today, in 2008, there are a fewer than 14,000.

If there is one date that will be forever etched on the mind of David Naish, it is 20 March 1996. It was on that day that health minister Stephen Dorrell stood up in the House of Commons and announced to a stunned world that the government was now of the opinion that there was a link between Human CJD and the consumption of beef. A new variant of CJD had been identified that looked very similar to BSE. Just as with Edwina Curry ten years before, Dorrell's short statement reverberated around the world and looked ready to topple a vital part of UK agriculture. What made matters worse was that, just a few days before, Dorrell was on record as saying a link between BSE and CJD was 'inconceivable'. Three headlines from the following day's *Daily Mirror* give a flavour of the sensationalist media reaction that followed:

MAD COW CAN KILL YOU
Government to admit it today [and they did, after denying it until 12 o'clock]

WE'VE ALREADY EATEN 1,000,000 MAD COWS
Borrowed time fear. Up to 500,000 could succumb to CJD

YOU'RE RIGHT TO BE ANGRY
[Professor Lacey writing to say that consumers should have been treated better and not misled.]

Ten years on it is becoming clear it was a huge overreaction to the risk presented to human health from BSE in 1996, but at the time it was very difficult to contain the backlash. After Dorrell's announcement it was clear that the impact on beef sales at home could be calamitous and export bans would now be inevitable. Not surprisingly, an increasingly cynical public would pay little heed to government reassurance that beef was now currently safe due to the offal ban put in place in 1989. The sense of shock in the farming community was palpable.

Consulting with the good contacts he had in the supermarkets, Naish realised that animals over 30 months would now be, more or less, unsaleable. Over the next few days the NFU machine laid down a ground plan to limit the damage. Consultation was made at DEFRA and EU level. On the Monday, Naish phoned No. 10 and asked for an urgent meeting with Prime Minister Major. It was in that meeting that the OTMS (Over Thirty Months) scheme was hammered out to help save the British beef industry. The meeting between Naish and Major was reminiscent of one of those 'one to one' moments men like Plumb and Turner had had at No. 10 when the hopes and prospects of the farming industry lay on the shoulders of the NFU president. Naish rose to that challenge. As the *Times* noted in its columns the week following the Dorrell announcement, Naish almost single-handedly forced the government to abandon the 'do-nothing' policy.

Over the next few weeks the NFU called for, and achieved, further support measures to keep beef farmers afloat; market support though firmer intervention buying; a calf-processing scheme; a £110 million aid package for increased premium schemes and the Hill Livestock Compensatory Allowances scheme. With a 24 per cent reduction in the home market for beef and an export ban leading to a decline in the UK beef market of 36 per cent, the schemes the NFU lobbied hard for proved a lifeline for many farmers. Mercifully, over time, it was also clear that the British public had not deserted British beef in the manner the media suggested they should.

The irony for the NFU was that, at the time of the Dorrell announcement, it was clear from epidemological studies that the existing control measures had the disease under control and it was clearly diminishing. Cases in 1996 were at around 7,000, whereas at their peak in 1992 it was 36,000. There were some in the NFU membership who wanted to resist any extra regulation, including Naish's OTMS scheme, stemming from the Dorrell announcement. The export ban was also seen as nothing more than French and German protectionism. Naish's view was that, in order to try to regain consumer confidence and to get the EU to eventually lift the export ban, then there was little choice but to go the extra unpleasant mile. The EU demand for a selective cull of 100,000 cattle was agreed to. Cattle passports for all newborn cattle were introduced, as well as double tagging. The offal ban and meat rendering were also tightened up.

The BSE crisis had dominated 1996, and for Naish it was a stressful time. It had been an exhausting nine months that would have tested the best of men. The media interest was at fever pitch and NFU media relations became a matter of fire-fighting rather than industry promotion. There was a lot of high politics being played out. The beef ban, imposed largely at the behest of the French and Germans, became a pretext for the anti-Europeans in the John Major cabinet to confuse the situation rather than deal with it. On the Continent it became an opportunity to take revenge on 15 years of British 'non-communitaire' bile. It all just added more heat than light, and while the NFU tried to guide government to do the best for its beef farmers, other agendas subverted any sensible lobbying. Mr Hogg, in his silly hat, journeyed back and forth to Brussels with no clear policy steer as to what the British negotiating position should be. Finally, for Naish, there was a lot of disquiet among beef farmers, who were always going to be difficult to keep happy. In the South West there was a new NFU firebrand called Richard Haddock, who delighted in being a thorn in Naish's side.

One aspect of Naish's abilities that should not be forgotten was his political nous. Before becoming involved in the NFU he had a proven track record in local politics as a councillor. As president he worked hard to build bridges between the NFU and the political establishment in the way Plumb had done successfully in the 1970s. He went out of his way to build dialogue and rapport with senior figures in the Conservative Party, such as Michael Heseltine. It should also be remembered he was president of COPA, the pan-EU farmer representative organisation, and as such gave the NFU an influential position in Brussels. His good relations with governments generally meant he could effectively limit the damage BSE could have caused.

To compound Naish's BSE misery, in 1996 the pound was resurgent and the gains farming had made after the crash of 1992 were starting to evaporate. Commodity prices were on the slide again and area payments under the new IACS system were also going down. Just as farming fortunes had risen with the collapse of the pound in the first half of the '90s, in the second half they were to plummet to the miserable state they had been in 1990. At the end of 1997, Naish decided to stand down. Had he done so in 1995 he would have joined his uncle in a place in the sun in the history of the NFU.

One interesting but rather trivial observation is that Naish lost an appreciable amount of weight during the BSE crisis. Not only is this a neat comparison with his uncle, who waxed considerably during his presidency, it is also a reflection of the stress and sheer hard work Naish endured during the episode.

As with previous presidents who led the NFU in

time of crisis, Naish's personal sacrifice in leading his industry should not be forgotten or underestimated.

David Naish is an interesting man for anyone trying to write a 100-year narrative of the NFU. His mentor was his uncle, Jim Turner, and in turn Turner's mentor was Harry German, who was a contemporary and friend of Colin Campbell. Thus we span 100 years of history through close personal contact. What is more, they all lived and farmed within 30 miles of each other, with Naish, Turner and German all holding posts in Nottinghamshire NFU. They were all larger-than-life characters who left their imprint on the world around them. But there were differences. Campbell and Naish were wary of collectivised marketing and celebrated the importance of the individual yeoman farmer. Both were wary of the farmer becoming too dependent on the state, and felt the farmer's lot was best addressed through self-reliance. German and Turner, having experienced the misery of the 1920s and 1930s, came to the view that the free market could be a cruel mistress for the farmer, and that it was necessary for farmers to look to more corporate ideas whereby individuality was pooled and agriculture worked alongside an interventionist state.

Naish's belief in marketing and securing agriculture's place in the food chain was opportune and important. The irony was that, no matter how good your product and no matter how brilliant your marketing, one short statement on a Wednesday afternoon in the House of Commons could send your markets and your business into meltdown. The response to this did not lie in the hands of the farmer or in his business skills, it lay in the hands of those who represented him politically. The crisis of March 1996 presented David Naish and the union with the most testing of challenges. As president of the NFU, Naish rose to that challenge.

CHAPTER 32

Sir Ben Gill, 1998–2004

When Sir David Naish stepped down at the 1998 AGM, for the first time in 30 years there was a hard-fought electoral battle as to who would succeed. The choice was between two Yorkshiremen, Ben Gill and Tony Pexton, the deputy presidents. In the end Council showed a preference for the sharp, hyperactive, fiery Gill rather than the smooth, phlegmatic, blunt Pexton. The ballot was secret, but the gossip was that it came down to a handful of votes.

Ben Gill was born on the auspicious date of 01/01/50. He was brought up on a 350-acre farm near Easingwold, at the foot of the Howardian Hills, 12 miles north of York. On the Hawkhills Estate, 250 acres was owned and a further 100 acres was rented from the government. It was typical North Yorkshire vale countryside, with a mixture of soils and a mixture of farming. It was half arable (potatoes, sugar beet and wheat) and half grass (sheep and suckler cows). Gill recollects how, when he was a lad, the store cattle used to arrive by specially commissioned train from Oban in Scotland. Once the train got lost en route, and arrived three days late full of very hungry and thirsty cattle. Typical of many farms in the 30 years between 1945 and 1975, the farm saw its labour requirement shrink from seven men and 13 cart-horses to just one man and a couple of tractors.

Gill went to the local primary school and passed his 11-plus to attend a boarding school in Barnard Castle. Ben was a bright schoolboy and passed his O levels and A levels two years early. At Cambridge his year was the last to take a degree in agriculture at the leading university.

On returning to the farm, like many farming sons fresh out of college, Ben couldn't get on with his father. Blood and land can make for a heady brew, even in the most settled of farmyards, and the young Gill looked to expand his horizons beyond North Yorkshire. Spontaneously responding to an advert in a local paper, he ended up in Namasagali in Uganda, teaching in a secondary school. This was the early '70s, when the unstable rule of Idi Amin was making Uganda a dangerous place for a white man. On more than one occasion Gill found himself at the wrong end of a machine gun wielded with intent. Through thinking on his feet, he learned how to survive. Back in Easingwold in early 1978, Ben's father was ailing and wanted his son home. It was time to bury their differences, and the prodigal son returned to run the farm at Easingwold and to say his last goodbyes to his father, who died four months later.

Ben Gill on his Easingwold farm with the last man to lead MAFF – Nick Brown.

Over the next few years Gill expanded the arable side of the farm, built a large grainstore and scaled down the livestock enterprises.

Early in his farming career, Gill was attracted into agri-politics and the NFU. In the 1980s he carved out a reputation for his forcefulness in debate and as an original thinker. He was soon chairman of the Livestock Committee in London and chairman of the European Sheep Advisory Committee in Brussels. It was at this point that he bought more grazing land and brought sheep back to the farm.

As a man, Ben Gill is fiery and passionate. When you ask others what it was like to work with Ben Gill they smile and say 'not dull'. He is both excitable and exciting, with a 'full-on' personality. Some were not always sure how to take him, but it was those who gave as good as they got who got on with him best. He had a boisterous energy which he threw into whatever task lay before him. As a speaker he was lucid and could speak without notes, with a speciality of leaving the stage and walking amongst the audience. 'Hot-blooded' is a good way to describe Ben Gill, not least because he would delight in being comfortable in shirtsleeves while those around him were complaining of the cold. He was known for his capricious eccentricities. On more than one occasion while on presidential visits, he would bemuse farmers by greeting the growling farmyard dog by barking back in the dog's face. (No one would have been rude enough to describe Gill as barking mad, but at times they were tempted.) Gill was generally well regarded by the Europeans in Brussels, who liked his eccentricity and odd British sense of humour, as well as his energetic, but sometimes incomprehensible, French. The Dutch thought it highly appropriate that, as their 'G' is softly pronounced 'H', his name was pronounced 'Benny Hill' rather than Ben Gill.

His brilliance as a schoolboy was not just a childhood wonder; in between his ears there throbbed a fearsome computer which ran red hot, giving him an easy ability to read and store information. Gill could process the most complex of technical issues with ease. Physically he is a large man, 6ft 3ins tall, and has a large personality to go with it. He is fair-haired and ruddy in complexion. As with many North Yorkshiremen, you suspect there must have been a Viking raid somewhere in the dark past of the family history.

There is a considerable element of the academic about Ben Gill, and he took huge pride in his science background. While deputy president he received the CBE for his science contribution, particularly on the AFRC and BBSRC. As president he cultivated the friendship of both Lord May, president of the Royal Society and Sir David King, chief scientific adviser to government. Some in the green movement nicknamed him 'Bio-tech Ben' as a term of derision. It was a curious sign of the times in the 1990s that someone should be sneered at because of an interest in new science and technology.

The 1990s had seen the emergence of two new technologies, GPS and bio-technology, that had the potential to further revolutionise the way farmers produced food. GPS gave the ability to improve the way field operations were carried out. Through satellites in space talking to in-cab computers on the ground, field operations such as fertilising, harvesting and seeding could be undertaken with far more precision and efficiency. Although the technology had some impact, it is fair to say that the uptake was never as fast and as widespread as was envisaged when it first started to appear. The main reason for this was probably the downturn in farm profitability in the second half of the 1990s. In the ten years around the millennium, on-farm investment dropped significantly and farmers had to concentrate their money on the essentials rather than on new technologies. It is a very similar story to that in the 1930s, when there were exciting new technologies available to farmers, most notably the tractor, that were not widely taken up because of lack of profit and lack of investment.

The second new technology, genetic modification, stalled for a very different reason. As later became clear with his role as a governor at the pioneering John Innes centre in Norfolk, Gill was well versed in the potential GM had for advancing UK agriculture. By directly modifying a plant's genetics, research scientists were managing to breed plants that expressed useful traits that had advantages for both the farmer and the consumer. It was far faster and better targeted than traditional methods of plant breeding, but in the UK it fell foul of consumer acceptability and political intrigue. The 1980s and 1990s saw the rise of a consumer trend that was of the view that it was somehow better if nature provided food rather than science. There was no doubt that, as food became more plentiful and more affordable after the postwar privations, consumers could more easily indulge their own concerns. Suddenly supermarket shelves could be found full of products boasting they were 'naturally wholesome' or 'nature's choice'. This dovetailed with an increasingly fashionable view that somehow modern agriculture since the Second World War had moved too far away from 'natural or traditional' methods of producing food. The 1990s saw a significant rise in the organic movement. The BSE drama simply reinforced these trends. The Dorrell statement of March 1996 severely undermined the public's trust in government and scientists when it came to food safety. What, in essence, this all meant for farmers and the NFU was that the technology train that had carried agriculture so smoothly and swiftly since the Second World War had now suddenly hit the buffers. Given the science bias of his education, Gill was a great believer in science and its achievements for agriculture, and could be found at conferences, as president, urging farmers to 'grasp the nettle of technology'. At first the NFU took a clear pro-GM view, arguing that the technology should be allowed in the UK. But the lesson of the late 1990s was that science and technical improvement were no longer enough to justify changes in farm production. Consumer acceptability was just as important. Despite initial acceptance of the GM 'Flavor Savor' tomato, consumers became highly sceptical of GM's proven safety and, accordingly, retailers cleared it from their shelves. The media were generally hostile to the new technology, the most infamous being the *Daily Mail*, with its 'Frankenfoods' headlines. At the political level, the regulators refused to give the licences to grow the crops although, perversely, licences were granted to import them. Gill lost this particular battle and never saw GM crops grown commercially in the UK during his presidency. In his defence, he was not helped by some ham-fisted attempts to introduce the technology into Britain by some American corporations who didn't understand the new scepticism among UK consumers when it came to food safety.

The GM debate that emerged in the 1990s represented a new departure for British agriculture. There had been earlier indications of a wariness of new technology with the refusal to allow BST in dairy cows in the late 1980s. Gill had come across this as chairman of the Livestock Committee when the use of growth hormones was debated. Gill was a forceful

Ben Gill and Prime Minister Blair launching the Farm Assurance mark – the Little Red Tractor – an NFU initiative.

advocate for their introduction, as a safe technology, to make beef production more efficient. This was also lost, as government would not license their use on the spurious grounds of food safety. As the food shortages in the 1940s became a distant memory, if not completely forgotten, technologies that increased food production were not so readily taken up. No one in the 1950s had even thought to question the use of gamma-ray chromosome mutation in producing new crop varieties, but in the 1990s GM techniques were viewed with hostility. The emergence of 'the precautionary principle', along with the rise in 'consumerism' and 'environmentalism', had transformed the way society viewed technical developments in agriculture. It was also fair to say that, after BSE, many in the farming community had become more wary of change. Farmers felt that the BSE tragedy had lost them the confidence of the public when it came to food safety, when the real culprits were the corporations who provided the feed and the scientists who had changed the clandestine way its ingredients were processed. For farmers and the NFU the postwar world of Jim Turner was very different from the one in which Ben Gill was president.

In 1997 a new Labour Government came to power with Tony Blair as Prime Minister. After 18 years in the political wilderness, it was a long overdue return for the small group of Labour MPs who could remember life under Jim Callaghan. One of the few who had had any experience of government was Jack Cunningham. Cunningham was given the agricultural portfolio and proved a difficult man for the NFU to deal with. It was established protocol for the president of the NFU to meet the new minister within a few days of the new minister's appointment. With Cunningham, he kept President Naish waiting for two and a half weeks. Cunningham quickly became

known as 'Junket Jack' as he wined and dined his way through his ministerial brief in five-star luxury. He later explained that he had once nearly died at sea and at that point resolved never to stint himself again. By the time Gill became president, the NFU had learnt the place to do business with Cunningham was in the best restaurants with extensive wine cellars, rather than in his plush Smith Square offices. It should be said, though, that, compared to the likes of Butler and Naish, Gill was no 'dining-room diplomat'. Cunningham was replaced by the much more approachable and emollient Nick Brown in 1998. Gill built up a close, constructive relationship with the new minister. Not long after Brown's appointment, some gutter journalism in the *News of the World* forced the minister to admit he was gay. This he did with characteristic good humour, telling an NFU audience: 'It's a lovely day, the sun is out – and so am I.' Despite his background writing for *Jackie* magazine and penning advertising jingles for fabric conditioners, Brown proved one of the better Ministers of Agriculture the NFU had to deal with. As we shall see, he was also the last. At the 2000 NFU AGM Brown had the ignominy of having a chocolate éclair shoved in his face after being barracked by some NFU delegates over BSE compensation. The young lady with the éclair was nothing to do with the NFU. To his credit, Brown played down the seriousness of being attacked by someone armed with patisserie. To the delight of the NFU faithful, he mopped himself down with a large handkerchief and commented into the microphone: 'You will be relieved to know this is chocolate.' This good humour was somewhat in contrast to John Prescott who, when confronted by an egg-wielding farm-worker in 2001, lashed out with his fists.

With the advent of the New Labour Government, the NFU noticed that the corridors of power were more full of lobby groups than in the past. Blair was keen to be seen as inclusive of all 'stakeholders', which was particularly the case with environmental pressure groups. One flagship part of their manifesto had been 'the right to roam', largely at the behest of the Ramblers and to the horror of the CLA. The result was the Countryside and Rights of Way (CROW) Act in 2000, which gave the public access to common land, moor, mountain, heath and down. Initially, the NFU opposed the idea, but when they realised the head of steam behind it they concentrated their efforts on minimising its impact on practical farming. They were reasonably successful when the Act excluded cultivated land and was made more sensitive to the needs of livestock, for instance dogs were to be kept on leads at lambing time.

One of the key battles Gill inherited was the lifting of the beef ban that had followed the Dorrell announcement. It wasn't until 1998, after repeated lobbying by the NFU in Brussels, that the European Commission announced an easing of the ban.

Boneless beef from animals aged between six and 30 months was permitted for export within the EU after 1 August 1999. As British beef farmers prepared to re-conquer their lucrative continental markets, their patience was tested as the French and Germans defied the Commission and refused to lift the ban. German farmers had been annoyed by the collapse in their home beef prices because of the BSE health scare, which they saw as the fault of the British. Gill came face to face with this anger when he had to walk past 1,000 German farmers as he went into talks at the Commission in Brussels in the summer of 1999. The Germans aggressively chanted 'Schweinhund' as he walked past. Despite the animosity, the German Government decided to abide by the rules of the EU game and lifted their ban in the spring of 2000. Gill was to suffer similar personal demonisation later when, by chance, he came across some relatives of CJD victims in Downing Street. This time the catcall was 'murderer'. On that occasion Gill bravely defused the situation by approaching his foe and managing to have a constructive conversation about the issue. Both these incidents are good examples of how the president of the NFU is a publicly recognised, personal embodiment of the industry he represents. At times, such a position must be a joy and a privilege, but at others it is clearly not much fun.

Although the Germans lifted their illegal beef ban reasonably quickly, the French were happy to stick with their own agenda and pick and choose the rules they wanted to play by. Before the beef ban, the French market had been worth £179 million a year to British beef farmers. The row that ensued was reminiscent of the lamb wars that had raged 20 years earlier. Following the footsteps of President Butler in 1980, an outraged Ben Gill could be found making his way to the French Embassy armed with a letter of complaint threatening legal action. As the French refused to budge, Gill appealed to consumers to boycott French produce and buy British instead. In a famous publicity stunt, Gill was photographed squatting in a Soho gutter tipping some of the best French wines down the drain. The picture appeared in newspapers around Europe. There was some resulting damage to sales of French goods in the UK, much to Gill's amusement. Later, Gill held a beef barbecue outside the French Embassy and invited the ambassador who, to his credit, turned up and genially ate a British beefsteak, commenting to journalists that taking risks on behalf of his country was all part of his job.

As the financial situation for beef farmers, particularly in the West Country, became more desperate, farmers started to call for direct action against both French imports and the government, which was seen as indifferent to their plight. Just as with his forebears in the 1960s and 1970s, Gill was caught between leading direct action and keeping the NFU within the law. At the Labour Party Conference in September 1998, Gill led a protest march. The 9,000 farmer crowd had gathered first at the dilapidated Bloomfield Road, the home of Blackpool Football Club. One of the stewards commented to Gill that they had not seen a crowd like it since the days of Stanley Matthews. Despite leading this show of strength, Gill refused to join farmer blockades at ports. Inevitably, as the anger of farmers mounted, calls for the NFU to take a tougher, more proactive stance were made. In 1998 a group of farmers at Holyhead seized a lorryload of Irish beefburgers bound for Tesco and tipped them into the harbour. As ever, the NFU, for legal reasons, had to distance itself from such action. The row with the French rumbled on until they eventually lifted their illegal embargo in 2002.

Just as Wallace Day emerged in the 1960s to lead dissident NFU men in his Farmers Action Group, a new firebrand in the form of David Handley formed Farmers For Action in 2000. Handley's main grouse was low milk prices, but he was happy to have a snipe at Gill on any issue. Handley once delighted in creating a man of straw he called 'Ben Gill', putting it through a chopper for the benefit of the cameras.

Another grouse for the beef and dairy men at the time was the increase in TB cases. By the year 2000 over 8,000 cattle were being slaughtered each year, and the number of farmers suffering TB restrictions was growing by the day. The hotspots were in the South West and Wales, but it was also creeping into the West Midlands. Farmers and the NFU were still

Farmers on the march in Blackpool in September 1998.

188

adamant the disease was being spread by badgers, whose numbers and temerity were also growing by the day. Rather than take firm action, the government dithered as it sat between the farmers and the vets, who wanted targeted culling, and the badger conservation groups, who ranked cruelty to badgers as the ultimate sin. The government initiated the Krebs trials, which politically stalled the need to take any sort of comprehensive action.

Just as the fortunes of farming improved after Golden/Black Wednesday had weakened the pound in 1992, conversely, as sterling gained strength through the second half of the 1990s, so farm incomes fell. The year 2000 saw the fifth successive year of falling incomes and they hit new postwar lows. Self-sufficiency in indigenous produce, which had grown since the postwar period to over 80 per cent in the 1985–95 period, declined steadily thereafter to 71 per cent ten years later. Self-sufficiency in all foodstuffs declined even faster, going from over 70 per cent in the 1985–95 period to 58 per cent (an 18 per cent decline). Cripplingly low commodity prices were in part to blame here, but so also was set-aside and the OTMS scheme.

Furthermore, as consolidation continued apace in the retail sector, the multiple retailers grew in strength and farmers started to lose share of the food pound. This dropped 15 per cent between 1995 and 2005. In the same period cereals and livestock production fell 10–20 per cent. The price of cereals nearly halved, from £110 to £70. The milk price fell from 25ppl to 18ppl. The area of fallow land (excluding set-aside) more than tripled over the period, reaching 200,000 ha in 2005. Accordingly, the ten years between 1995 and 2005 also witnessed a 10 per cent loss of full-time farmers and a 20 per cent loss of farm workers. Gill had the misfortune to lead the farming industry through its worst financial crisis since the '30s.

To add to this misery, the NFU saw the loss of two of its brighter stars in the time of Gill's presidency. At

Beef farmers take their protest to the streets of London in 1998.

37, Richard Watson-Jones was one of the youngest men to fill the post of vice-president. He was highly rated by those around him and tipped for great things, and his tragic death from a brain tumour in 2000 robbed the NFU of a future leader. Ian Gardiner was head of policy at the NFU, a revered original thinker who did much to guide NFU thinking. Through a morbid coincidence he also succumbed to a brain tumour in the summer of 2003.

Just as British beef farmers thought things couldn't get much worse, with TB and BSE still affecting them, a ghost from the past suddenly reappeared to further haunt an industry on its knees. In mid-February 2001 the supervisory vet at Cheale's abattoir in South Essex noticed some of the pigs awaiting slaughter were lame. Although he had never seen foot and mouth disease before, the vet knew from his textbooks that the blisters he found on the pigs' feet were one of the symptoms. Tissue samples were sent to the MAFF labs at Pirbright and, on 20 February, FMD was confirmed.

Apart from a minor outbreak of FMD on the Isle of Wight in 1981, it was the first outbreak since 1968. The 2001 generation of British livestock farmers were the first ever not to have experienced a major national FMD outbreak. To call it a bolt from the blue was an understatement. Although, internationally, FMD had seen a resurgence in the years leading up to the millennium with a mutation of the virus, its eradication from Northern Europe from the 1970s onwards made it seem most unlikely the UK would succumb again. Contrary to all expectations, the 2001 FMD epidemic was to prove the worst ever to affect British agriculture.

The investigation of the Cheale pigs traced them back to Burnside Farm in Northumberland where, in a state of neglect, they had been swill fed. Although it was never proved, the best explanation was that the swill was inadequately boiled and could have included illegally smuggled meat from parts of the world where FMD was endemic. Hopes that the outbreak might be confined to this small, grubby farm were soon dashed when it became clear the virus had spread from the farm into neighbouring sheep flocks. The final and cruellest twist was that sheep from the flock had recently been through Hexham and Longtown markets. Thereby the seeds of disease had been spread as far as the South West, Wales and Scotland. Unlike the 1922 and 1967 outbreaks, which were primarily in dairy cows, the 2001 outbreak was mainly in the British sheep flock and as such was going to be all the more difficult to stamp out. One key problem with sheep was that, whereas cows and pigs displayed FMD symptoms quite clearly, sheep did not, and so identification was more reliant on laboratory analysis of tissue samples, which all required time and veterinary resources. Another hindrance was the severe cuts the State Veterinary Service had suffered over the previous 20 years. Although on 20 February FMD confirmation triggered an immediate ban on the export of meat and livestock, it took a full three days to prohibit movement of stock within the UK. Tony Blair was in Washington meeting the newly elected President, George W. Bush. Their discussion, amongst other things, concerned what to do with Iraqi leader Saddam Hussein, who, they thought, was accumulating weapons of mass destruction. A national livestock standstill order needed Blair's approval, hence the delay. Meanwhile, thousands of infected animals had spread far and wide.

By early March it was clear the disease was spreading fast the length of the western half of Britain and throughout Northumberland. It was then realised that probably as many as 80 cases spread around the country were unidentified at the time of the first confirmation. It was also clear that MAFF was not coping. Many farming families were finding themselves confined to farmyards full of heaps of rotting corpses that no one seemed to have the responsibility to remove. Just as in 1968, the NFU worked hard on the ground through national, regional and branch channels to make sure someone was talking direct to farmers and providing them with regular FMD updates. For many farmers, bunkered away in their farmyards, fearful of where the virus would appear next, the NFU was the key link with the outside world. It was the NFU that farmers turned to if they wanted information on movement licences or just a therapeutic chat. At national and local level NFU personnel worked hard with the media to keep some sort of perspective on what was becoming an emotive and depressing issue. A key difference with 1968 and 2001 was that the world had entered the age of the '24/7' media, and the NFU had to cope with the constant, insatiable demand for comment or information.

On 18 March Gill was in Downing Street to convince the Prime Minister the outbreak was not under control and more resources would have to thrown at the situation. Blair decided to take personal responsibility for the situation and to call in the Army in order to improve logistics and add manpower. At this point communication between the NFU and government improved enormously, with the NFU attending daily briefing sessions with MAFF, Cabinet and veterinary officials, sessions known as the 'bird table'. Returning to Downing Street on 20 March, Gill gave Blair a progress report from what the NFU had learnt on the ground.

The policy moved from waiting for confirmation of the disease to slaughter on suspicion. As the disease swept up the M6 into Cumbria a further policy of contiguous culling was developed in order to try to create firebreaks. (Some called the contiguous cull policy 'computerised carnage'). To make matters worse, the winter of 2000/01 was filthy wet, and soon the media was awash with pictures of young lambs drowning in mud because, under FMD movement restrictions, they could not be moved from the hills and marshes they had been born on. Following NFU lobbying, MAFF implemented a compensated welfare cull.

It was clear that, as time went on, more and more animals that did not actually have FMD were being slaughtered. Throughout this time Gill was adamant that the slaughter policy was correct and must be persevered with. The government enquiry after the 1968 outbreak had suggested scenarios where ring vaccination might isolate the disease in certain areas. The problem in 2001 was that the disease was occurring in hundreds of widespread outbreaks, not just in a few clusters. Furthermore, vaccinating sheep would always be problematic. Many in the hills were not kept in tightly controlled flocks. Of course, the accusation the NFU had to face in all of this was that their real concern was that a vaccination policy would delay any resumption of exports. What should also be remembered is that the UK was home to a third of the EU's 70 million sheep and very dependent on good export markets. But, as the NFU pointed out, the live export trade of sheep was negligible and, in the case of cows, it was banned. This showed that resumption of exports was not the NFU's main concern but rather the effective eradication of the disease.

By Easter 2001 it was clear there were even more considerations complicating the disease control agenda. Firstly, the countryside had been rendered largely inaccessible through the closing of footpaths in an attempt to stop tourists and ramblers from spreading the disease. As winter turned to spring, the tourist industry was growing impatient of the lack of progress in halting the disease. The closing of the countryside was causing economic damage that went well beyond agriculture. Secondly, after four years of administration, the Labour Government was keen to call an election. The Tories, under William Hague, were in a state of disarray, and the time was opportune for Blair to secure another term of office. The problem for Blair and his PR guru, Campbell, was that a closed countryside riven with an out-of-control disease was not the best backdrop against which to go to the country seeking re-election. One further factor was that there was a small body of high-profile farmers, largely outside the NFU and led by the Soil Association and their patron, Prince Charles, who were putting pressure on government to adopt a vaccination policy.

Late on Maundy Thursday Gill became aware that a high-level summit to discuss the situation had been called and, ominously, the NFU was not invited. On the following Tuesday Gill was summoned to Chequers to be told that a policy of vaccination was to be brought in. Gill was deeply suspicious that the Prince of Wales had been exceeding his constitutional position and interfering in executive policy. It was at times like this that Gill's fighting mettle and single-mindedness came to the fore. He took it upon himself to convince Blair that the vaccination policy would not work. He urged the Prime Minister to stick with the science and not to let the emotion or the desire to call a May election cloud his judgement. Blair was convinced by Gill and changed his mind. The vaccination plan was scuppered and the slaughter policy was continued with. The election was put off until June, much to the frustration of Labour MPs and electoral hopefuls, who had been given the wink that they should prepare for one in mid-May. It must have been the only time in its history that the NFU has been instrumental in post-poning a general election. Throughout May Campbell was in regular contact with Gill and NFU director-general Macdonald as to how the NFU should be presenting the FMD crisis to the general public. Suffice to say, Gill was no one's political poodle and continued to call it as he saw it.

A curious media increasingly turned their focus on Gill. The 'Newsnight' opening shots on the evening of the post-Easter meeting showed Gill and Blair on the steps of No. 10 Downing Street. Paxman, in his voice-over couldn't resist the snide remark: 'Two men standing outside No. 10 Downing Street. One runs the country, the other is the Prime Minister.' Paxman was not the only journalist to suggest Gill and the NFU had too much influence in government. It is neat to remember this observation about the NFU and government had been made since the 1930s. On the other hand, David Handley could be found complaining that the NFU and government were too close for farming's own good. The NFU's critics wanted it both ways.

In May 2001 Gill and his advisers felt a long-planned trip to Australia on IFAP business was opportune. Unfortunately, Gill managed to take the FMD controversy with him. When a journalist asked if he thought there was any mileage in the idea that the FMD virus might be spread by terrorists, Gill replied that it was unlikely, but you couldn't rule it out. Some of the more lurid press duly reported that Gill thought the FMD pandemic was started by terrorists. We recollect here how the IRA had tried to intimidate Williams and Plumb with threats of germ warfare 30 years earlier. By 2001, the IRA were no longer the terrorist threat they had been; now it was Muslim extremists who had taken on that mantle. Gill also managed to upset the Australians by making the observation that the shorter the supply chain, the greater the probity of the product. Not suprisingly, such comments were given a frosty reception Down Under . It was reminiscent of the reaction the likes of President Baxter and President Dorman-Smith had excited in the 1930s when they suggested quotas on antipodean meat exports. The Australians had got the impression that, because of the extensive FMD cull, the Brits were short of beef.

Obviously, with the export restrictions facing UK farmers, the opposite was the case.

The spread of FMD slowed towards the end of April but did not actually die out until September. The final statistics make grim reading. There had been 2,026 outbreaks and over ten million animals had been culled. The number of outbreaks was actually fewer1 than the numbers recorded in 1922–24 and 1967–68, but the death toll was 20–30 times higher. There is no doubt that month after month of pictures of animals being burned on pyres or buried in mass pits left a nasty taste in the mouth of the viewers when it came to the image of British farming. Some within the NFU criticised Gill for appearing so dogmatic about the need for slaughter, and felt a softer line could and should have been taken. Nonetheless, in hindsight, the slaughter policy had eventually worked, and there was no certainty that vaccination would have led to a better outcome. What is for sure is that Gill had the strength of his convictions to stand up for what he believed was right, and stood by his guns in the face of enormous pressure to back down.

Apart from ten million sheep, cows and pigs, there was one further casualty in the FMD crisis – the MAFF. Following the June election and the return of the Blair government, the ministry was merged with the Department of the Environment to become DEFRA.

After 82 years of acting as the farmers' regulator and adviser, the ministry was no more, and suddenly the NFU road map of Whitehall looked very different. The history of the NFU is very closely intertwined with the history of MAFF. Since the Second World War there had been a keen sense of partnership between the two, with the single purpose of meeting the food needs of the UK from its own resources. The ministry was at the height of its powers in the 1960s and early '70s, when it had 15,000 staff. The largest group were scientific, professional and technical specialists who worked out in the regions alongside farmers on the ground. Accession to the EEC and cuts in state services in the Thatcher years led to a diminution of the ministry, but even so, in the 1990s the MAFF/NFU nexus remained an important one. After 2001 the NFU found itself operating on a broad number of fronts across Whitehall and its associated quangos. With the demise of MAFF also came the demise of a Minister of Agriculture. Nick Brown was the last of a long line of 31 men and one woman who had held the post around the Cabinet table. With the demise of MAFF, DEFRA now had in its midst a minister for sustainable food and farming. To date, the post has always been held by a member of the House of Lords, namely their Lordships Whitty, Bach and Rooker.

Another consequence of the FMD outbreak was the Curry Commission, which went on to make several recommendations concerning agricultural policy. The careers of Gill and Curry were curiously intertwined. They had first met on York Station in the 1980s, travelling to their first NFU Council. The rumour was that on one train journey they agreed between them that if one went for the presidency of the NFU then the other would be allowed a clear run at becoming chairman of the MLC. Curry ended up at the MLC. Over time, their respective roles frequently found them working alongside one another due to issues such as BSE, the beef ban and FMD.

Apart from the beef ban and FMD, the third key issue Gill had to deal with under his presidency was CAP reform. In 1992 he had been charged by President Naish to head up an NFU team to look at the issue and present a report to Council. The resulting document, 'Real Choices', considered four different directions the CAP could take: the bond system, leading to long-term removal of support; de-coupling, whereby direct payments were made to farmers unrelated to production; indirect quotas, restricting such practices as nitrogen usage to limit production while maintaining production subsidies; direct quotas, directly limiting production at farm level while maintaining production subsidies.

Council chose the de-coupling option, and this became the central plank of the NFU's proposed CAP reform. In 1995 a new EU agricultural commissioner, Franz Fischler, had taken office. The rotund Austrian announced his intent to review the CAP under a discussion document known as 'Agenda 2000'. After the millenium it became clear the review was actually going to be a fundamental reform. The GATT negotiations that had now morphed into the WTO Doha round was still demanding the removal of market-interfering mechanisms in the CAP.

The NFU's de-coupling proposal was seen, both in Britain and Brussels, as a credible reform proposal. Amongst the continentals, particularly the French and the Mediterraneans, the de-coupling model was far from enthusiastically received. The fear was that it would take away much-needed production support in rural areas and thus lead to desertification. Gill worked hard on some of the floating voters, such as the Belgians, to agree with the proposed reforms. Eventually, in 2003, de-coupling was accepted and written into the CAP to begin the following year.

And so we reach the end of Ben Gill's presidency at the beginning of a new era for British agriculture. With the notable exceptions of poultry, pigs and horticulture, for 60 years, through price support, government had directed what farmers produced. With the advent of de-coupling this was no longer the case. Of the £16.5 billion total output from farming in 2004, £2.2 billion was from subsidies. The problem for many farmers was that their subsidy cheque represented their total profit margin and more besides.

Before we finish with Ben Gill, it is worth observing that, in the 13 years he was an office-holder, there was a technical revolution that completely changed farming and the NFU. When Gill was livestock chairman, mobile phones were the size of housebricks and only used by yuppies. It was impossible to contact a farmer in his fields or a staff member away from the office. By the time Gill stepped down, mobile phones were small enough to fit in shirt pockets, everyone had one and anyone could be contacted at any time, anywhere in the world. In the 1980s the NFU had one large main-frame computer in the economics department which spewed out reams of paper. By Gill's time everyone in NFU HQ had computers, many of them small enough to fit in a briefcase, with many thousands of times the power of the old mainframe. It was during this time that the NFU joined the virtual world and launched its own website. Just as the NFU had campaigned for better access for farmers to the tele-phone network before the Second World War, in the Gill years it demanded better broadband facilities for the rural areas. Gill was the first e-enabled president, and he became a fanatical e-mailer, sending messages to all and sundry at all times of the day and night from wherever he was in the globe. Life was never to be the same again.

In 2004 Gill decided to stand down from the presidency. He had been knighted in 2003. Ironically, the royal who waved the sword around Gill's shoulders was the man with whom he had often clashed – Prince Charles.

Returning to his Easingwold farm, Gill decided to sell up. His four sons were not going into farming and the farm was struggling to make a profit. At the time, Gill noted:

I've got to the stage in my life where the family farm, in terms of lowland farming, is not as viable as it would have been 20 years ago. When my father started farming Home Farm was a big farm. It doesn't take a mathematician to see that, with wheat at £65/t, it's not going to be profitable.

It was a symptomatic of what had happened to British agriculture since the 1980s. Sir Ben Gill was far from alone, as a farmer on less than 500 acres who was struggling to make a living out of farming. Another sign of the times was the fact that, while Gill sold the land, he held onto the traditional farm build-ings so he could convert them into offices or indus-trial lets. While incomes from farming had collapsed in the decade after the mid-1990s, the value of real estate had climbed significantly. By the first decade of the new millennium, many farmers were aware that their outbuildings were worth infinitely more if they could get them out of the loss-making business of farming. The phrase 'asset rich, cash poor' became an apt way to describe many farm businesses.

Tim Bennett, 2004–06

CHAPTER 33

Of all the presidents of the NFU, Tim Bennett has one of the least agricultural backgrounds. His father was a coach-tour operator from Stourbridge in the West Midlands. By the age of 12 the young Bennett was pedalling his bike out into the surrounding Black-countryside and somehow got to know a dairy farmer in the village of Halesowen. Soon he had a weekend job milking cows and, much to his parents' horror, decided farming was to be his career of choice. They hoped and prayed he would grow out of it, but he never did.

On leaving school, the West Midlands lad was introduced into the farming community at Seale-Hayne Agricultural College, where he studied for, and passed, his National Diploma in Agriculture. During the following gap year he was odd-jobbing in France and met his future wife, Sue, who was training to be a translator in Brussels. They had a dream of running a farm in France, but somehow they returned to Sue's native Carmarthenshire in 1978 to take over her family's farm at Maesybont. It was a small 80-acre grassland farm, where Bennett milked 100 pedigree Holstein Friesians and established an 8,000-hen battery egg unit with a farm shop and an egg round. The environment of his farm was a testing one, sitting as it did 400–800 ft above sea level with an annual rainfall of 68 inches. Some was in a Less Favoured Area (LFA). Not long after taking over the farm, Bennett purchased more land with an AMC mortgage to expand the farm to over 200 acres.

The establishment of milk quotas in 1984 was a blow, as it came at a time when, as a keen young farmer, Bennett was trying to expand his business. Conversely and perversely, five years later, Mrs Currie and her salmonella scare actually increased the sales in the egg round. Bennett found that the growing concern over food safety among consumers could play into the farmer's hands in that, by selling the idea of 'provenance' with the product, he could grow his market. In keeping with the overused phrase of the time, by thinking 'outside the box', Bennett found he could turn what appeared to be a disaster into an opportunity. It was a good example of a farmer integrating himself into the food chain at a local level and selling direct. In the 1990s many farmers got wise to this concept and converted their outbuildings into farm shops. It was a similar tale with the burgeoning farmhouse bed and breakfast market. At the political level, the NFU fought hard to secure rate relief, planning dispensation and grant aid for such ventures. It is interesting to note that,

Tim Bennett at the NFU AGM flanked by the Agriculture Minister, Nick Brown, and Prime Minister, Tony Blair.

whereas in the 1950s and '60s the government were giving grants to encourage increased farm production, 20 years later, in the 1980s and 1990s, such grants had largely been replaced by ones encouraging barn conversions, so that farmers might diversify away from agriculture.

In the '80s Bennett rose through the ranks of Camarthenshire NFU, eventually becoming chairman in 1988. Today, he wryly recollects that the early NFU roles he was given were sometimes more at the behest of others than of his own volition. His tales of being voted into jobs while not being aware he had put himself forward are reminiscent of the stories told by Tom Baxter 80 years earlier, when Baxter unwittingly found himself in the chair of his local branch at the first-ever meeting he attended. The NFU has always found devilish ways to make sure the talent in its ranks is not too shy to come forward.

Eventually, Bennett found himself chairing the Marginal Lands Committee at Knightsbridge. It was at this time it merged with the Hill Committee in the Gourlay restructuring of the late '80s. Bennett became chairman of the new committee and remained in that post until he became deputy president in 1998.

The farmers who farm the hills, mountains and moors of Britain have always been a hardy bunch, who experience agriculture at the sharp end. The topography and climate in these areas severely limit the type of farming that can be undertaken. Consequently, farm businesses in these areas can be fragile, but in terms of the social fabric and the environment, farming is of key importance. There are also special issues over access and tourism that affect these areas more than most. We remember the NFU

193

first came across the demands for greater access to farmland by ramblers in the 1930s in the Lake District. We also remember it was farmers on Exmoor in the 1970s who initiated some of the first discussions about preserving landscape in the face of the farmers' need for agricultural improvement. Also, it should be remembered that the hills were the last and least affected by the postwar changes in technology and mechanisation. As lowland farmers enjoyed the delights of tractors and mains electricity, the farmers in the remote hills went without. Bennett observes how it was the introduction of the quad bike in the 1980s and the mobile phone in the 1990s that first revolutionised the life of the hill farmer. He could remember visiting many farms in the 1980s with no mains electricity and where the pony was still the main form of transport around the farm.

Because of their special nature, the NFU recognised early on that the hills and moors justified their own committees and their own NFU staff. Official designation of these areas as in some way less favoured and requiring separate government policy emerged in the 1940s with hill payment schemes. With entry into the EU, these schemes became more elaborate, with hill livestock allowances and other sheep-support mechanisms part funded at EU level and part funded from the UK treasury. Negotiations between government and the NFU would take place yearly as to the funding levels and the design of the schemes. It was here that Bennett gained a reputation as a solid negotiator and someone who could master a brief.

Of key importance was where the lines were drawn on maps so farms qualified for these special payments. Over time, the NFU has pushed for an extension of these areas to include more farmers in their ambit. Such policies increased stocking and concentrated sheep farming in the hills. In the 1980s a new debate emerged as the conservation lobby alleged the policies were causing environmental damage through over-grazing. This led to demands for reduction of stocking and adjustments in the ways the schemes worked. When Bennett chaired the LFA committee he was always insistent that good science rather than anecdotal generalisation should guide the policy. The result was land management schemes that secured another form of income for the hill men.

As a man, Bennett was short in stature but big hearted. With his Midland accent and cheerful disposition, people warmed to his good nature and understated modesty. He had a sedate pace and the president's office did not have the same high-charged energy once Gill had vacated it. Members appreciated Bennett's interpersonal skills and his genuine empathy with their problems. In the farming community you come across many testimonies of Bennett taking the time and trouble to speak to individual farmers and do what he could to help them. It

was an approach that rightly won him many friends. At the political level he had a quiet competence that inspired respect both from NFU staff and from DEFRA officials. He was effective in ministerial meetings, where he was determined, stuck to the point, knew what he wanted, and was good on detail. His weakness was that this competence did not always manifest itself on the bigger stage in front of a larger audience.

He is yet another president who farmed in Wales but was not born there. There are no fewer than five NFU presidents who could claim to have a foot in both the English and Welsh camps. On reflection, it makes sense that men who could appeal to both the English and Welsh votes on Council should be popular when it came to elections.

On taking the presidency in 2004, Bennett led the NFU through another period of reform. As the farming recession continued to bite and farming lost more farmers, the NFU was obliged once again to tighten its belt. By 2005 NFU membership had shrunk to 60,000 full members and 60,000 countryside, but it still kept its claim of representing 70–80 per cent of English and Welsh agriculture. One increasing problem with this figure was that, as the industry restructured fast during the 1995–2005 recession, what constituted a 'farmer' became even more difficult to define. With some farmers covering far more land through FBTs and share farming arrangements, the distinction between contractors and farmers was becoming more blurred. Furthermore, as the value of real estate boomed in the face of poor returns on farming, many farmhouses and surrounding paddocks were being sold away from the land and the practice of commercial farming. The industry was in a state of flux, which made it difficult to be sure what was happening to farmer numbers. It is probably most accurate to say that the NFU, then and now, represents 75 per cent of production, production being easier to measure.

As deputy president under Gill, Bennett was charged with the task of leading a fundamental review. On becoming president he executed much of what had been proposed. A decision was taken to move the headquarters out of London to the Royal Show Ground at Stoneleigh, near Coventry. The building at Shaftesbury Avenue had never proven the most accommodating or the most salubrious of premises for the NFU, and few were sorry to leave the place. However, the move out of London was more controversial. For nearly 90 years the NFU had chosen to have its HQ in the capital, close to Whitehall and Westminster. Some felt it should retain this strategic link. Others took the view that a rurally based industry should find a home outside the metropolis and should be more centrally located in the Midlands. There were also savings to be made by moving out of the increasingly expensive and increasingly congested city. Another factor in favour

Tim Bennett (right) on top of the new NFU HQ at Stoneleigh.

of leaving London was that the old NFU–MAFF nexus had weakened over the previous decade. Now the NFU had to lobby and liaise on a number of fronts and with a number of government departments, quangos, RDAs and NGOs that did not have headquarters in London. Another factor was that, over the previous 20 years Brussels had become just as important as London in the NFU's 'lobbying sphere'.

After some debate, Council agreed to leave London and move 100 miles north. Construction at Stoneleigh was started in 2004 and the new building opened in December 2005. In design, the exterior of the building was striking and managed to make a statement in much the same way the Knightsbridge building must have done. Inside there was an emphasis on functional open-plan office design and pleasant pastoral views over Stoneleigh Park, and the building provided a good work environment for the 100 or so staff who duly moved into it. To retain the London connection. office space was rented in Smith Square alongside the DEFRA buildings.

Bennett also initiated simplification of the NFU committee structure and changed the composition of Council. By 2004 the NFU had slimmed down its HQ committee structure from 34 in the 1980s to just 13 under Gill. The Bennett reforms reduced this further, to nine: Governance, Policy and Audit, along with six commodity boards covering dairy, combinable crops, horticulture, livestock, poultry and sugar beet. Also under the review, there were reductions in and restructuring of staff. One final change that should be noted – the president's car and driver were consigned to history. NFU 1 was no more.

The main purpose of the review was to put the NFU on a sound financial footing, which, in hindsight, was achieved. Some of the reforms did not make Bennett popular, but his diligence in preparing his case won the day. They proved a testimony to his quiet determination and intelligent analysis.

Despite the disruption of the move and all the other changes, it should be noted that, in terms of workload and achievement, 2005 was a year no

different from the ten that preceded it. It is worth remembering that, despite the changes in the NFU and in Whitehall, the NFU continued to lobby on both the broad and the detailed areas of policy. Farmers continued to be affected by legislation and regulation in a myriad of ways, and needed effective political representation as much as ever. By way of a few examples, in 2005 the NFU successfully called for changes in support for the Severely Disadvantaged Areas (SDAs) and secured an agreement from DEFRA to pay slaughter premium on animals under the Livestock Welfare Disposal Scheme (LWDs). The latter was worth £5.5m to the industry. Similarly, under Bennett's presidency the NFU moved to resist calls to erode the tax breaks agriculture gained from red diesel. These were lucrative concessions the NFU had won for farmers in the 1940s and had defended ever since. In terms of new legislation, the NFU did much to ensure the new gangmaster licensing regulations that followed the Morecombe Bay cocklepickers disaster in 2005 were practical and workable for farmers dependent on casual labour. In this instance, President Bennett took particular pride in the fact that an industry in the middle of a recession could support a Bill that tried to protect people from abuse. The NFU had been calling for such legislation to ensure its agriculture had world-class labour standards for a world-class industry for 20 years. The legislation came from a Private Members' Bill which both the NFU and TGWU jointly backed as an unstoppable alliance

Similarly, the evergreen question as to why farming should be a special case when it came to rating was raised by the Lyons Report, which looked into local government financing. The NFU did much to ensure agriculture retained this exemption, which was worth an estimated £400 million a year. We recollect it was a victory won in 1929 under the Baldwin government, when it was worth £5 million a year. Today the NFU continues to fight a rearguard action to maintain this benefit for farmers.

A final example of the way the NFU provided the industry voice in the corridors of power in Whitehall was the levy board review, whereby the future use and direction of millions of pounds worth of farmer levy-payers' money was up for discussion.

Through the legal assistance scheme, the union continued to empower individuals to achieve justice. During Bennett's presidency there were notable victories in areas such as set-aside definitions, eligibility for the organic farming scheme and the powers of Trading Standard officers when it came to animal health and welfare.

The union also retained its key advisory role for members. Litigation against the NFU in the early 1990s over advice given on milk quotas at that time had meant the way the NFU gave advice had become more formalised. The days of giving advice through friendly chats in branch or county offices were over.

The launch of NFU (Services Ltd) in 1998, which became Associa in 2003, changed the way advice was given out through the 'call first' facility.

In terms of the profitability of the industry he led, Bennett did not have any more luck than his predecessor, Gill. Commodity prices remained in the doldrums for most sectors. Farmers continued to leave the industry or restructured their businesses so they became less dependent on food production for their income. Under the de-coupled payment they were encouraged only to respond to market signals and not use their support payment to prop up unprofitable production. The irony for most farmers was that profitable milk production at 18p a litre or wheat production at £60 a tonne was hardly possible, and their farm businesses remained dependent on their SPS payment. This came home in the winter of 2005–06, when, due to administrative problems at the RPA, farmers were kept waiting several months for their support payments. Part of the problem was that, contrary to the NFU's lobbying in favour of a system based on historic claims, DEFRA, under the guidance of Environment Minister Margaret Beckett, had opted for a complicated hybrid model which was too complex for the Civil Service to master. This was all the more the case when some intellectual heavyweight in DEFRA decided there was no need to phase things in to allow time for proper administrative preparation. One result of the chosen non-historic area model was that it brought out of the woodwork thousands of small, newly registered claimants who clogged up the system. As the inability of the RPA to process the claims became apparent in early 2006, Lord Bach told Bennett: 'This could cost me my job.' Bennett replied: 'Mine too.' Both were proved correct with their forecast. The frustration from the delays in receiving the money provoked NFU Council, in early 2006, to 'pass a motion of no confidence in both Environment Minister Beckett and her agricultural junior, Lord Bach'.

To the increased chagrin of the farmers, who waited for the SPS cheques like Vladimir and Estragon waited for Godot, there came the revelation in the press that at the RPA offices in Newcastle, where their claims sat unprocessed, there were wild parties taking place where staff 'leapt naked from filing cabinets'. As more than one farmer observed at the time, it put paid to the lie that the RPA couldn't organise an orgy in a brothel.

As farmers became more dismayed at the government ineptitude over SPS payments, it was inevitable that some of the ire was directed at the president of the NFU. As we have noted before, when times are tough and farmers are in an ugly mood, the NFU president can get caught in the crossfire. Bennett was never the most forceful or passionate of speakers on

the public platform, and he lacked the force of personality to keep the confidence of NFU Council when strong leadership was needed. He also had the ill-luck of being an NFU president under the reign of Mrs Beckett at DEFRA. Behind the scenes, Beckett was not the nightmare most farmers took her for, but in public she gave off a dismissive arrogance that seemed completely disinterested in the serious economic situation in which most farmers found themselves. Farmers desperately wanted a heavyweight champion to lay a few blows on Beckett's apparent disregard. Bennett struggled to give them what they wanted. His preferred arena was round the farmhouse breakfast table or one to one with the minister. He did not thrive in front of farming crowds wanting a bit of heavyweight action. He also had the misfortune of having an ambitious deputy president in the form of Peter Kendall, who, like Plumb and Gourlay as deputy presidents before him, made no secret of a desire to take the president's job before the incumbent wanted to go. To add to the intrigue, David Handley, the tub-thumping leader of Farmers For Action, made loud his low opinion of Bennett's leadership and, along with Kendall, challenged Bennett at the 2006 AGM. It was Kendall who came out the victor.

To add to the disappointments of 2006 for Bennett, his beloved West Bromich Albion played like the blind school all season and were duly relegated from the premiership.

Bennett returned to his Carmarthenshire farm, where he had closed down the dairy and the egg business to concentrate on beef. As was the case with many farmers' sons and daughters at the time, both Tim's children sought careers away from the farm. Today Tim Bennett expresses some regret that neither of his children was interested in taking over the family farm, but then he also wryly recollects that he himself had ignored his father's wishes when he decided to become a farmer.

Today Tim Bennett holds a number of posts in agriculture. He sits on the boards of Food From Britain, the Food Standards Agency and the Meat Hygiene Service, which is appropriate given his first-hand knowledge of farming on the front line, milking cows and supplying an egg round. He also has a voluntary role with FWAG in Wales, which means he revisits those landscape issues he worked hard with in his time on the LFA Committee. Finally, he is the chairman of the new Dairy Co. levy body.

All in all, it seems only right that a coach driver's son who decided at the age of 12 that agriculture was his calling should continue to serve the industry he chose in this energetic way. Farming has always benefited from injections of blood from outside the industry, and Tim Bennett has provided exactly that.

CHAPTER 34

Peter Kendall, 2006 Onwards

And so we come to the final chapter of this long saga, which charts 100 years of the history of the NFU and the agriculture it represented over that century. Peter Kendall is the 33rd man to hold the title of president of the National Farmers' Union. Although he is the last president in this book and thus concludes the story, we should remember he is certainly not the end of the line. Just as he heads up the NFU as it celebrates 100 years of history, so too he leads it into its second century. Already, in his first two years as president, Kendall has had good cause to look forward with optimism, but has also been haunted by some ghosts from the past.

It is probably too early to give Kendall his place in the annals of the NFU, as his presidency is only a couple of years old and is ongoing. Most reckon, given Kendall's popularity and ability, he will serve as president for a number of years. Despite the fact we cannot fully evaluate the Kendall record, as an NFU president he makes for an interesting comparison with those who have gone before him. He is very much his own man in his own time, but it is tempting to place him within the context of this 100-year narrative.

He hails from Eyeworth in Bedfordshire. As such, he is atypical in that he is the first president to come from that county, but, then again, it is not unusual for presidents to come from locations that are within reasonable striking distance of London (or now of Stoneleigh). Most of the NFU presidents either came from the South East or had farms close to the A1 or the GNR. The reason why NFU presidents tend to come from areas with below-average travel times to the NFU's HQ is self-evident. It is interesting that, although the NFU has always spanned the length and breadth of England and Wales, few presidents have ever come from the further outreaches. For instance, none has come from Norfolk or Suffolk in the East, and none has come from Cornwall, Devon or Somerset in the West. Furthermore, apart from Gill, none has come from within 100 miles of the Scottish border. Few have farmed near the coast, which is odd, given that Britain is an island with an agriculture characterised by a maritime climate.

Throughout its history the NFU has often stood accused of not evenly representing all British farmers and of the president reflecting this bias. As we have seen, the West Country has liked to claim the eastern region is too influential and, conversely, the arable men have suggested livestock issues have absorbed a disproportionate amount of the NFU's time. The fact

Peter Kendall.

that most members are equally convinced that their particular sector or region gets a raw deal perversely suggests the NFU has done a reasonable job in being even handed and representative of a very diverse industry. What is true is that the presidents have tended to come from larger farms and none has farmed less than 100 acres. A good number of them have been tenants, and eight have been first-generation farmers.

Kendall is an arable man with a large farm. In this respect he is not average but, then again, he is very much of his time. Farming in partnership with his brother, Richard, they own 1,350 acres which were inherited. In recent years the brothers have branched out to cover a further 3,000 acres, all of which is owned by non-farming third parties. As we have seen, the story of postwar agriculture is one of fewer farmers covering more acres. There are two reasons for this: mechanisation and declining returns.

Machinery powered by internal combustion engines has taken over from horsepower and hand labour. Whereas Colin Campbell in 1908 (or even Nevile in 1943) needed a small army of men and horses equipped with scores of different kit, Kendall manages to cover ten times Campbell's arable acres with just three full-time staff, four tractors and two combines. Kendall prides himself on having new, top-of-the-range large machinery that works to optimum efficiency and allows him to cover more acres in a working day than Campbell would have covered in weeks, if not in a month. It is a sobering thought that Campbell would probably have been more familiar with the workings of a Roman farm than he would have been on Kendall's Eyeworth cereal empire. What is more, Kendall's cereal yields (8.5 tonnes per ha) are three to four times what Campbell could have boasted. The productivity per man on Kendall's farm is probably up to 50 times more than that on Campbell's. We recollect that in 1908 1.5 million farmers and farm workers were tied up producing 40 per cent of the nation's food with a population of 40 million. Today under half a million produce 60 per cent of the needs of 60 million.

But while they had their differences, there are things Campbell and Kendall have very much in common. Campbell let the hunt use his land, so does Kendall. Of course, after 17 February 2005 the hounds that ran across Kendall's land suddenly lost the intent to kill foxes. As a countryman, Campbell enjoyed a farmed vista broken by woods, copses, hedges and spinneys. So, too, does Kendall. Intertwined with the hardcore arable production at Eyeworth is a significant element of conservation. Under the Countryside Stewardship Scheme, and through the Entry Level Scheme, Kendall places margins of fulsome biodiversity around each field. He also plants new hedges and trees where his father took them out. In this respect Kendall has followed the shift in direction of the CAP, where subsidies no longer support production but rather support environmental management. Like most farmers of the baby-boomer generation, he has embraced the conservation schemes that came in after the 1980s and has spurned the rapacious appetite to plough and crop every last square inch of dirt that characterised the previous generation.

One frustration Kendall shares with many other farmers of his generation is that, while he has clearly moved on a long way in terms of his attitude to conservation since Marion Shoard wrote *The Theft of the Countryside* in 1980, his public image has not. This is largely because, in the last 20 years, the voice of the conservation lobby has got louder, better funded and more politicised. It has clearly been in the interests of these groups to talk up the negative environmental impact of agriculture and turn a blind eye to the myriad of positive benefits for which conservation-minded farmers such as Kendall have been respon-

sible. In recent years the NFU has initiated frequent campaigns, such as 'Care of the Countryside' in 2002 and 'Making Green Ground' in 2005. They have all played their part in getting over key messages about farming's positive contribution to countryside management, but they have lacked the impact better-funded campaigns with contrary messages, launched by groups such as the RSPB, have had. The NFU has always been the main player when it comes to championing agriculture and its environmental record. Kendall recognises that the challenge in this respect will become more demanding for the NFU in the future. In 2006 the NFU launched their latest campaign, 'Why Farming Matters'. It seemed to have more punch than many of its predecessors, and its sound-bites even found their way onto government ministers' lips.

Like the very first president, Colin Campbell, Kendall is primarily a tenant, but the nature of his tenancies is very different. The response of many farmers to the decline in returns on farming in the last 20 years has been to cover more acres to achieve greater economies of scale. This Kendall does *par excellence*. This has largely been done through short-term tenancy agreements and share-farming arrangements made possible by the legislation that relaxed tenant rights in the '80s and '90s. These arrangements are in great contrast to the traditional tenancies based on the old social nexus between landlord and tenant of which Campbell was such an advocate. The short-term farm business tenancies that Kendall likes to use are also at variance with the old union policy of establishing greater security of tenure that reached its culmination under the 1976 Miscellaneous Provisions Act, which secured tenure for three generations. Since then new, more flexible, arrangements have enabled farmers such as Kendall to respond swiftly to the lower returns and survive. What it has also meant is that farming, in particular combinable crop farming, is now characterised by far fewer, much larger, farmers.

Kendall is also typical of his time in that his farming is highly specialised. His soils are primarily Gault and Hanslope clay. Bedfordshire clay is long renowned for its ability to grow good crops of wheat. In the past his father also farmed brussels sprouts and potatoes, along with pigs, sheep and suckler cows. Now the Kendall brothers only grow combinable crops such as wheat and oilseed rape. Increasingly, as we have noticed through the farming of the NFU presidents over the century, there has been a movement away from mixed farming, whereby farmers no longer have a variety of crops or livestock on their farms. If Colin Campbell could have visited Kendall's silent, stockless steel and concrete farmyard, he would have found it an eerie place. He would also have been boggle-eyed at the various in-cab technologies that link Kendall's machinery with satellites in space so that they might locate themselves on planet earth to the nearest square foot.

Nor would Campbell have recognised the oilseed rape that grows in abundance around Eyeworth, some of which goes for bio-diesel. However, Campbell was au fait with the concept of growing fuel to generate horsepower for transport, traction and haulage. Like most arable farms before the Second World War, up to a fifth of the acreage on Campbell's farm was down to horse fodder in the form of hay and oats. We remember Jim Turner's family first went into farming so that they might produce fuel for their quarrying business. In this analysis, Kendall's production of bio-diesel is the story come full circle.

As president of the NFU, Kendall has been keen to promote the possibility of farmers producing renewable fuel such as bio-mass, bio-gas and bio-diesel. They are potentially important new markets for farmers at a time when the world is looking to wean itself away from using mineral oil. We recall how, 100 years ago, Campbell thought ethanol from potatoes could be used to power the new-fangled motor cars that were starting to appear in country lanes. In Campbell's time roads were mainly unsurfaced country lanes, and only a tiny percentage of the population had cars. Today, in Bedfordshire, Kendall farms within spitting distance of the A1, while just 20 miles further west reverberates the mighty M1. Between them these two Bedfordshire roads carry 200,000 vehicles a day through the county. Bedfordshire also has more than its fair share of urban sprawl. Milton Keynes, that exemplar of postwar development, lies not far from his farm, 20 miles to the west, while 20 miles east lies Stansted, with its plans to greatly increase capacity and pour yet more concrete to create another runway. In the 100 years between 1908 and 2008, the amount of agricultural land in England Wales has shrunk by 15 per cent from 12.6 million ha to 11 million. There is no doubt that, given the projections as to population pressure and housing needs, this area will continue to shrink, especially in counties such as Bedfordshire.

For Kendall, the presidency of the NFU is a 'five days a week plus some of the weekend' job. Just like Campbell, he travels the length and breadth of the land on NFU business. The difference is that Campbell was dependent on pony and trap in order to arrive at NFU meetings, where he exercised a bit of soapbox oratory. Kendall travels by bio-diesel-powered car. He still manages a bit of old-style soap-box oratory at NFU meetings, but also uses new media such as pod-casts, automated voice mails and text messages in order to speak to the membership. Compared to previous presidents, he is very informal within the NFU and relatively low-maintenance. The chauffered car, the London flat, the personal secretaries and the private advisers are no longer part of presidential trappings. On planes Kendall travels economy class. He sensibly recognises that the financial rigours of the last ten years have meant that his staff and his members have had to make sacrifices. Like a previous son of Bedfordshire, John Bunyan, he prudently leads by Puritan example.

In terms of his age, Kendall is in his 40s (he was born in 1960), which makes him a youngish president, but when we remember Dorman-Smith and Turner were in their 30s, we realise he is far from the youngest. Having said that, Kendall exudes a youthful energy which distinguishes him from most of his peers. Furthermore, he has three young children, all under the age of eight. He tells amusing tales of doing early morning live interviews from home for the 'Today' programme on Radio Four while hiding in the bedroom with his foot against the door. Small children wanting to play with their dad are no respecters of the importance of the media role of the president of the NFU. He also recollects how, in a breathless, sweaty state while trampolining with the kids, he was handed the phone by his wife, Emma, only to find he was talking to the newly appointed Environment Minister, David Miliband.

As a man, Kendall is very much in the mould of the men who preceded him as president. He has a rugged character with a forceful nature. The phrase which a journalist used to describe the first president, Campbell, in 1908, 'an honest John Bull', also aptly describes Peter Kendall. He was educated at Uppingham and then studied economics and agriculture at Nottingham University. David Handley once derisively referred to him as 'an economist', as if it was a term of abuse. Despite this absurdly alleged impediment, Kendall is highly regarded for his analytical mind and his insight into the issues that surround the agricultural scene.

Just like past presidents German and Turner, he enjoys the sport of rugby. There is something of the rugby-club bar about Peter Kendall. Like Campbell, he has a boisterous sense of humour which can get the better of him. Whereas Campbell was known for making risqué remarks in polite society, Kendall's first ever address as president was to a Cambridgeshire NFU branch dinner, where he prompted a complaint that it was not appropriate for him to include jokes about porn stars. He also somewhat shocked a RSPB/NFU audience by using the 'F' word when describing the predatory nature of magpies. (No doubt the ornithological element of the audience were more taken aback than the farming side.) But all this is not to say he is foul mouthed or disrespectful. He is highly regarded for his professionalism and widely liked for his pleasant nature and good manners. On a stage he is lucid and, just like Naish and Gill, most comfortable in his no-nonsense shirtsleeves. As a speaker he is relentlessly positive and forcefully upbeat, which is something farming audiences find refreshing and uplifting. Having said this, farmers also recognise he is aware

NFU Vice President Paul Temple (right) visits John Lund and Tracy Atkinson at their farm in Driffield, Yorkshire, caught in the eye of the storm in July 2007.

of their problems, and his members trust him to fight their corner with government. In all these respects, some compare him to Plumb.

However, like all good presidents, he does not escape the criticism of the ever-present malcontents in the NFU. When he was asked to review Kendall's first year in office, Somerset NFU delegate Derek Mead commented that: 'Kendall's achievements wouldn't fill a postage stamp.' In this regard, Mead is a loner who struggles to find many in the NFU to agree with him, but nonetheless he exemplifies a tradition of sniping at the president that is as old as the NFU itself.

Like most of the presidents, Kendall is a hard worker known for his early starts. It is sometimes noted that if you get up at 5a.m. and send him an e-mail you will quickly get one back.

In terms of his pre-presidential CV, Kendall's is rather thin. Most men who make it to the top of the NFU do so through long years of committee work, struggling their way up the greasy pole. In contrast, Kendall's rise was positively meteoric. He came onto NFU Council in 2000, was then chairman of the Cereals Committee in 2003, deputy president in 2004 and president in 2006. He is also the first man to have openly challenged a sitting president and won. The fact he managed to break this deep-seated NFU

tradition says a lot for the respect and trust he easily engenders. The minority on Council who opposed Kendall's challenge to the sitting incumbent in 2006 made the point that the NFU would regret his lack of experience. It is interesting to note that the only man in the past to come close to matching Kendall's inexperience when taking on the presidency was Turner, yet Turner turned out to be one of the greatest leaders the NFU ever had. Some feel Kendall has the potential to do the same.

Kendall's first year as president was reasonably uneventful, but the second, 2007, gave him what he described as 'the summer from hell'. It was a year that neatly reflected the remark that history is 'just one damn thing after another'. After a spring drought there was severe flooding across great swathes of the Midlands in June and July, as inches of rain fell in short, severe bursts. Farmers suffered the misery of having thousands of acres under water. Kendall put it down to climate change, but also hedged his bets on a long-range weather forecast by saying that, in the future, 'farmers would have to get used to drier summers with heavier rain'. We also note here that, throughout this 100-year story, farmers suffer freak weather with perverse regularity. Extremes of drought, flood, Arctic winters, heatwaves and gales (or, as farmers call it, 'rather unseasonable weather') seem to pepper every farming decade. Indeed, we remember that the deepest roots of the NFU lie in the years at the end of the 1870s, which were known as 'the three years without a summer'. What was notably peculiar about the seasons in the 1990s and 2000s was the absence of hard winters.

What was also true was that by 2007 the climate change debate was firmly on the agenda and was becoming increasingly politically charged. Through the first years of the new millenium, Kendall and the NFU recognised that the debate was gathering steam. The issue not only represented opportunities for farmers in the form of new markets for farm-produced forms of renewable energy, but it also involved possible threats in the form of taxes on farm essentials. Farm inputs such as fertilisers and farm outputs such as muck and methane were increasingly in the frame as causing global warming. Kendall sensibly recognises that the NFU must get involved in the debate on behalf of farming and not watch it unravel from the sidelines. In one analysis, the present perceived need for a national response to the threat of global warming has parallels with the position in which the NFU and agriculture found themselves in 1916 and 1939. They are all moments in history where agriculture is called upon to play its part for the common good. The point is that, at such times, agriculture needs to have good political representation and needs to be part of the debate. Just as the NFU heavily engaged on behalf of farmers with government in 1916 and 1939 at a time of national crisis, so to it must engage with government today.

In 2006 Kendall attacked the government for its poor record in encouraging the farm production of renewable fuels, pointing out that Blair was good at 'doing the least while talking the most'.

Just as many farmers were recovering from the floods in August, an isolated outbreak of foot and mouth disease in Surrey put the livestock industry into several crippling months of standstill. Almost immediately, Kendall found himself in the footsteps of many previous NFU presidents, making his way up Downing Street to see the Prime Minister at No. 10. This time the man he was going to see was the newly appointed Gordon Brown. Just as with Blair in 2001, Brown was considering the possibility of an election and so was sensitive to how the government was seen to be handling the FMD outbreak.

Unbelievably the source of the outbreak was not the usual imported beef but rather the laboratories in Pirbright, in Surrey, where the virus was manufactured and experimented with. At the time of writing it is still not clear if the virus came from the government's own research laboratory at Pirbright or the neighbouring one, where a private firm manufactured vaccines. The Pirbright facility had been set up after the 1922 outbreak to investigate the creation of FMD vaccines. Ironically, those vaccines have done

In the footsteps of many of his predecessors, President Peter Kendall emerges from No.10 having discussed the Foot and Mouth outbreak with the Prime Minister.

much to eradicate FMD around the world but have never been used in the UK. Just to add to the irony, 2007 was not the only time Pirbright has infected nearby cattle farmers with FMD – virus leaks also occurred in the 1960s.

Although in these earlier incidents, and in the one in 2007, the outbreak was locally contained, the big difference for British farming was that in the 1960s the standstill was localised, but in 2007 it was national. The economic damage was felt right across England and Wales. It was indicative of how jumpy the severe outbreak of 2001 has made the authorities and the farming community. It was also indicative of how many more animals were moving about across the country. Before 2001, FMD was tackled on a county-by-county basis, but the 2001 epidemic shut down the whole of English and Welsh livestock farming. The Pirbright debacle raised key legal issues as to negligence, fault and consequential loss. At the moment of writing the NFU, through its Legal Aid Scheme, is leading the challenge in this regard. So far over £100,000 has been spent looking at the case. It is an excellent example of the NFU yet again seeking justice for the small individual farmer in the face of large corporations or all-powerful government departments.

Foot and mouth disease is interwoven throughout the history of the NFU. The union has always called for better controls on the import of meat into the UK from countries where FMD is endemic. In December 2007 the NFU backed Irish calls on the EU authorities to restrict the import of meat from Brazil because of proven irregularities in the way the Brazilians were tracing animal movements between endemic FMD states and non-endemic ones.

Hard on the heels of FMD in the summer of 2007 came the previously unseen blue tongue disease, first arriving in Suffolk in September. Again, it caused disruption with animal movements, causing economic loss to livestock farmers. Finally, avian 'flu, the third of a 2007 hat-trick of animal diseases, appeared in two outbreaks on the Norfolk/Suffolk border. Avian 'flu was different from the other two in that it had human health connotations. In the Far East there had been cases where the virus had crossed into humans. No matter how small the risk, as ever, the media struggled to keep their reporting proportionate. The NFU communications team needed to do its best to remind consumers that there was no health risk from eating British poultry. While FMD, AI and blue tongue appeared over the horizon, TB rumbled on in the background. By late 2007 in England and Wales there were an alarming 7,113 herds under TB movement restrictions, and over 23,000 animals had been culled that year. Still the NFU called for selective culls on badgers and still the government prevaricated.

So 2007 will be remembered as the year when the NFU found itself fighting four major diseases on four fronts. In terms of animals slaughtered because of FMD, the year was relatively small beer. Compared to previous cull figures, most notably the ones in 1922, 1968 and 2001, the figures are hardly significant, but 2007 is a reminder that the British livestock industry often finds itself wrestling with bio-security issues. Throughout its first century the NFU has been integral to the industry response to an endless list of animal disease, such as FMD, TB, brucellosis, swine vesicular disease, anthrax, BSE, avian influenza and Newcastle and Aujeszky's diseases. Some diseases have been eradicated, some seem to keep reappearing and others appear that have never been seen before. The list goes on and on. There has not been a year go by in its 100-year history that the NFU has not had to throw some of its resources at animal health issues. One suspects it will remain that way in the future. To further complicate the issue, at the time of writing there is a lively political debate as to who should pay for the measures needed to combat disease and compensate for animals culled. The government is insisting that it is only equitable that the livestock industry should shoulder a good proportion of the financial burden. The NFU response is to point out that it is government which has ultimate responsibility for bio-security. One reason why British farmers have been repeatedly visited by disease outbreaks where their counterparts in countries such as America and Australia have not is because of contrasting attitudes to the import and control of meat at national borders. As ever, the NFU is at the heart of the debate, putting forward the industry's case.

But 2007 was not all bad news for President Kendall. After a long wait of ten years, prices for arable and dairy farmers suddenly picked up to give a much-needed return to sustainable prices. An increased demand for food was caused, in part, by the rapidly developing economies in the Far East, where newly affluent consumers were wanting more protein in their diet. Futhermore, new schemes hatched in Washington to promote the use of bio-fuel were increasing the demand for commodities such as maize and soya. This increase in demand collided with problems with supply, as the world experienced a number of poor harvests in 2007. World wheat stocks fell to just 65 days, their lowest level since 1983.

Through 2006 and 2007 milk prices picked up 30 per cent and cereals more than doubled. In the summer of 2007 Kendall announced: 'The era of cheap food is over and I for one am not sorry to see it go.' He was echoing exactly what President Turner had said in 1945. Subsequently, Turner led British agriculture into 30 years of unrivalled growth and prosperity. NFU members must hope that Kendall's term of office will herald an equally prosperous period. Where Turner looked to government to guarantee prices in 1945, in 2008 Kendall is optimistic that such state interference in the market is consigned to history and will not be needed. He is hopeful that, in the future, the demand for food and fuel, coupled with problems with supply, will provide the dynamics to reinvigorate farm incomes. Quite what his view is on the future of the £2.2 billion English and Welsh farmers receive in the way of support payments is more complex. Unlike Turner, Kendall has no aspirations to be found negotiating levels of farm support with government ministers by reference to figures scrawled on the back of fag packets.

One reaction to declining world wheat stocks was the decision of the EU Commission in late 2007 to reduce the set-aside level to zero. This decision, coupled with buoyant prices, encouraged British farmers to get their ploughs out in the autumn of 2007 and increase their arable acreage. It was vaguely reminiscent of the plough-up campaigns of 1917 and 1940. It also reignited a very old debate as to how much of Britain should be ploughed then cropped, and how much should be grazed by livestock. In previous times the plough had come to symbolise the means by which Britain produced more food from her own resources. In 2008 this

NFU Headquarters, Stoneleigh.

debate continues, but drags in some new agendas. Some champions of vegetarianism, such as Sir Paul McCartney, are of the view that the best way to feed the world's burgeoning population from an over-stretched planet is through farming crops rather than livestock. McCartney makes the same point that occurred to medieval kings and wartime politicians in the past, that there are more calories of food produced on a cropped acre than on a grazed one. Conversely, conservationists such as the RSPB were warning the government in 2008 of the damage to bio-diversity that would be done if too much of the landscape was ploughed and cropped. Meanwhile, it is worth noting that the arable area in England and Wales had shrunk from 5.5 million hectares in 1958 to 3.8 million in 2008. Many farmers feel that for too long productive agriculture has not been given due regard at policy level in government. As the supply and demand equation starts to move in favour of supply, the hope is that this policy might be at last changing. Kendall has become a poster-boy for productive agriculture, just as Dorman-Smith, Turner and Plumb were in their day.

A key point of differentiation is that Kendall realises that there will be no return to the rapacious change of the 1970s, when there was too little regard for the impact on landscape and bio-diversity. No matter how high the wheat price, the established conservation margins and recently planted landscape features that enclose Kendall's arable fields will remain. Just as it is for most of the nation's farmers, the land around his house in Eyeworth is part of his home. Like his peers, Peter Kendall takes pride in his home and intends to leave it in better heart than when he found it.

Postscript

The last date in this book is 10 December 2008. It marks exactly 100 years from when the inaugural meeting was held that led to the founding of the NFU. Hopefully, the occasion of this date in late 2008 will cause many glasses to be raised, both to the health of the NFU and to congratulate it for its many achievements. At the same time, many stories should be told of great leadership and of great unity. Of how Colin Campbell inspired and cajoled 'the one class of men who would never combine' to see the need for a single union. Of how Rowland Robbins tried to pick up the pieces of a broken industry which had been 'greatly betrayed' in 1921. Of how Tom Baxter, in 1933, led 120,000 dairy farmers to form the greatest co-operative venture British agriculture had ever seen. Of how, in 1939, Reginald Dorman-Smith led both ministry and union into the challenge of ploughing for victory and for freedom. Of how Jim Turner, in 1945, worked to form a pioneering part-nership between government, union and industry so that Britain would never fear hunger again. Of how Henry Plumb, in 1970, was hoisted onto the shoulders of a seething crowd of farmers in Whitehall so that he might deliver them a better future and a more just reward. And of how, in more recent times, men such as David Naish and Ben Gill dug deep into their characters to lead a fight against overwhelming disease in the nation's livestock.

At the same time, toasts will be made to the next 100 years, and thoughts will be of the future as well as the past. Young men will consider how their generation of farmers will take on the new challenges of tomorrow and what legacy they will eventually leave. Some may even wonder what it might be like to lead the NFU as its president in the decades to come.

Agriculture is one of the grand old industries of Britain and, when compared to some others, such as coalmining or shipbuilding, it has survived a century of great change in reasonable shape. The same is true

of the organisation that has represented English and Welsh agriculture throughout that period. Just as with the farming industry, the NFU doesn't have as many farmers as it used to, but it retains a healthy and impressive share.

While British agriculture may have downsized in terms of numbers of farmers, it has retained its enormous diversity. Over its history the NFU has achieved many things, but maybe its crowning glory is that it has pulled together a motley crew of fractious individuals and united them into a single band of brothers. As such, they have managed to speak with one forceful voice and have managed to work purposefully together towards common ends. Such is the enormity of the challenges and changes that have faced farmers over the last 100 years it would have been foolhardy not to unite under one banner and take leadership from one man– the President of the National Farmers' Union of England and Wales.